UNDERSTANDING OUR ENVIRONMENT

SECOND EDITION

Stewart Dunlop / Michael Jackson

TORONTO
OXFORD UNIVERSITY PRESS
1996

Oxford University Press Canada
70 Wynford Drive Don Mills Ontario M3C 1J9

Oxford New York
Athens Auckland Bangkok Calcutta
Cape Town Chennai Dar es Salaam Delhi
Florence Hong Kong Istanbul Karachi
Kuala Lumpur Madrid Melbourne
Mexico City Mumbai Nairobi Paris
Singapore Tapei Tokyo Toronto

and associated companies in
Berlin Ibadan

Canadian Cataloguing in Publication Data

Dunlop, Stewart
Understanding our environment
2nd ed.
Includes index.
ISBN 0-19-541241-9

1. Ecology. 2. Man — Influence on nature.
3. Environmental protection.
I. Jackson, Michael. II. Title.

GF75.D86 1997 333.7′2 C96-931872-3

Managing Editor: Loralee Case
Editors: Micaëla Gates and Karen Ross
Design: Marie Bartholomew
Photo Researchers: Natalie Pavlenko Lomaga and Patricia Buckley
Cover Design: Brett Miller
Cover Photo: Arnulf Husmo/Tony Stone Images
Illustrators: Susan Calverley, David Edmunds, Catherine Farley & Associates, Julian Mulock, and VisuTronX.
Compositor: Gandalf Communications Inc.
Printed in Canada by Friesens

This book is printed on permanent (acid-free) paper .

1 2 3 4 5 — 01 00 99 98 97

Acknowledgements

The publisher would like to thank Lex Mackenzie of Stephen Leacock Collegiate Institute and Ron Bonham, formerly of the York Region Board of Education, for their reviews of the manuscript and their participation in the preparation of question material.

CONTENTS

8: Land 114

9: Energy 135

10: Waste Disposal 155

UNIT 3: MANAGEMENT AND CONSERVATION 171

11: The Environment and Politics 172

12: Rural Management and Conservation 187

13: Urban Management 200

14: The Environment and You 213

Glossary 226

Index 231

PHOTO CREDITS

page iii Stewart Dunlop; page 1 Stewart Dunlop; page 2 Stewart Dunlop; page 7 David Woodfall/Tony Stone Images; page 9 (top and bottom) Stewart Dunlop; page 10 Victor Last/Geographical Visual Aids, Wiarton, Ontario; page 11 R. Nowitz/ VALAN; page 12 NASA; page 17 Janet Dwyer/First Light; page 18 Victor Last/Geographical Visual Aids, Wiarton, Ontario; page 21 (left and right) Canapress Photo Service; page 22 Victor Last/Geographical Visual Aids, Wiarton, Ontario; page 23 R. Maiman/Sygma-Publiphoto; page 24 Canapress Photo Service; page 25 Stewart Dunlop; page 27 Miller Comstock; page 33 Michael Jackson; page 36 Janet Dwyer/First Light; page 38 Stewart Dunlop; page 43 Victor Last/Geographical Visual Aids, Wiarton, Ontario; page 44 (left and right) Michael Jackson; page 45 Bill Ross/First Light; page 46 Stewart Dunlop; page 47 Stewart Dunlop; page 48 Pat Morrow/First Light; page 49 Ron Watts/First Light; page 51 Michael Jackson; page 53 Brian Milne/First Light; page 54 Stewart Dunlop; page 55 Manitoba Department of Agriculture (Winnipeg); page 57 P. Durand/Sygma-Publiphoto; page 58 World Wildlife Fund; page 61 (top) Mary Evans Picture Library; page 61 (centre) Bill Majesky/The Toronto Sun Syndicated Services (Formerly — Canada Wide Feature Services); page 61 (bottom) Stewart Dunlop; page 63 (top and bottom) Michael Jackson; page 64 Jeff Foott/VALAN; page 65 Michael Jackson; page 67 Gilbert van Ryckervorsel/VALAN; page 74 P. Brunet/Publiphoto; page 75 Victor Last/Geographical Visual Aids, Wiarton, Ontario; page 77 Mark Stephenson/First Light; page 84 Val Wilkinson/VALAN; page 86 Stewart Dunlop; page 92 Stewart Dunlop; page 95 Stewart Dunlop; page 96 (top and bottom) Stewart Dunlop; page 97 J.L. Atlan/Sygma-Publiphoto; page 104 Chris Dunlop; page 105 RADARSAT INTERNATIONAL; page 109 Ken Graham/Pono Presse; page 117 (top) D. Marchand; page 117 (bottom) Stewart Dunlop; page 118 (top) Jim Brandenburg/First Light; page 118 (bottom) Thomas Kitchin/First Light; page 119 (top and bottom) Stewart Dunlop; page 121 (bottom right) International Centre for Research in Agroforestry (ICRAF) (other photos) Stewart Dunlop; page 125 Michael Jackson; page 128 (left) Vinai/Greenpeace; Page 128 (right) Garth Lenz/Greenpeace; page 130 Province of BC – Ministry of Forests; page 132 Al Harvey; page 137 TransAlta Utilities Corporation; page 139 Saskatchewan Tourism; page 141 Atlan/Sygma-Publiphoto; page 142 Strathcona Park Lodge, BC; page 147 (top and bottom) Stewart Dunlop; page 148 (left) Michael Jackson; page 148 (right) A. Cornu/Publiphoto; page 150 McMillan Bloedel; page 152 Stewart Dunlop; page 153 (top and bottom) World Vision Canada; page 160 Tricil Ltd.; page 161 M. Ponomareff/Pono Presse; page 162 (top) Simon Parent/Pono Presse; page 162 (bottom) Stewart Dunlop; page 163 John McNeill/*The Globe and Mail*; page 164 Quebec and Ontario Paper Co. Ltd.; page 165 (top) Ron Watts/First Light; page 165 (bottom) Simon Parent/Pono Presse; page 166 Uniphoto Worldwide/Canapress Photo Service; page 167 David Prichard/First Light; page 168 M. Ponomareff/Pono Presse; page 169 Maritime Resource Management Service; page 171 P. Brunet/Publiphoto; page 172 (left) Louis Fernandez/First Light; page 172 (right) Victor Last/Geographical Visual Aids, Wiarton, Ontario; page 175 Paul G. Adam/Publiphoto; page 177 AP/Canapress Photo Service; page 178 Baldev/Sygma-Publiphoto; page 180 Brian Milne/First Light; page 181 Canapress Photo Service; page 182 Andrew Vaughan/Canapress Photo Service; page 184 Lorraine C. Parow/First Light; page 187 Michael Jackson; page 189 W.J. Brown; page 192 Dave Prichard/First Light; page 193 Ken Straiton/First Light; page 195 Victor Last/Geographical Visual Aids, Wiarton, Ontario; page 201 Giansanti/Sygma-Publiphoto; page 202 Stewart Dunlop; page 204 G.E. Hasse/Publiphoto; page 205 (left) Chris Dunlop; page 205 (right) D. Aubert/Sygma-Publiphoto; page 206 Stewart Dunlop; page 211 Al Harvey; page 213 (top) R. Poissant/Publiphoto; page 213 (bottom) Stewart Dunlop; page 214 (both photos) Stewart Dunlop; page 215 Victor Last/ Geographical Visual Aids, Wiarton, Ontario; page 216 (top) Victor Last/Geographical Visual Aids, Wiarton, Ontario; page 216 (bottom) The Toronto Sun Syndicated Services (Formerly — Canada Wide Feature Services); page 217 Victor Last/ Geographical Visual Aids, Wiarton, Ontario; page 221 The Toronto Sun Syndicated Services (Formerly — Canada Wide Feature Services); page 222 Victor Last/Geographical Visual Aids, Wiarton, Ontario; page 223 Brian Milne/First Light; page 225 Thomas Kitchin/First Light.

Every effort has been made to trace the original source of all material and photographs contained in this book. Where the attempt has been unsuccessful the publisher would be pleased to hear from copyright holders to rectify any omissions.

INTRODUCTION

There is a growing awareness today of the importance of the environment. Many events have helped to make us conscious of environmental issues. Disasters such as Chernobyl have illustrated how rapidly contaminated air can spread over great distances. The increase in the instances of diseases such as cancer has caused concern about the effects of toxic chemicals in our environment. Holes in the ozone layer of the upper atmosphere and global warming have created fears that the future of our planet is seriously at risk. In addition, we have come to realize that the extremes of wealth and poverty found between rich nations and poor nations are contributing to the rapid rate of environmental destruction. The wealth of the industrialized countries enables people to consume huge quantities of resources. But in the process they rob the earth of these same resources and create environmental problems such as toxic waste and air, water, and land pollution. Extreme poverty causes increasingly larger numbers of people to over-exploit the land. This is turn causes desertification or the loss of rain forest, both of which have environmental consequences on a global scale.

The growth of technology is a powerful force affecting our lives in countless ways. Technology impacts on the environment both positively and negatively. For example, some fear that biotechnology will release new types of organisms into the environment that it will be unable to cope with. Technology also creates numerous deadly substances that sooner or later have to be disposed of. On the other hand, technology gives us unique ways of monitoring the environment for our own safety. These include satellite imagery, which gives a constant global overview of the environment, and computer controlled devices to monitor local conditions.

The environment is also affected by political activities, including war. For example, in 1991 retreating Iraqi forces set fire to hundreds of Kuwaiti oil wells polluting the skies with thick black smoke and killing much of the wildlife in the area. Perhaps of even greater importance is the realization that the environment can be an easy target for terrorism.

Many environmental issues have received extensive coverage in newspapers and on television. However, it is important to recognize the danger in absorbing information from journalistic sources alone. Often the media are reporting events which may involve only one point of view. In addition, there may be little emphasis on understanding the processes that cause environmental problems. There are usually no simple or clear-cut answers to questions about the environment. Between the extremes of opposing viewpoints on any issue there are various shades of opinion. There may be scientific opinions that are uncertain due to the complex nature of ecology. Often political opinions may be sharply polarized and economic issues are frequently seen from only a short-term perspective. Responsible citizens should be aware of the many sides of the issues so that they can reach informed decisions about environmental problems.

Understanding Our Environment is designed to help students make these informed decisions. In this book we will look at environmental issues that might affect you in your own community. We will also learn about vastly different threats to the environment in other parts of the world. We will see that, no matter what the issue, human activity affects the physical world and the natural world in turn affects humans. Finally, we will look at what each of us can do to help preserve and protect our environment. We all recognize the need to take better care of the earth in order to ensure a habitable world for future generations. As a piece of graffiti painted on a bridge in Rock Creek park in Washington, D.C., so aptly put it, "Good planets are hard to find."

UNIT 1

ECOSYSTEMS AND THE EARTH'S ENVIRONMENT

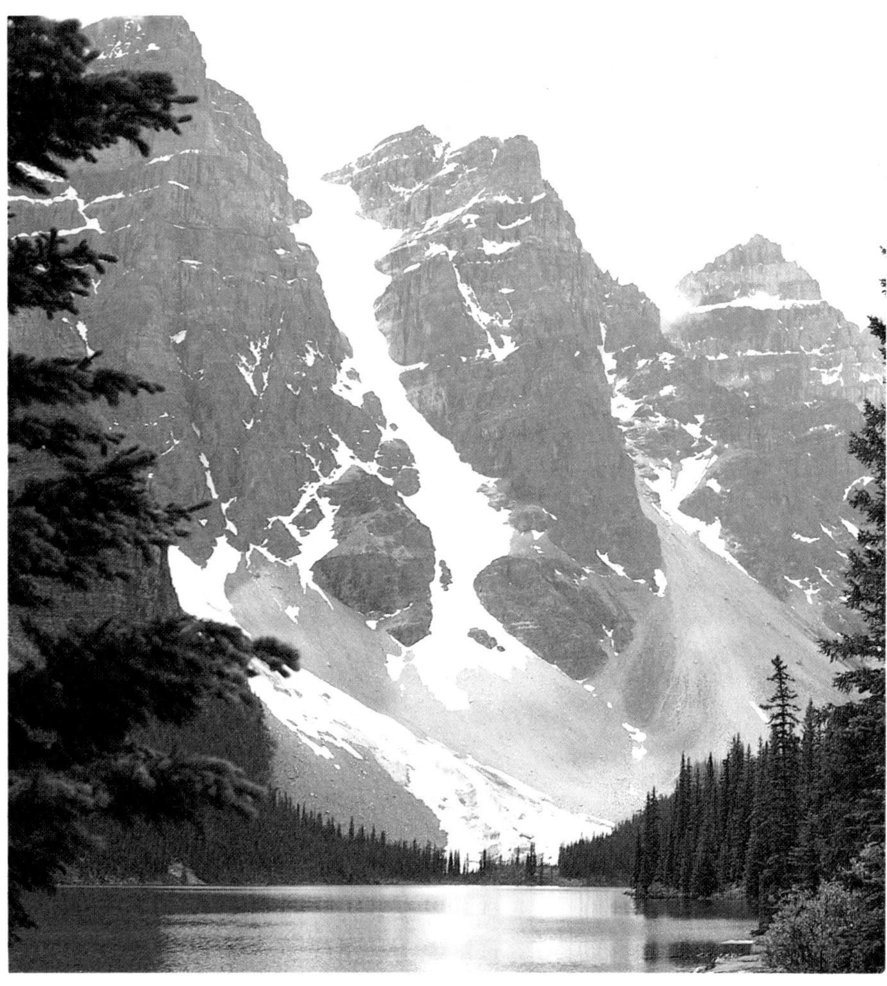

Moraine Lake is located near Lake Louise in the Canadian Rockies.

1 THE ENVIRONMENT

When the first astronauts viewed the earth from space, they remarked that they could not see any international boundaries. To them the earth was a single unit — the home of all living creatures.

We have always depended on the environment for survival. Without air, water, and soil none of us could exist. Yet if we do not take care of our planet, the day may come when life as we know it will become impossible.

Today we are aware that the global environment is fragile. The pollution of air and water has become a major threat to our health. The buildup of chemicals in wildlife and in the foods we eat has reached levels we can no longer ignore. Soil erosion threatens more than one-third of the world's farmland. Figure 1.2 on page 4 shows a few of the world's major environmental "hot spots." Others will undoubtedly arise as time passes.

Many people have begun to question the ability of the planet to support the growing population if our present ways continue. The result is that, while twenty years ago most people would not have given the environment more than a passing thought, today many people are taking a keen interest in environmental problems.

What is the environment?

According to *The Shorter Oxford English Dictionary*, the environment is "the conditions or influences under which any person or thing lives." Therefore the environment includes the surface of the land, rivers, and oceans, as well as soils, vegetation, and animal life. It also includes the atmosphere we breathe every day. Yet the environment is not something separate from us that we can choose to ignore. We are a part of the environment. Everything we do affects it in some way. Driving a car or using a washing machine affects the environment just as smoke from a factory does.

Because we in Canada have a high standard of living, we consume a relatively large share of the world's resources. For example, Canadians account for only 0.5 percent of the world's people. Yet we use about 4 percent of the world's energy supply. The impact Canadians have on the environment is therefore many times greater than the impact of people in developing countries. We use far more resources and create much more waste than they do.

The environment as a system

It is useful to think of the environment as a **system**. A system is a set of different elements that interact with one another in a particular way. An aquarium is such a system. Water and oxygen must be present for fish to survive. The temperature of the tank must be relatively constant and an energy supply in the form of food must be added from outside the system.

The world in which we live can be thought of as a giant system. Life within it depends upon the delicately balanced relationships between climate, vegetation, and soil. When these relationships are in balance, a state of environmental equilibrium exists. This may be upset in a number of ways — for example, by a change in climate or by people removing the vegetation cover. The result usually is a change in the number of plants and animals that live in the area. Like the aquarium, the earth receives its energy from an outside source — the sun. Unlike the aquarium, which can be cleaned from time to time, all of our wastes remain on earth.

An aquarium is an example of an environmental system.

Today we frequently speak about **ecosystems**. An ecosystem is a system consisting of living things and the environment in which they live. **Ecology** is the study of living things in their environment.

The idea of ecosystems helps us to understand the relationships that exist between people and their environments. In this book we will:

- identify the world's major environmental problems and the processes that cause them;
- examine the risks posed by environmental problems, both to human health and the physical environment;
- discover what policies and programs are being implemented to solve environmental problems;
- focus on our own role in creating a cleaner and healthier world.

Opinions on the environment

In the late 1980s, Canadians for the first time placed the environment at the top of the list of national problems, ahead of the state of the economy and the possibility of nuclear war. The importance of environmental issues tends to decline in periods of economic recession, however, when people are concerned with job security. A poll taken in 1989 and 1992 (Figure 1.1) shows that the number of Canadians concerned about some issues increased, while concern for other issues declined. You may want to produce a class average for concern about each of the issues today.

The surge of interest in the environment has suddenly converted many politicians to the environmental cause. This highlights the truth of the saying, "Where the people lead, governments will follow." The environmental movement has also become a political force, with "green parties" gaining votes in many countries. Industry, too, has joined the environmental bandwagon. Many companies have appointed environmental officers to help them with their expansion plans and to deal with public concerns about the environment.

An important event was the establishment by the United Nations of the World Commission on Environment and Development. In 1987 the commission published a report entitled *Our Common Future*. This widely acclaimed book is often referred to as the Brundtland Report after the commission's chairperson, Norwegian prime minister Gro Brundtland. It quickly became the handbook for environmental policies and programs.

Figure 1.1 (a) Major Global Environmental Concerns, 1989 and 1992

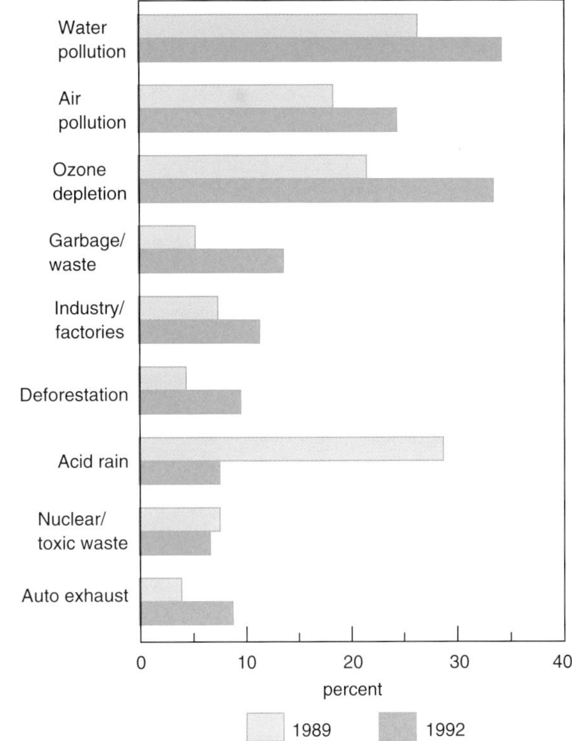

From Angus Reid Group, Canadians and the Environment Survey. Reprinted from the *Toronto Star*, 1 September 1992, by permission.

Figure 1.1 (b) Major Global Environmental Concerns of Canadians by regions, 1991

ISSUE	CANADA	ATLANTIC PROVINCES	PQ	ON	MB/ SK	AB	BC
	percent						
Water pollution	34	26	40	38	28	25	28
Air pollution	25	21	23	27	24	26	24
Ozone depletion	20	16	19	22	17	20	19
Garbage/waste	12	12	8	13	18	12	11
Oil spills	12	14	6	13	10	16	22
Industry/ factories	11	8	21	6	2	7	11
Deforestation	10	2	9	9	11	18	16
Acid rain	10	13	9	12	7	8	6
Rain forest destruction	10	6	6	10	15	14	12
Nuclear/ toxic waste	8	8	8	9	10	3	7
Pollution general	7	16	6	5	11	11	5
Greenhouse effect	7	8	4	8	7	7	6

Note: Respondents were asked to name the two most serious problems facing the world, but not necessarily their community. Up to two answers were accepted; therefore responses will add to more than 100%.

Adapted from Angus Reid Group, *Canadians and the Environment* (Toronto 1991).

Figure 1.2 Ecological hot spots

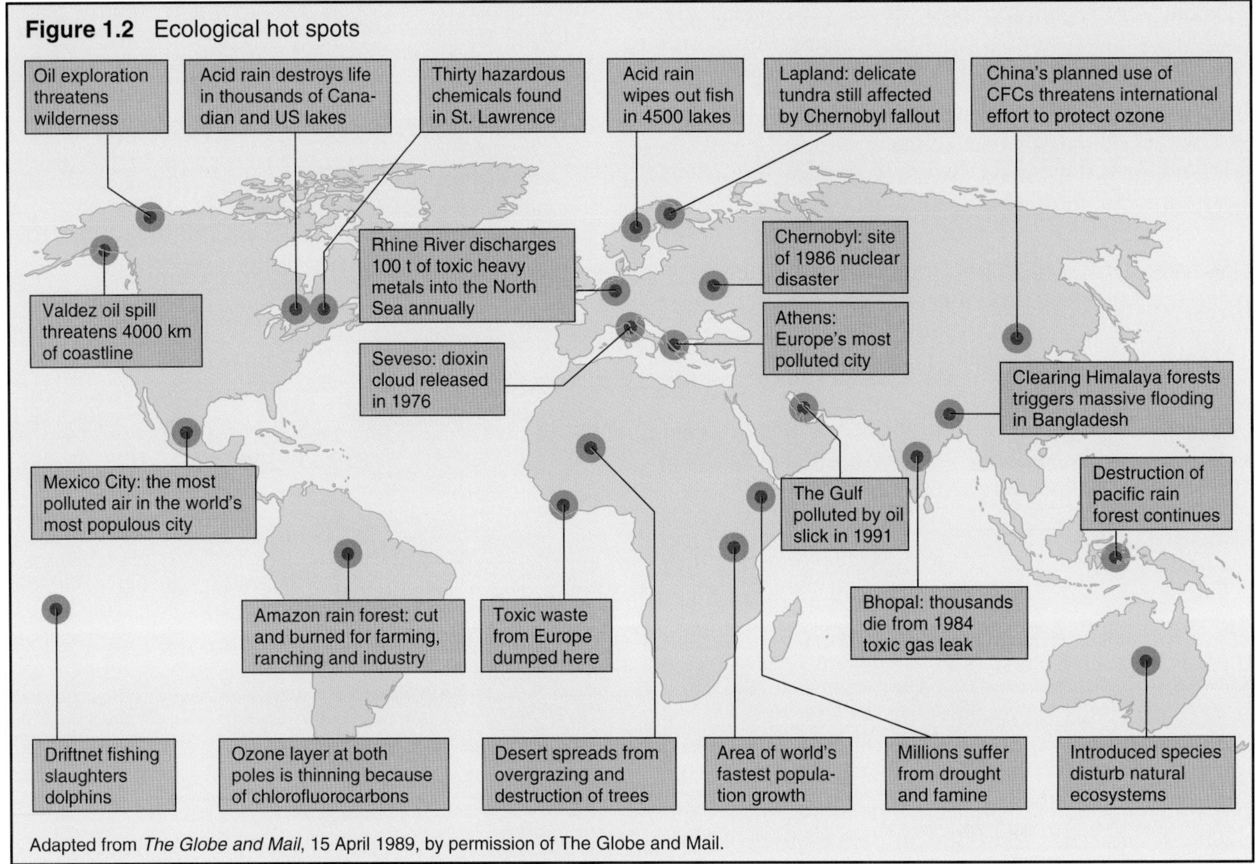
Oil exploration threatens wilderness
Acid rain destroys life in thousands of Canadian and US lakes
Thirty hazardous chemicals found in St. Lawrence
Acid rain wipes out fish in 4500 lakes
Lapland: delicate tundra still affected by Chernobyl fallout
China's planned use of CFCs threatens international effort to protect ozone
Valdez oil spill threatens 4000 km of coastline
Rhine River discharges 100 t of toxic heavy metals into the North Sea annually
Chernobyl: site of 1986 nuclear disaster
Athens: Europe's most polluted city
Seveso: dioxin cloud released in 1976
Clearing Himalaya forests triggers massive flooding in Bangladesh
Mexico City: the most polluted air in the world's most populous city
The Gulf polluted by oil slick in 1991
Destruction of pacific rain forest continues
Amazon rain forest: cut and burned for farming, ranching and industry
Toxic waste from Europe dumped here
Bhopal: thousands die from 1984 toxic gas leak
Driftnet fishing slaughters dolphins
Ozone layer at both poles is thinning because of chlorofluorocarbons
Desert spreads from overgrazing and destruction of trees
Area of world's fastest population growth
Millions suffer from drought and famine
Introduced species disturb natural ecosystems

Adapted from *The Globe and Mail*, 15 April 1989, by permission of The Globe and Mail.

SOME MISUNDERSTANDINGS ABOUT THE ENVIRONMENT

A number of false views about the environment should be dispelled right away. First, as we have already noted, the environment is not an issue that we can take an interest in or ignore at will. Problems such as air and water pollution are important to everyone. Only through an understanding of the environment can many of these problems be solved.

Second, environmental problems are not new. People in Roman times died of poisoning from lead pipes. Open sewers caused countless deaths from cholera in early cities. Air pollution reached high levels in the towns of the Industrial Revolution. However, toxic chemicals have now added a new range of environmental problems.

Third, environmental problems are not simply the fault of industry. We like to blame chemical companies or metal smelters for creating pollution, or perhaps politicians for not doing much about it. Yet all of us buy the products of companies that create pollution. And most of us drive cars. Cars have been described as the greatest source of pollution. We also create pollution in other ways. Think of what we throw out as waste or dispose of through the sewage systems.

Fourth, few environmental problems have a purely local effect. Most problems eventually influence large areas and possibly the entire world. A chemical spill into a creek, for example, quickly affects the river system and finds its way into the ocean. Although the effect of the spill may be diluted, the gradual buildup of chemicals from many spills can seriously pollute the world's lakes and oceans. Pollution is impossible to confine to a particular part of the world. The continuous movement of the world's winds and ocean currents spreads the pollution of air and water over the globe without regard for national boundaries.

Finally, environmental problems do not exist only in the rich Western world, even though our large-scale use of resources does create serious pollution problems. Consider the two newspaper clippings on page 5, which suggest that air pollution may be at its worst in the cities of developing countries. The reference to Africa tells us that extreme poverty, like extreme wealth, can cause serious degradation of the environment.

BEIJING'S AIR 35 TIMES DIRTIER THAN LONDON'S

Reuters, Beijing

Beijing has become one of the world's most polluted capitals, with air 35 times dirtier than London's and 16 times more contaminated than crowded Tokyo's, the Chinese media said yesterday.

Soot from the burning of coal and sulphur dioxide emissions from heavy industry send air pollution above state limits in the capital and 59 other cities, the *China Youth News* said, quoting the results of China's first survey of industrial pollution.

The country has 168 000 "polluting factories" despite an environmental protection law in force for nine years, the paper quoted the head of the state environmental protection agency as telling a news conference.

ACID RAIN REPORTED OVER AFRICAN RAIN FOREST

Associated Press, Frankfurt, West Germany

Scientists have discovered air pollution over much of Africa, says Meinrat Andreae, a chemist with West Germany's Max Planck Institute. He said the deliberate burning of huge savanna areas produces acid rain and ozone pollution that settles over Africa's rain forests.

The problem of the "commons"

In earlier times the **commons** were the pastures that were shared by all the villagers. Today we use the term to refer to any natural resource that people can use freely. The air we breathe is a common resource, available to all of us and not even taxed! Water, especially in the oceans, is another, as is wildlife. Because these resources have been freely available to us, they have often been taken for granted and abused. Common resources belong to everyone, and thus everyone feels that they have the same "right" to use them. Without proper resource management, however, resources will inevitably become overused.

Population and resources

Imagine a test tube containing bacteria that double in number every day. Suppose the tube fills completely after fifty days. How full would the tube be after forty-eight days? If the bacteria double each day, then on the forty-ninth day the test tube would be only half full. On the forty-eighth day it would be only one-quarter full. At this stage a crisis level would not be apparent in the tube, yet only two days would remain before the tube is completely full. In the same way, only a very short period of time may remain before world population exceeds the ability of this planet to sustain the human species.

This rapid rate of world population growth is a relatively recent trend. Figure 1.3 shows that rapid growth began only with the Industrial Revolution in the middle of the eighteenth century and has been particularly rapid in the past fifty years. Today the population of the world continues to grow at an alarming rate. In one minute, about 260 babies are born and 100 people die. Therefore there is an increase of 160 people per minute. Convert this figure to an annual total and you will see that the world's population rises by about 84 million people per year or by nearly three times the population of Canada! In 1995 total world population was estimated to be at least 5.75 billion, with 75 percent of that number living in developing countries.

Figure 1.3 The growth of world population since 1650

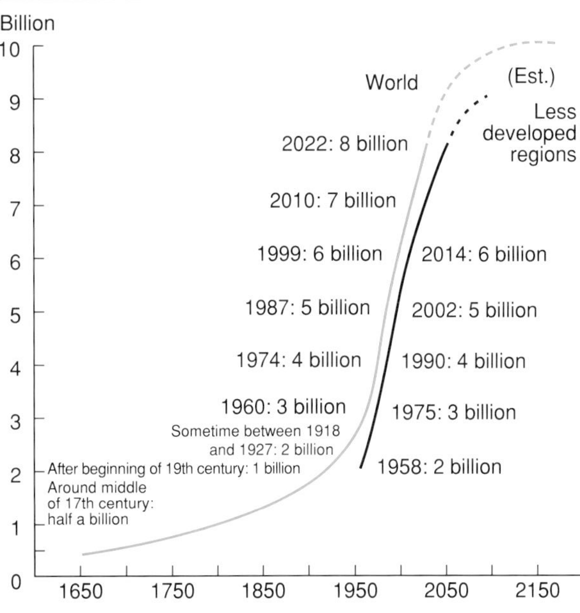

The population of 5.7 billion in 1995 is expected to continue growing until after 2200 when the population could stabilize at around 11.6 billion. The graph illustrates only what could happen under certain assumptions of fertility and mortality.

From *Vital Signs 1996*, Worldwatch Institute and *The Economist*, 24 September 1994

According to estimates made by the United Nations, the world's population is likely to double over the next fifty to one hundred years. This rise in world population will have an enormous impact on the use of world resources. The pressure of population increase underlies most environmental problems. Merely to support today's population, the world's ecosystems have been greatly modified. Ten billion people will have a much greater impact on the environment than five billion, especially since the rate of consumption per capita of goods and services is continually rising.

One of the phrases frequently used today is **sustainable development**. This term is defined in *Our Common Future* as meeting "the needs of the present without compromising the ability of future generations to meet their own needs." What we see as needs depends very much on where we live and what our expectations are. In developing countries the basic needs of food, clothing, and shelter are often barely met, with only a minimum of health and educational facilities. In richer, developed countries our expectations are much higher. An enormous variety of consumer goods and services is available to the majority of people. Our wants are much greater than our needs, and we all seem to want more tomorrow than we have today.

Our use of resources

All the goods and most of the services we use in everyday life depend upon resources. The use of resources affects the environment in one way or another. Each member of the world's population is a consumer. Each of us must eat and have some form of shelter and comfort and, as a result, all of us use a wide variety of products in different ways. In economically developed societies the number of products available for sale is so great that it is difficult to count them. Have you considered what it must be like to keep track of all the products in a department store or supermarket?

The production of these goods requires the use of **natural resources**, which may be defined as all of earth's materials that are of use to people. Resources may be classified as **renewable** and **nonrenewable**. Renewable resources are produced by natural, or biological, processes. These include all useful plants (including forests), wildlife, and fish. Water, since it is renewed by a natural process, may also be called a renewable resource.

On the other hand, nonrenewable resources include all materials that can be obtained from the earth only once. Although natural processes have created these resources and will do so again, the process takes millions of years. Therefore these resources are termed nonrenewable. They include mineral ores and **fossil fuels**.

Cultural development and energy use

Geologically speaking, humans have been present on earth for a very short period of time. Only in recent years have people come to dominate the landscape. Until about 10 000 years ago, human society consisted of small groups of hunter-gatherers. These primitive people mastered the arts of fire- and tool-making. They survived by hunting wild game and gathering wild fruits, nuts, and roots. Hunting and gathering societies needed large amounts of land to sustain them. Their lifestyles often included seasonal migrations to follow game.

Figure 1.4 Use of energy throughout history. Note that the uppermost bar represents energy use in today's technological society.

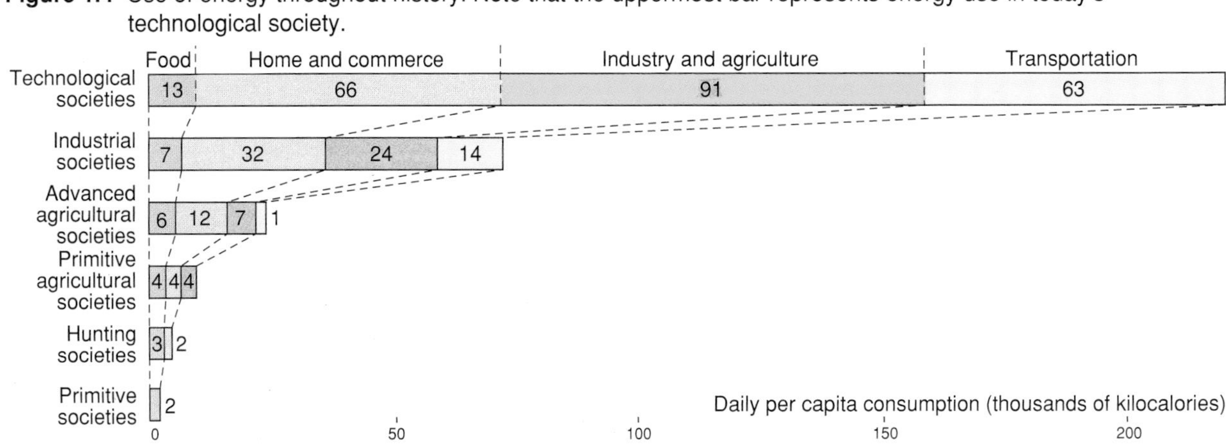

Between 10 000 and 5000 years ago, people discovered that they could domesticate many of the plants and animals needed for survival. Settlements and a more intensive use of land developed in some areas. As a result of this agricultural revolution, people started to shape the plant and animal communities instead of simply being a part of them. New tools such as the wheel and the plough were developed, and people began to use animals for work as well as for food.

Over thousands of years more and more tools were developed and other sources of energy were harnessed to meet the needs of agriculture and the growing industries. The smelting of metals, for example, required large amounts of heat energy, and wood was used to supply this. Water and wind were used to drive the machinery that pumped water and ground grain. Figure 1.4 shows how the use of energy has changed through history.

During the eighteenth century, coal replaced wood as a fuel and mechanization increased as a result of the Industrial Revolution. Since that time our ability to change the environment has grown by leaps and bounds. Today few places on earth have not been affected by human activities. The combination of our numbers, technology, and resource use is having a tremendous impact on our planet.

Moving things around

We talk about "using up" our resources. However, the elements contained in these resources are not used up or destroyed but remain on our planet. We in fact merely move materials around and change the form in which they are found. For example, we take coal (mainly carbon) out of the ground and move it from one place to another. When it is burned, the carbon is converted to carbon dioxide (CO_2), much of which goes into the air. The residues, including some toxic materials, are dumped as ash. The moving of materials, as well as their manufacture, uses a great deal of energy, mainly derived from fossil fuels.

The use of resources creates serious problems for society. Consider just two of these problems.

First, some elements, such as metals, may be concentrated by human activity. Mercury, for example, is found in rocks and even in soils. When used in an industrial process, it may be discharged in a concentrated and toxic form as **methyl-mercury**. It can then find its way into the **food chain** — that is, it is taken in by small creatures, which in turn fall prey to larger creatures, and so on. The mercury then becomes concentrated in higher levels in the food chain.

Second, industrial processes may combine chemicals to produce deadly compounds. Carbon, hydrogen, oxygen, and chlorine, when combined in particular ways, can produce poisonous chemicals, many of which are available for use in our gardens as organic pesticides. Other dangerous materials may be by-products of industry, such as the **dioxins** produced by the pulp and paper industry. A study of the main groups of chemicals is on pages 12 to 14.

Large volumes of resources are brought into towns and cities where they are manufactured or consumed. Finally, the wastes are discharged into the environment. Think for a moment of the concentration of materials brought into a large city such as Toronto. Food is imported for Toronto's 4.2 million inhabitants, both from within North America and from around the world. A large volume of manufactured goods is also assembled, including clothing, chemical products, home appliances, and cars. Most goods are carefully packaged, which uses further volumes of materials. Everyday the sum total of human waste, discarded goods, discharged chemicals and gases, and empty bottles and packages creates volumes of sewage and mountains of waste. All of this output has to be absorbed by the environment in and around the city. And every other city in the world has a problem similar to that of Toronto.

A typical landfill site for domestic waste.

Cities and technology

A growing number of the world's inhabitants live in cities. In Canada the figure has risen to about 80 percent. In the world as a whole, once dominated by rural farmers, almost 50 percent of people live in towns and cities. (See Figure 1.5.)

The growth of cities, or **urbanization**, is closely related to improvements in technology. Towns grew when the first farmers learned how to produce more food than they needed. Many people then left farming for other occupations, such as trading or the making of implements. The first towns were small but later expanded as transportation of food over greater distances became possible. Later the empires of Greece and Rome sustained large capital cities by creating networks of sea and road links.

Figure 1.5 Urban population growth, 1950–2025

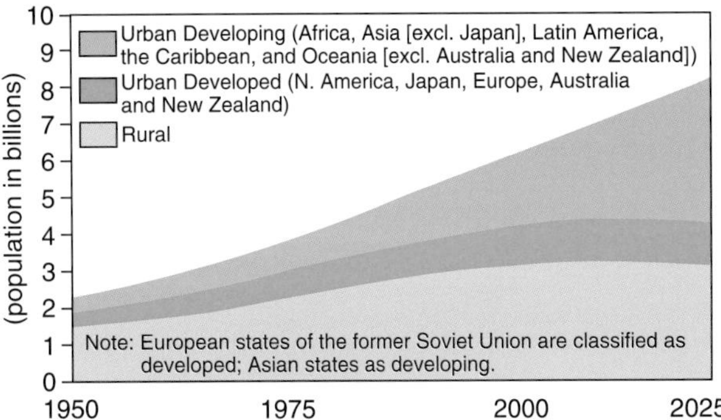

From *World Resources 1996-97* by permission of Oxford University Press, Inc.

In the past two centuries the development of mechanical power gave a great boost to urban development, creating jobs for thousands of factory workers. Along with factory work, other service jobs were created in offices and shops.

The modern city is an elaborate system that brings resources to a large number of people concentrated in a small area. In return the urban population manufactures goods and provides services for the benefit of people living in the city and elsewhere. Today only a small percentage of the population is required to produce food and obtain other natural resources, thus freeing the majority of people for city-based jobs.

Figure 1.6 shows the city as a type of system. The city uses large volumes of resources and creates corresponding masses of waste. Energy or materials, such as rainfall and imported products, that enter the system from outside may be called inputs. Materials that leave it, either as exports or waste, are called outputs.

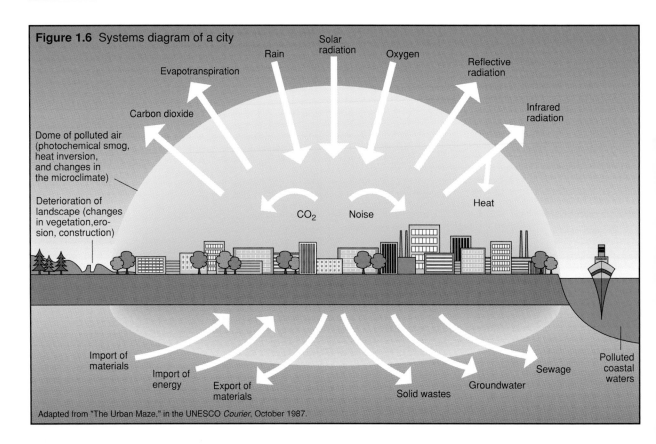

Figure 1.6 Systems diagram of a city

Rain
Solar radiation
Oxygen
Evapotranspiration
Reflective radiation
Carbon dioxide
Infrared radiation
Dome of polluted air (photochemical smog, heat inversion, and changes in the microclimate)
Deterioration of landscape (changes in vegetation, erosion, construction)
CO_2
Noise
Heat
Import of materials
Import of energy
Export of materials
Solid wastes
Groundwater
Sewage
Polluted coastal waters

Adapted from "The Urban Maze," in the UNESCO *Courier*, October 1987.

The attractions of cities

Cities have obvious attractions in the form of their amenities. These are the facilities they provide, particularly in health, education, and recreation. Cities also provide job opportunities in manufacturing and services. Today services provide most jobs in Western cities.

Information handling has become an important part of our way of life. Cities have become centres of information, providing many jobs in the fields of education, finance, communications, and decision-making.

We may ask whether the choice of city living has any drawbacks. Is the urban or built environment as desirable to live in as the rural or **natural environment**? The rural environment creates images of forests, lakes, and green fields. The urban environment consists of buildings, streets, factories, and perhaps some parks. The rural environment suggests quietness and clean air; the urban environment has more noise and dirt.

Some people in Western society have the opportunity to enjoy the best of both worlds. Subdivisions on the outskirts of cities give homes a rural quality, while urban jobs and amenities are relatively close. These people are able to work in one environment and live in another, though the price they pay is often a long trip to work either by car or commuter transportation. Both can be expensive. Other people have no choice. For many in North America the inner city slum is a trap from which they can rarely escape.

In cities in developing countries, where migrants arrive by the thousands every year, the situation is even worse. Many people live in makeshift shantytowns. Their urban environment is one of dust, dirt, and odour. Compare the urban scenes shown below to gain a sense of the contrasts in urban living in just one country.

Industrial areas, such as the one above in Glasgow, Scotland, are unattractive environments in which to live, but other cities, such as Chester, England (below), are greatly admired for their architectural beauty.

Technology and the environment

While technology has made the growth of cities possible, it has also affected the environment. First, it has provided people with more elaborate and powerful machines. Think of the environmental impact of a bulldozer compared with a flint axe. Second, technology has created demand for many materials that were previously of little or no use. Uranium, the raw material of the nuclear power industry, is an example.

The Industrial Revolution

In the eighteenth century coal was first used to smelt iron. It was also used to power steam engines, which were gradually adapted to many manufacturing processes. The age of coal brought with it some serious environmental problems. One was the long hours worked by coal miners in dangerous underground conditions. The towns that grew up on the coal fields provided cramped, unsanitary conditions for workers. Another was the air pollution in coal-based industrial areas. Death rates were high as a result of the unhealthy environment.

Improvements in urban health

By the early twentieth century the environments of industrial towns had improved greatly resulting in falling death rates. The health of city dwellers benefitted from the installation of water supply and sewage systems. Improved transport, first by rail and then by road, and the introduction of electricity allowed industries to be located away from coal fields. Newer industrial towns enjoyed cleaner air and a less grubby appearance. Nevertheless, the burning of coal continued to create serious atmospheric pollution.

Changes in energy use

The middle of the twentieth century saw a major shift from coal to oil in most industrialized countries. Oil has three main advantages over coal: it is cleaner to burn, it contains more energy per unit of volume, and it is easier to transport both by tanker and pipeline. Coal quickly lost a number of its traditional markets, particularly in transport, industry, and home heating. Since the Second World War the use of oil continued to increase at the expense of coal. After 1973 coal made something of a comeback, as the price of oil rose tenfold between 1973 and 1980 and the consumption of oil dropped for the first time.

A new technological advance in energy — nuclear power — occurred in the 1950s. Requiring much less transport of raw materials and creating no atmospheric smoke, nuclear power seemed likely to become the power source of the future. However, the problem of how to dispose of highly toxic nuclear waste remains. In addition, two major accidents (at Three Mile Island in the United States in 1979 and at Chernobyl in Ukraine in 1986 in what was then the Soviet Union showed the dangers of nuclear power.

The chemical revolution

Another area of rapid change since the Second World War has been in the field of applied science. The research laboratories of chemical companies have created a steady stream of new products. Agriculture has been a major market for the chemical industry. Herbicides and pesticides, along with chemical fertilizers, are used in large quantities on modern farms. Selective weed killers, such as 2,4-D, have revolutionized prairie farming by controlling weeds. Check a garden store to see the range of chemical compounds available for use in your own garden. Many of these pose a threat to our immediate environment.

Another major sector of the chemical industry produces drugs and medicinal products. Yet another produces chemicals for industrial use, including products such as **PCBs (polychlorinated biphenyls)** and **CFCs (chlorofluorocarbons)**. These were used in electrical transformers and refrigeration equipment respectively.

Pesticides are used extensively in modern agriculture. Here herbicides are being sprayed on orchards in the Niagara fruit belt.

Electronics

Technology has made great contributions to modern society in the field of electronics. Moving parts in some machines have been replaced by electronic impulses. Computers can design and control machines. They can also perform complicated calculations in very little time. These advances have created a late twentieth-century technological revolution. Computer technology has resulted in automated production of many articles. This automation has the effect of lowering prices, bringing products within reach of millions of people. The computer revolution has created many more information-based and service jobs. At the same time, the number of resource extraction and manufacturing jobs has been greatly reduced.

The expansion of computer and chip manufacturing has had one positive effect on the environment. Much less energy is required both to make and to operate electronic equipment than was required for older "heavy" industries. There is therefore less air pollution from the burning of fossil fuels. Nevertheless, some health problems have been observed in places such as Silicon Valley in California. For example, some of the chemicals used in the production of microelectronics have been linked to birth defects. The office environment, where computer operators sit continually in front of video display units, may also prove harmful to our health.

Industrial and technological progress have therefore had a variety of effects on the environment. Increasing energy use is a major problem, not only now but in the foreseeable future as population growth in developing countries continues. The increasing use of chemical compounds is another threat that will require more and more attention. High technology, on the other hand, seems to be less threatening to the environment than heavy industry since it uses much less energy.

Technology as an environmental aid

Technology can also be used in the battle to protect the environment. For example, air photographs and satellite images can be used to monitor the environment. Air photographs can be used to check the spread of crop diseases and to measure the amount of tree growth. Both air photos and satellite images can be used to pinpoint areas where emissions into the atmosphere or water are made; they have also been used to monitor the decline in Canada's wetlands, which are so important to migrating birds. Satellite images can be used to estimate the rate at which the tropical rain forests are being destroyed. Monitoring the burning of the rain forests would be almost impossible to do by ground survey since the areas involved are so vast and inaccessible. Finally, use of the Internet opens up a wealth of information that can help us become more aware of environmental problems.

While computers have revolutionized the business world, there is some concern that they may be harmful to our health.

Images from satellites show features in different colours. In this photograph of the Amazonian rain forest, the cleared rectangles have been converted to pasture or agricultural land. One brush fire is still burning.

MEASURING TOXIC CHEMICALS

Toxic chemicals are usually measured by their concentration in air, water, or food. For example, we talk about parts per billion (ppb) or parts per trillion (ppt).

1 ppb = 1 drop of water in an Olympic size swimming pool.
1 ppt = the size of a $5 bill in relation to the area of the whole of Canada.

CHEMICALS IN THE ENVIRONMENT

Some 80 000 chemicals are in regular use, with an annual addition of at least 1000 new ones. Most of these are **toxic**, which literally means poisonous. The degree of toxicity varies. Some chemicals, such as dioxins, are among the deadliest substances currently known. Tiny amounts can kill people. Others are only mildly toxic, or toxic only if taken in excess, which would be true of most of the medicines we use. In this book the term toxic applies to those chemicals that have serious health risks for human beings, even when taken in small quantities.

Organic chemicals

Many toxic chemicals belong to a group known as **organo-chlorides**. DDT is a well known organo-chloride. Its use has been banned since 1969 in North America, but DDT is still widely used in developing countries. Many pesticides, such as heptachlor, belong to this family of chemicals. Most organo-chlorides accumulate in the fatty tissues of creatures at various levels in the food chain.

Another group of widely used chemicals is **organo-phosphates**. An example is parathion, an extremely dangerous insecticide that kills insects by interfering with the nervous system, causing paralysis and death. Parathion has been replaced in Western countries by less toxic organo-phosphates such as malathion. Nevertheless, even malathion can be extremely hazardous if used incorrectly, and all pesticides have the disadvantage of killing more than their intended targets.

Polychlorinated biphenyls (PCBs)

These chlorinated organic compounds have been widely used in industry because of their special properties. PCBs are stable and have good insulating properties, including fire resistance. They quickly became a standard material for use in electrical transformers. They were also used in electrical capacitors, such as those found in fluorescent lights, and in the making of carbonless copy papers.

Monsanto Chemicals had a monopoly on the manufacture of PCBs in North America. The total produced was 635 000 t, of which 40 000 t was exported to Canada. Although the production of PCBs has been banned in North America since 1977, the inert nature of PCBs ensures that virtually all of the production ever made still exists, either in use, in storage, or in the environment. In Canada, PCBs in use can legally remain until the end of the life of the equipment containing them. Detailed inventories of PCB stocks are kept, with Ontario, Québec, and Alberta having 83 percent of the total.

Problems with the use of PCBs were first noticed in the 1960s. Deformities began to show up in birds that had absorbed significant quantities of PCBs. Since PCBs are soluble in body fats and not in water, they quickly accumulate in the food chain. Many people working in the electrical industry came into contact with PCBs. The most observable effects on humans were outbreaks of chloracne, a painful skin condition. It has been suggested, but not yet proven, that PCBs lead to liver damage and cancer.

The disposal of PCBs is a political rather than a technical problem. PCBs can be disposed of by high temperature incineration (over 1100°C), but it is extremely costly and risks the formation of dioxins. For these reasons, nobody seems to want to take the initiative to do so. In 1989 a cargo of PCBs from Québec crossed the Atlantic for disposal in Wales, only to be refused entry into Britain. Its arrival back in Canada caused an embarrassment to the Québec government, which was in the middle of a provincial election.

Chlorofluorocarbons (CFCs) or freon gases

CFCs are a group of chlorine-based gases that, although much less toxic than PCBs, are similarly stable and inert. The most commonly used CFCs are CFC-11 ($CFCl_3$) and CFC-12 (CF_2Cl_2). CFC-11 has been widely used in aerosols and as a foam-blowing agent in the production of styrofoam and plastics. CFC-12 is used in refrigeration units. A further product, CFC-113, is a dry-cleaning agent. The chemical stability of CFCs that makes them so suitable for these purposes also enables them to survive and rise into the upper atmosphere. There they may last for 75 to 110 years. At high altitudes they release chlorine, which has the capacity to destroy ozone molecules (O_3) in the ozone layer. Low density ozone in the stratosphere protects our planet against ultraviolet radiation.

Dioxins and furans

Dioxins are a family of seventy-five chemical compounds, the most toxic of which is 2,3,7,8-TCDD. This particular dioxin is said to be 1000 times more lethal than cyanide. Dioxins are not intentionally created, but are the result of the incomplete combustion of organo-chlorides. The burning of solid wastes and sewage sludge, as well as wood waste, creates most of the dioxins in the environment. Small amounts may come from fossil fuel-burning plants, cars, and even cigarettes. Forest fires create an unknown quantity of dioxins. Some dioxins come from the bleaching process in pulp and paper industries or from the wood preservative pentachlorophenate. The emission of dioxins from the pulp and paper industry has been largely responsible for the closing of fisheries in Howe Sound, British Columbia. (See page 193.)

Furans are a related family of toxic chemicals with 135 varieties. They have similar properties to dioxins. Furans also accumulate in the food chain and are not readily **biodegradable**. Some furans are known to be highly toxic in animals.

Heavy metals

Lead, mercury, and cadmium are among the many **heavy metals** found in small quantities in soils, water, and the atmosphere. Traces of these elements are natural since they are part of the earth's crust. However, our use of these metals has created higher concentrations, which in many cases creates serious health hazards. For example, lead poisoning can result from the use of lead pipes, and lead from automobile exhaust creates pollution for those who live next to busy roadways. Fortunately, the use of lead pipes has declined greatly, and lead-free gasoline has helped to reduce pollution from automobiles.

Mercury has many valuable properties for industrial use. It is used in batteries, thermometers, and paints, and in the electrolysis of salt to produce chlorine and caustic soda. When absorbed into the body, mercury can damage the central nervous system in adults and children. Exposure to mercury before birth can produce mental retardation.

Cadmium is a heavy metal produced in many industrial processes. It is also used in some types of batteries. Cadmium is highly toxic to organisms at the lower end of the food chain.

Plastics

We live in a plastic age. Since the Second World War the number of plastics and the uses for them have multiplied at an extraordinary rate.

While most plastics are made from oil, a nonrenewable resource, resource depletion is not the only problem they pose to the environment. Plastics are composed of long chains of hydrogen and carbon atoms, called polymers. These polymers create a surface that is not easily penetrated by the bacteria that break down substances. In addition, plastics are waterproof and do not decay easily, nor do they break under sudden or continuous pressure. Thus the features that made plastics so desirable are the very ones that make them so damaging to the environment.

Unfortunately, attempts to find a biodegradable plastic have so far failed. Plastics create mountains of waste and take up space in landfills. However, they do not degrade easily into toxic materials that might damage groundwater. Plastics present great natural hazards to wildlife both on land and at sea.

Oil

Oil, or petroleum, refers to a variety of liquid **hydrocarbons**. These compounds have formed over millions of years from the accumulation of organisms on the ocean floor. Oil is often found at great depths, both on land and offshore. Its use as a source of energy has grown rapidly since the Second World War. It is also an important raw material, especially for plastics and synthetic rubber. Oil is cleaner and has a higher heating value than coal. It is also more easily transported.

However, oil is the source of a variety of environmental problems. The most obvious problem is the oil spills that occur during the recovery and transport of oil. In spite of the great efforts to avoid them, oil spills seem to be occurring with increasing frequency. The effects on wildlife are disastrous. (See Figure 1.7).

Oil is also the leading source of fuel for most forms of transport. Emissions from gasoline-burning engines is one of the world's greatest sources of atmospheric pollution. In addition, a great deal of oil leaks from our cars, ending up on the roads and seeping into groundwater.

Figure 1.7 Main tanker routes and major oil spills

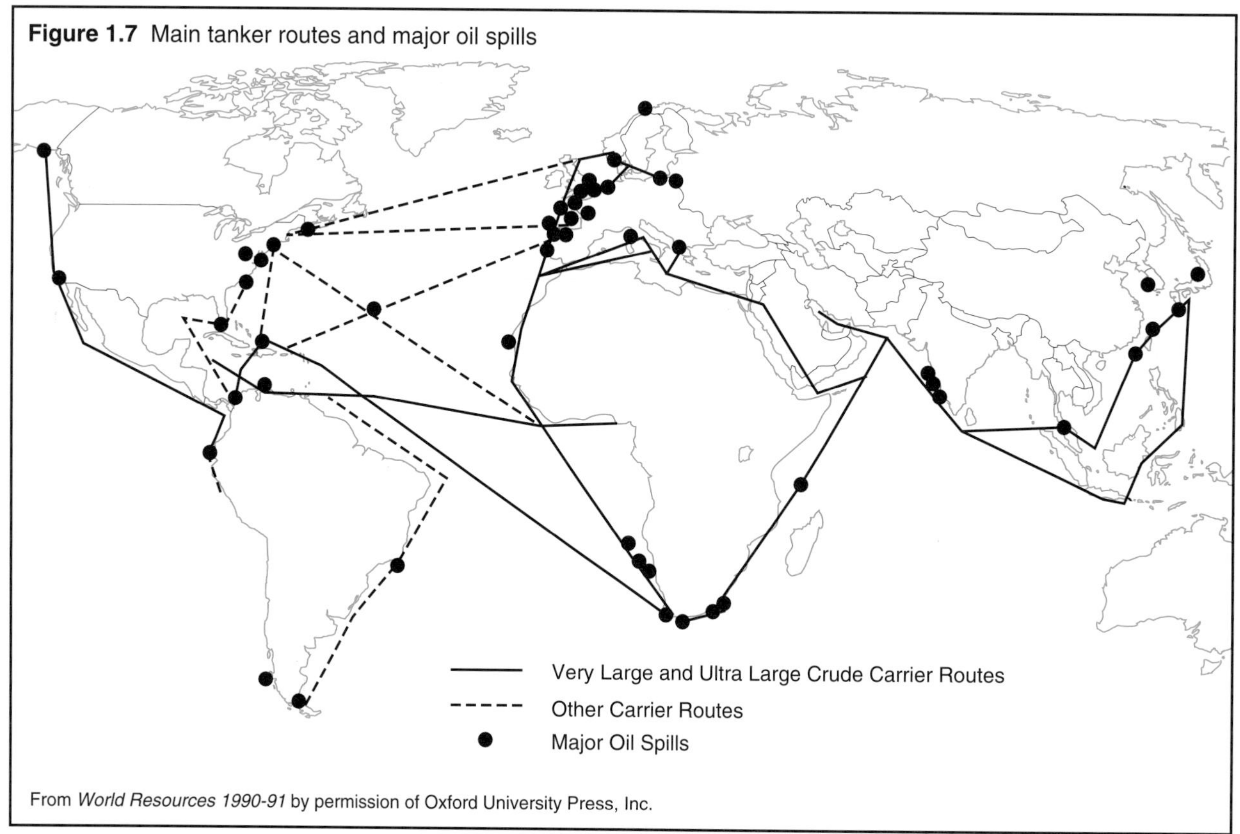

From *World Resources 1990-91* by permission of Oxford University Press, Inc.

Looking back

1. (a) What are the *component parts* of the environment?
   (b) Describe the difference between an ecosystem and an environment.
2. How do human *wants* differ from human *needs*?
3. In what ways does the consumption of resources create environmental problems?
4. List some historical events that show that technological improvements were responsible for the development of cities.

Applying your knowledge

1. Create a table to compare the similarities and differences between a local environment and a global environment.
2. Describe a specific example that explains how a local environmental problem can affect a much larger area.
3. Examine Figure 1.2.
   (a) Where are the hot spots located?
   (b) Is there a pattern to the locations? If so, what is it?
   (c) Look at a world population distribution map and compare it with Figure 1.2. Explain any problems your comparison suggests.
   (d) What conclusions can you draw from your observations?
4. Examine the photograph of the garbage dump on page 7. List three items that should not be in dumps for each of the following categories:
   (a) products that are toxic;
   (b) products that take up too much space; and
   (c) products that can be recycled.
5. Give examples to show how chemicals harm the environment and create health problems.
6. (a) From Figure 1.6, make a list of the inputs into the city system and the outputs from it. What benefits and problems are associated with the outputs?
   (b) Explain why cities contribute more to environmental problems than rural areas do.

Extending your thinking

1. (a) Why is the impact that Canadians have on the environment far greater than that of people in many other countries?
   (b) Have a class debate about whether the situation in (a) is fair.
   (c) If your debate concludes that this situation is *not* fair, have a brainstorming session to determine what Canadians can or should do about it.
2. In groups of three, select a "common" resource, research it, and prepare a presentation to show how it relates to an environmental issue.
3. Discuss how technology both attacks and protects the environment.
4. (a) Figure 1.1 shows the results of a poll taken in Canada in 1989 and 1992. Prepare a questionnaire that lists the nine issues cited in the poll. In a column across the top, list the responses 'Don't know,' 'Not too serious,' 'Somewhat serious,' and 'Very serious.' As a class project, organize the distribution of the questionnaire to 100 people in the school and the community. Have each person respond as to how serious he or she considers each of the issues to be.
   (b) Tabulate the results of your questionnaire. List the issues in descending order of importance — that is, beginning with the 'Very serious' issues. Keep in mind that the results show only the way respondents perceive the problems. If we don't fully understand a problem, we may not be able to make accurate judgments.
5. Fill in your own responses to the questionnaire and review them at the end of this course.
6. Use the Internet or other computer sources to make a list of chemicals that can damage the environment. Then write a list of guidelines to explain how these products should be used (if at all).
7. Prepare an organizer or table highlighting the most serious environmental problems in your community. In the first column list the environmental issues. In the second column describe the problems they create. In the third column suggest some possible solutions to the problems.

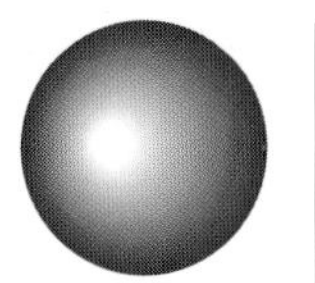

2 THE PHYSICAL WORLD

The themes discussed in chapter 1, such as population growth and the increased use of mechanical power, help to explain some of our environmental problems. However, we cannot fully understand these problems without considering some of the processes that take place in the physical world around us.

Environmental pollution is spread worldwide by the movements of winds and water. These movements require large amounts of energy. Although some energy is available as heat from the interior of the earth, by far the largest part of the energy on this planet comes from the sun.

Solar energy is important to us in several ways. First, it maintains the process of **photosynthesis** by which carbon dioxide (CO_2) and water are converted into carbohydrates and oxygen. This process is the source of all the energy in the foods we eat. Even when we eat animal products, the energy we receive comes from the plants the animals have eaten.

Solar energy also powers the atmospheric engine that causes winds and changing weather. Without solar energy there would be no precipitation and therefore no natural vegetation or life on earth.

Finally, solar energy may be harnessed directly either to heat water or to generate electricity.

The hydrological cycle

Precipitation is just one part of an important natural system known as the **hydrological** or **water cycle**. Figure 2.1 shows that solar energy lifts water vapour by evaporation from the surface of the globe, especially from the oceans. The sun also provides the energy that drives the world's wind systems. These systems carry moist winds from the oceans to the world's land masses. This moisture eventually falls as precipitation, which drains back to the oceans by river systems or **groundwater.**

Figure 2 .1 The hydrological cycle

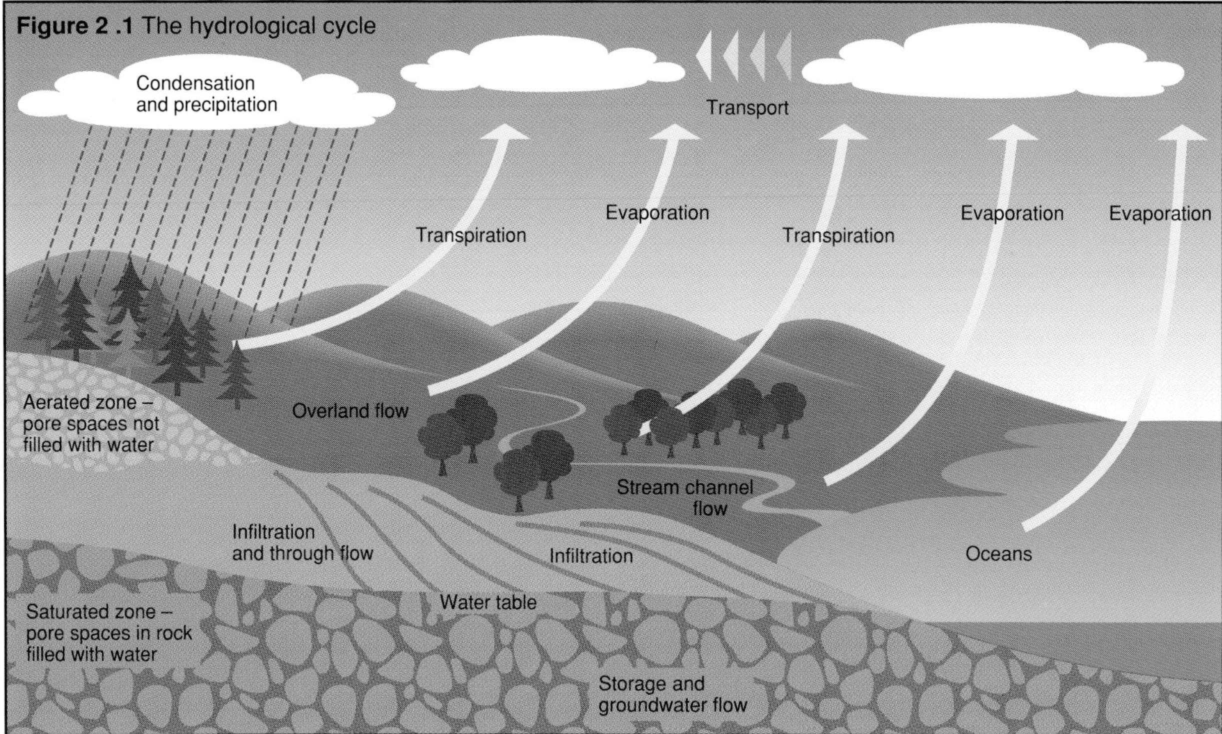

The important final part of the hydrological cycle is the large number of streams and rivers that return the water to the oceans. The world's river systems are vital to human life. They provide us with water for drinking, irrigation, and other purposes. Their energy can also be harnessed for hydroelectric power.

Rivers also create physical features of their own. As water flows downstream it carves its bed and carries loose material and sediment with it. Running water can carve out some spectacular landforms, such as the canyons in the southwestern United States. Overflowing rivers can flood farmlands and settlements, often causing great damage or loss of life.

Not all water that falls on land finds its way immediately back to the oceans. Figure 2.1 shows that much of this water seeps into the large reservoir of groundwater, where it may stay for many years. In many areas people rely on groundwater for their domestic water supplies.

Oceans

The oceans cover a much greater proportion (70.9 percent) of the earth's surface than the land masses on which we live. The oceans act as an enormous water reservoir for the hydrological cycle. Not only do they provide much of the moisture that falls on earth, but they have a moderating effect on the temperatures of nearby land masses. For example, on the southern coast of British Columbia the ocean causes the summers to be cooler and the winters to be warmer than they are inland.

The beach in this part of Nova Scotia has been used as a dumping ground.

The action of winds and tides keeps ocean water on the move. Major currents carry large volumes of water over great distances. The action of currents and tides ensures that pollution in one part of the ocean is likely to affect other areas. Unfortunately, the oceans have been widely used to dispose of all kinds of wastes. Many Canadian beaches are littered with plastic containers and other forms of debris that have been carried from afar by currents and tides.

The world's second most important source of food, after agriculture, is fishing. Solar energy sustains the micro-organisms that are the basis of fish life. Millions of people throughout the world depend on fishing as a basic source of food. If aquatic life is upset, a large portion of the world's population will be deprived of a major source of nutrition.

Ocean water is also a storehouse of dissolved minerals, including several kinds of salts. Another element found in ocean water is carbon. Carbon dioxide is absorbed by the oceans from the atmosphere in the form of carbonate (CO_3^{2-}), helping to some extent to offset the increase in atmospheric CO_2.

Because of their size, we often take the oceans for granted. We assume that they will be able to absorb all the waste dumped into them. The oceans do indeed have a great capacity to break down many waste products, but they cannot handle major marine disasters, such as the oil spill near Valdez, Alaska, in 1989. Heavy metals and toxic chemicals may also build up to levels that can prove harmful to life in ocean waters.

The atmosphere

Consider for a moment how much we depend on the atmosphere. We breathe its gases continuously and adjust our lives every day to the weather around us. The oxygen in the atmosphere is necessary for breathing and for life. The atmosphere provides water for the land and supplies the nitrogen and carbon dioxide required for plant growth.

Differences in temperature and precipitation affect the ability of the environment to cope with pollution. Hot, wet weather, for example, supports the bacteria that break down pollutants and render them harmless. Heavy rainfall may dissolve and carry away many undesirable materials. Cold, dry conditions, on the other hand, are not likely to encourage either the breakdown or the transport of waste materials.

Weather and climate affect our environment in several other ways. In the first place, the world's wind systems are responsible for circulating air around the planet, as shown in Figure 2.2. This circulation ensures that air pollution is spread widely. Weather also has a direct effect on all of us. It influences the types of houses in which we live and even our health. Extremes of weather can have drastic effects on the lives of people.

Figure 2.2 Planetary winds (generalized)

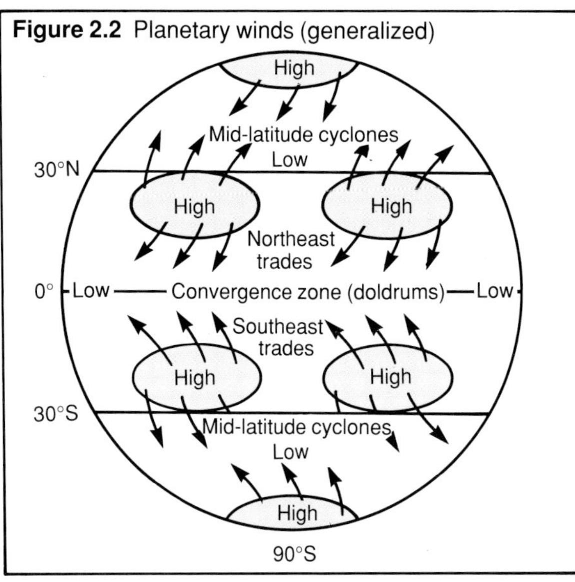

Climate and people

Weather and climate affect the lives of people in many ways. The world pattern of climates provides a framework for the world's agricultural production. The weather at any given time can help or hinder that production. Cold snaps in Florida can damage the citrus crops and thus raise the price of orange juice. Frost in Brazil can have the same effect on coffee. The 1988 drought in the American Midwest and the Canadian Prairies caused a rise in grain prices, which, in turn, led to an increase in prices in North American supermarkets. On the other hand, favourable weather can lead to a glut of fruit or vegetables, resulting in a price decrease.

Weather is also a great potential hazard to transportation and communication. Most delays and accidents involving aircraft are related to bad weather. Road and rail traffic are also frequently upset by snow, ice, and fog.

Climate and health

One aspect of human life that is greatly influenced by

Heavy snowfall often interferes with the movement of traffic and can cause delays of several hours.

climate is health. In much of the tropics disease is easily spread because of the warm, humid climate and the countless insects and other organisms that act as **vectors**, or carriers. Unfortunately, the poverty in much of the tropical world makes badly needed medical services impossible to provide.

Weather and the human body Weather conditions around us change greatly, but we adapt to these changes in many ways. We wear clothes for all kinds of weather. Just think of how different a Canadian's summer and winter clothing is. We also heat or cool our homes and other buildings. Housing styles around the world vary with the need to keep comfortable in different climates. Figure 2.3 shows how some housing types suit climatic conditions in particular parts of the world.

In combination with wind and humidity, extremes of temperature can cause great discomfort and even death. You have probably heard about the effects of wind chill in the Arctic or heatstroke in the tropics. Consider the reactions to extremes of heat or cold given in Figure 2.4. Each extreme will ultimately lead to death if the situation is not corrected.

Climate is also said to influence how we feel and even how we behave. For example, a dull, cloudy climate tends to be depressing, whereas a dry, sunny climate has a more cheering effect. Humidity increases our sense of lethargy, whereas dry weather is said to be more exhilarating. Can you think of any occasions when the weather may have something to do with the way you feel?

Figure 2.4 Human responses to extreme heat and cold

RESPONSES TO COLD	RESPONSES TO HEAT
Constriction of skin, blood vessels	Dilation of skin, blood vessels
Concentration of blood	Dilution of blood
Increased muscle tone	Decreased muscle tone
Shivering	Sweating
Inclination to increase activity	Inclination to decrease activity
Increased urine volume	Thirst and dehydration
Danger of frostbite in fingers and toes	Decreased blood supply to the brain
Increased hunger	Decreased appetite
Falling body temperature	Rising body temperature
	Difficulty maintaining salt balance; cramps

Adapted from John F. Griffiths, *Climate and the Environment*, Grafton Books, Harper Collins Publishers.

Figure 2.3 Some house types associated with various climates

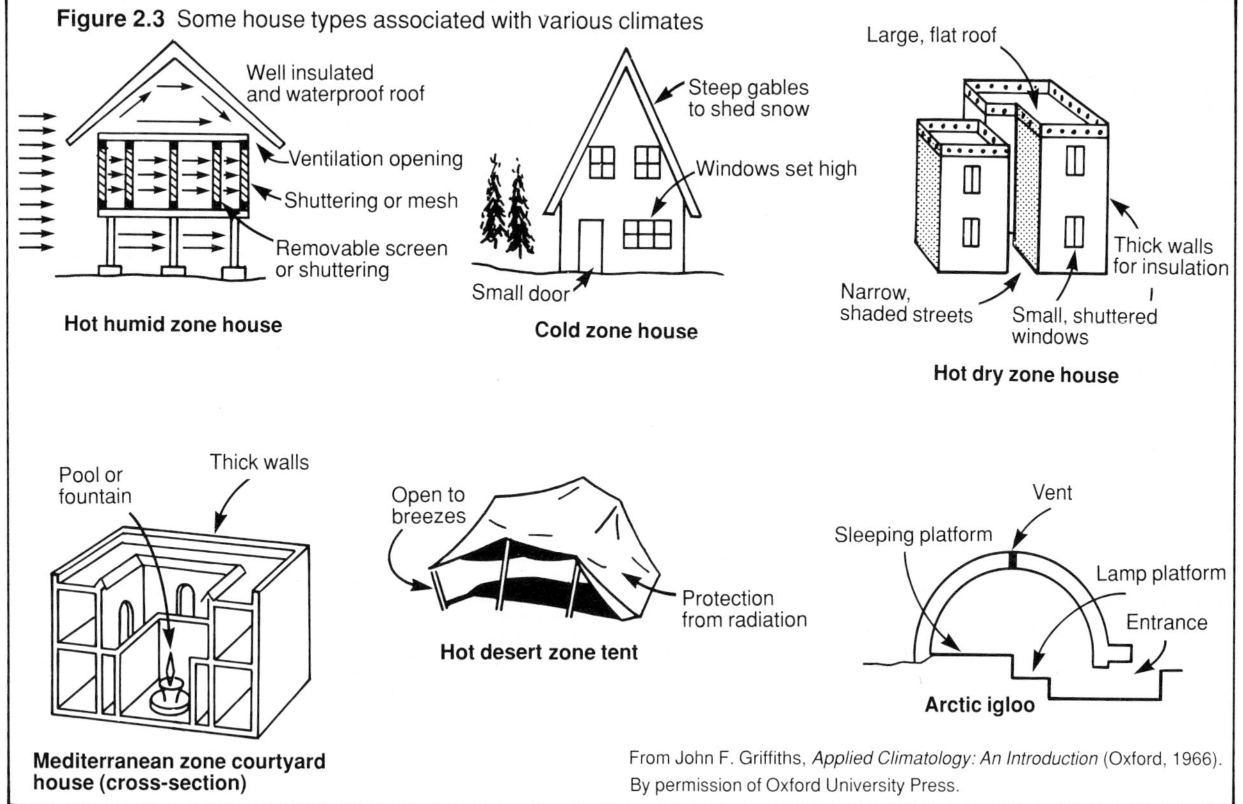

From John F. Griffiths, *Applied Climatology: An Introduction* (Oxford, 1966). By permission of Oxford University Press.

Natural disasters

Natural disasters include events such as floods, droughts, and earthquakes. (See Figure 2.5.) They have increased markedly in recent years. The average disaster causes many more deaths in a poor country than in a rich country, suggesting that overpopulation and poverty may increase the severity of a disaster. In the 1970s an average of 143 000 people were killed each year in natural disasters according to the Red Cross. In 1995 an estimated 133 million people worldwide were affected in some way by natural disasters.

Extremes of weather

If the weather in an area maintains an average, it creates few problems for people. But most farmers will tell you that an average year of weather does not exist. The extremes of weather damage crops and property and even cause loss of life. There are several types of extreme weather conditions. Some, like a hurricane, can create sudden, and often violent, effects. Others, like an extended drought, can spread their damage over a period of years.

Tropical storms (hurricanes, typhoons, and cyclones)
Tropical storms have different names depending on the region of the world in which they occur. **Hurricanes** happen around the Caribbean and the Gulf of Mexico and the nearby parts of the United States. **Typhoons** occur in the Pacific Ocean near China and Japan. **Tropical cyclones** occur around the Indian Ocean and Southeast Asia.

Most of these tropical storms originate in late summer, usually in latitudes around 10° to 15° north or south of the equator. They form in moist air over warm oceans. Their very strong winds spiral toward the low-pressure centre or **eye** of the storm, which is a calm, clear area. The spiralling winds, which can reach strengths of 200 km/hour or more, often cause great damage.

Many hurricanes occur in the Caribbean Sea area. On 24 August 1992 one of the most powerful storms of the 20th century moved across the Miami area of southeast Florida. Hurricane Andrew, as it was called, had sustained wind speeds of 230 km/hour with gusts reaching 280 km/hour. Later it reached Louisiana causing further damage even though by then it had

Figure 2.5 Natural disaster areas

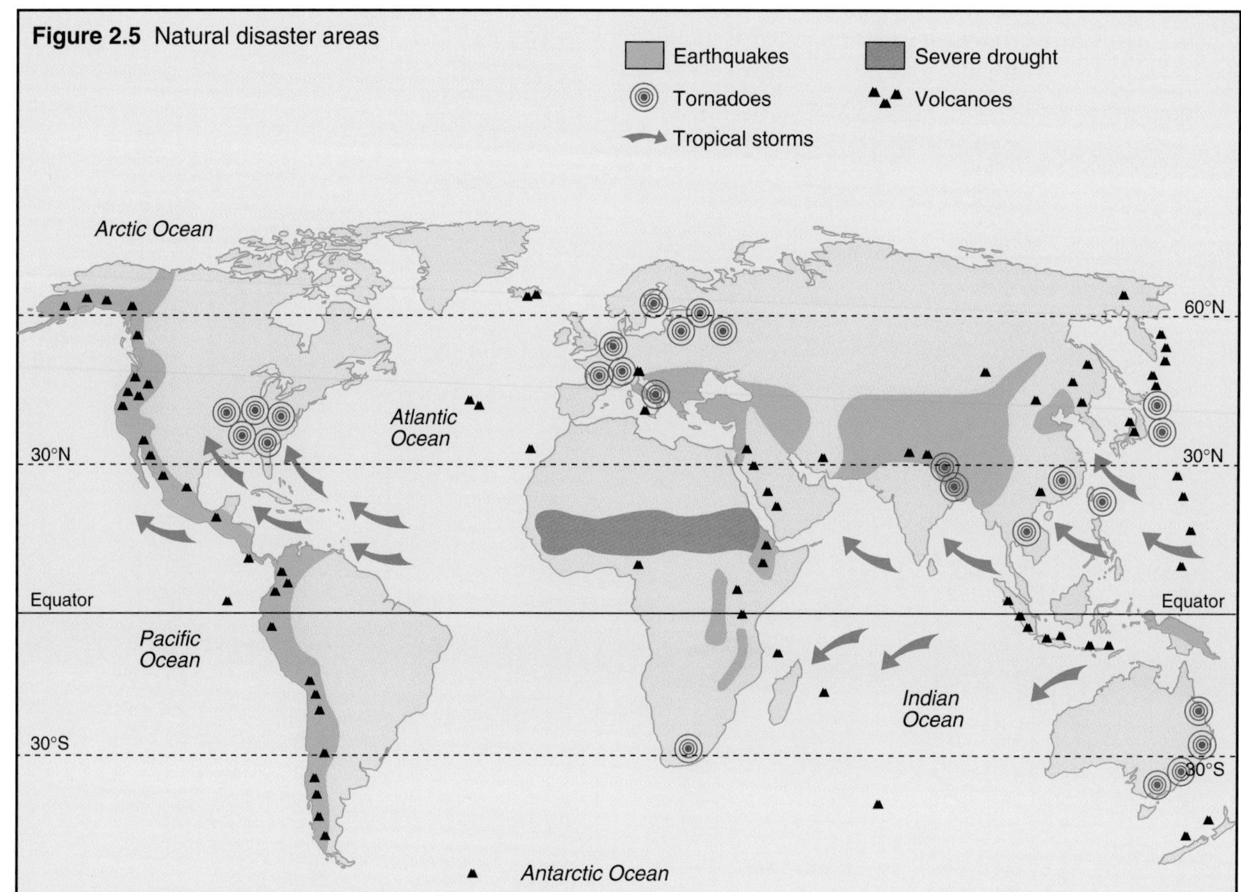

been downgraded to a Category 3 storm. Hurricane Andrew caused at least 62 deaths and caused damage of $20 billion to $30 billion. It was the costliest natural disaster in US history.

The Philippines, to the southeast of China, has been the victim of no less than nine typhoons since 1970. Over 4500 people have been killed. Typhoon Ike claimed the most lives — 1363 — on 2 September 1984. The worst storm since then, Typhoon Angela, claimed over 800 lives on 6 November 1995.

The Bay of Bengal produces many tropical cyclones. On the low-lying shores of Bangladesh, these storms can cause massive damage and loss of life. When the storms coincide with high tides, the people cannot escape. A severe cyclone struck Bangladesh on 30 April 1991. At least 125 000 people either drowned or died from diseases.

Tornadoes Unlike tropical storms, which originate over oceans, **tornadoes** form over land. They usually occur in spring or early summer in conditions where cold, dry air meets hot, moist air. The central and southern areas of the United States provide such conditions, although tornadoes can move as far north as the Canadian Prairies and Ontario.

The tornado is a narrow, spiralling storm that is 100 to 500 m in width at ground level. It resembles a funnel in shape and has the fastest known winds on earth — up to 600 km/hour — and very low pressure in the centre. The powerful winds, coupled with the low pressure, can cause buildings to "explode" outward. The tornado that struck Edmonton in the summer of 1987 killed twenty-six people.

Droughts A drought is an extended period of below average rainfall. The most famous drought in the history of North America lasted from 1930 to 1937. Its effects were worst in the American Midwest and the Canadian Prairies. The very low yields, coupled with the rock-bottom prices paid for those crops that were harvested, caused many farmers to go bankrupt. History was to some extent repeated in the mid-1980s (culminating in the very dry year of 1988) when drought and low prices struck again.

The most severe drought in recent decades has been in the Sahel region of Africa, south of the Sahara Desert. Figure 2.6 shows that rainfall was below average in the Sahel every year except one from 1968 to 1993. The drought alone would have been serious enough. Unfortunately, rapid population growth led to overcropping and overgrazing. The cutting down of trees for fuel wood was another contributing factor. Starvation was widespread and international aid on a large scale was necessary.

The floods created by the cyclone in Bangladesh in April 1991 left over 10 million people homeless.

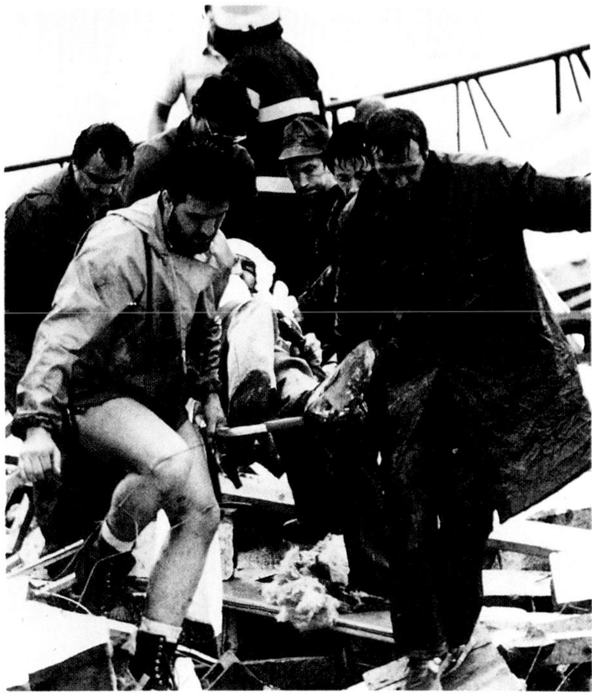

The tornado that struck Edmonton in 1987 killed twenty-six people and caused serious damage to property.

Floods Unlike droughts, which develop slowly, unexpected heavy rainfall can cause serious flooding. On 4 August 1988 the city of Khartoum, the capital of Sudan, received a total of 210 mm of rainfall in a single evening. To put this figure in perspective, the average rainfall for Khartoum *for the whole year* is only 160 mm!

Not surprisingly, flood waters covered 75 percent of Khartoum. Several hundred thousand poor people lost what little they had. Relief camps were set up to administer aid, but the lack of clean drinking water led to outbreaks of cholera and other diseases.

Figure 2.6 Average rainfall in the Sahel over fifty years

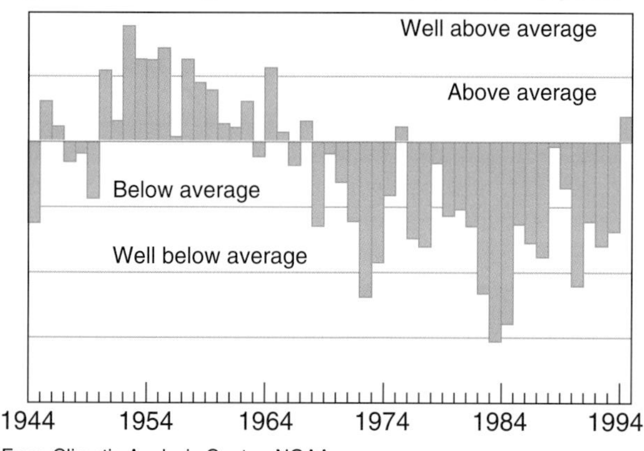

From Climatic Analysis Centre, NOAA.

The unstable earth

The surface of the earth on which we live is unstable in many areas. There are three main causes of instability, each of which may seriously affect human life.

Landslips On sloping ground, landslips may occur where the surface of the ground is loose. The ground may gradually slip downhill, especially if it has been lubricated by heavy rainfall. Or the slide may be sudden, as in the Hope Slide in British Columbia that killed three people in 1965. Houses built on eroding coastlines may experience slumping as the land is eroded from beneath. Evidence of this slumping can be seen on the shores of Lake Ontario near Toronto.

Earthquakes Earthquakes are caused by the release of shock waves from a sudden movement in rocks at or near the surface of the earth. The severity of earthquakes is measured on the **Richter scale**, named after a Californian seismologist, Charles Richter. Each number on the scale indicates a vibration ten times higher than the number below it. Structural damage can be very serious above 5.5 on the scale.

There are two main kinds of earthquakes. Earthquakes can occur when one tectonic plate slowly moves below another (**subduction**). The buildup of stress between the plates eventually overcomes the friction that locks them together. The sudden movement releases shock waves, which shake the earth's surface. The Mexico City earthquake of 1985 was of

Land slippage can threaten homes like this one in Ontario.

this type. Much of British Columbia is under the constant threat of a subduction earthquake.

San Francisco's earthquake in October 1989 was caused by a horizontal movement between two earth plates along the San Andreas fault. In the San Francisco earthquake of 1906, the land on either side of the fault was suddenly displaced by as much as 5 or 6 m, breaking power and gas lines and causing great damage to buildings. The October 1989 earthquake was about 7.2 on the Richter scale. The 1906 San Francisco earthquake was about 8.2.

Those who live in an earthquake-prone environment have three options. They may build on solid rock rather than on soft clay, which tends to liquefy during the tremors (as in the 1985 Mexico City earthquake). They may rely on insurance, which is expensive, and on some basic knowledge of what to do in an earthquake situation. Or they may do nothing. Even in San Francisco, some people feel that disasters happen only to others. Figure 2.7 shows the results of a study of residents living within 1.6 km of the San Andreas Fault.

The 1995 earthquake in Kobe, Japan was 7.2 on the Richter scale. It caused massive damage to housing and port facilities, and caused the death of 5501 people. Damage was estimated at over $150 billion (US).

Earthquakes occurring near or under the oceans may give rise to **tsunamis**. These are ocean waves produced by the shock of the earthquake. They are

Figure 2.7 Deaths, injuries, and losses in the Kobe earthquake

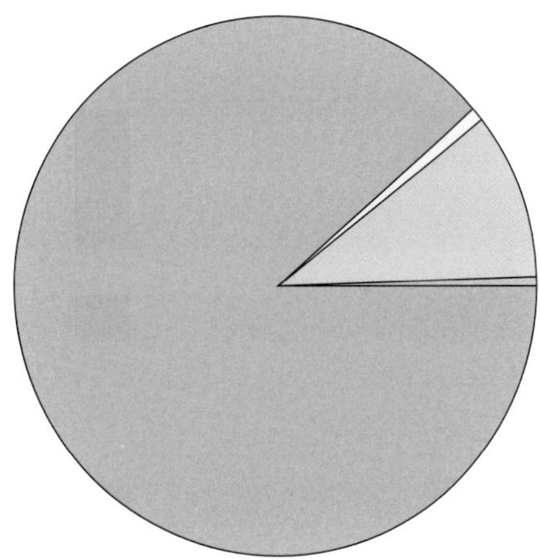

Number of people in the affected area 4 000 000 (100%)
- Number of people killed 5 501 (0.1%)
- Number of people who lost their homes 319 000 (7.3%)
- Number of people injured 36 918 (0.8%)

Extensive damage was caused to houses in San Francisco during the 1989 earthquake.

often incorrectly called tidal waves. A tsunami caused by the 1964 earthquake in Alaska swept down the Pacific coast of North America, causing over twenty deaths in Crescent City, California.

Volcanoes There are three main types of volcanoes, each posing a different form of natural hazard. **Cinder cones** have steep sides, creating the tendency for viscous lava to plug the neck of the volcano. The result is that a major explosion can occur, like that at Krakatoa, Indonesia, in 1883. This explosion created an enormous tsunami that killed about 30 000 people in the Pacific region. **Shield volcanoes**, such as Mauna Loa in Hawaii, produce a more liquid lava and do not usually explode, but they do pose the threat of running lava flows. **Composite cones** contain alternate layers of ash and lava. The massive explosion that blew off the top of Mount St. Helens in 1980 is proof that this type of volcano can also be explosive.

An important effect of volcanoes is the nature of the ash and lava they produce. A lava flow from a shield volcano can form the basis of fertile soil. Cinder cones, however, produce a less useful lava.

The explosion of the Mount St. Helens volcano was a spectacular sight. The ash eventually spread over hundreds of kilometres.

Soils

Soils are the most vital resource for human existence, since they provide an environment for plant life. In turn, plants provide photosynthesis, from which we receive our food energy.

Soils consist of biotic (living) and abiotic (non-living) elements. The non-living, or inorganic, components consist of weathered rock (called parent material). These are mixed with organic materials from decaying plants, animals, and insects. The remaining ingredients of soils are air and water.

Soil formation

Soils are formed over long periods of time, perhaps as much as thousands of years. Soil formation processes include the physical weathering of rock, and the gradual buildup of **humus** from decaying organic material. However, soils can be destroyed in a matter of days or months. The loss of soil by the action of wind or water is known as **soil erosion**.

Climate plays an important role in the formation of soils. Consider Figure 2.8, which shows the relation-

Figure 2.8 The relationship between precipitation and evapotranspiration

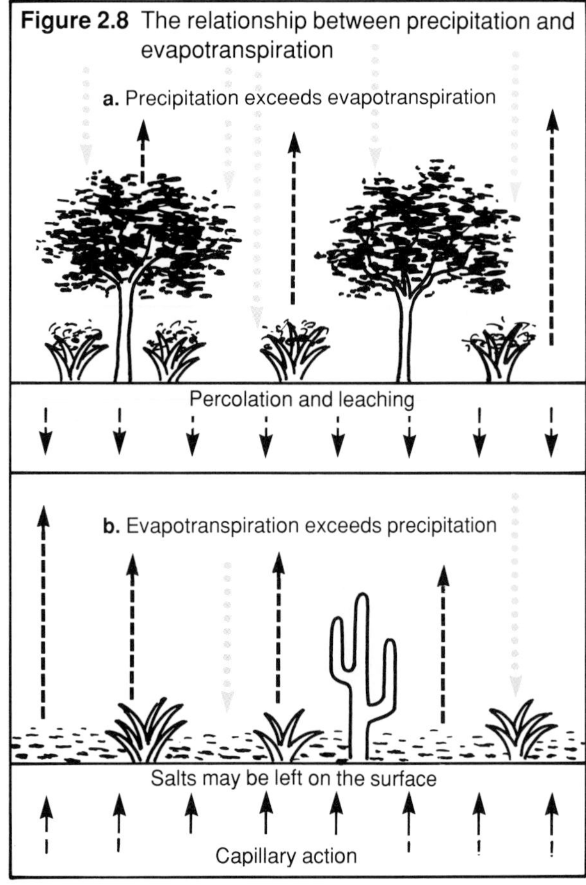

ship between precipitation and evapotranspiration or rising water vapour. If precipitation exceeds evapotranspiration, the result is a downward percolation of water in the soil, assuming that rainwater does not run off along the surface of the ground. If water carries dissolved materials downward, the process is known as leaching. It is common in humid climates and occurs most readily in coarse soils. Leaching may remove many of the nutrients and chemicals from soils. The upper layer of a leached soil therefore tends to be low in nitrates and other nutrients. Leaching can also carry pollutants into groundwater.

The opposite of leaching is **capillary action**. If evapotranspiration exceeds precipitation then water in the soil is likely to move upwards. Capillary action may happen after a heavy rainfall in an arid or semiarid climate. First, rainwater penetrates the ground to a certain depth, dissolving some minerals in the process. Then surface water begins to evaporate, causing an upward movement of water. The salts that were dissolved in the water are left behind on the surface.

Calcium carbonate ($CaCO_3$) is a common surface deposit in arid or semiarid climates. Few plants will grow in a surface encrusted with $CaCO_3$. Poor irrigation practices can also increase the formation of calcium carbonate deposits.

Over time, the soil-forming processes normally produce a soil with several distinct layers or **horizons**. The typical section or **soil profile** has three main layers. The largest amount of organic material occurs in the top or A horizon.

One important variable in soils is the degree to which they are acid or alkaline, as measured by the **pH scale**. A pH of 7 is neutral. The pH of soils ranges from 4 (strongly acid) to about 9 (strongly alkaline).

This soil profile illustrates a chernozem (black earth) soil in Manitoba.

Soil texture and structure

Soil texture is related to the proportions of different sizes of mineral particles. (See Figure 2.9.)

A sandy soil has a high proportion of sand particles, which gives it a coarse texture. Such a soil will drain easily but is easily leached for the same reason. An advantage of a sandy soil is that it warms up quickly in the spring.

A clay soil, on the other hand, is slow to warm up and has poor natural drainage. It is hard to work but is richer in nutrients since the leaching process is slow A loam soil combines the best of each type, having a variety of nutrients as well as being reasonably well drained and easy to work.

Figure 2.9 Soil particle size

PARTICLE	DIAMETER
Coarse sand	0.5 to I mm
Medium sand	0.25 to 0.5 mm
Fine sand	0.1 to 0.25 mm
Silt	0.002 to 0.1 mm
Clay	below 0.002 mm

Soil structure is the degree to which the soil forms crumbs or clods, as opposed to being loose like pure sand. This stickiness is caused by the amount of humus that the soil contains. The organic matter is also able to hold much more moisture than the mineral particles alone could carry. Humus therefore helps to reduce wind erosion. Unfortunately, constant cultivation without replenishing the humus can break down the soil structure. The overuse of chemical fertilizers has the same effect. If the soil becomes powdery, which happened in the Prairies in the 1930s, it can easily be blown away. In the thirties, much of the interior of North America was turned into a "dust bowl."

World soils

Many different soil types can be found throughout the world. Each main climatic region, for example, has its own soil type. (These will be discussed in chapter 4.) Other soil types reflect particular local conditions. For example, a river such as the Nile floods on a regular basis producing a fine water-deposited soil known as **alluvium**. In Canada, many soils are the result of the weathering of glacial materials. Parts of the prairies have fertile soil as a result of the deposition of glacial materials that are rich in lime and other nutrients. On the other hand, glacial sands and gravels are responsible for poor, infertile soils. Where the ground is regularly flooded, the decomposition of organic materials by bacteria is slow. The result is a heavy wetland soil that usually contains peat.

● | A local environmental survey

The area in which you live may or may not have serious environmental problems. Before you can analyse any problems, you will need to survey your environment in general. This survey will help you to become more familiar with the area around you and to notice any problems that may arise. Below are some suggestions for activities you could undertake.

The land surface

Obtain a topographic map of the area around your home and/or school. An oblique air photograph would also be useful. Maps are published by Energy, Mines, and Resources Canada.

A topographic map is a valuable source of information. From it you can see the patterns of relief and drainage. You can also note the date of the map and compare it with the area as it is today. In this way you can determine how much change has taken place in the form of new construction.

An extract from the Niagara Falls 1:50 000 topographic map is shown in Figure 2.10. The air photograph covers some of the areas shown on the map. Consult your atlas to find out where this area is located. Study the map to locate the falls, the gorge, and the whirlpool. Note that the map and the photograph help you to identify industries and other human activities.

Weather and climate

The Atmospheric Environment Service of Environment Canada maintains a network of weather recording stations. These stations publish the Monthly Meteorological Summary that gives details of the weather month by month. The daily and monthly data can be compared with long-term climatic averages for your area. You can recognize droughts, hot and cold spells, and other departures from average weather.

Air quality information is available locally for most cities in Canada. As well, Environment Canada has an air quality index. (See Figure 6.11.) You may be able to correlate extremes on this index with unusually hot or dry weather spells.

Changes in vegetation and animal life

An ecosystem consists of all the living plants and animals and their surrounding physical environment. Record the main types of vegetation and wildlife in your area on a map. If you live in the heart of a city or even in the suburbs, this environment may be largely artificial. However, it is still your local environment and awareness of the plants and animals that live there is important. Try to find out what the environment was like before your town or city developed. Many plants and some animals may have died out as their habitats were disturbed. If so, their existence may have been recorded in documents in a local library.

Land and water use

Your observations should include how the land and local water systems are used. If you can obtain a large scale plan from the local planning department, you can shade in different types of land use such as residential housing, industry, commerce, and recreation. Which types of land use have an impact on land and water? Do local industries discharge any waste products? If so, how are they disposed of? Do you notice any evidence of soil erosion or landslides? Is the water in rivers or streams clean? Does it contain any chemicals? You may be able to discover chemical contaminants by asking your local municipality. You can also test the water for alkalinity or acidity using litmus paper.

Transport

Some urban environments contain little open space. A heavily built up environment is likely to contain a great deal of traffic. To conduct a traffic density survey, construct a sheet to record the volume of traffic at particular intersections. Such surveys can be used to show how traffic density varies with the time of day. You may also be able to devise a means of recording traffic noise and other types of common urban problems.

Another test of the urban environment also requires the use of a large-scale plan. First locate all the "green space" in your area. Estimate the walking distance in minutes from a number of homes to the nearest green space. Plot this data on your map. Then draw a line for "less than five minutes" from the nearest green space, "five to ten minutes," "over ten minutes," and so on. In this way you can see what proportion of your town or city is close to green space.

Activities such as these can help you to evaluate your local environment. In this way you will not only be better informed, but also more able to contribute to the solution of local environmental problems.

This photograph of Niagara Falls looks southeast. In the upper left is Niagara Falls, New York, which is an important centre of the chemical industry.

Examine the above photograph of Niagara Falls and the topographic map on page 28.

1. Identify as many features as you can on both the map and the photograph. Which appears to be more up-to-date?
2. What attractive features make this a prime location for tourism?
3. Many chemical industries located in this area years ago, especially in Niagara Falls, USA. What advantages did the area provide for these industries?
4. The Love Canal (see pages 103-104) is located near the Robert Moses Parkway and the Niagara River, just east of the area shown in Figure 2.10. How might chemicals in this dump reach Lake Ontario?
5. The map shows other examples of environmental "black spots." What are some of these?

Figure 2.10 A topographic map of the Niagara Falls area.

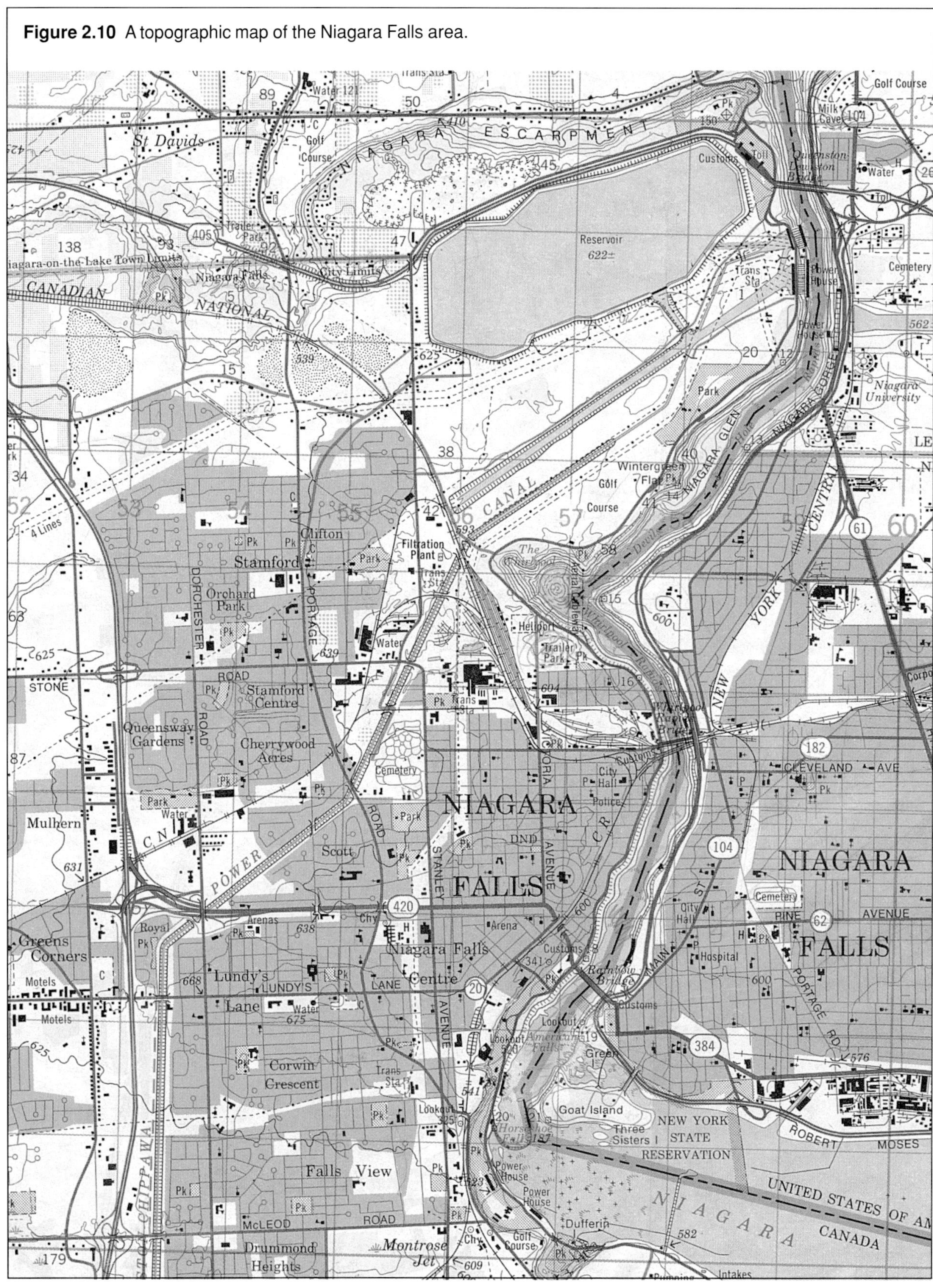

Looking back

1. (a) Pollution in the oceans cannot be easily confined to one area. Explain why this is so.
   (b) Give two examples of how the world's wind systems can spread environmental problems to different parts of the world.
2. Explain how solar energy powers all the systems in the natural environment. Make specific references to the hydrological cycle, the wind systems, and the ocean currents.
3. Give two reasons why the organic content of a soil is so important.
4. Why are some events that occur in the natural environment considered disasters?

Applying your knowledge

1. (a) As a class, brainstorm a list of at least ten questions about how the following systems in an environment affect or interact with one another: (i) hydrological cycle; (ii) wind systems; (iii) soils; (iv) vegetation; and (v) the human component.
   (b) Divide the class into five groups. Each group should take two of the questions from the brainstorming session and prepare answers to the questions for presentation to the class.
2. (a) What types of weather extremes do the most damage in your area?
   (b) How do these extremes affect the environment and the lives of people?
   (c) What measures might people take to prepare for these weather extremes?
3. (a) Describe the natural and human factors that contribute to natural disasters such as floods and droughts.
   (b) Which factors may act as "triggers" for these disasters?
4. Describe the differences between the forces that produced the problems shown in the photographs on pages 21 to 24.
5. Explain how biotic and abiotic factors combine to produce a particular type of soil.

Extending your thinking

1. (a) Review newspapers, magazines, the Internet, and other sources for information about environmental issues. Set up your own vertical file of these articles.
   (b) Choose one environmental issue from your file and prepare a report that discusses the threat to the environment, any conflicting viewpoints that may exist over the issue, and what proposals have been made and/or what actions have been taken to resolve the issue.
2. Find out if your community has an emergency plan in case of natural or human-caused disasters. Interview someone involved with the plan and prepare a report describing when and how the emergency plan would be put into effect.
3. In small groups, prepare a large diagram and an oral presentation to illustrate one of the following:
   (a) ways in which pollution is created;
   (b) types of pollution;
   (c) how pollution enters the environment;
   (d) systems that concentrate pollution;
   (e) how natural systems transport (spread) pollution to other environments.
4. Gather water samples from as many different local sources as possible (taps, streams, ponds, lakes, swimming pools, wells, etc.). Test each sample for its pH level. Record the results on an organizer. Develop hypotheses for the similarities and differences you observe. If some results show high levels of acidity, try to determine the source of the acid.

3 ECOSYSTEM PROCESSES

All life on earth exists within a narrow zone called the **biosphere**. The biosphere is a band circling the surface of the earth, including the lower layers of the atmosphere and the top few metres of the soil. The biosphere is important because it receives solar energy and contains the solid matter, water, and gases that are necessary for life. We may think of it as the human habitat.

Ecosystems

An **ecosystem** is a community of living things and the environment or **habitat** in which they live. An ecosystem therefore contains both **biotic** (living) components, such as people and animals, and **abiotic** (nonliving) elements, such as rocks and water. Ecosystems may exist at many different scales. A decaying log is a small-scale ecosystem, while the earth itself makes up a vast ecosystem. A simple ecosystem is shown in Figure 3.1.

The essential idea of any ecosystem is that the elements within it are interrelated. If a particular element is changed, the system as a whole will be affected. For example, a forest ecosystem consists of air, water, animals, birds, insects, soil, and trees. If some of the trees are cut down, each of the other elements will be affected. Animals and birds will lose their habitats. Soils will erode. Even the flow of rivers will change. Rainfall will run more directly into rivers and may carry some of the soil with it, resulting in silting and flooding downstream. The pattern of high and low flows in the river would also be more extreme.

The ecosystem concept is the foundation of environmental science. The best known examples of ecosystems are the great vegetation regions or **biomes** of the world, such as the tropical rain forests and the **tundra**. Human activity has greatly modified these biomes. For example, by clearing a piece of land for agriculture, people change a natural ecosystem into an artificial one. As a result, the number of plant and animal species (and their genes) in the ecosystem are greatly reduced.

Figure 3.1 An ecosystem

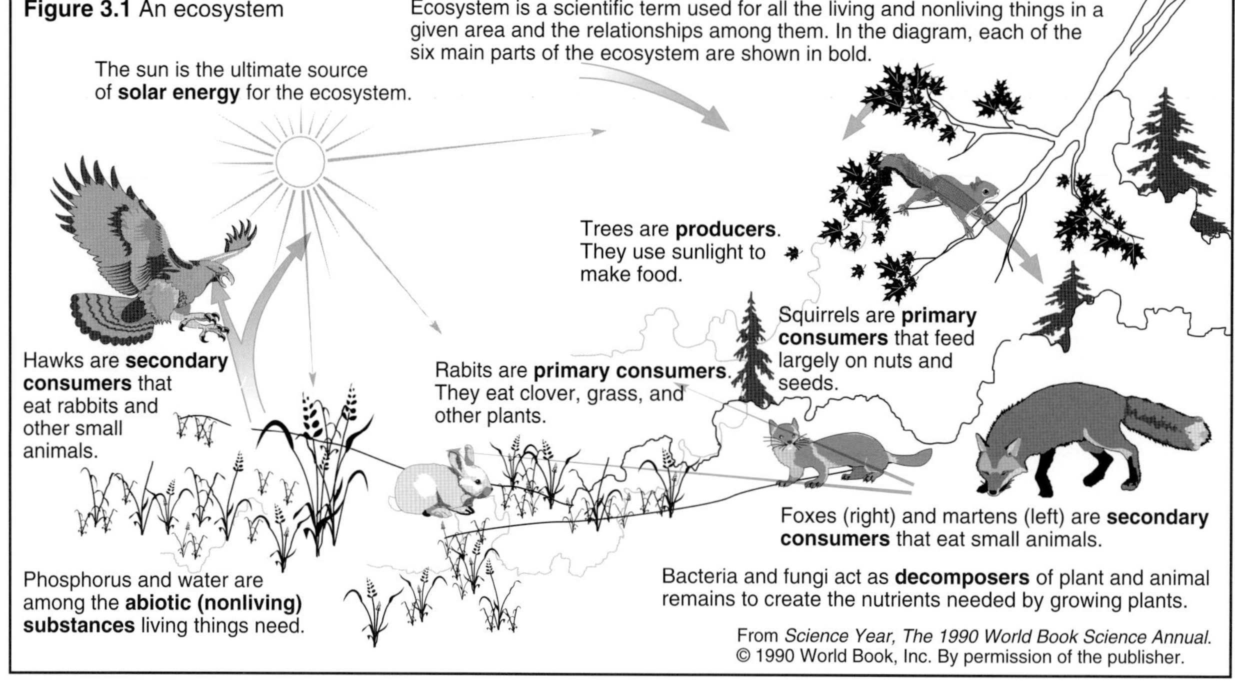

Ecosystem is a scientific term used for all the living and nonliving things in a given area and the relationships among them. In the diagram, each of the six main parts of the ecosystem are shown in bold.
The sun is the ultimate source of **solar energy** for the ecosystem.
Trees are **producers**. They use sunlight to make food.
Squirrels are **primary consumers** that feed largely on nuts and seeds.
Hawks are **secondary consumers** that eat rabbits and other small animals.
Rabits are **primary consumers**. They eat clover, grass, and other plants.
Foxes (right) and martens (left) are **secondary consumers** that eat small animals.
Phosphorus and water are among the **abiotic (nonliving) substances** living things need.
Bacteria and fungi act as **decomposers** of plant and animal remains to create the nutrients needed by growing plants.

Ecosystem structures

Food pyramids

Organisms in an ecosystem form a **food pyramid.** (See Figure 3.2.) At the base of this pyramid are the **producers.** These are the plants that have converted solar energy into carbohydrates through **photosynthesis.** Above the producers are the consumers. The first category of consumers is the **herbivores,** or plant eaters, which live off the carbohydrates created by the producers. Next are the **carnivores,** or flesh eaters, which feed only on consumers. Omnivores are both herbivores and carnivores, eating both plants and animals. Human beings are omnivores since we live off a broad range of plants and animals.

Also in the food pyramid are the **decomposers,** such as bacteria and fungi, that break down dead organic materials and recycle them into their inorganic elements. These elements are then available to start another cycle.

Figure 3.2 A typical food pyramid with four levels. This pyramid may refer to numbers, biomass, or energy.

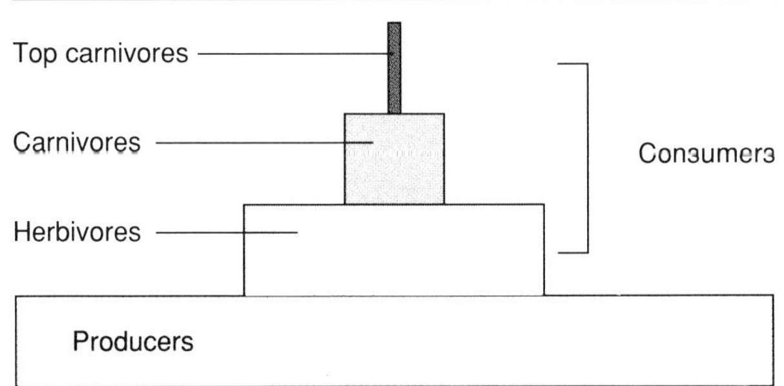

Food webs

Organisms in an ecosystem are linked together in a complex set of relationships. Many of these relationships are based on feeding. Energy and chemicals pass through an ecosystem by way of **food chains** or **food webs.** (See Figure 3.3.) A simple food chain consists of one organism eating a plant and in turn being eaten by another animal and so on. Few, if any, species feed exclusively on one type of food. Most species also have several predators. A simple food chain therefore develops into a complex food web.

Changes to one component of the food web will affect other components. For example, removing wolves from an area may cause the deer population to expand, leading to the overuse of the plants on which

Figure 3.3 A food web showing the complicated feeding relationships between producers, herbivores, and carnivores in an ecosystem

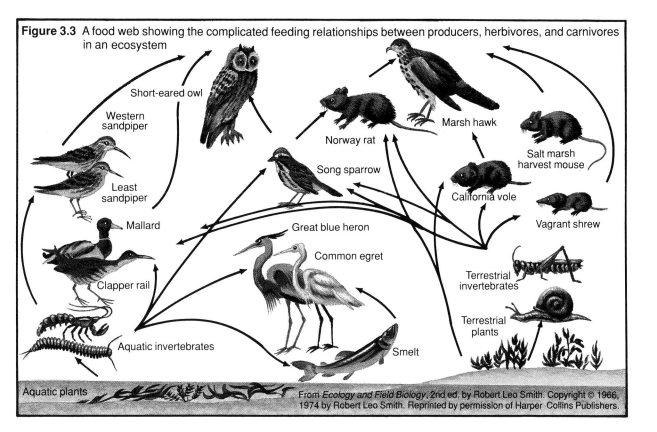

Short-eared owl
Western sandpiper
Least sandpiper
Mallard
Clapper rail
Aquatic invertebrates
Aquatic plants
Norway rat
Marsh hawk
Song sparrow
Great blue heron
Common egret
Smelt
Salt marsh harvest mouse
California vole
Vagrant shrew
Terrestrial invertebrates
Terrestrial plants

From *Ecology and Field Biology*, 2nd ed. by Robert Leo Smith. Copyright © 1966, 1974 by Robert Leo Smith. Reprinted by permission of Harper Collins Publishers.

the deer feed. The results may be a large population of undernourished deer and damage to the local vegetation.

Predators and prey

Predators have an important role to play. They help to maintain balance and diversity in ecosystems. Their numbers are closely linked to the numbers of the species on which they prey. If a predator feeds on only a few types of prey, a linked cycle of predator and prey populations results. For example, the population cycles of the snowshoe hare and the lynx are closely related, as shown by the Hudson's Bay Company trapping records between 1845 and 1935. (See Figure 3.4.) During this period the population of both species cycled from low to high numbers nine times. The population cycles stayed in step with one another.

In most ecosystems, predators tend to cause a greater diversity of species within the system because a generalist predator will feed on whatever prey is abundant at a particular time. Thus any prey species is prevented from dominating the scene to the exclusion of others.

Figure 3.4 Population fluctuations of snowshoe hare and lynx in the Arctic

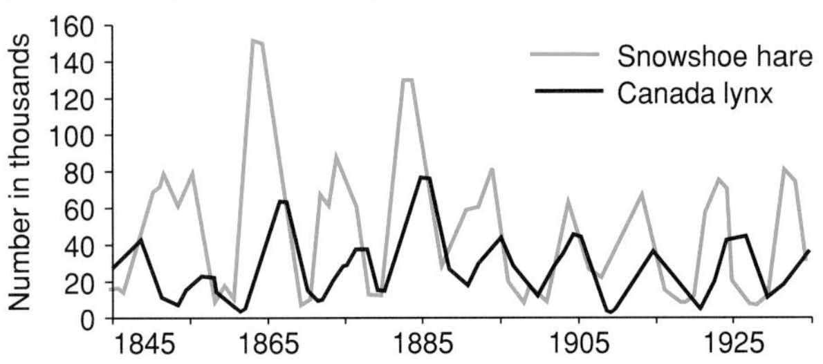

Reprinted with permission from *Science Probe 9* by Bullard *et al*, © John Wiley & Sons Canada Limited, 1986.

Special relationships between species

Organisms in an ecosystem are interrelated primarily by links in the food chain, but a variety of associations between species deserve special mention. These relationships include parasitism, commensalism, mutualism, and competition.

Parasitism Parasites are organisms that live on or in other living organisms from which they obtain food and, frequently, shelter. The organisms that parasites live with are called **hosts.** (See Figure 3.5.) **Ectoparasites,** such as fleas, lice, and mites, live outside the body of their hosts. **Endoparasites,** such as worms,

Figure 3.5 Predator, prey, and parasites

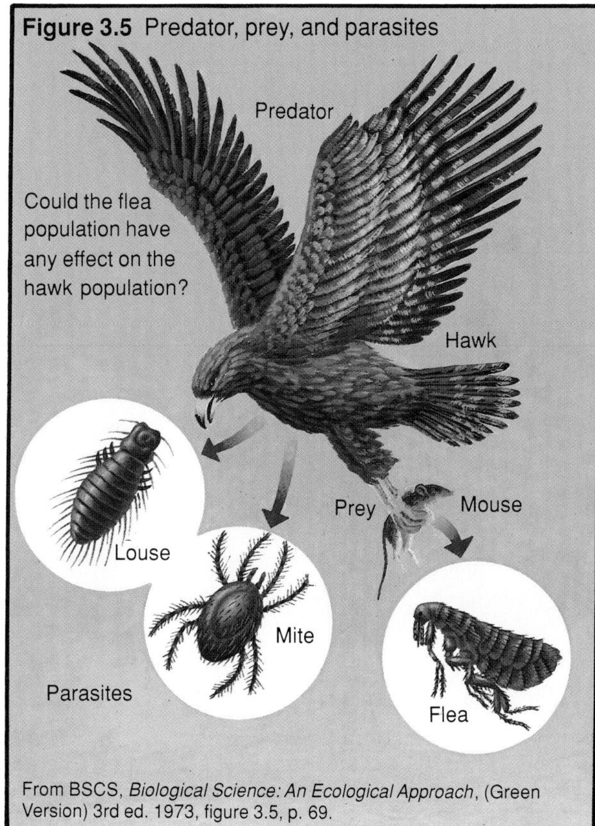

From BSCS, *Biological Science: An Ecological Approach*, (Green Version) 3rd ed. 1973, figure 3.5, p. 69.

flukes, and microscopic parasites, live within the body of their hosts and in some cases within the cells of the hosts. While predators kill their prey, parasites *may* kill their hosts. However, the death of the hosts is a serious disadvantage for parasites because their food and shelter is gone.

Because they live within the body of the hosts, reproduction and dispersal are problems for many endoparasites. Several of these parasites rely on secondary hosts or simple carriers, such as insects, to spread from one primary host to another. For example, the mosquito carries the malaria parasite from one person to another, and freshwater snails transmit the parasite that causes bilharzia. Parasites play an important ecological role. They can reduce host populations either by killing them or reducing their ability to reproduce. Parasites that prey on insects can be used to control pests without the use of pesticides.

Commensalism Commensalism is an association between organisms of different species in which one (the commensal) gains from the relationship while the other (the host) neither benefits nor loses. For example, a remora fish is able to attach itself to a larger animal, such as a shark. The remora probably does not affect the shark, but it benefits by being transported by the shark and being able to feed on pieces of the shark's prey as they float by. However, commensalism does not necessarily involve feeding relationships. Several kinds of birds, such as bluebirds, like to nest in abandoned woodpecker holes. The bluebirds benefit from the woodpeckers, but of course the woodpeckers gain nothing from the bluebirds.

Lichens are an example of a symbiotic relationship.

Symbiosis or mutualism Symbiosis, or mutualism, is an association where both members benefit from the relationship. Lichens provide a good example of symbiosis. Lichens are the small plant-like organisms that cling to rocks and trees. They are composed of two separate organisms, a fungus and an alga, that live in close association. The alga produces food by photosynthesis, while the fungus consumes the food the alga produces. In turn, the fungus provides protection for the alga.

Another example of symbiosis can be found in the **ruminants**. Ruminants are cud-chewing animals, such as goats, deer, cattle, and antelope, that have multi-chambered stomachs. One of the stomach chambers hosts a multitude of cellulose-digesting micro-organisms. Cellulose is a type of plant fibre that is indigestible to most mammals. They do not have the appropriate enzymes to break it down. The ruminants could not use the cellulose, a major component of grasses, without the micro-organisms, while the micro-organisms receive shelter and a steady supply of food.

Legumes, such as peas, beans, clover, and alfalfa, are unique plants in that they harbour symbiotic nitrogen-fixing bacteria in root nodules. The bacteria are able to "fix" inert atmospheric nitrogen into nutrients that are suitable for uptake by the plants. As a result, legumes such as soya beans are protein-rich, and alfalfa and clover can be planted to improve soil quality. Legumes and their symbiotic bacteria play an important role in the nitrogen cycle. (See page 35.)

Competition Many species compete with one another for resources in the environment. Two or more species of herbivores may compete for the same plant species. Two species of birds may compete for the same type of nesting site. For example, bluebirds and starlings both nest in holes in trees and poles. Neither can make their own holes, so the presence of one species limits the abundance of the other. Competition within a species can limit the size of its population if any resources become scarce. In many situations where competition between species exists, one species fares better than others and may end the competition altogether. For example, the competition between humans and many animal species for food and living space has resulted in the disappearance of these species. Humans are the better competitors in most situations, and we have succeeded in pushing many species out of their natural habitats.

Materials and energy in ecosystems

The organisms found in the food pyramid (biotic components) are interrelated with the materials and energy (abiotic components) in ecosystems. For example, plants and animals ingest minerals and water. Materials are returned by excretion and by the decay of plant and animal remains.

Nutrient cycles

Unlike energy, chemicals are not used up as they pass through an ecosystem, but are merely changed. Chemical nutrients therefore are a part of **closed systems**. Carbon, oxygen, and hydrogen are the main elements that pass through an ecosystem. Plants also require large amounts of nitrogen, phosphorus, and potassium. Smaller amounts of chemical elements such as calcium and magnesium are needed, as well as traces of minerals such as iron, zinc, cobalt, and molybdenum. We shall examine two chemical nutrients as they cycle through an ecosystem — carbon and nitrogen.

The carbon cycle

Carbon is a vital ingredient of living things. It exists in sedimentary rocks such as limestone and in the form of carbon dioxide (CO_2) in the atmosphere and carbonate (CO_3^{2-}) in the oceans. Carbon moves in a continual cycle between living things and the atmosphere. The process of **photosynthesis** converts carbon dioxide to green matter. This process is represented by the formula $6CO_2 + 6H_2O \rightarrow C_6H_{12}O_6 + 6O_2$. The plants thus convert carbon dioxide and water to sugars and oxygen. By the reverse of this formula, living creatures convert oxygen and sugars into carbon dioxide and water through **respiration**.

From Figure 3.6 we can see that organic material makes up one of the main carbon reservoirs. By depleting the earth's forests we are reducing this reservoir and increasing the amount of CO_2 in the atmosphere. The burning of **fossil fuels** also adds to the amount of atmospheric CO_2. The likely effects of increased amounts of CO_2 in the atmosphere is an overall warming of global climates.

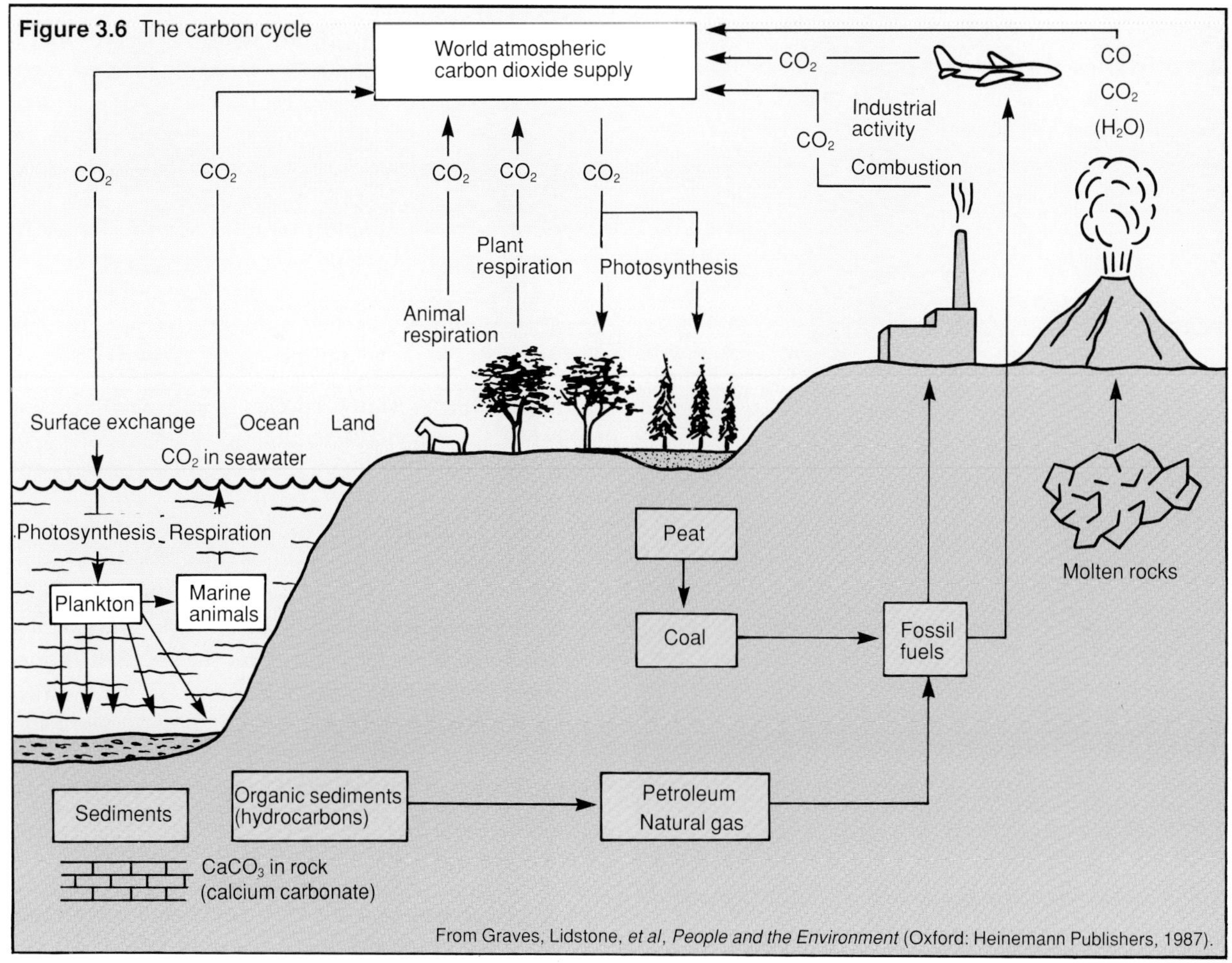

Figure 3.6 The carbon cycle

From Graves, Lidstone, *et al*, *People and the Environment* (Oxford: Heinemann Publishers, 1987).

The nitrogen cycle

Nitrogen is an essential nutrient for plant growth. It makes up 78 percent of the dry atmosphere, but to be used by plants it first must be converted to nitrates (NO_3^-). This conversion is done by nitrogen-fixing bacteria that are found in the soil and the root nodules of legumes. Other sources of nitrates include the erosion of nitrate-rich rocks and the fixing of nitrogen by atmospheric lightning. The nitrogen cycle is shown in Figure 3.7.

When plants and animals die and decay, the nitrogen is converted first to ammonia (NH_3), then to nitrites (NO_2^-), and finally to nitrates (NO_3^-). The nitrates can be used again by plants or returned to the atmosphere as nitrogen gas.

Human activity has altered the nitrogen cycle in two ways. First, since nitrates are important for farming, large quantities of nitrogen fertilizer are produced and used each year. Much of the fertilizer that is spread on fields seeps down into groundwater, then into rivers and lakes, causing serious water pollution. Second, the burning of fossil fuels releases nitrogen oxides into the atmosphere, thus contributing to acid rain.

Bioaccumulation

As materials pass through an ecosystem they may become concentrated in the tissues of living creatures. This phenomenon is known as **bioaccumulation, biological magnification**, or **food chain concentration.** Organisms at the bottom of a food chain, such as microscopic algae, may absorb minute quantities of toxic chemicals, such as the insecticide DDT. Many such chemicals are fat soluble and are not excreted easily. Therefore they become more concentrated toward the top of the food chain. (See Figure 3.8.) In the top predators, the chemicals may be concentrated enough to have damaging effects. For example, the concentration of DDT in birds of prey leads to deficiencies in calcium, causing thin eggshells and poor nesting success. Because humans are at the top of several food chains, we are also affected by the problem of bioaccumulation.

Figure 3.7 The nitrogen cycle

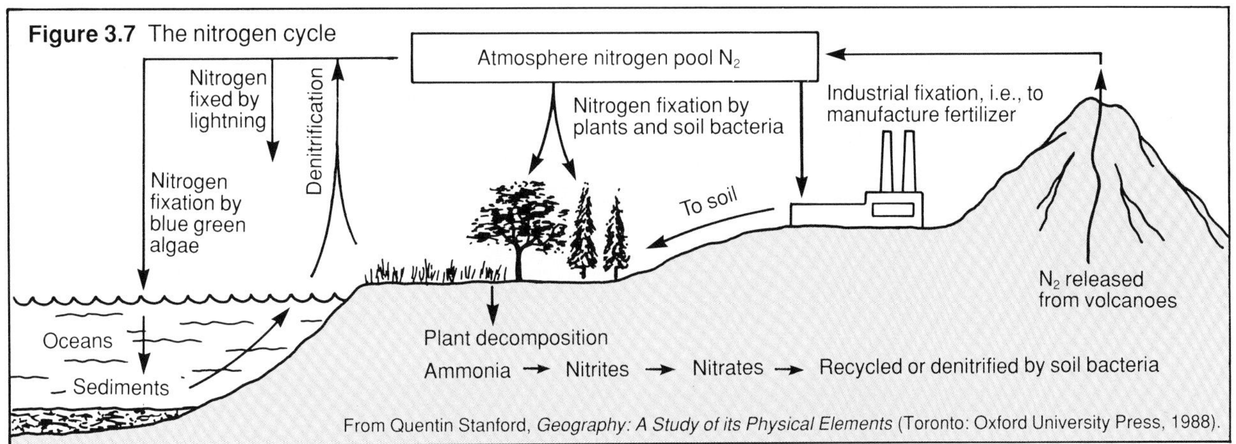

From Quentin Stanford, *Geography: A Study of its Physical Elements* (Toronto: Oxford University Press, 1988).

Figure 3.8 Bioaccumulation of toxic chemicals in the food chain

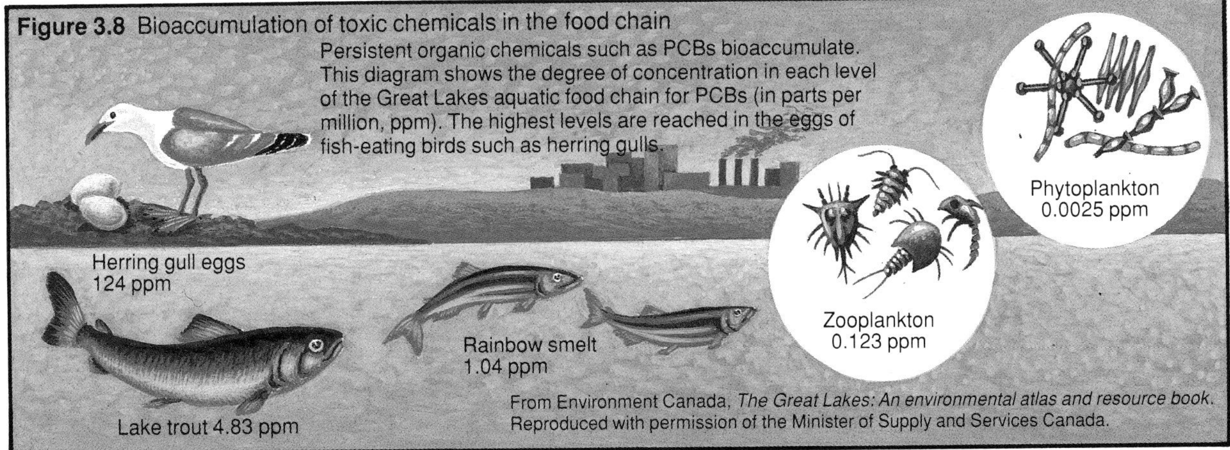

From Environment Canada, *The Great Lakes: An environmental atlas and resource book.* Reproduced with permission of the Minister of Supply and Services Canada.

Filter feeding

Many human activities tend to disperse undesirable chemicals into the environment. In the past we have practised the "dilution solution to pollution"—that is, we have assumed the atmosphere and the oceans are large enough to dilute the pollutants we put into them so they will eventually disappear. We are now finding, however, that many of these toxic chemicals are coming back to haunt us through the process of bioaccumulation. This may occur as a result of the way that materials pass through an ecosystem or through the action of **filter feeders**.

Several marine organisms, such as barnacles, clams, oysters, and mussels, feed by filtering their environment for food. An individual mussel may filter 60 L of water daily or 75 000 L in its three- or four-year lifespan. Any diluted chemical in the water may be rapidly concentrated in such filter feeders. An unfortunate natural result of this phenomenon is the **red tide** that periodically breaks out on the west coast of Canada. A poison produced by microscopic marine plants or algae is absorbed by the shellfish that feed upon them. The shellfish do not seem to be harmed by the poison, but humans eating the shellfish may suffer paralytic poisoning.

The widespread dumping of sewage and industrial wastes into our oceans has led to the concentration of contaminants in the shellfish. The result is that many of our coasts have been closed to shellfish harvesting. Filter-feeding shellfish may be useful for ecological monitoring. They may concentrate pollutants sufficiently to measure otherwise undetectable quantities of chemicals.

Mussels and barnacles feed by filtering food particles from the sea water.

Energy in an ecosystem

Solar energy is converted into vegetable matter by photosynthesis. When this vegetable matter is consumed, energy passes to the consumer. In turn, when the herbivore is consumed, energy passes again. This process continues up the pyramid. However, much energy is lost at each stage. Only about 10 percent of the energy absorbed by one level in the pyramid can be stored by the level above it. The rest is lost to the atmosphere through respiration, as Figure 3.9 shows.

To see how the energy is lost, imagine cattle eating grass. In the first place, not all the grass is consumed; some is left to decompose. Some of the energy consumed is used up by the movements of the animals and to maintain their body heat; some is lost by excretion. When the animal is killed for food, only a part of it is actually eaten. Only 10 to 15 percent of the plants that animals consume are converted into edible products. For these reasons, pastoral farming is much less energy efficient than crop farming. In many parts of the world the need for food is so great that people cannot afford the luxury of feeding animals. They live directly off the energy created by crops. Figure 3.10 compares the energy available from pastoral farming with crop farming.

The decomposers use up the balance of the energy originally derived by photosynthesis. This residual energy, like the energy used up in earlier stages, is eventually lost by radiation into outer space, roughly balancing incoming solar energy. Thus energy is lost as it passes through an ecosystem. Energy supply is an example of an **open system.**

Figure 3.9 The flow of energy in an ecosystem

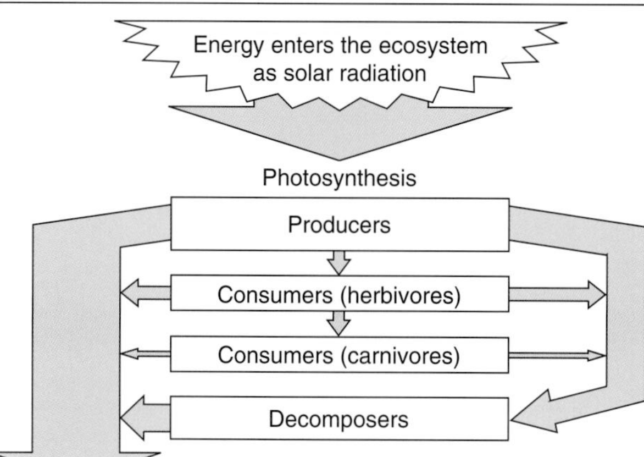

From Quentin Stanford, *Geography: A Study of Its Physical Elements*, (Toronto: Oxford University Press, 1976).

Figure 3.10 Plants and animals as converters of energy

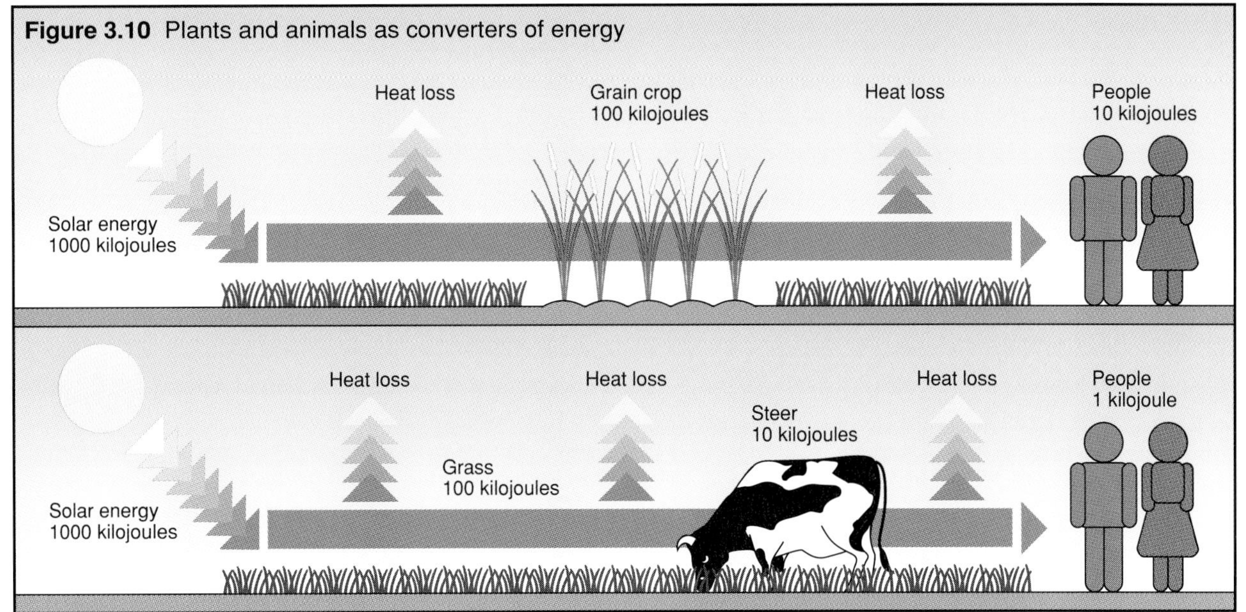

Vegetation

Our dependence on plants

In spite of our technological progress, our diet still has a vegetable base. By far, the largest part of what we eat comes either from plants or from animals that depend on plants. This situation is not likely to change in the foreseeable future, even though the varieties of plants from which we obtain our food may change over time.

We are dependent on a small number of plants for most of our food. Although several hundred edible plants exist, only a few are eaten to any significant extent throughout the world. Three main food grains—wheat, rice, and corn—provide more than half of the world's food energy. The twelve most important food crops are shown in Figure 3.11.

Many useful materials also come from vegetable sources; the most obvious example is timber. Approximately 3 billion cubic metres of timber are used throughout the world every year. Just over half is used as fuel, while less than half is used for industrial purposes. In addition, a large amount of timber is burned to make way for farming. The world's timber resources are being depleted much faster than nature can replace them.

Vegetable matter is widely used as a fuel. Figure 3.12 shows the dependence on fuel wood in a variety of countries. Other types of vegetable matter provide material for other non-food products. For example, bamboo is used in tropical countries for a variety of purposes, and grasses and leaves are often used to roof houses.

Finally, plants are a vitally important source of medicines. For example, aspirin has a botanical origin as do many other well-known medications. Since so many plant species are as yet unresearched, the contribution of plants to medicine could become even greater in the future.

Figure 3.11 Major food groups

CROP	FOOD GROUP	CROP	FOOD GROUP
Wheat Rice Corn	Cereal grains	Sugar cane Sugar beet	Sugar
		Beans Soy beans	Legume
Potato Sweet potato Cassava	Roots or tubers	Coconut Banana	Tree crops

Figure 3.12 The percentage of total energy supply from fuel-wood sources

Brazil	33	Mali	97
Chad	94	Nepal	98
Ethiopia	93	Nigeria	82
India	36	Pakistan	37
Kenya	70	Sudan	81
Malaysia	8	Honduras	45

From Food and Agriculture Organization 1991.

Natural vegetation and climate

Plants depend closely on climatic conditions. Each has an optimum set of temperature and moisture needs. Some survive only in tropical conditions, while others are adapted to moderate or cooler temperatures. All plants require moisture, but they differ in their rates of **transpiration**, that is, the evaporation of water through pores or **stomata** in the leaves and stems. The total amount of water transpired in a year is often astonishingly large.

Some plants, called **hydrophytes**, require a particularly large amount of water. Others, called **xerophytes**, are adapted to an acute scarcity of water. Hydrophytes may be found either in water (for example, water lilies) or in damp locations. They often have shallow roots and thin, fragile leaves. Xerophytes are found in arid climates or in climates with a hot dry season. They have adapted to drought in several ways. Their root systems may be long, as in the case of vines. They may have thick stems or bark, like the cork oak. Or the leaves may be thick and hard, with a small number of stomata to reduce transpiration. (They may have a hairy or waxy surface for the same purpose). Prickly pear cacti have several xerophytic characteristics as well as some sharp thorns to keep predators away. Many xerophytes shed their leaves during the dry season. Others survive the drought by compressing their growth cycle and producing seeds to await the next rains.

Plants that have adapted to climates with contrasting wet and dry seasons may act as hydrophytes in one season and xerophytes in another. They may adapt by shedding leaves in the dry season, which eliminates most of the transpiration and conserves water.

All plants photosynthesize, but their light requirements differ greatly. Sun-loving plants reach upward for light but are intolerant of shade. The upper layers of tropical forest vegetation provide a good example. On the other hand, shade-loving plants are intolerant of open sunshine. Some plants require shade from other plants during the early stages of their growth but eventually grow upward into sunshine.

The reproductive systems of some plants are also affected by the length of day and night. Some plants cannot flower in the longer summer days of high latitudes, whereas others require this type of climate in order to reproduce. Varieties of wheat that do well in Saskatchewan often cannot grow in India or Pakistan. For this reason, the new high-yielding varieties of wheat introduced to these countries in the 1960s were bred in Mexico, which has similar lengths of day and night. Any plant that requires a particular length of day and night to flower and reproduce is called **photoperiodic**.

Other adaptations that plants make to their environment include the ability to withstand strong winds. Grasses can bend under winds of any strength. Some plants are able to survive burning. Most grasses again have this ability, as do trees such as the jack pine. The lodgepole pine and savanna spruce need fire to open their cones.

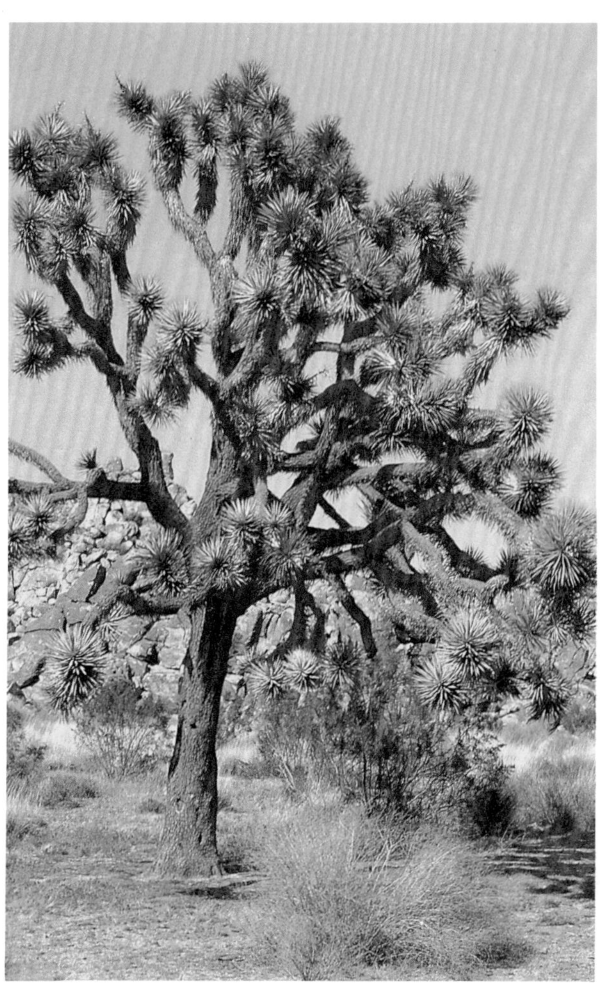

The Joshua tree, shown here in southern California, is an example of a xerophyte.

Plant communities

Plants do not grow in isolation. Like people, they form communities. Groups of plants that grow together under similar conditions are known as **plant associations**. Within these associations plants may have similar roles, as do different species of trees in a forest. On the other hand, they may complement each other in the sense that trees and shrubs or grasses may be part of the same association. The trees provide shade and draw nutrients from a greater depth. The shade-loving shrubs and grasses tap the shallower soil.

Associations such as these need time to develop. In any given area several plant associations may develop before the maximum vegetation is attained. These stages form a **succession**, the end product of which is **climax vegetation.** The climax vegetation of any area is determined by climate and to a lesser extent by the drainage, soil type, and frequency of fires.

The first plant community in the sequence toward climax vegetation is called a **pioneer community**. (See Figure 3.13.) This community usually consists of grasses, herbs, and small shrubs that can live on bare sites with a minimum of soil. Gradually these sites are colonized by a more complex set of plants with a longer growth cycle. As the vegetation becomes more complex, the soil also develops. Biomass production is usually greater in the earlier stages of a sequence, whereas diversity of species increases in the later stages. For example, old growth forests do not create much biomass growth but have many species.

If the sequence is not interrupted, climax vegetation eventually will be established. The whole process may take over a century to complete or, in the case of tropical rain forests, several centuries.

Resiliency of ecosystems

Some ecosystems are more resilient than others, meaning that they are better able to recover from alteration by natural or human causes. When considering the effects of environmental changes, consider how resilient the ecosystem under discussion is. A grassland ecosystem may return to its original state within a few years of a fire, while a tropical rain forest may take over 1000 years to recover from logging.

The resiliency of an ecosystem depends on many factors, such as the climate, soils, complexity of the system, and life span of the species involved. Cold polar climates result in slow regeneration even though the ecosystems themselves are relatively simple, while warmer climates tend to regenerate at a faster rate. Ecosystems with deep soils tend to regenerate quickly if the soil is not removed by the disturbance. Many tropical forests have shallow soils, which slow down the rate of recovery. The more complex a system is, the longer it will take to return to its original state. The complex interactions of a mature forest take a long time to develop, especially when the organisms involved are long-lived. An ecosystem composed largely of annual grasses can regenerate far more rapidly than one of giant trees with a life span of several hundred years.

Figure 3.13 A vegetation sequence that might occur on abandoned farmland in eastern Canada

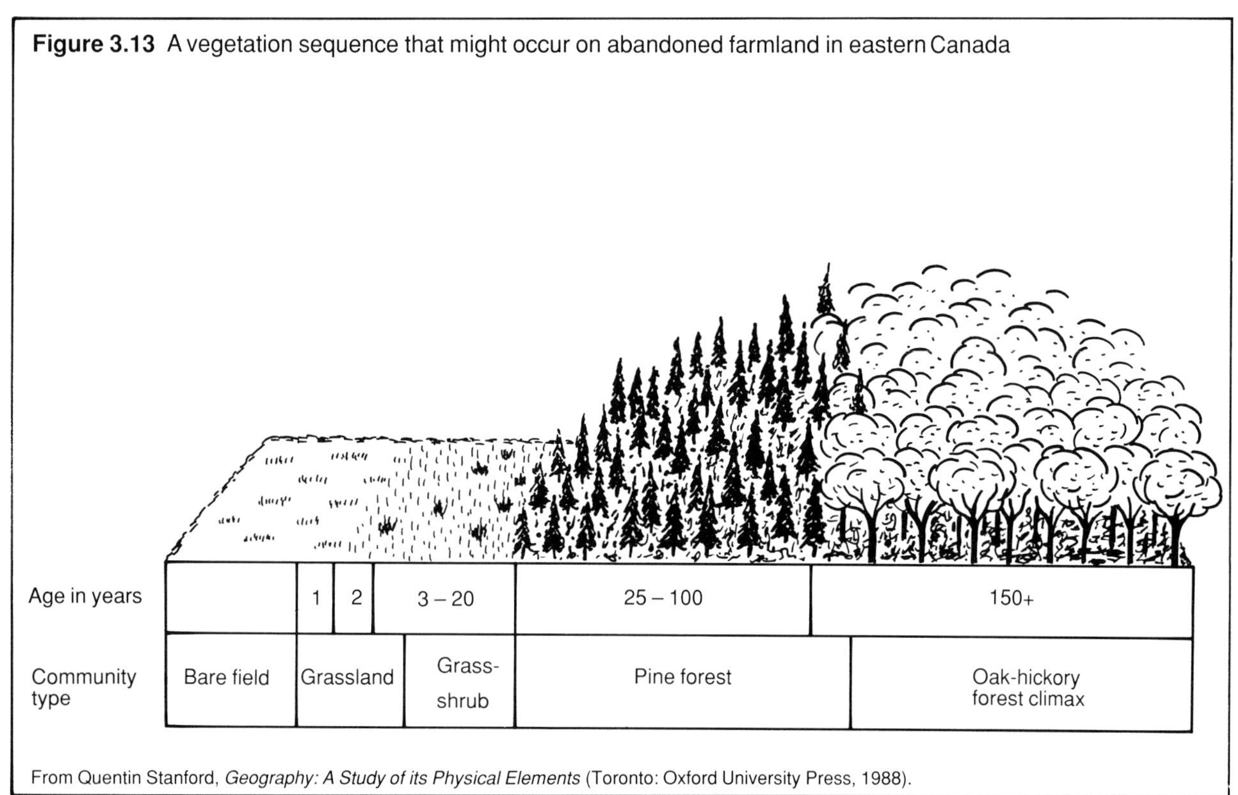

From Quentin Stanford, *Geography: A Study of its Physical Elements* (Toronto: Oxford University Press, 1988).

Looking back

1. Describe the role of decomposers in an ecosystem.
2. (a) State two different ways in which parasites exist in relation to their hosts.
   (b) Explain how a parasite differs from a predator in its ecological role.
3. In what three ways can forestry seriously interfere with an ecosystem?
4. How has human interference in the nitrogen cycle created problems in ecosystems?
5. Explain how energy is lost at each stage of the food pyramid.

Applying your knowledge

1. Draw a diagram to illustrate and explain a food web that includes the following species: snakes, mice, grass, hawks, sheep, cows, people, cougars, and white-tailed deer.
2. (a) In Figure 3.4, the population of one of the two species lags behind that of the other. Which species is this? Explain why this time lag occurs based on the ecological relationship between them.
   (b) Which of the species' populations seems to reach higher levels than the other? Explain why this might be so based on their position in the food pyramid.
3. (a) Using Figure 3.8, calculate how many times more concentrated the PCBs are in the gull eggs than in the phytoplankton.
   (b) Discuss how the position of humans in the food web relates to bioaccumulation.
4. (a) Explain why livestock farming is less energy efficient than crop farming. (See Figure 3.10.)
   (b) Which type of farming should be emphasized as world population increases? Why?
5. Using Figure 3.6, discuss how cutting down and burning large areas of forest would affect levels of carbon dioxide in the atmosphere.
6. Discuss why a prairie grassland ecosystem might be more resilient than a west coast forest ecosystem.
7. Human activities often result in a natural nutrient cycle being converted to a simple chain. Give an example of a situation where this has happened and discuss the ecological implications.

Extending your thinking

1. Select one of the environmental hot spots from Figure 1.2. Research and prepare a presentation which outlines the reason for the area being designated a hot spot and how the food chain has been affected by this environmental problem.
2. Set up a classroom aquarium to observe a small-scale ecosystem. Obtain an aquarium with a gravel-type filter and a minimum capacity of 75 L. Decide whether you want a cold or a warm water system for either salt or fresh water species. To manage the aquarium successfully, you must control many environmental factors, including the number of plants and animals and the temperature and oxygen levels of the water. You should also keep track of the pH, nitrite, and nitrate levels. Carefully research the requirements for your type of aquarium before starting.
3. Use newspaper and periodical sources, as well as your school library, to find an example of an ecosystem that has been threatened by human activities. List the species whose habitats have been disrupted and describe the efforts being made to protect the ecosystem and its species.
4. With a partner, prepare a comparison organizer that identifies what you consider to be the most important environmental issues in (a) your local area, (b) Canada, and (c) the world. Your organizer should show the similarities and differences among the issues as well as whether or not the issues are related.

4 WORLD ECOSYSTEMS

Earth is a remarkably varied place. Life is found in almost every part of the globe, both on land and in the oceans. In this chapter we will look at the major life zones of the planet. We will see how conditions in these zones vary and how these conditions determine the kinds of organisms that live in these zones. We will also see how people are disturbing more and more of the earth's natural environment.

Biomes

The world contains several major land-based ecosystems or **biomes**. A biome may be considered to be a large ecosystem. It is sometimes called a **bio-geo-climatic zone**. In a biome a particular type of climate and geology produces a certain form of vegetation. In turn, the vegetation interacts with the soil and provides habitats for its own range of living creatures — that is, it is an ecosystem.

Biomes are sometimes identified and named on the basis of the characteristic plants found in the area. Plants are the producers that convert solar energy into food for all the other members of an ecosystem. Therefore it makes sense to use them to classify the major ecological regions of the world.

The relationship between biomes and climate

Figure 4.1 shows the locations of the world's major biomes. Variations in local geography cause the edges of biomes to be blurred, but the patterns are clear. One

Figure 4.1 Worldwide distribution of biomes

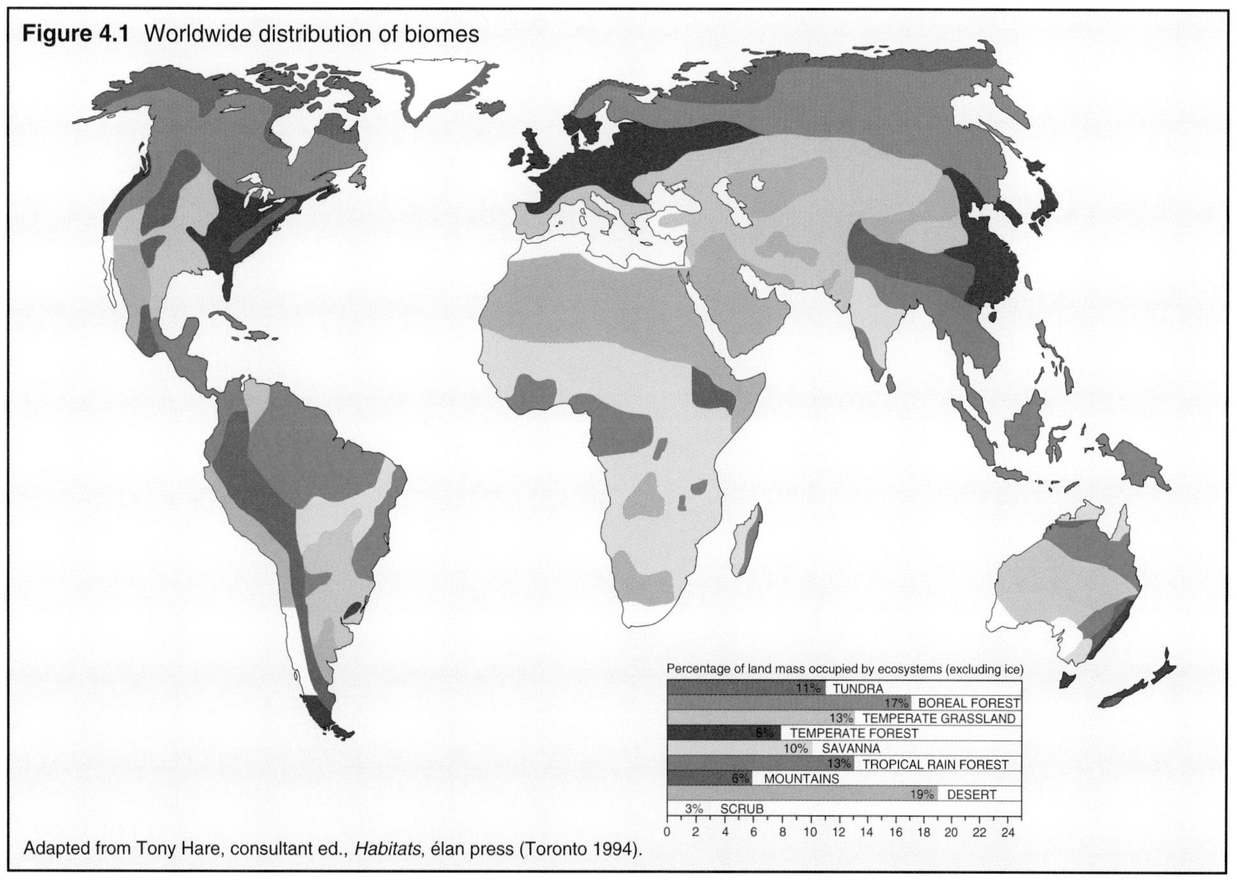

Adapted from Tony Hare, consultant ed., *Habitats*, élan press (Toronto 1994).

of the most striking features of the worldwide distribution of biomes is that it roughly follows lines of latitude. As one moves north or south, climates become drier or wetter, colder or warmer, and more or less seasonal.

The distribution of the world's biomes is related mainly to climate. One of the best ways to show the climate of a particular region is with a climate graph. Climate graphs show the average monthly temperatures and precipitation of an area. They indicate both the amount of precipitation and warmth as well as the season in which each occurs. Figure 4.2 shows climate graphs for each of the biomes described in this chapter.

Figure 4.2 Six climate graphs

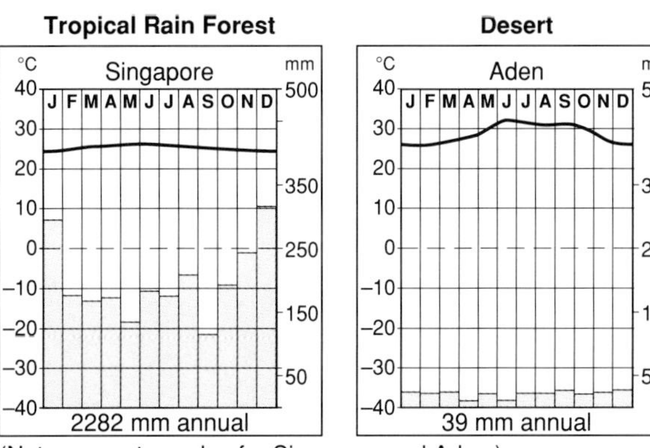

(Note separate scales for Singapore and Aden.)

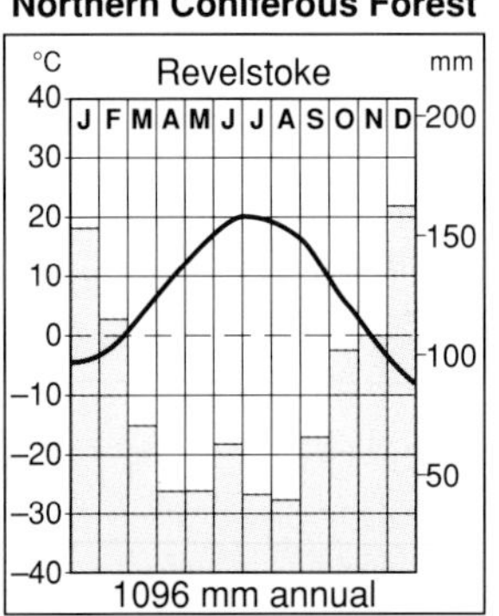

Tundra

Frobisher Bay

415 mm annual

Temperate Grassland

Medicine Hat

379 mm annual

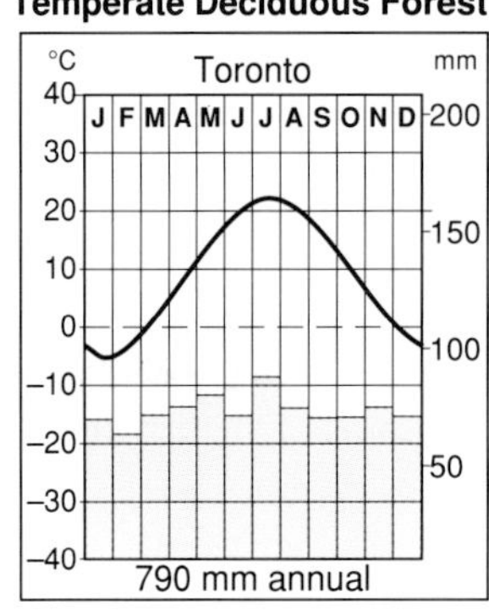

If you drive to Mexico during a Canadian winter, the temperature will increase gradually as you travel southward. Likewise, climates and their associated biomes change gradually and blend together at their boundaries. The biomes are not separated by sharp lines, even though maps suggest that they are. The world's major climate and vegetation regions grade into each other through transitional zones.

Biomes may be classified in various ways. Large biomes can be subdivided to achieve more precision in describing regional environments. This precision is important in environmental science, since the representative life zones of an area are important when planning a parks system. For the purposes of the national parks system, the major biomes of Canada have been subdivided into thirty-nine "Terrestrial Natural Regions." (See Figure 12.9.) This division helps the park planners to identify regions with significant conservation areas. At another level, Ontario has been subdivided into thirteen natural regions for the purposes of provincial park planning. These regions are like biomes, but on a smaller scale.

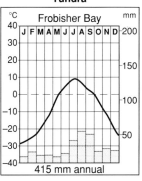

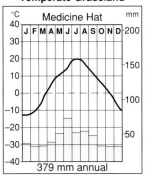

Two other factors influencing biomes

Altitude Life zones are also greatly affected by altitude. A mountainous region will have a very different climate from surrounding lowland areas. Mountain chains also create different climates as a result of rain shadow effects. Mountain climates are cold and severe. As you climb a mountain range you can see changes similar to those seen when travelling north or south from the equator. While remaining on the equator in the Andes of South America, you can climb from tropical rain forest, through temperate regions and tundra, to permanent ice.

Human modification The biomes in Figure 4.1 show the natural vegetation that would exist had these biomes not been modified by people. Large portions of the biomes have been replaced by other forms of vegetation. For example, in all farmed regions natural ecosystems have been replaced by artificial ecosystems. Nevertheless, studying the world's natural biomes is worthwhile since they sum up the links between climate, soils, vegetation, and all forms of life.

As you learn about the major biomes or life zones in this chapter, keep in mind the relationships between climate, vegetation, and animal life that cause biomes to exist.

The world's main biomes

Tropical rain forests

Tropical rain forests are the most productive and the most diverse of all the world's ecosystems. Rain forests are found in low-lying areas at low latitudes. In these locations the climate is hot with high and fairly continuous precipitation. Ideally, precipitation should total 2000 mm per year or more. The red soils are often poor in nutrients and contain much aluminum and iron.

The dominant vegetation is hardwood evergreens with a layered structure. This layering is caused by the struggle of plants to reach their required amount of light. In a dense tropical rain forest a closed canopy of trees creates deep shade. Therefore relatively little ground vegetation exists. Animal and bird life is concentrated in the various layers of the trees.

More species of plants and animals are found in the tropical rain forest than in all other biomes combined. A hectare of forest may contain more than 100 different tree species. The ecology of tropical rain forests is full of complex interactions between species. Many insect species feed only on a particular plant species. Rain forest flowers may be pollinated by such diverse animals as insects, bats, mice, and hummingbirds.

While the tropical rain forest is dense and luxuriant, it exists in a delicate relationship with the soils. In the hot, wet conditions decomposition is so fast that the soils require a continuous leaf fall to maintain a thin surface layer of humus. But even though leaves are constantly falling, the forest as a whole always remains green. Nutrients are quickly absorbed from the decaying leaves before they are washed away. Most trees have shallow roots to tap into the thin layer of nutrients.

Tropical rain forests are one of the fastest disappearing habitats. They are being cut and burned at a rapid rate. Many of the species of plants and animals are becoming extinct before they have been discovered and described by scientists. The enormous diversity of these forests is a unique biological resource.

Tropical rain forests contain several layers of dense foliage and are the habitat of countless bird and animal species.

Figure 4.3 Cross-section of the prairies

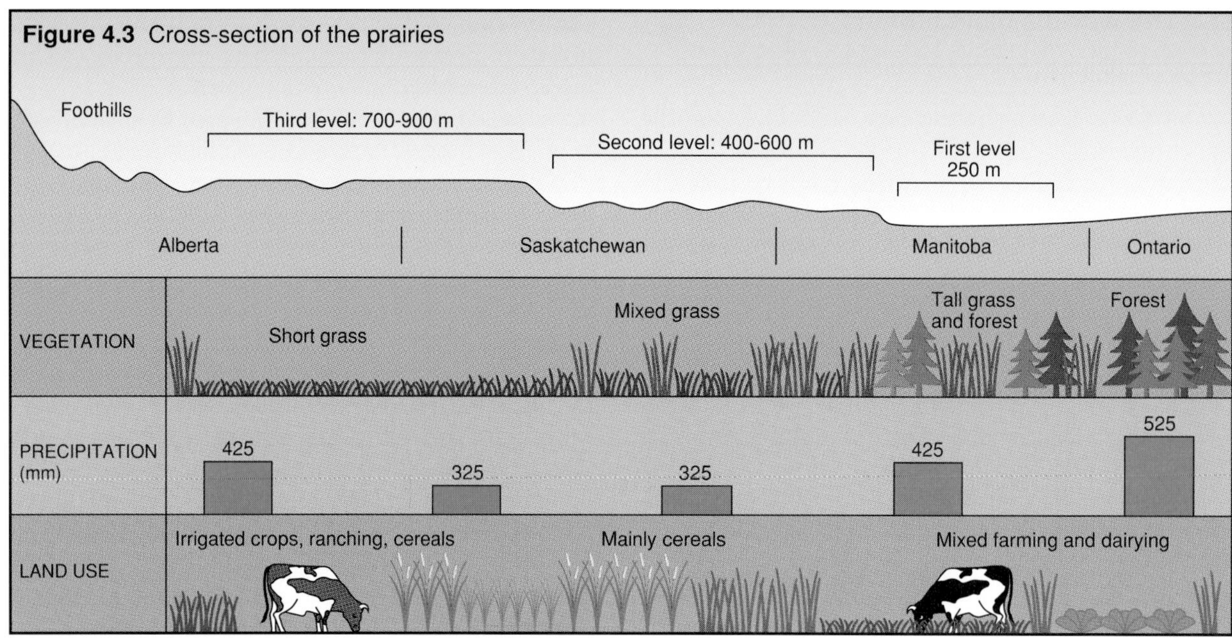

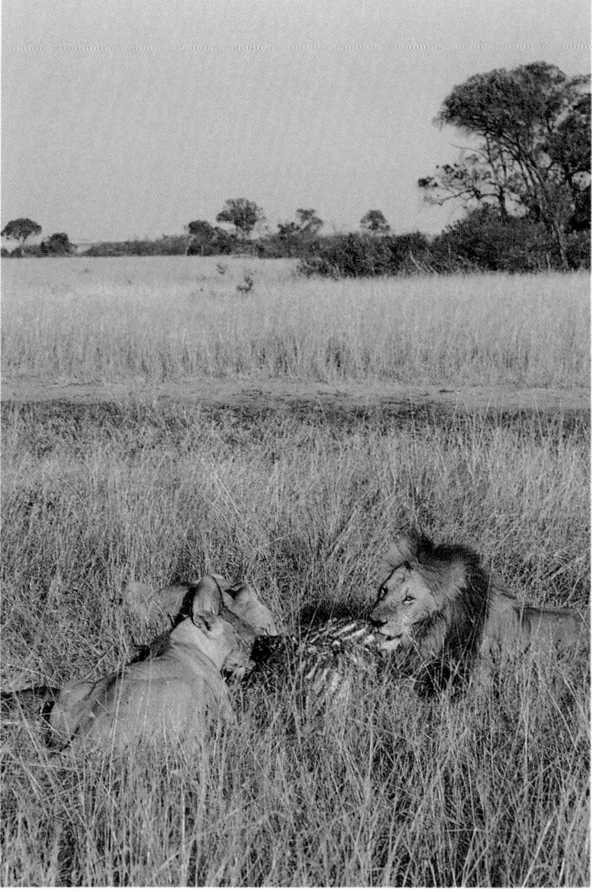

Giraffes are herbivores, eating only vegetation, while lions are carnivores, stalking other animals for their food. These animals are in the Masai Mara game reserve in Kenya.

Grasslands

Tropical grasslands The tropical grasslands, or **savannas** as they are called in Africa, are located to the north and south of the tropical rain forests. In these areas precipitation is very high in one season and virtually absent in another. The coarse grasses grow in the wet season and remain dormant during the period of drought. The frequency of fires is another factor that has led to the dominance of grasses over trees. Africa has the largest area of tropical grasslands, but they also exist in South America and Australia.

The African savannas support a wide variety of herbivores. Elephants and giraffes browse on trees, while huge herds of antelope (such as the wildebeest) and zebras help to maintain the grasslands by grazing. They are preyed upon by carnivores such as lions and cheetahs.

Temperate grasslands The temperate grasslands are found in the interior of the northern continents. They are located in areas that are too dry or too frequently burned to permit the growth of forests. The southern continents also contain areas of natural grassland, though in less extreme climatic conditions.

Figure 4.3 shows the relationships between different aspects of the environment in the Canadian Prairies. The transect shows a transition from west to east, beginning with the mixed and short grass areas that, like the Russian **steppes**, have few trees. The short grasses are low growing and tufted. If overgrazed they are easily invaded by xerophytic shrubs such as the prickly pear. Farther east tall grasses, such as bluestem, are native to the Red River Valley in Manitoba. These grasses are the vegetation type the French called **prairie**.

The temperate grasslands have a distinctive fauna with many burrowing rodents, including gophers and prairie dogs, and some large herbivores, such as antelope and bison.

Throughout the world the temperate grasslands have been largely replaced by artificial ecosystems based on grain farming or ranching. In the drier areas this change has led to problems of soil erosion by both wind and water.

Deserts

On the fringes of the savanna farthest from the equator, the vegetation becomes semidesert scrub and then desert. Precipitation is generally below 200 mm a year in a desert and below 300 mm in a semidesert.

Desert vegetation is highly xerophytic, adapting to the arid climate and the thin, stony soils. Perennial plants adapt by having long roots or thick stems and leaves.

Desert animals have also adapted to survive on a minimum of moisture. Many hunt for their food during the cool desert nights, burrowing underground in the heat of the day. Rodents such as the kangaroo rat and pocket mouse survive in the desert without needing to drink.

About one-third of the earth's land is arid enough to be desert or semidesert. Yet based on present vegetation, over 40 percent appears to be desert or semidesert. This increase has been caused by human activity. The drier margins of the savannas have been turning into desert at an alarming rate. Observers point to a southward spread of the Sahara Desert at the rate of several kilometres per year. In the past half century 700 000 km^2 of land have been turned into desert or seriously degraded. Formerly prosperous towns, such as Timbuktu in Mali, have been engulfed by sand and dust.

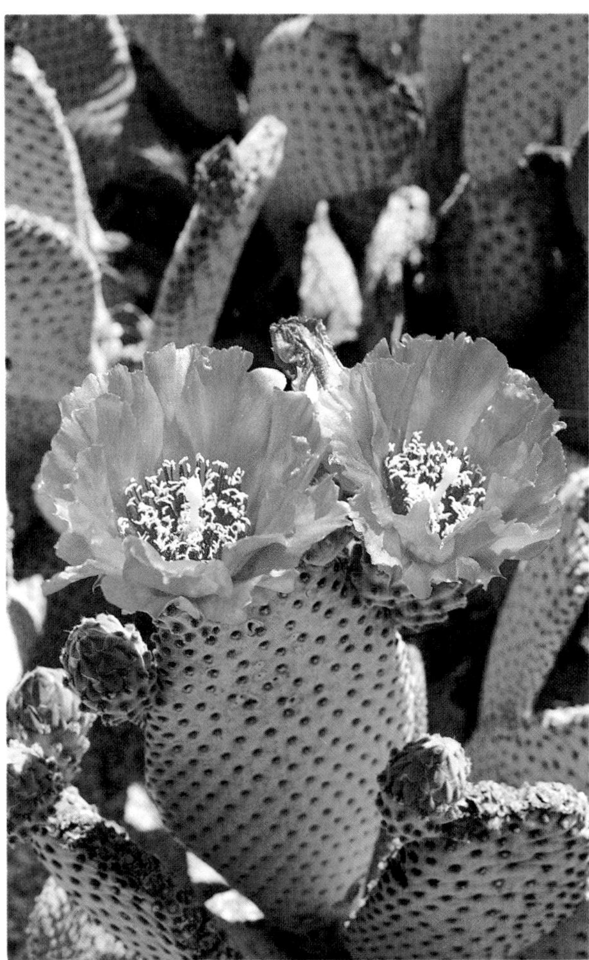

A cactus adds colour to the desert.

Temperate deciduous (broadleaf) forests

Temperate deciduous forests are found around the world in temperate latitudes where winters are cold enough to restrict growth and precipitation is over 750 mm per year. Trees are **deciduous**, which means they shed their leaves in autumn. Many variations exist, including the birch/maple forests of the St. Lawrence Valley and the oak/hickory forests of the Appalachians. Where soils and climatic conditions are less favourable, coniferous trees, such as pine and spruce, are often mixed with deciduous. The leaf fall from deciduous trees provides a richer source of humus than in coniferous forests. As a result, the soils are rich and usually quite deep. Since much of the natural habitat in the temperate forest biome has been lost, the wild animals are no longer abundant. Bears and wolves are found in some areas, while deer and smaller mammals are quite common. Many species of birds also inhabit this biome.

The broadleaf forests of the world have been largely cut down. In Western Europe the demand for timber for ships and construction since the Middle Ages has left little broadleaf forest standing. Most land that was originally under broadleaf forest in Europe and North America is now used for commercial farming or has been urbanized.

Northern coniferous forests (taiga)

An almost unbroken zone of coniferous forest stretches across the subarctic regions of North America, Europe, and Asia. This region is the **taiga**, which is Russian for primeval forest or **boreal forest**, meaning northern forest. It consists of conifers, such as firs, spruces, and pines. These are adapted to short summers and long, cold, snowy winters. The waxy, needle-like leaves protect against the cold conditions that make water difficult to absorb from the soil. Most conifers are evergreen, enabling trees to make the best use of the short growing season. They can survive the tough climate, since less energy is wasted in annual leaf loss than with deciduous species. Finally, the shape of conifers helps them to shed snow. The needles contribute to the formation of acid soils, known as **podzols**, which comes from a Russian term meaning ash-coloured.

The taiga is the home of many fur-bearing animals, such as the beaver and muskrat, with predators such as wolves and lynx. The forests provide food for many seed-eating birds such as crossbills and grey jays.

On the west coast of North America, rainfall is sufficient for a temperate rain forest to develop. Here conifers such as Douglas firs and redwoods often exceed 60 m in height and can reach as high as 95 m, like the "Carmanah giant" spruce. These huge trees form the basis of British Columbia's coastal forest industry.

Douglas firs reach towards the sky in Cathedral Grove, British Columbia.

The tundra

To the north of the coniferous forest lies the treeless tundra. Here the climate is too cold for tree growth. Strong winds further increase the chilling effect on these northern plains. Tundra also exists above the **tree line** in mountainous regions, even near the equator.

Much of the north is affected by **permafrost**, which is the name given to any ground with a permanently frozen layer beneath its surface. In all but the extreme north, summers are warm enough to melt some of the ground surface, forming what is called the **active layer**. Plants grow slowly and stay close to the ground to take advantage of whatever warmth can be absorbed from the sun. They have shallow roots because of the permafrost. The vegetation consists of grasses, mosses, lichens, and dwarf shrubs, some of which can be very colourful for a brief period. Since water cannot drain through the frozen soils, much of the tundra is flat and waterlogged during the summer.

Plant life is significantly affected by permafrost. Roots cannot penetrate the frozen zone and are thus confined to the active layer. Plants are subjected to widely differing temperatures as the active layer freezes and thaws. Expansion and contraction of the soil also occurs, placing further stress on plants.

The number of resident plant and animal species is low in the tundra. One reason is the slow growth of producers (vegetation) in the cold temperatures. Another is the fact that the tundra has only recently been recolonized after the Ice Age. Tundra animals include arctic hares and lemmings, with some large-bodied mammals such as caribou. Polar bears are common on the coast. Many birds migrate to the Arctic during their breeding season. They feed on the enormous populations of mosquitoes, blackflies, and other insects that abound during the long summer days. These species do not remain for the long, cold winter nights, however. Overall, the tundra is an ecosystem of low productivity. It can support only small numbers of people on the basis of its ability to produce food. The slow rate of growth makes the tundra a very fragile ecosystem. When damaged, it takes years to recover.

Permafrost poses several problems for people living in northern areas. Structures built on soils containing significant amounts of water, such as clay, loam, and organic soils, are apt to move. Heat from within a house, plus pressure from its weight, can cause the permafrost to melt and the building to subside. Similar problems affect transport. Sheets or wedges of ice can form below the surface of roads, causing heaving (when the ice freezes) or subsidence (when it melts). Water supply and sewage disposal are difficult in areas subject to permafrost. Pipes cannot be buried and must be enclosed in a heated jacket.

The Canadian tundra near Churchill, Manitoba, is close to the northern limit of tree growth.

The ice sheets

Until 10 000 years ago, ice sheets covered much of North America and Eurasia. Now large ice sheets are found only in Greenland and Antarctica. Within these enormous bodies of ice lie tremendous reserves of water, which could have dramatic effects on sea levels if they were to melt. The ice sheets themselves are home to few species, but they hold climatic and environmental records for the last few hundred thousand years locked up in their chemistry.

The Antarctic continent makes up about 10 percent of the world's land surface, but only 2 percent of it is ice free, and then only in summer. It also contains 90 percent of the world's ice, locking up nearly 75 percent of the world's freshwater.

The margins of the ice sheets are important for many kinds of seabirds and marine mammals. The waters surrounding the ice sheets have stable temperatures and support a diversity of species that need both land and sea. These include walruses, narwhals, seals, sea lions, albatrosses, and penguins. The Adélie penguins of the Antarctic live on and around the ice pack all year long, where they feed upon the abundant **krill** (small shrimp-like animals that thrive in the Antarctic waters).

Hundreds of Adélie penguins gather in the Antarctic. These flightless birds live in colonies but mates often form long-lasting relationships.

Ocean ecosystems

Perhaps "planet earth" should be called "planet water." Water covers about 71 percent of the earth's surface. The **hydrosphere**, or the water in the atmosphere and on the surface of the planet, helps regulate the temperature of the earth and the balance of chemicals such as carbon dioxide. Fossil evidence suggests that life on earth began in the ocean waters. Water can be classified into two main types: ocean and inland, which roughly corresponds to the division into salt- and freshwater systems.

Though the aquatic environment is far more extensive than the land environment, it does not show as much variation. Despite their large extent, aquatic ecosystems are not as well understood as land-based ones because of the difficulties of exploration. The deepest part of the oceans, in the Marianas trench, is approximately 11 000 m below sea level—about 2 km deeper than Mt. Everest (8848 m) is high!

The open oceans

The oceans and seas are huge bodies of saltwater that cover about 71 percent of the earth's surface and account for 97 percent of the world's water. The total mass of organisms in the oceans also far exceeds that on land. Most life in the oceans is found close to the surface. The microscopic algae or **phytoplankton** must be close to the surface to receive enough light for photosynthesis. These plant-like organisms (see Figure 4.4) form the basis of large food chains, which include most marine species and are responsible for producing much of the world's oxygen. The chief producers of the oxygen are diatoms and dinoflagellates, which exist in vast numbers in the surface water layers. In 1 L of water more than 5 million producers may exist. Even huge whales are dependent upon these tiny organisms.

The phytoplankton are eaten by small crustaceans (**zooplankton**), which in turn provide food for larger animals. In Antarctic waters enormous populations of krill provide food for the baleen whales, which are able to filter the krill out of the water.

The productivity of the oceans largely depends on the nutrient content of the waters. Dead organisms tend to sink below the surface layers, taking nutrients with them. These nutrients may be returned to the surface through a process of upwelling when offshore winds move surface water away and deep water rises to take its place. Nutrients may also be washed in from the land by rivers. These two factors make the coastal waters in mid-latitudes very productive. The Grand Banks of Newfoundland and the North Sea are among the world's richest fishing areas, although recently they have been seriously overfished.

Several of the ocean's biological resources have been so overused that renewable resources have become nonrenewable. The whale hunt is an example of how a marine resource has been so heavily used that the organisms involved have been driven to the brink of extinction. Only a few hundred blue whales remain. Even though hunting them is now illegal, their population may not recover.

Coral reefs

A special example of marine environments is the coral reef. Coral reefs are diverse and are widely distributed in tropical oceans. The characteristic organisms of a coral reef are the corals themselves, a group of soft-bodied animals that produce a skeleton of calcium carbonate. When the animal dies, this skeleton forms a foundation upon which new coral animals can grow, resulting in the continual growth of coral reefs.

There are three main types of coral reef: the **fringing reef**, which grows as an extension of a coastline; the **barrier reef**, which is located some distance from the shore with a lagoon in between; and the **atoll reef**, which is a more or less circular structure with no visible land mass. Coral reefs are highly productive despite living in nutrient-poor ocean waters. This productivity is largely because many corals harbour symbiotic algae, which capture energy from the sun and receive nutrients from the coral animals. The coral animals receive most of their food directly from the algae that live inside them, forming a tight cycle of nutrients.

Despite their richness and diversity, coral reefs, like the tropical rain forests, are fragile systems. They are easily destroyed by silting, the buildup of sediment in the water, which affects the ability of the algae to photosynthesize. In some areas silting is due to poor logging or agricultural practices. One of the most serious threats to coral reefs is the crown-of-thorns starfish. This species is a predator of corals, and its population has exploded as human activity has removed the starfish's own natural predators. One of these is the giant triton, which is harvested for food and its shell. Coral reefs are also being destroyed by the use of poisons to capture fish for the aquarium trade.

The destruction of the coral reefs is not just the loss of one of the world's most spectacular biological systems. The reefs also act as natural wave breakers for coastlines and tropical islands. Their destruction could lead to serious erosion.

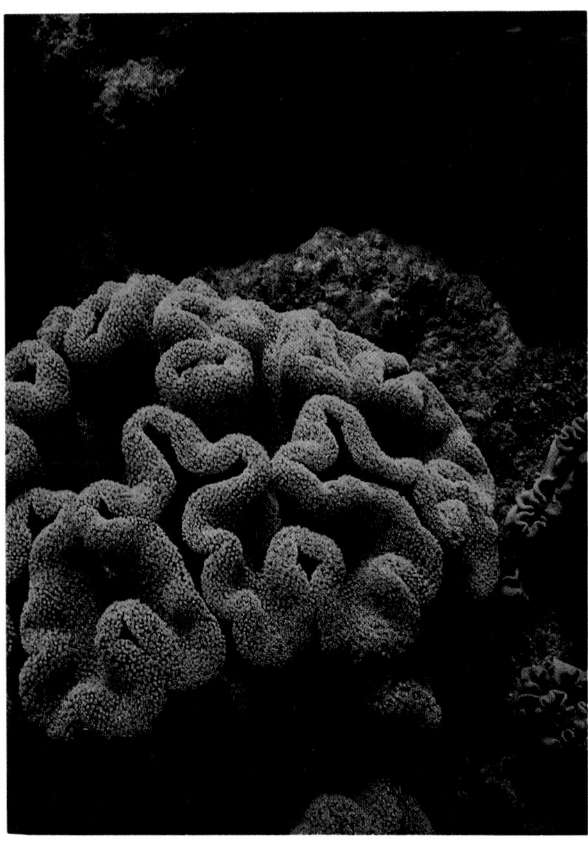

Corals such as these on the Great Barrier Reef in Australia are being threatened by human activity.

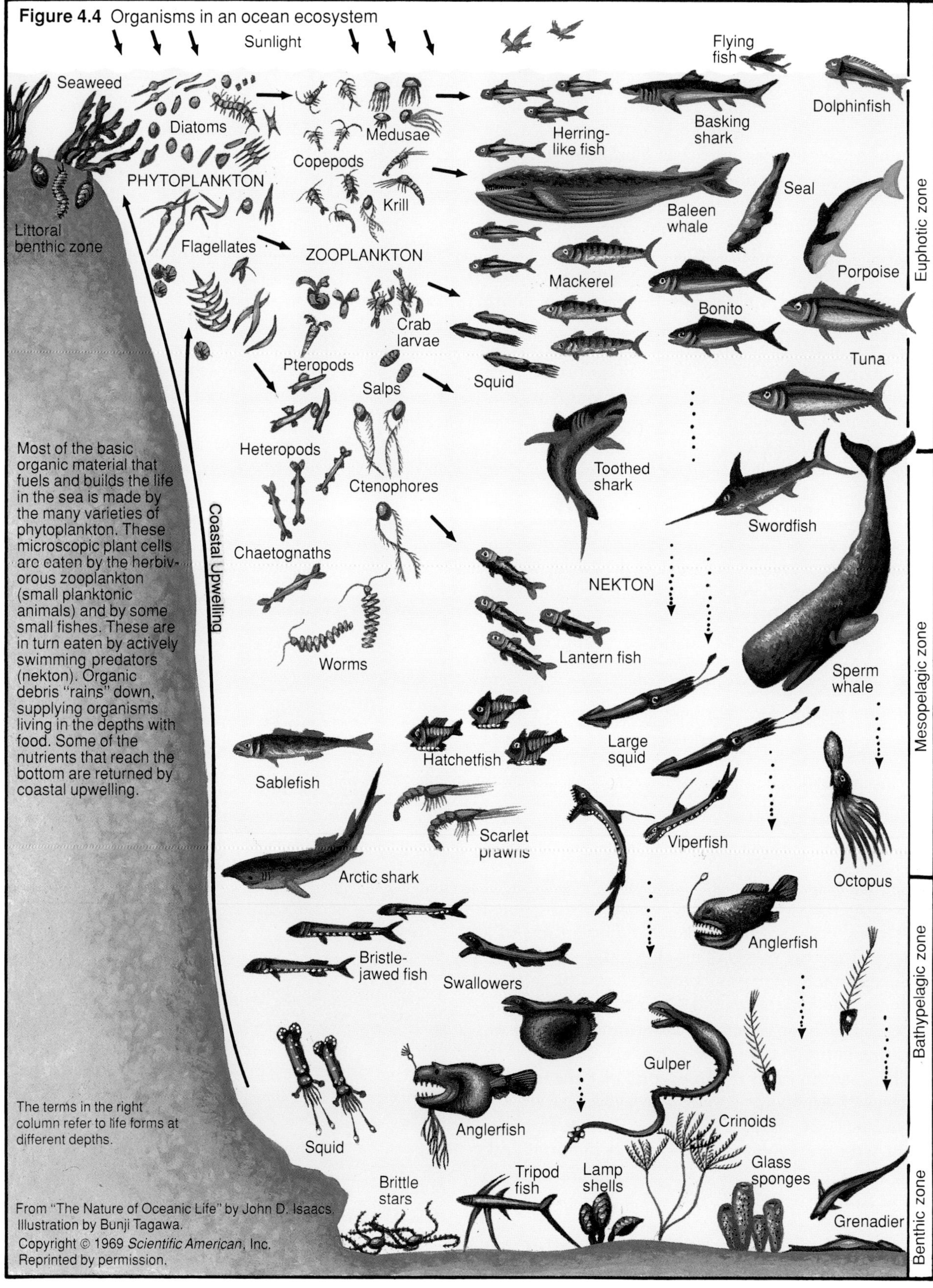

Figure 4.4 Organisms in an ocean ecosystem

From "The Nature of Oceanic Life" by John D. Isaacs. Illustration by Bunji Tagawa.

The ocean margins

At the edges of the oceans are several inshore ecosystems that bridge the gap between salt- and freshwater or land and sea. These include **estuaries, mangrove swamps**, and **intertidal zones**.

Estuaries are found where rivers empty into the sea and thus have a rich supply of nutrients and sediment as well as varying concentrations of salt in the water. The young of many fish species spend time in estuaries as a part of their life cycle, where they take advantage of the rich food supply and the lack of deep-water predators. The estuarine habitat is an important feeding area for shorebirds on migration, but it is being lost in many areas due to land reclamation.

Mangrove swamps are found on most tropical coastlines. The trees that make up these systems are unique in that they can obtain their moisture from saltwater and their nutrients from the sediments in marine lagoons. The upper layers of the mangroves are part of the land ecosystems. They provide food and shelter for insects and birds. The lower layers are important as shelter for fish and support for filter-feeding shellfish such as oysters.

The intertidal zones of the world are extensive. British Columbia alone has some 27 000 km of coastline. As their name suggests, these zones are subject to the daily ebb and flow of tides. The tidal action creates a region where organisms must spend part of their lives in the water and part out. Many organisms in intertidal zones are restricted to narrow zones. Despite the problems of the intertidal environment, a great variety of life forms can be found, including several commercially important species such as crabs, clams, and mussels.

Inshore ecosystems are highly productive because of the rich supply of nutrients. The organic sediment and the organisms that feed upon it provide an excellent food source for the young or larval stages of many species of fish and crustaceans. The larvae can also find shelter from predators among the seaweeds and grasses of estuaries and the roots of mangroves. They are thus important nursery grounds for species that are commercially exploited.

Mangrove swamps, such as this one at Turtle Cove in the Galapagos Islands, are common in tropical areas.

Inland water ecosystems

Freshwater systems may be split into still and flowing waters. Still waters include lakes, ponds, and wetlands. Flowing waters include rivers and streams. Most inland waters are fresh, containing few dissolved minerals, though some bodies of water such as the Caspian Sea, the Great Salt Lake, and the Dead Sea are very salty. Inland water ecosystems change over time as lakes and ponds fill up and rivers change their courses.

Lakes and ponds

Lakes and ponds range in size from tiny puddles to huge lakes such as the Caspian Sea, Lake Victoria, and Lake Superior. Canada has a great deal of freshwater, covering about 8 percent of its surface area. As with ocean environments, the primary producers in lakes and ponds are phytoplankton. These tiny green or brown organisms are responsible for the murkiness of many lakes and ponds during the summer. The phytoplankton are food for the zooplankton. (See Figure 4.5.) The food chain continues upward, including small crustaceans, insects, fish, freshwater mussels, birds, and some mammals, such as otters.

The boundaries of aquatic ecosystems are sometimes hard to define since several plants may have their roots in the water and their leaves out. Many insects, such as mosquitoes, dragonflies, and mayflies, spend their larval stages in the water but emerge to spend their adult stages in the air.

Most lakes and ponds have both inflow and outflow by means of streams and rivers. Some, however, have no outflow and tend to accumulate minerals that are washed in from the surrounding land. If the lake is in a dry region where evaporation is high, it can become very salty. In the Great Salt Lake or the Dead Sea, conditions are unfavourable for most life forms.

Ponds and lakes are temporary features of the earth's surface. The material produced by organisms in the pond or lake eventually settle to the bottom and gradually fill up the body of water. This process can be hastened by an inflow of sediment from streams and rivers or by the addition of nutrients. Many lakes, such as the Aral or Caspian seas, are shrinking because of the increased diversion of water from inflowing rivers.

Rivers and streams

Some of the water that falls to the earth flows on the surface as creeks, streams, and rivers. Many flowing waters begin from springs where groundwater reaches the surface. As the water flows over rocks, down rapids, and over falls, it traps many air bubbles. Thus the oxygen content of running water is usually greater than that of still water. The oxygen content is also determined by the temperature of the water. Cooler water is able to absorb more oxygen than warmer water. Both the oxygen content and the speed of the water influence the kinds and numbers of species.

Small streams meet, forming larger streams, which in turn join to form rivers. As a body of flowing water becomes larger, its flow usually becomes slower, its bed wider, and the water less shaded by overhanging plant life. Slower flow and more sunlight encourage the growth of phytoplankton. Some larger plants can take root in the stream sediments. The flow of an individual stream may vary by more than a hundredfold between the driest time of year and floods. During floods many organisms are washed away to become food for organisms farther downstream.

Flowing waters often change their courses. Streams and rivers have great powers of erosion and deposi-

Figure 4.5 An aquatic food chain in a lake

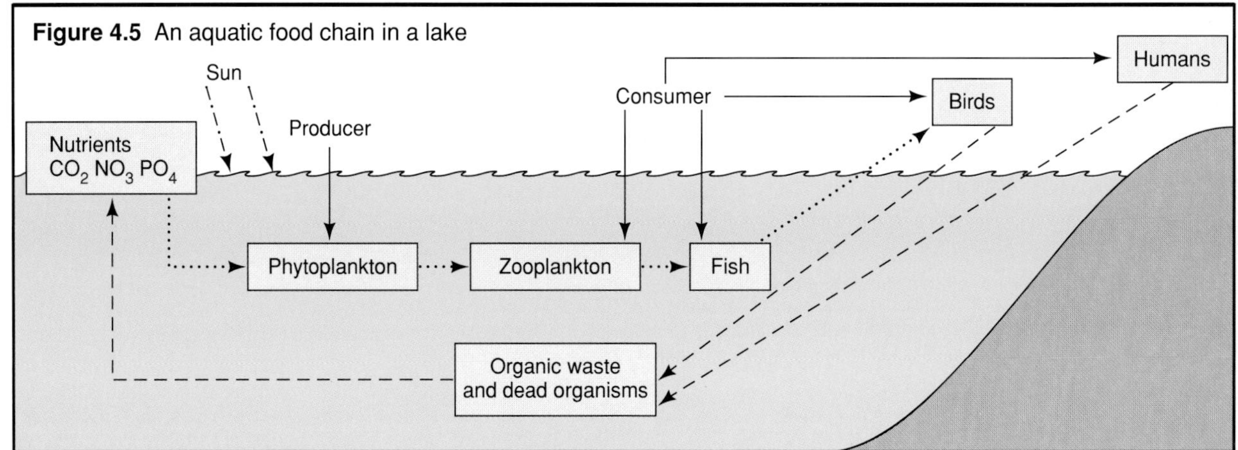

tion that alter their courses over time. Land near a body of flowing water is liable to be flooded or even washed away. At the mouth of a river, sediments are dropped because water flow slows and deltas form. Thus a river can both build up and break down the landscape.

Many organisms depend on flowing waters. Some animals, such as beavers and otters, spend time both in the water and on land. Many waterfowl and other birds depend on streams and rivers for their food and nest along the banks of flowing waters. People also depend on flowing waters for food, drinking water, transportation, irrigation, and waste disposal. We have drastically altered many bodies of flowing water, especially by building dams. Dams usually reduce the risk of flooding and harness the water for energy production and water supply.

Wetlands

Wetlands are areas of land that are covered by water for a part of the day or year and include marshes, swamps, bogs, and temporary ponds and sloughs. Wetlands may be the result of heavy spring rains, flooding rivers, or the daily ebb and flow of the tides.

Wetlands are found all over the world. In Canada they account for over 10 percent of the land area. Some of the well-known Canadian wetlands include the marshes in the Great Lakes basin, the Peace-Athabasca River delta, the peatlands of Newfoundland, the muskeg of northern Canada, the Fraser River delta, and the prairie pothole region. The vast prairie region of Alberta, Saskatchewan, and Manitoba is pitted with millions of depressions of varying sizes. Many of these fill up in the spring from melting snow and rain, only to dry up later in the year. These potholes and sloughs are important breeding and feeding grounds for wildfowl.

Many of our wetlands are being drained or filled to create new land for industry or agriculture. Undisturbed, wetlands are unsuitable for most human uses. We cannot build, farm, swim, or boat on them. As a result, farmers often drain them. Environment Canada estimates that more than two-thirds of southern Canada's wetlands have been converted into urban or agricultural uses. However, wetlands are important as wildlife refuges. Over 100 species of birds inhabit or make use of Canada's wetlands, particularly during migration.

Wetlands are common on the Canadian Prairies.

Artificial ecosystems

Natural ecosystems have been modified for so long and so thoroughly that many human environments can be considered ecosystems in their own right. These artificial ecosystems are characterized by a lack of biological diversity. Certain species are actively encouraged while others are suppressed. The maintenance of these ecosystems requires an input of both energy and materials. These systems therefore cannot be considered stable. Many artificial ecosystems also show interrupted or incomplete nutrient cycles.

Plant life is present, though scarce, in this urban ecosystem in Portimao, Portugal.

Urban ecosystems

The most drastically altered ecosystems are the urban ecosystems found in towns and cities around the world. Here the land is smothered with asphalt and concrete. Some streets are lined with trees, gardens, and lawns. Some scattered parks may resemble the natural environment. People dominate the ecosystems in cities such as Mexico City, which may have populations of over 20 million. Like other human-dominated ecosystems, the urban environment does not vary greatly between biomes as it is built for the convenience of people rather than plants or animals.

City dwellers get their food from many places. A person in Toronto may eat wheat from the Prairies, bananas from Ecuador, coffee from Colombia, lobster from the Atlantic provinces, tomatoes from California, apples from British Columbia, and oranges from Florida. The urban food web extends all over the world. The waste products of a city are not usually recycled or are only partially recycled. Sewage may or may not be treated and is discharged into lakes, rivers, and oceans. Garbage is collected and may be either incinerated or buried in a landfill.

Humans are not the only organisms found living in a city. Several species, such as mice, rats, squirrels, cockroaches, sparrows, and starlings, have adapted to urban conditions. Others, such as dogs, cats, and flowers, have been imported by humans. Many trees are planted because they can tolerate the poor soil and polluted atmosphere, while weeds spring up in vacant lots and in cracks in the sidewalks.

Agricultural ecosystems

People have transported the species that they want to cultivate all over the globe. Wheat from Asia has been transferred to the grassland biomes of North America and has also replaced many of the world's deciduous forests. In some cases deserts have been transformed into wheat fields by irrigation. Agricultural ecosystems often appear to be similar to one another, regardless of the natural biome in which they are found. A wheat field in Ontario (temperate forest biome) shares many similarities with a wheat field in the Prairies (grassland biome).

Agricultural ecosystems tend to be **monocultures** or fields of a single plant species. Monocultures are not favourable to wildlife and require a great deal of energy and pesticides to maintain them. To produce crops, agricultural land must be maintained in an early stage of succession. The land is tilled to loosen the soil and cleared of vegetation to give the crop a start against competing weeds. The crop is usually

Figure 4.6 A farm system

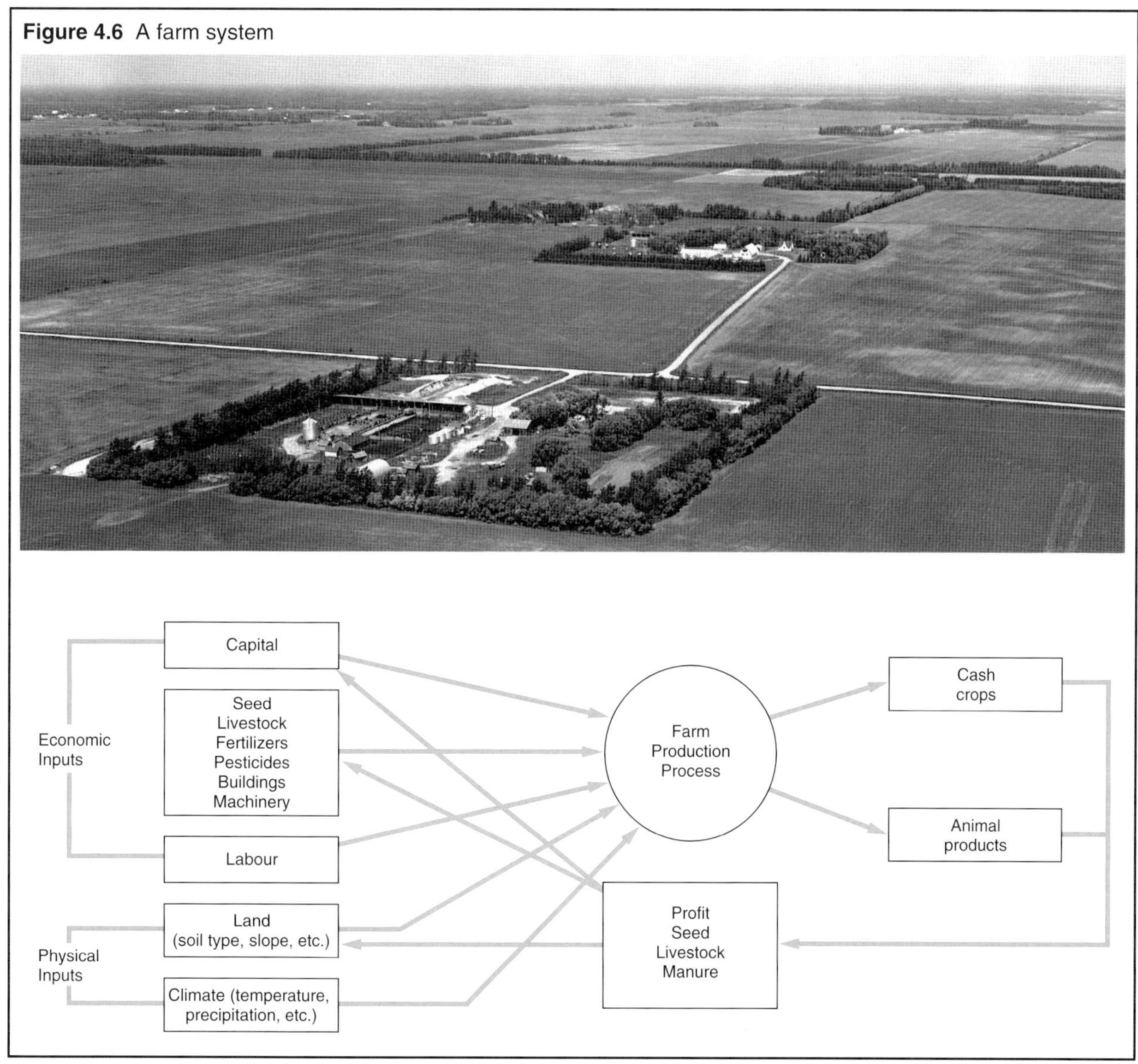

sprayed with pesticides to keep competing plant and animal species under control.

Another feature of agricultural land is that the nutrients that are in the soil are exported in the crops to other places. Most soil nutrients end up in cities and are not returned to the land. This breaks the nutrient cycles, and therefore the land must be supplied with extra nutrients in the form of costly fertilizers. If left alone, many agricultural ecosystems would slowly revert to the natural vegetation that is characteristic of the region. However, this process could take more than a century.

Timberland ecosystems

When a forest is cut for lumber, the natural forest is usually not allowed to regenerate. The new forest is treated much like a crop. The land is cleared and the vegetation may be slashed and burned before planting. The trees that are planted are often of a single species and may be **genetic clones**, with a corresponding lack of genetic diversity. This lack of diversity can lead to a greater risk of disease and pest infestation.

These second-growth forests may be managed to varying degrees. Some are left to develop through a process of natural succession. Others are planted, thinned, fertilized, and sprayed with pesticides. The natural cycle of forest fires is also controlled where possible to maximize lumber yields. The harvesting techniques may be detrimental to the soil, and clear-cutting can lead to severe soil erosion. Clear-cutting in the upper parts of river basins greatly reduces the ability of soils to hold water.

Looking back

1. (a) Which major biomes are found in Canada?
   (b) Describe the relationship between climate and the plants and animals found in each biome.
2. (a) Refer to Figure 4.3. Describe the relationships between precipitation and vegetation, precipitation and land use, and vegetation and land use in the Canadian Prairies.
   (b) In what ways has the prairie grassland ecosystem been changed by human activity?
3. List the reasons why polar ecosystems are so fragile.
4. Coral reefs are found in some of the most nutrient poor waters of the world. How do these rich and diverse systems maintain themselves?

Applying your knowledge

1. With a partner, construct a two-stage diagram explaining one of the following:
   (a) why, how, and when the seasonal differences in rainfall lead to soil erosion in tropical grasslands;
   (b) why a broadleaf forest biome is more suitable for farming than a taiga biome;
   (c) why coastal waters are generally more productive than open oceans and which is more susceptible to pollution.
2. Compare the similarities and differences in the climates of the biomes as indicated in the climate graphs in this chapter.
3. Create an organizational chart that shows which climatic hazards can affect human life in each of the major biomes.
4. Discuss why wetland conservation is particularly important in Canada.
5. Examine the farm shown on page 55. Describe how each of the boxes and arrows in Figure 4.6 might apply to this Prairie farm.

Extending your thinking

1. (a) Brainstorm a list of ways in which humans modify environments.
   (b) Which type of modification is most important in (i) your local area, (ii) your province, and (iii) Canada?
2. As a class, carry out an in-depth analysis of your local environment. The purpose of the analysis is to answer such questions as:
   - What parts of the environment are natural/artificial?
   - What biome is represented?
   - What natural ecosystems exist in this environment?
   - How has the human population enhanced/disturbed this environment?
   - In what ways do you contribute to the enhancing/disturbing?
   - What are the main environmental issues and how are they being addressed?

   (You may want to investigate other questions as well.)

   To carry out your investigation, begin by studying topographic maps and air photos, then arrange to take a bus or walking tour of the area. Working in small groups, complete the following tasks as part of a presentation to be made to the class:
   (a) Photograph the features of the area that are of environmental significance.
   (b) Draw a sketch map and diagrams of these features.
   (c) Prepare a videotape of your tour.
   (d) Interview people who live in the area.
3. Choose a biome from those discussed in this chapter. Use the resources of the school library to find information about the following aspects of this biome:
   (a) the climate (refer to the appropriate climate graph in Figure 4.2);
   (b) the flora and fauna and how they relate to the climate;
   (c) the ways in which this biome is threatened by human activity.

UNIT 2

THE ENVIRONMENT

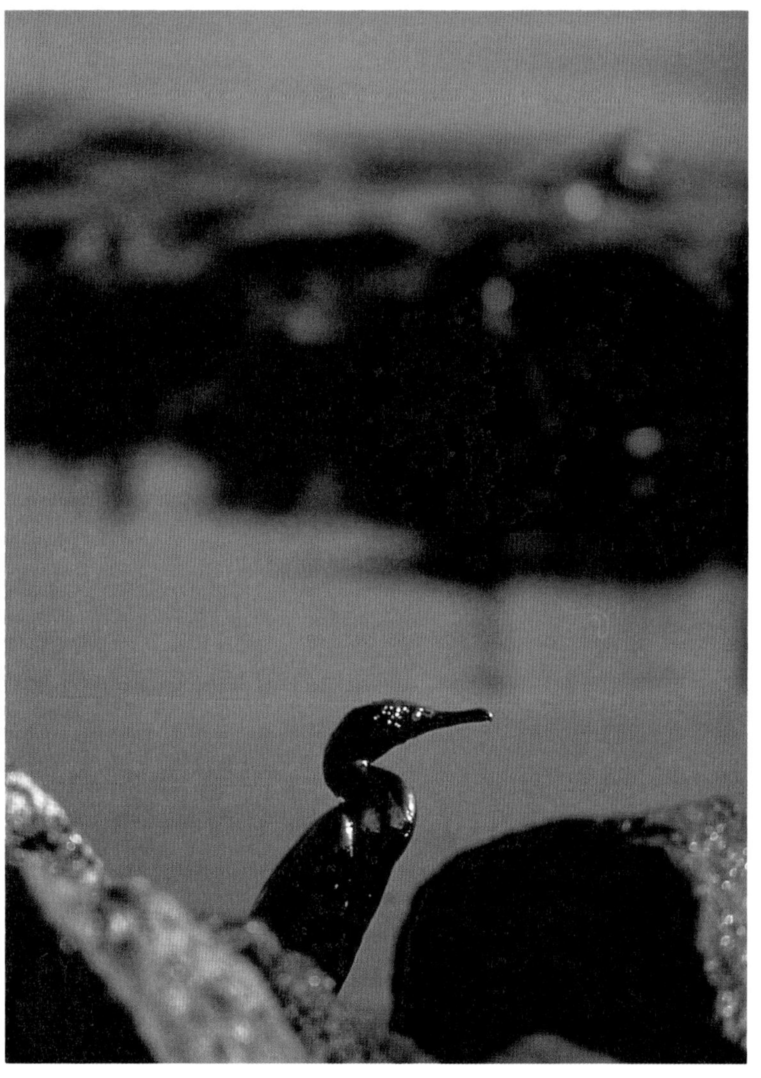

The oil slick released into the Persian Gulf created one of the world's greatest ecological disasters.

5 LIFE

We know approximately how many stars are in the Milky Way. We also know how many atoms make up complex proteins in our body. But we do not know exactly how many **species** of organisms live on earth. Human beings are just one of these species, but our impact is enormous. While life is thought to have existed on earth for the past 3 billion years or more, the human species may have been around for only about 3 million years. In the past few centuries we have become so powerful that we are now capable of dramatically altering the patterns of life on earth.

One way that we have altered these patterns is by causing many species to disappear forever, leaving other species to dominate an ecosystem. We can now modify species to conform to our own needs, but in doing so we may create a situation that we cannot handle. The world stands to lose many potential benefits unless we can find a way to conserve many wild species.

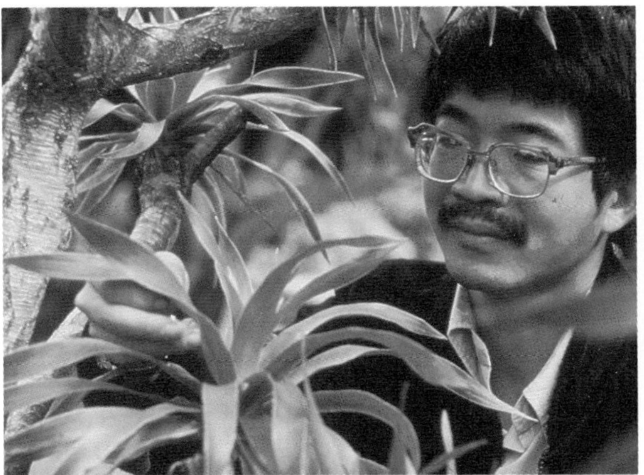

Many useful medicines are obtained from the forest.

The diversity of life

How many species of organisms live on our planet? Estimates range anywhere from 2 million to 50 million. We have a good idea of the numbers of larger organisms such as mammals and birds, but we are just beginning to discover how many invertebrates (animals without backbones or spinal columns) there are. Why can we not make more accurate estimates? Scientists have described and named about 1.4 million species and are adding new ones at the rate of around 5000 per year. When a new species is found, it must be checked against existing species and then fully described. This process takes an individual researcher months or years for each species. And often, by the time a new species is accurately identified, several other species have been eliminated.

Though new species are being found worldwide, most are being discovered in the tropics. As scientists begin to explore the diversity of these species, they are staggered by the numbers. For instance, as many as 160 species of beetles may depend on a single species of tropical tree. Even in temperate regions, diversity is high. More than twenty species of ladybird beetles are found in British Columbia alone. A west coast forest harbours more than 1000 species of insects.

These estimates are obtained by counting the number of new species found when exploring a sample area of a biome and extending the results to the biome as a whole. As with any projection, however, the results should be treated with caution. But even the most conservative estimates reveal the tremendous variety of life on earth.

The genetic information carried in a single species is immense. The information carried in the genetic code of a house mouse would fill a disk of 1250 MB capacity if converted into computer code. (The text of this book by comparison would fill only 0.75 MB.) When a species becomes extinct, this information is lost.

The loss of species

Throughout geological history there has been some loss of species, although this has been relatively slow. Perhaps a few species per million years have become extinct. At times, however, this rate has risen dramatically. In a relatively short space of time, around 65 million years ago, 75 percent of the species known from the fossil record, including dinosaurs, disappeared. The cause of this mass extinction is uncertain, but it may have been the result of a collision with an asteroid or comet. About forty species of mammals and ninety species of birds have been confirmed as extinct since 1600. However, the problem of extinction extends to all species of plants and animals, including insects, fishes, and micro-organisms.

The extinction rate is now as high as several species per day. Species are being lost mainly because of changes to their habitat. This is also true in Canada. (See Figure 5.1.) The tropical and temperate forests of the world are being cut down to make way for agriculture and grassland. Natural habitats are also being fragmented. Small areas cannot support the diversity that large ones can. For example, many North American parks have lost species. (See Figure 5.2.) Another example is the reserve on Barro Colorado Island, which was formed in 1914 by the flooding of the Panama Canal. The 15 km² island was set aside as a reserve in 1923, when it was home to 208 species of breeding birds. Since then, it has been protected continuously but has still lost forty-five of these species. These extinctions have occurred despite the fact that the island is only 200 m from the mainland.

We cannot easily predict the rate of extinction. There is little historical data, and few places have a sufficiently well-known **biota**. Human beings have increased the rate of extinction of species in some cases. For example, at least eighty-eight species of

Figure 5.2 Habitat area and loss of large animal species from North American parks

PARK	AREA (KM²)	PERCENTAGE OF ORIGINAL SPECIES LOST
Bryce Canyon	144	36
Lassen Volcano	426	43
Zion	588	36
Crater Lake	641	31
Mount Rainier	976	32
Rocky Mountains	1 049	31
Yosemite	2 083	25
Sequoia-Kings Canyon	3 389	23
Waterton-Glacier	4 627	7
Grand Teton-Yellowstone	10 328	4
Banff-Jasper-Kootenay-Yoho	20 736	0

From the Worldwatch Institute.

Figure 5.1 Some extinct, extirpated, and endangered species in Canada in 1996

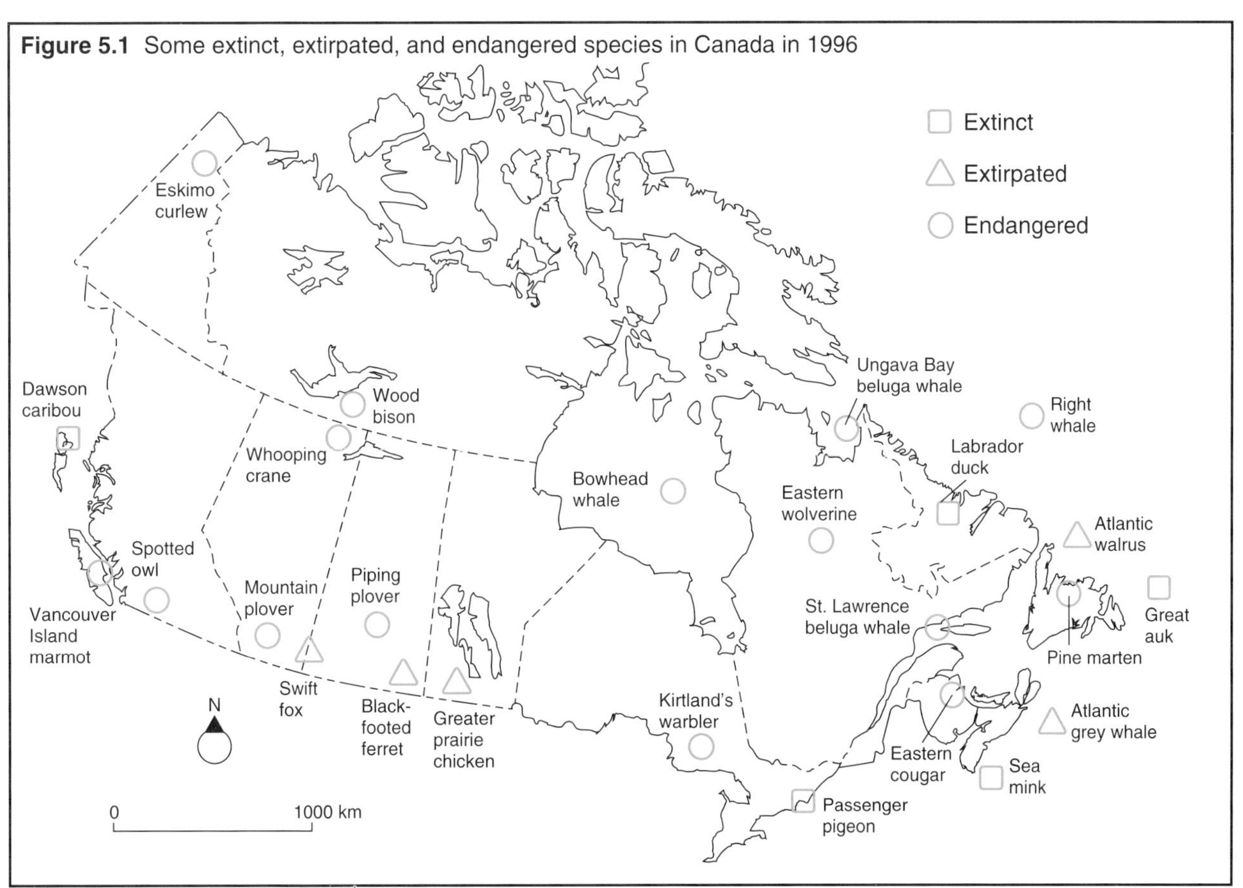

land birds lived on the Hawaiian Islands when the Polynesians arrived, forty-three when Captain Cook explored the islands, and only twenty-three today—two-thirds of which are endangered.

Species at risk

Some species are more at risk than others as a result of human activity. Large animals usually need much more space than small animals. When a habitat is reduced, the larger animals feel the impact first. For example, grizzly bears are no longer found in many of North America's parks. If the larger animals are driven toward extinction, smaller animals, such as parasites, will also be threatened. Species that reproduce slowly, such as whales and elephants, are at risk because it takes them a long time to rebuild their numbers.

Some species are naturally rare because of their way of life. These creatures are particularly vulnerable. For example, the Dawson caribou was found only on the Queen Charlotte Islands. It was wiped out by hunters at the turn of the twentieth century. Seabirds, which often nest in enormous colonies, are at risk if their nesting sites are disturbed. Half of the population of ancient murrelets, a small diving seabird, nests in only two sites off the coast of northern British Columbia.

Species that are used to produce a valuable commodity, such as oil, medicine, fur, or food, are at risk from over-exploitation. We have a poor record of managing species to yield a sustained harvest. Whales are an example. Some species of whales yield valuable oils. Several species of Atlantic whales were hunted until low numbers made it no longer economical to pursue them. The St. Lawrence River population of the Atlantic walrus disappeared between the 1600s and 1800s for the same reason. Chimpanzees, whose numbers have declined as a result of habitat loss, are also threatened by their use in medical research.

The value of species

You may well wonder if the planet could not do without some of the millions of species of insects and plants that exist. Many of them appear to be unnecessary, or even to be a nuisance, especially to farmers. However, before making up your mind, consider the following points:

The loss of genetic resources All living creatures contain genes that transmit their characteristics to the next generation. The extinction of any species means the loss of its genes for all time. Some of these genes enable plants and animals to adapt to particular features of their environments. Preserving the world's pool of genes became increasingly important with the discovery of **DNA** in 1953 and the techniques of **recombining genes** or **gene splicing** in 1973. This procedure basically involves transferring genes from one species to another to create desirable traits. If the genes of any one organism can be spliced into those of another, then the bank of genetic raw material should be sustained.

The loss of potentially useful species The possible uses of threatened species are difficult to estimate. Many of these species have never been studied. But they almost certainly contain materials that could be useful in the future, possibly in the making of new medicines. For example, disease resistance in our tomatoes comes from wild relatives in South America. A wild relative of corn, found in Mexico in 1978, is providing resistance to a fungus that can wipe out our hybrid species. This wild corn may also allow us to develop a perennial species, which means it will produce year after year without replanting. Cyclosporin, a drug used to prevent transplant rejection in humans, was recently isolated from a fungus growing in Norwegian soils.

Many of our most useful species have come from tropical rain forests. Coffee, tea, cashews, rice, cassava, cacao, bananas, citrus fruits, pineapples, avocados, vanilla, mangoes, cardamon, cloves, peanuts, pepper, ginger, cinnamon, and rubber have their origins in tropical forests. Many medicines also have wild origins. The drug quinine, used to fight the deadly disease malaria, comes from the forests of Peru. A valuable drug used in the fight against leukemia and Hodgkin's disease comes from the rosy periwinkle. We have only begun to explore the variety of species in these forests, yet we are already extinguishing some of them. No one can predict which species will turn out to be important to human existence by providing valuable material benefits in years to come.

The possible effects on ecosystems Although it is not certain, the loss of species may threaten the stability of ecosystems. We do not fully understand how living creatures interact within an ecosystem. The loss of some plants or animals could upset the delicate relationships within an ecosystem.

The aesthetic value of species Some species have an aesthetic value—that is, the existence of the species improves our lives in a non-material way. Many birds are valued for their beauty and interesting habits. This value is significant, judging by the number of birdwatchers. Species have a value in themselves, independent of any human use.

Endangered species

Extinction is forever. Once a species is gone it cannot be brought back. Each lost species means a piece of our heritage is gone. By showing our concern for endangered species, we can try to maintain these valuable resources. The loss of a species from an ecosystem may also indicate deeper problems with that ecosystem. For example, birds of prey were endangered by the buildup of DDT in the ecosystem.

The term **endangered species** refers to those species with population numbers so low that they could become **extirpated** or **extinct**. Extirpated refers to a species that no longer exists in a country or region but does exist elsewhere. An extinct species is one that no longer exists anywhere.

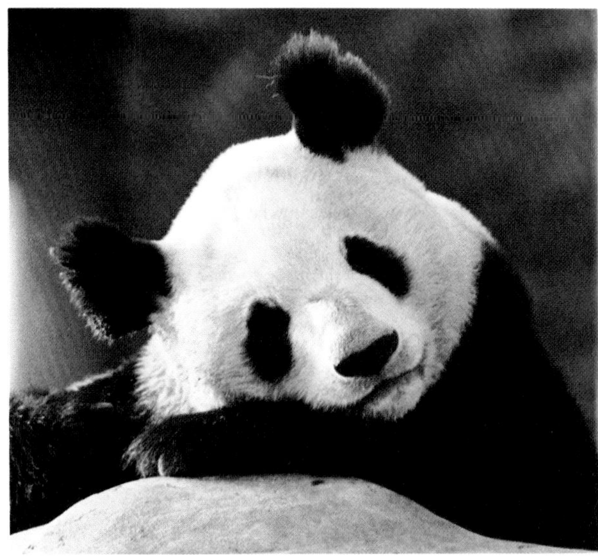

The panda is a well-known endangered species.

The sea otter has recovered from the verge of extinction, and was upgraded in 1996 from 'endangered' to 'threatened.'

The passenger pigeon became extinct in 1914.

Endangered species in Canada

As of April 1996, the Committee on the Status of Endangered Wildlife in Canada listed 272 species of Canadian organisms as either extinct (10), extirpated (11), endangered (63), threatened (66), or vulnerable (122). Figure 5.1 shows some extinct, extirpated, or endangered mammals and birds in Canada.

The major factors that lead to the endangering of Canadian species are over-exploitation (hunting, fishing, gathering of eggs), habitat destruction, and pollution. For example, the sea otter was hunted for its fur during the eighteenth and nineteenth centuries. By the start of the twentieth century the sea otter was on the verge of extinction. The few remaining sea otters in Alaska were protected by international treaty, and the population grew to about 30 000 individuals by 1960. Sea otters were successfully reintroduced to British Columbia between 1969 and 1972.

The great auk was a large and flightless penguin-like seabird that lived off the Atlantic coast of Canada. It was exploited by early explorers for fresh food, for bait, and for its feathers. The birds were too easy to kill and their eggs were easy to collect. The last-known pair of auks was killed and stuffed as museum specimens in 1844.

The greater prairie chicken has lost its prairie grassland habitat because of agriculture and cattle ranching. It is now missing from most of its natural range. The black-footed ferret may be North America's rarest mammal. It is extirpated in Canada and may number less than 100 individuals.

As late as the 1860s, the passenger pigeon was one of America's most common birds. Before 1840 it was estimated that there were between 5 billion and

9 billion individuals. Its uncountable numbers were one of the continent's natural wonders. Vast flocks, numbering in the millions, would darken the sky and bring down telegraph wires by the sheer weight of their numbers when they settled. However, they were slaughtered in equally huge numbers. The birds were attacked at their roosts and nesting sites, where they were easy targets. The breast meat was tasty and cheap; the feathers were even used for filling pot-holes! By 1905 they were no longer found in the wild, and the last known bird died in the Cincinnati Zoo in 1914.

Endangered species around the world

Since the diversity of species in many parts of the world is poorly understood, it is hard to know how many have disappeared or are in danger of doing so. However, over 350 species of mammals, birds, reptiles, and amphibians are known to be in danger of extinction. The numbers for fishes, plants, insects, and other invertebrates are not known.

Only 400 mountain gorillas remain in Africa, while less than 1000 pandas survive in the wild. Both of these species have suffered primarily from the loss and fragmentation of their habitat. Farmers cut trees and build their homes in low-lying areas, forcing small colonies of animals to the tops of mountains. These colonies are usually too small to make effective breeding groups.

Many plants around the world are also threatened with extinction, but in most countries the flora is not yet well known. Of the 3300 native plant species in Canada, about 500 are endangered.

Island species are particularly susceptible. At the turn of the century two tropical island plant species, the Juan Fernández sandalwood and the wine palm, became extinct due to commercial exploitation. The African violet is one of the world's most common house plants. In the wild it is close to extinction as a result of habitat loss to logging and agriculture. It is only known in a few mountainous areas of Tanzania. The Rio Palenque mahogany is from the lowland tropical forest of western Ecuador. There are now only twelve reproducing individuals left in a highly vulnerable 0.8 km^2 reserve. This species is a wild relative of the avocado and has commercial potential as a lumber species.

What is being done about endangered species?

The problem of endangered species involves political, cultural, and economic issues as well as ecological ones. Basically, further decline must be prevented, current numbers boosted, and habitats protected and enhanced. But these seemingly simple solutions fail to indicate how complex the problem is.

Since 1973, 102 countries have supported the **International Union for Conservation of Nature and Natural Resources** (**IUCN**). All or most of these countries have signed the **Convention on International Trade in Endangered Species of Wild Fauna and Flora** (**CITES**). The aim of the convention is to prevent commercial trade in plants and animals from speeding up the decline of endangered species. Another international organization, the **World Wildlife Fund** (**WWF**), now known as the **World Wide Fund for Nature**, has been instrumental in raising millions of dollars to help save endangered species. The WWF also advises governments on how to protect endangered species. Other national and local organizations also exist in many countries.

Captive breeding programs Two species of mammals recently became extinct in the wild, but they have been rescued through captive breeding programs. Przewalski's horse (the only remaining wild horse species) became extinct in the wild during the 1950s. Animals from zoos were used to start a captive breeding herd that now numbers over twenty individuals. When the herd numbers eighty, some of the horses will be released into their former pastures in the Xinjiang province of China. A similar program involving the Arabian oryx (a kind of antelope) was successful in Oman in 1982. The oryx had become extinct in the wild by 1972, but ten years later a captive-bred herd was released into the central regions of the country.

Protecting Africa's animals — the elephant and the rhinoceros In 1980 about 1.3 million elephants were living in Africa. Now there are less than 500 000. This decline is caused by the illegal slaughter of elephants for ivory. The poachers are servicing the demand for luxury trinkets in the more affluent countries. As a result of several years of lobbying and political bargaining, the elephant is now on the CITES Appendix I. This means that trade in elephant products is banned between member countries. The three main markets for ivory — the US, the European Economic Community (EEC), and Japan — have already imposed trade bans. Several Canadian companies have recently removed ivory products from their stores. However, some countries are upset and may not participate. Zimbabwe and other southern African countries have healthy elephant populations and good management programs. These countries cull elephants and sell the elephant products to help support their conservation programs. They say that the ban on the ivory trade will harm their management programs, which are based on the elephant as an economic resource. The next few years will prove crucial in determining the fate of the African elephant.

There are five species of rhinoceroses, all of which are endangered. The black rhinoceros of Africa numbered about 65 000 during the 1960s but now numbers only about 2500. As with the elephant, their slaughter is driven by greed, but their plight is more extreme. In the Far East, the rhino's horn is ground up as a medicinal powder with supposed magical aphrodisiac properties, and in North Yemen a rhino-horn dagger is a status symbol. Fetching up to $40 000 (US) per kilogram, rhino horns are about four times more expensive than gold. Rhino numbers are now so low that they are too scattered to breed effectively — the solitary animals simply do not meet often enough. Wildlife managers are desperately trying to protect the dwindling populations from well-organized and well-armed poachers. Some countries, such as Kenya, have set up strike forces with instructions to kill poachers on sight. Others have tried to dehorn all the rhinoceroses in an area to make poaching useless.

The African elephant is hunted for its ivory tusks.

The black rhinoceros is becoming so rare that finding a mate is a problem.

Some successes in Canada In Canada we have had some success in preserving endangered wildlife. In 1987 the white pelican was taken off the endangered species list. The rebuilding of the population was a result of five years' work by the WWF to enhance and protect nesting sites. In 1988 the wood bison was down-listed from endangered to threatened as a result of reintroducing animals from Elk Island National Park and Metro Toronto Zoo to areas in northern Manitoba, the Yukon, and the Northwest Territories. In the Prairies, a program has begun to reintroduce the extirpated swift fox into its former habitat using captive-bred stock.

Perhaps the most impressive recovery of a Canadian species is that of the whooping crane. In 1941 only sixteen individuals were left. The whooping crane breeds in and around Wood Buffalo National Park and winters in the southern states of Texas and Arkansas. As a result of an intensive program on the part of the Canadian Wildlife Service, the population is recovering. The nests are checked each spring. Any extra eggs are used to stock nests with infertile eggs, and some eggs are artificially incubated. This is done using sandhill cranes as "foster parents." Since the program began in 1966 the population of whooping cranes has risen from just 43 to 149 birds in the US, and to about 300 worldwide.

Although still an endangered species, the whooping crane is making a recovery.

The American bison, commonly called the buffalo, almost became extinct in the late 1800s. Its population is estimated to have been over 60 million individuals, ranging from Florida to Alaska. The slaughter was partly for meat and hides but also for sport and because they often damaged fences. Sometimes just the tongue was taken as a delicacy. "Buffalo Bill" Cody records killing 4280 animals in one twelve-month period for food for the railway crews. The plains bison may have disappeared completely had it not been for four calves captured by a Native person named Walking Coyote and five more saved by a Winnipeg fur dealer. These animals are the ancestors of the more than 40 000 bison that now live in protected areas of North America.

Wildlife

Wildlife is important to most Canadians, but it means different things to different people. A trapper, a naturalist, and a hunter may share many attitudes toward wildlife, but they see it in ways that reflect their special interests. Most people think of wildlife as all wild animals, but government agencies often define it more narrowly as game and other designated species. Wildlife is important for recreation and, in some instances, as a source of livelihood.

Canada is known worldwide for its abundance and diversity of wildlife, with 163 species of mammals, some 600 species of birds, and several species of reptiles and amphibians. We have many species that are unique to this country. Canada also has a large share of the world's Stone sheep, mountain goats, grizzly bears, and bald eagles.

The value of wildlife

One question facing wildlife management agencies is the value of wildlife. Although efforts to put a dollar value on wildlife have met with resistance, wildlife managers are trying to maintain wildlife in the same areas that are also used for other purposes, such as forestry, mining, agriculture, power development, and transportation. These uses of land are readily valued in dollar terms. To determine the value of wildlife

Tourists are often fascinated by wildlife such as this iguana in the Galapagos Islands.

resources, environment ministries have conducted surveys and socio-economic studies. A recent study by the British Columbia Ministry of Environment, Lands and Parks produced the following data:

- About 115 000 provincial residents and 4700 visitors hunt each year in British Columbia. The revenue from fees and surcharges from the sale of hunting licences is about $8 million (CDN) per year.
- About 1600 licensed trappers and about 1600 unlicensed Native trappers take pelts with a total value of about $1.4 million (CDN) annually.
- About 1.8 million provincial residents do wildlife-related activities around their homes and cottages.
- Nearly one-half of people surveyed find their trips enhanced by incidental wildlife encounters.
- Almost one-quarter of the provincial population take trips specifically to watch, feed, photograph, or study wildlife in the field.
- Over 90% of the provincial population are familiar with wildlife through reading, films, and television.
- Altogether British Columbians spend about $850 million (CDN) (1995 dollars) yearly on wildlife-related recreation.

Used by permission of the Wildlife Branch of BC Environment.

These results show that in dollar terms alone, wildlife is a significant resource in British Columbia. The numbers would have been much higher if sport fishing had been included. But the results also show that people greatly enjoy and often seek out experiences with wildlife. Wildlife is becoming increasingly valued across the country and in many parts of the world.

Introduced species

Many species are now introduced into an area that would not normally support them. Some of these species have caused the elimination of local species. Other species have altered the habitat, changing the kinds of species that can survive in that environment. Most introduced species are difficult to get rid of because they reproduce and disperse rapidly. They also adapt to new environmental challenges easily. These biological invasions have occurred on every continent, but island areas are easily affected.

The ability of some species to spread is enormous. One hundred European starlings were introduced to New York City in 1890 and 1891, and now millions of them are found throughout much of North America. (See Figure 5.3.) The starling's success lies in its omnivorous habits and its ability to live around people.

The Indian mongoose was introduced to several Hawaiian and Caribbean islands to control rats, but it proved much more efficient at eliminating native species of reptiles and ground-dwelling birds. The Hawaiian or dark-rumped petrel (a species of sea bird) is in danger of extinction as a result of the introduction of the mongoose. In Hawaii 28 percent of the insects and 65 percent of the plants are non-native species. In Australia one species of hibiscus (a plant species) is reduced to about eight individuals on Philip Island as a result of the introduction of rabbits. About 10 percent of Australia's flora is composed of "invaders."

The cane toad was introduced to Australia in 1935 to kill the greyback beetle, a pest of sugar-cane plantations in Queensland. The toad is indigenous to South America but has adapted well to conditions in Australia. It has a voracious appetite and eats virtually anything, from insects to lizards, birds, and small mammals. Its range is spreading by 27 km a year, and it is threatening one of Australia's most important wildlife parks, Kakadu National Park.

The sea lamprey, a type of fish, was introduced to the Great Lakes in the early part of this century. Since then, it has radically altered the variety and abundance of species in the lake ecosystems. The lamprey attacks other fish, sucking their blood and eating their flesh. The population of lake trout in particular has declined since the lamprey's introduction through the Welland Canal.

Eurasian milfoil, Russian thistle (tumbleweed), quack grass, Canadian thistle, dandelion, and knapweed are among the plant species that have invaded Canada. Knapweed is a particular problem in British Columbia where it has invaded over 24 000 ha of rangeland, eliminating desirable forage species (food for grazing animals) by competition. Forage production may be reduced by 85 percent.

The Mediterranean fruitfly has caused considerable economic loss to the citrus industry in California and has led to costly pesticide spraying programs. Similarly, the Africanized honey bee, which has recently colonized the southern United States, is also the subject of a costly and vigorous control effort. (See Figure 5.4.) A recent survey found that over 1300 non-native insect species were established in the United States

Figure 5.3 The spread of the European starling in North America

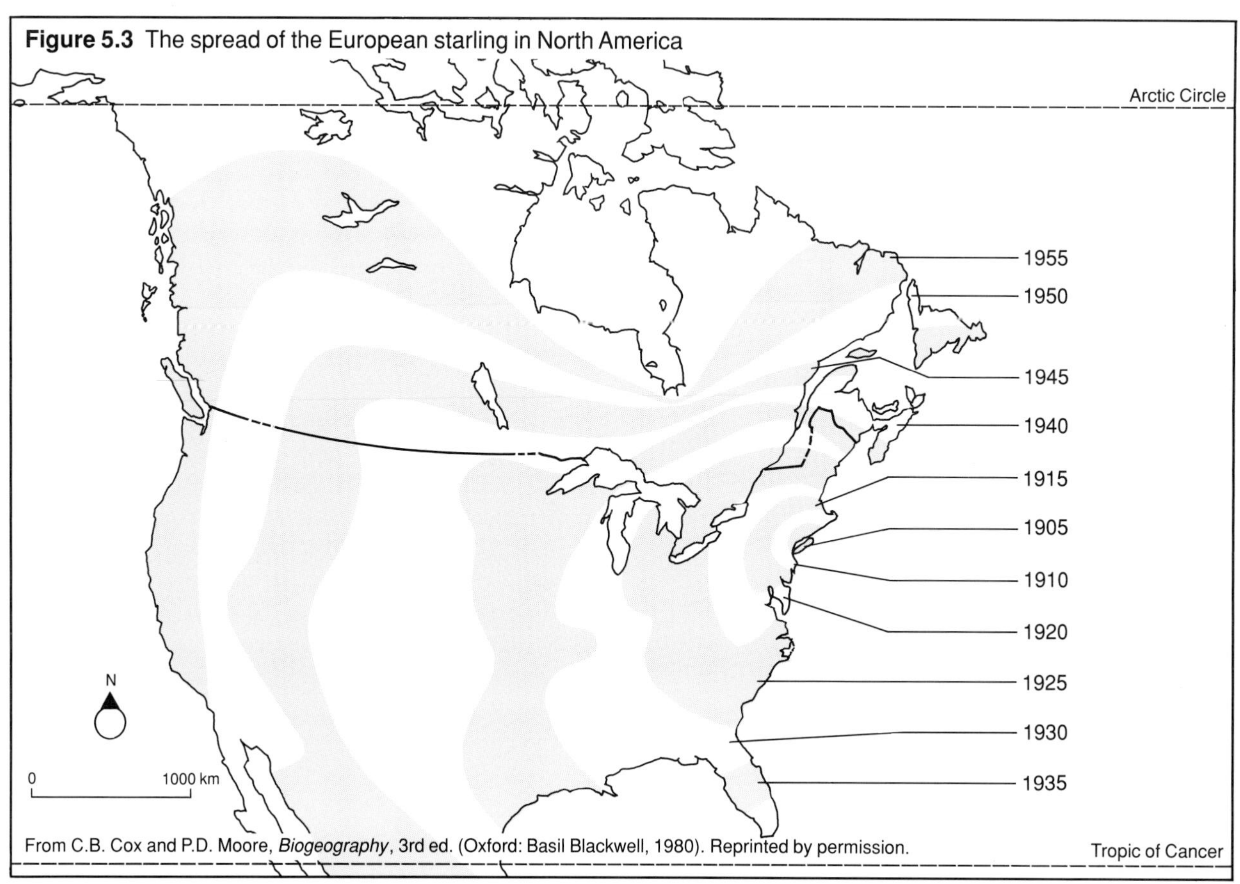

From C.B. Cox and P.D. Moore, *Biogeography*, 3rd ed. (Oxford: Basil Blackwell, 1980). Reprinted by permission.

The Sea Lamprey is threatening Great Lakes ecosystems.

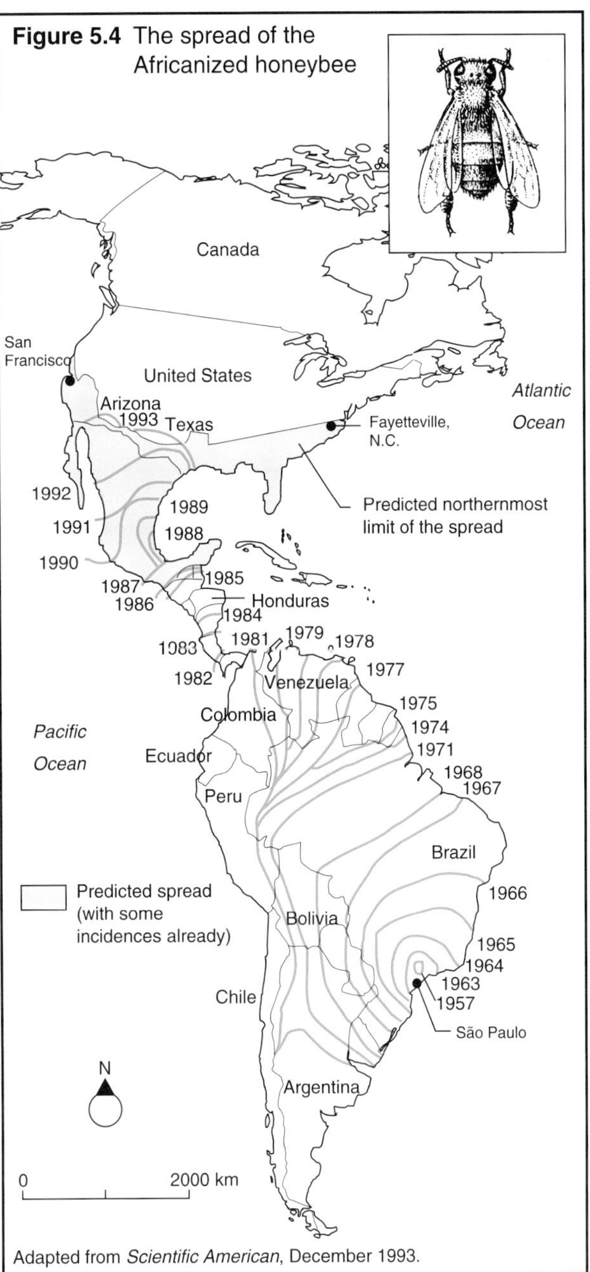

Figure 5.4 The spread of the Africanized honeybee

Adapted from *Scientific American*, December 1993.

between 1640 and 1977. This number continues to grow at the rate of about eleven a year.

A recent problem is that of the zebra mussel, a tiny brown mollusc with stripes on its shell. These minuscule creatures (up to 3 cm long) are thought to have been introduced from Europe into Lake Ontario and Lake Erie by ships' bilges. They can multiply at phenomenal rates and clog water pipes. This is causing severe problems for hydro, nuclear, and municipal water treatment plants. Multimillion-dollar abatement programs are now being organized by some municipalities and hydro companies.

Introduced species are a particular problem in island areas. Island species tend to be poor competitors. The introduction of several domestic species to the Galápagos Islands has had disastrous effects on the native flora and fauna. These species include dogs, cats, horses, donkeys, goats, cattle, pigs, rats, and mice. The species have become **feral** or wild, and they either prey upon or compete with native species. Feral goats have seriously altered the vegetation on several islands, while dogs, pigs, cats, and rats prey upon young giant tortoises, lizards, iguanas, and birds. Eradication programs are costly and so far have worked only on the smallest islands.

A success story — the prickly pear cactus

Many of our pest problems are the result of careless introductions of species that are often hard to eradicate. One success story, however, concerns the prickly pear cactus in Australia. By the 1920s, the prickly pear, a native of the Americas, had colonized some 24 000 000 ha of rangeland, making grazing land useless. Chemical treatment was uneconomical. It was decided to introduce an insect enemy of the cactus. The choice of pest had to be made with great care, lest it in turn became a pest. Eventually a moth species, *Cactoblastis*, was chosen and reared in captivity. Between 1920 and 1930, some 3 billion eggs were released. This resulted in a rapid decrease in the cactus population, and the two species now exist in balance with a much lower density of cacti.

The Green Revolution

People have been modifying domestic species to suit their own ends for thousands of years. New breeds or varieties with favourable characteristics have been created through **mutation** and recombination. The variations themselves are natural — we have simply capitalized on the features that suit us, such as increased crop yield or animal weight.

The term **Green Revolution** was first used by journalists in the 1960s to describe the use of **high-yield varieties** (HYVs) of crops in places with serious food shortages. The introduction of the HYVs has helped to create more food even in famine areas and has been a major advance in the ability of the planet to sustain its growing population. In spite of its success, however, the Green Revolution still has not been adopted by all developing countries. Only a little more than one-third of the total area devoted to cereal grains uses high-yield varieties. Asia leads in their use, while Africa is at the bottom of the list.

Gains from the Green Revolution

Jonathan Swift in *Gulliver's Travels* states that a person can do good for this planet by making "two blades of grass grow where one grew before." The Green Revolution promised to do even better. Early results showed that three grains of wheat could grow where one grew before. A whole new system of farming was introduced. For example, high-yield, drought-resistant wheats helped India recover from the disastrous famines of 1964 to 1966. Wheat production in India rose from 11.2 million tonnes in 1964-65 to 59.1 million tonnes in 1994 and yield per hectare tripled.

The gains in rice production have been less impressive. The first crossbred varieties were prematurely hailed as "miracle rices," but they proved unpopular in the areas where they were grown. Since rice is grown in a hot and humid climate, the crop faced greater problems of pests and disease than wheat. The new varieties also required precise water control. This was often impossible given the primitive forms of irrigation that exist.

Problems of the Green Revolution

In many parts of the world the Green Revolution is being adopted very slowly. The reason lies in the complex nature of the changes involved. New seeds that produce heavier grain heads have to be developed. These plants need short stems in order to support the heavier grains. HYVs require more nutrients from the soil, and probably more irrigation water, as shown in Figure 5.5. The farmers therefore have to use more fertilizers and pesticides, which means using more fossil fuels. They may require some machines, more irrigation water, and better water control.

Other off-farm conditions have to be met as well. Farmers who were once merely self-sufficient and grew food only for their own consumption now have a surplus to sell. They need markets where they can sell the surplus grain and new roads to reach them. Many farmers require loans in order to pay for the equipment and seeds they need to get started. Most also require more education in agricultural techniques.

The Green Revolution has also created social problems, since farmers with initiative and capital are favoured. The benefits of the Green Revolution have passed the world's poorest farmers by. It may have also widened the gap between the rich and poor in developing countries.

Finally, the Green Revolution has made people more dependent on a smaller number of varieties of crops and therefore on a more restricted gene pool. Any major outbreak of disease could have a serious

Figure 5.5 Traditional and green revolution farming

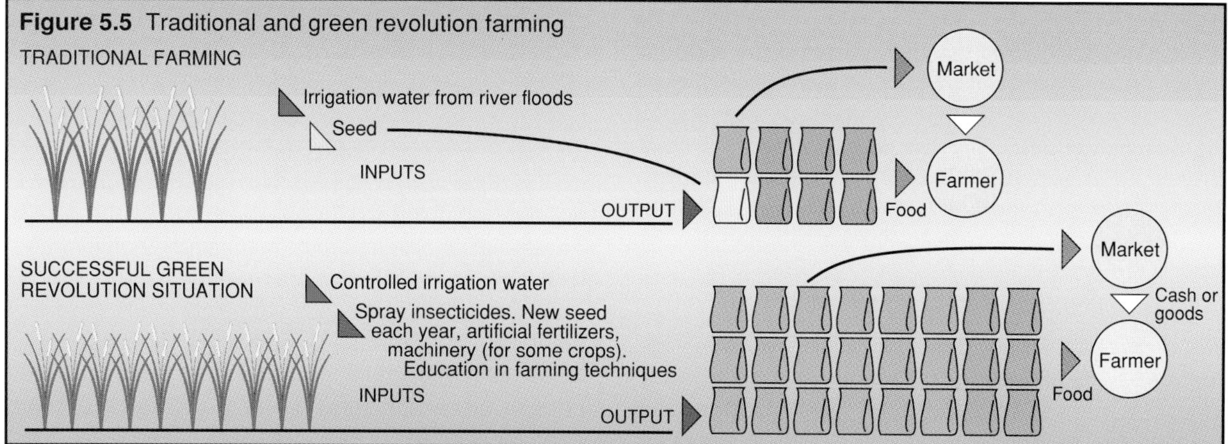

effect on areas influenced by the Green Revolution. To avoid such dangers, plant breeders must continue to produce varieties that will be able to stay ahead of the spreading diseases. For the benefits of the Green Revolution to be maintained, we must continue to research and invest.

Preserving the genetic base

Because of the dangers of trying to replace the whole farming system, scientists are no longer relying exclusively on Green Revolution methods. Traditional farming systems have developed over many years, and traditional varieties are usually well adapted to local conditions. In some parts of the world the aim is to improve traditional systems rather than to replace them by entirely new scientific systems. This approach is thought by many to be a safer method of improving farming. It helps to protect the environment and maintain a broader genetic base.

One cause for concern is that we depend on relatively few species of plants and animals to provide our food. Today 95 percent of human nutrition is derived from about thirty species. In most areas of the world traditional cultures have made use of a much larger variety of species. In North America, Native peoples dined upon more than 1100 different species of plants, while people in the deserts of southern Africa make regular use of 85 wild vegetables.

The source areas of many of our crop varieties deserve the same special protection as wildlife. Areas with a wide variety of plant genes are especially valuable to us. Most of our domestic plant and animal species originate from only a dozen or so geographic areas. (See Figure 5.6.) These areas are known as Vavilov centres of diversity after the Russian scientist who identified them. Wild relatives of our current domesticated species still exist in these areas and may provide useful genetic material.

One method of preserving the genetic diversity of crop species and their relatives is to use **seedbanks**. Botanists travel around the world collecting seeds from rare and endangered varieties and bring these to the "bank." Here the seeds are kept in cold storage and are periodically planted to maintain viability. Many varieties were lost during the Ethiopian famine of 1984 to 1985. This was because people were consuming virtually every grain they could find and not storing any for future use. The use of seedbanks can help to protect the great variety of the world's plant life for the benefit of future generations. This will make a great contribution to preserving the diversity of life.

Figure 5.6 Vavilov's centres of diversity

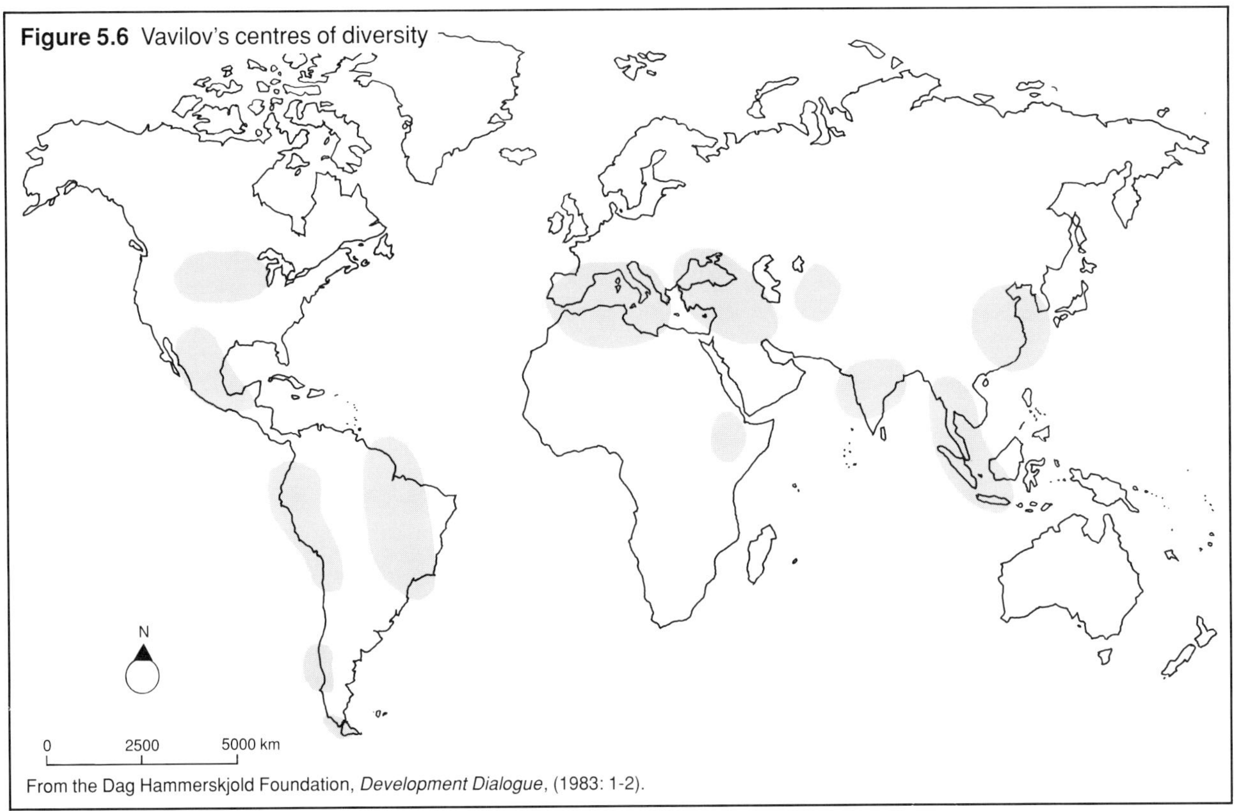

From the Dag Hammerskjold Foundation, *Development Dialogue*, (1983: 1-2).

Biotechnology

Since the Green Revolution, scientists have developed the capacity to create new variations through the recently developed techniques of **genetic engineering**. By taking genes from one organism and transplanting them into another, we can create varieties of life that would never have occurred naturally. This ability to alter life has tremendous potential but carries with it great responsibility. Genetic engineering will artificially change the course and speed of evolution.

A "gene revolution"

Genes are found in every cell of every plant and animal and contain the instructions for life. They determine whether a person has light or dark hair, whether a corn plant makes large or small ears, and whether wheat resists or succumbs to disease. If researchers can alter genes or add new ones, they can design "superorganisms" that may have higher yields and greater resistance to disease. The possibilities are enormous, but the field is still in its infancy.

Genetic tinkering has already created a type of tobacco that kills attacking insects, plants that resist herbicides, bacteria that prevent frost formation on crops, and even tobacco that glows in the dark. A human gene was transferred to mice suffering from anaemia, a blood disease, and the cure was passed on to the offspring. The disease was most likely caused by the lack of a particular **enzyme**, which the human gene replaced. Bacteria have been developed that can produce human insulin for the treatment of diabetes.

The process of gene splicing is technically difficult though simple in principle. Figure 5.7 shows how a fragment of DNA, containing the desired gene from one organism, can be joined with the DNA of another.

Figure 5.7 How gene splicing is done.

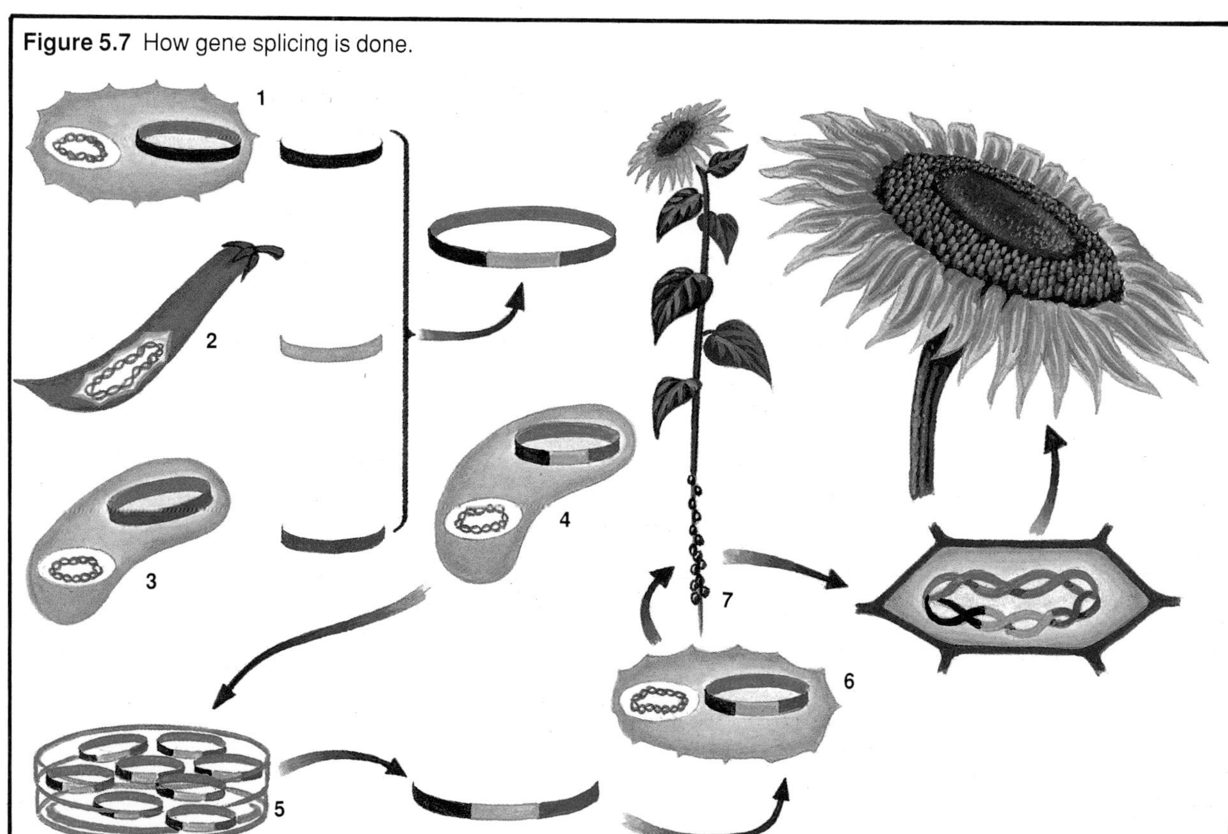

It is possible to graft the gene of one plant onto a cell of another plant in order to modify certain characteristics, such as protein content. One of the first experiments with such genetic manipulation was the grafting onto sunflower cells of bean genes, producing hybrid cells that were nicknamed "sunbean." The first step is the isolation of a transfer gene from an agrobacterium (1). The phaseolin protein gene is isolated from the bean DNA (2) and is crossed with the coliform bacterium, *Escherichia coli* (3), resulting in hybrid bacteria (4). Bacteria with the phaseolin gene are isolated (5) and crossed with the agrobacterium (6). These infect the sunflower (7), transmitting the alien genes. The phaseolin protein gene has now become part of the sunflower's genetic makeup.

From Alexandre Doroz, "The Newer Technologies' Agricultural Applications," in *FAO-CERES*, Vol. 17, No. 6, November-December 1984.

Genes may also be transferred between organisms using viruses. DNA segments exchanged between organisms of different species are known as **recombinant DNA**.

The dangers of gene splicing

Research involving recombinant DNA poses several potential hazards. Recombinants may accidentally enter the environment, where they may have unforeseen effects. Few people fear that scientists will create killer tomatoes, but many ecologists worry that genetically engineered species may behave as an introduced pest. Genetically engineered bacteria, which may be used to control insects, are potentially more dangerous than pesticides. We can stop using pesticides, but we may not be able to stop a species of bacteria from reproducing. Oil-eating bacteria are excellent for an oil spill but would be dangerous if let loose on an oilfield. Scientists are setting strict guidelines on the use of these organisms to help guard against these potential dangers. Debate continues, however, as to whether the potential advantages outweigh the potential hazards.

Looking back

1. List as many causes/reasons for the extinction of species as you can.
2. Write a sentence that states the relationships between the size of an environment and the diversity of species it can support.
3. Explain what is meant by an *introduced species*.
4. State how humans have used and profited from the products of mutation and recombination.

Applying your knowledge

1. From your list in question 1 above, generate a list of questions that should be answered in any study of extinction.
2. People have modified plant and animal species through domestication to satisfy particular wants and needs.
   (a) Brainstorm a list of wants and needs for which species have been domesticated.
   (b) For each want or need list the main species that have been domesticated for this purpose.
3. Create an organizational table that compares the pros and cons of the following efforts to restore the ecological balance:
   (a) bans on the sale of such items as ivory, fur, alligator, leather, etc.;
   (b) quotas on fishing, hunting, trapping, etc.;
   (c) the establishment of sanctuaries, national parks, and conservation areas.
4. Use diagrams, graphs, or a collage of pictures to show how the data produced by the British Columbia Ministry of Environment and Parks indicates the social and economic importance of wildlife and natural environments.
5. On a blank map of your province, locate and identify the areas where there has been some effort to protect the natural environment and its ecosystems. How much of the area does this represent as a percentage?
6. Prepare a comparison organizer to show the advantages and disadvantages of traditional farming and Green Revolution farming. (See Figure 5.5.)

Extending your thinking

1. Write an essay or prepare an oral presentation based on the resource list you created in question 2(c) in "Applying your knowledge." Be sure that your final product discusses the following points:
   - the characteristics of the species that has been modified;
   - why and how humans modified the species;
   - the effects human interference had on the species; and
   - your opinion as to whether or not human interference with the species was justified.
2. (a) Find out how important wildlife is in your area by listing those occupations and recreational activities that are wildlife related.
   (b) Does wildlife have an importance in your life? List the uses you have for wildlife and the amount of time you spend on wildlife-related activities. Organize your values into categories such aesthetics, food, clothing, medicine, recreation, etc.
3. With a partner use library catalogues, indexes to periodicals, films, videotapes, data bases, or the Internet to research and report on an introduced species, other than the ones already mentioned in the text.
4. Develop lists of arguments for and against the use of biotechnology. What conclusions can you draw from your lists?
5. Develop lists of arguments for and against the use of biotechnology. What conclusions can you draw from your lists?

6 AIR

We take the atmosphere for granted. We expect clean, fresh air to be present everywhere, both indoors and outdoors. Yet we expel a variety of our wastes into the atmosphere and assume that the air will be able to absorb it all. However, by discharging these wastes we have seriously damaged the quality of the air in many parts of the earth. The result is damage to the health of vegetation, animal life, and people.

When the air is clear, as it may be after rainfall, visibility can extend 200 km or more. Today, however, such occasions are rare. The air around us contains a great deal of dust and many polluting gases. Some of the dust is carried by the wind. Some is natural and comes from pollen, as sufferers from hay fever know only too well. A great deal more comes from the burning of coal and from industrial processes. Transport and mining activities also generate dust.

Of all types of pollution, air pollution is the most difficult to contain. The circulation of winds is unpredictable, ensuring that areas far removed from the pollution source experience its effects. Even the Arctic regions, once famous for clear air, now experience **Arctic haze**, which can cut visibility to 30 km or less. Arctic haze is caused by suspended particles (mainly sulphates) that come from industrial regions.

In this chapter we will examine the four commonly recognized forms of air pollution and the actions being taken to combat them. We will also look at the problems in our indoor environments, where we spend most of our time.

Acid rain

The term **acid rain** was first used in 1872 by a Scottish chemist, but only in recent years has it become a global problem. The more accurate name is **acid deposition**, since dry matter as well as rain and snow carry acids. Normal precipitation is slightly acidic because water droplets absorb some carbon dioxide to form a very diluted carbonic acid. The term **toxic rain** has been used to refer to rain containing heavy metals and other toxic materials.

Acidity is measured on the pH scale, as shown in Figure 6.1. Each drop of one point on the pH scale is a tenfold increase in acidity. Thus pH 6 is ten times as acid as pH 7, which is neutral. Normal, or pure, rainfall is about pH 5.6. In some parts of the globe, including Ontario, precipitation can measure pH 4 or even worse. In parts of the eastern United States the average pH of rainfall has decreased from 6.0 to 4.5 since 1930.

The sources of acid deposition are illustrated in Figure 6.2. Large volumes of gases and dust are discharged into the atmosphere. Sulphur dioxide (SO_2) and nitrogen oxides (NO_x) mix with water droplets in clouds to form diluted sulphuric and nitric acids respectively. Once these pollutants are in the atmosphere they do not recognize international boundaries. For example, pollution from power stations in the Ohio Valley are a major cause of acid deposition in eastern Canada. Figure 6.3 shows the areas of the

Figure 6.1 The pH scale

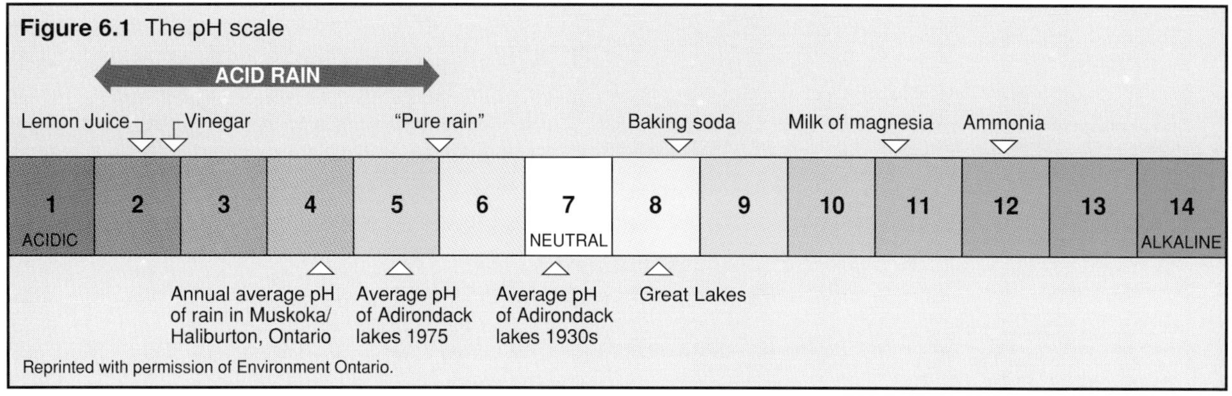

Reprinted with permission of Environment Ontario.

Figure 6.2 The causes of acid rain

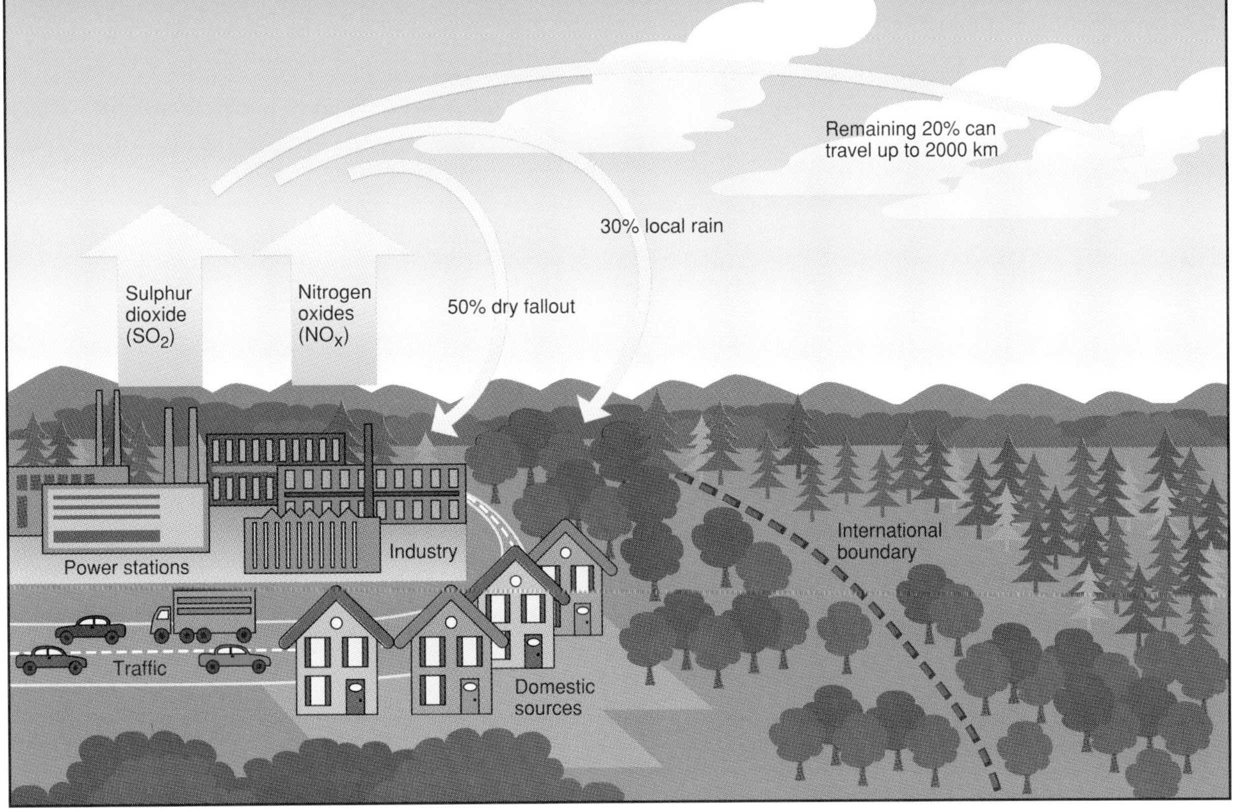

Figure 6.3 Estimated world distribution of acid rain in the late 1980s

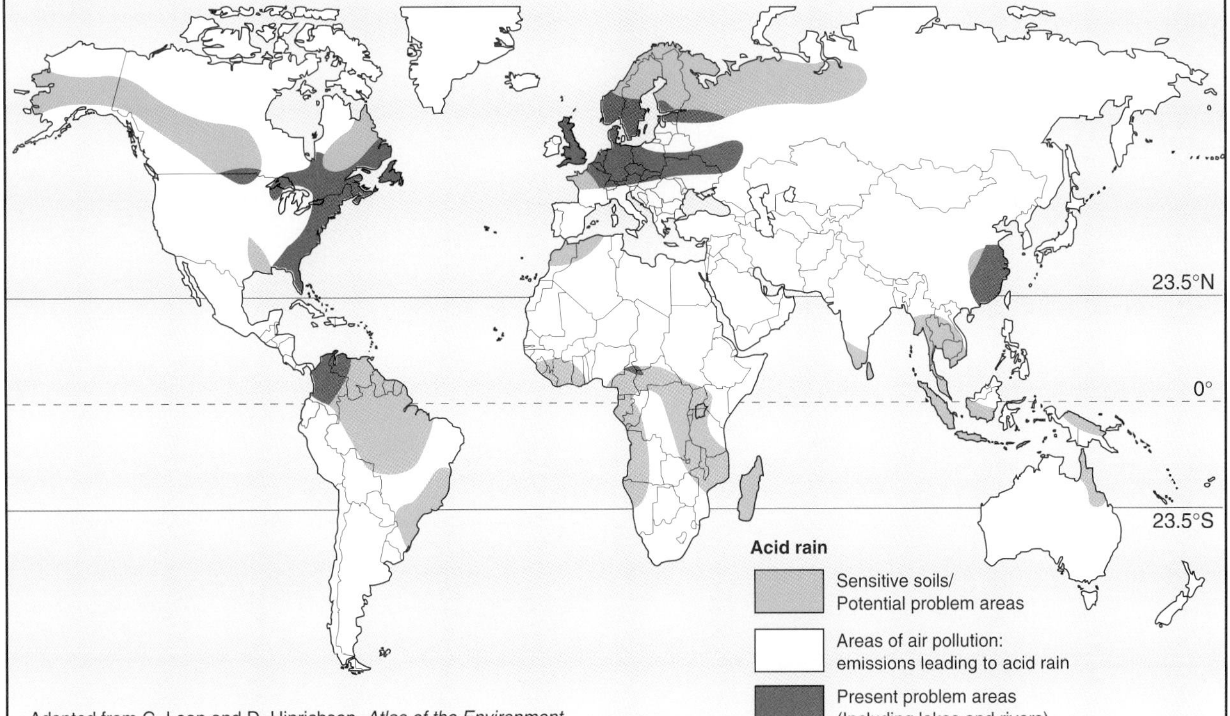

Adapted from G. Lean and D. Hinrichsen, *Atlas of the Environment*, © Banson Marketing Ltd, 1990, 1992.

world most affected by acid rain in the late 1980s.

The gases that cause acid rain come from several sources. Figure 6.4 shows that power utilities, especially those that burn coal, are the main cause of sulphur dioxide. On the other hand, vehicles are the leading source of nitrogen oxides.

The effects of acid rain

Forestry, fisheries, wildlife, and farming may all be seriously affected by acid rain, as are buildings, vehicles, and even human health. However, it is wrong to attribute all problems to this one single cause. For example, in the 1980s the sugar maple forests of Québec and Ontario were believed to be slowly dying as a result of acid rain. The losses in the industry were estimated at about $100 million (CDN). It was claimed that acidity was affecting the root systems of trees, causing metal poisoning and nutrient starvation. While acid rain may have been a factor in the sugar maple's decline in the 1980s, there has been an improvement in the 1990s, leading to the theory that bad weather may have been another cause of the problem.

Forests There is strong evidence, however, that acid rain leads to lower resistance to disease and insects in forests. The growth of seedlings is also harmed by acidity. Since our forests play a vital role in regulating water supply, preventing soil erosion and maintaining wildlife, we cannot take the risk of allowing acidity to harm them.

Lakes and rivers Acid deposition seriously affects the water cycle as acidity works its way through streams, lakes, and rivers. The problem of acidification in eastern Canada is particularly severe and not just because the level of pollutants is high. It is made

Figure 6.4 Emissions of gases that cause acid rain (1992)

	SULPHUR DIOXIDE (%)		NITROGEN OXIDES (%)	
Canada	Industry	61	Transport	59
	Utilities	23	Industry	23
	Other	16	Utilities	14
	Transport	0	Other	4
United States	Utilities	70	Transport	45
	Industry	23	Utilities	32
	Other	7	Industry	19
	Transport	0	Other	4

From EPA and Environment Canada

Acid rain is causing this forest at Mt. Mégantic, Québec, to die slowly.

worse by the lack of alkaline materials in the rocks and soils that could act as a natural "buffer" or neutralizer for the acidity. Sometimes lime is added to lakes to counteract the acidity. Adding lime is similar to taking an antacid tablet to settle your stomach.

Most aquatic life dies when the acidity reaches pH 5 or below. (See Figure 6.5.) The lowest pH levels often occur in the spring when acid snowmelt is suddenly released into lakes, creating **acid shock**. This coincides with spawning time and inhibits the reproduction of many species of fish.

The effects on lake ecosystems are serious. Eggs fail to hatch and young fish die. The predators also become affected and soon struggle to survive. Waterfowl migrate elsewhere. However, some varieties of algal blooms begin to spread and give the lake a bad odour. At the end of the process, a lake with an initial pH of 6.5 may be reduced to an acid reservoir with a pH of 4.3.

Acid rain also leads to the accumulation of toxic metals, which are leached by the rain into lakes and rivers. Higher than normal levels of metals, such as aluminum and mercury, are dangerous both to fish and to humans who may eat them.

According to Environment Canada, 150 000 lakes are being damaged in eastern Canada, 14 000 of them seriously. Some have become so acidified that they are unable to support aquatic life, and many more are approaching that condition. Sweden has about 18 000 acidified lakes. The Baltic Shield in Scandinavia has a nonalkaline bedrock like that of eastern Canada.

Figure 6.5 The impact of acidity on aquatic life

pH	6.5	6.0	5.5	5.0	4.5	4.0	3.5
Water boatman	○	○	○	○	○	○	○
Whirligig	○	○	○	○	○	○	○
Yellow perch	○	○	○	○	○		
Lake trout	○	○	○	○	○		
Brown trout	○	○	○	○			
Salamander	○	○	○	○			
Mayfly	○	○	○				
Smallmouth bass	○	○	○				
Mussel	○	○					

The circles indicate at what point aquatic life dies due to acidity.

From Daniel D. Chiras, "A framework for Decision Making," in *Environmental Science*, 2nd ed. (Menlo Park, CA: 1988.)

Farming In eastern Canada, particularly in Ontario, 84 percent of productive farmlands are affected by acid rain. The root systems of crops are unable to absorb nutrients properly. As a result, crop yields fall and millions of dollars are lost.

Buildings and Vehicles Acid rain causes the corrosion of buildings. Classic monuments such as the Sphinx in Egypt and the Parthenon in Greece have deteriorated more during the past half a century than during the previous thousands of years of their existence. Stained glass windows in Europe's cathedrals are suffering the same fate. Acid rain is also blamed for about half the corrosion of vehicles in Canada.

Egypt's famous Sphinx has been badly disfigured by acidity.

Health Evidence shows that the pollutants that cause acid rain also create health hazards. One study compares children living in an acid rain location (Tillsonburg, Ontario) with those living in an area relatively free of it (Portage la Prairie, Manitoba). It shows a significant difference in the occurrence of colds, allergies, and respiratory diseases. Researchers working at the University of California claim that high levels of sulphur dioxide can lead to colon and breast cancer. The increased leaching of mercury and aluminum by acid rainwater can also damage health through contamination of the drinking water.

Stopping acid rain

The United Nations Environment Program (UNEP) calculates that the damage caused by acid rain in a Western country may be equivalent to 1 or 2 percent of the entire **GNP (Gross National Product)**. Therefore there is a strong economic incentive to control acid rain.

Since the early 1970s some Western countries have had considerable success in reducing emissions of SO_2 and other pollutants, indicating that clean air laws have had some effect. Canadian reductions in air pollutants are shown in Figure 6.6.

Figure 6.6 Reduction in air pollutants in Canadian cities

POLLUTANT	CHANGE (%) 1974-1992
Sulphur dioxide	–61
Carbon monoxide	–70
Nitrogen dioxide	–38
Suspended particulates	–54

From Environment Canada

"He wasn't always bald. It's acid rain."

Reductions of sulphur dioxide, carbon monoxide, and nitrogen dioxide have reduced acid rain significantly. The burning of fuels containing less sulphur has helped air quality considerably. Many factories have installed desulphurizing or **scrubbing devices** in chimneys. New techniques for burning coal can also help to reduce the problem. In New Brunswick and Prince Edward Island, demonstration plants show how **fluidized bed combustion** can remove 90 percent of sulphur and nitrogen emissions. This technology burns finely ground limestone along with coal. Coal-water fuel technology is used in Nova Scotia with similar results. This technique removes sulphur from finely ground coal mixed with water. In addition to burning coal efficiently, the coal-water mixture can be transported by pipeline. In Alberta, a method called Low NO_x/SO_x Burner (LNSB) is being used to reduce emissions.

On a global scale, however, the burning of fossil fuels continues to increase. Acid rain is likely to become a growing problem in developing countries where laws curbing emissions are less strict. This problem is particularly true in China, where low-grade coal is being used on a large scale in the nation's rush to become industrialized. These countries insist that since the developed countries created the problem of acid rain in the first place, they should help poorer countries in their efforts to protect the environment. This suggestion would involve financial assistance and the availability of anti-pollution technology at minimal cost.

Monitoring acid deposition in Canada

In order to regulate emissions of air pollutants, the environment must be monitored carefully. Figure 6.7 shows the air pollution standards accepted in various parts of Canada in the late 1980s. Note that these standards distinguish between *acceptable* and *desirable* levels, the latter being a strict standard to be attained over the long term. Of course, pollutants cannot be eliminated from the environment completely. For example, forest fires started by lightning will create smoke.

Acid rain control in Ontario Eighty percent of Ontario's sulphur dioxide comes from only four companies — Ontario Hydro, Falconbridge, the International Nickel Company (INCO), and Algoma Steel. Each of these companies has already greatly reduced its output of SO_2. INCO had a peak emission of 5500 t of SO_2 per day in the 1960s and reduced that amount to just over 2000 t by the early 1980s. In 1994 it achieved a low of 444 t per day. Ontario Hydro, Canada's largest power utility has cut its SO_2 emissions from 1240 t a day in 1980 to 285 t a day in 1994.

Further reductions will be needed to solve the acid rain problem, but the progress made so far is clearly visible on the landscape. Around Sudbury, Ontario, vegetation has reappeared near the INCO and Falconbridge smelters. In Trail, British Columbia, where the Cominco smelter has installed scrubbers to recover its emissions of sulphur and other chemicals, the forests are well on their way to regrowth. Cominco now makes fertilizers from the recovered materials.

Figure 6.7 Maximum 1-hour ozone concentrations in the Vancouver/Chilliwack area, based on an average of the three highest years during 1983–89

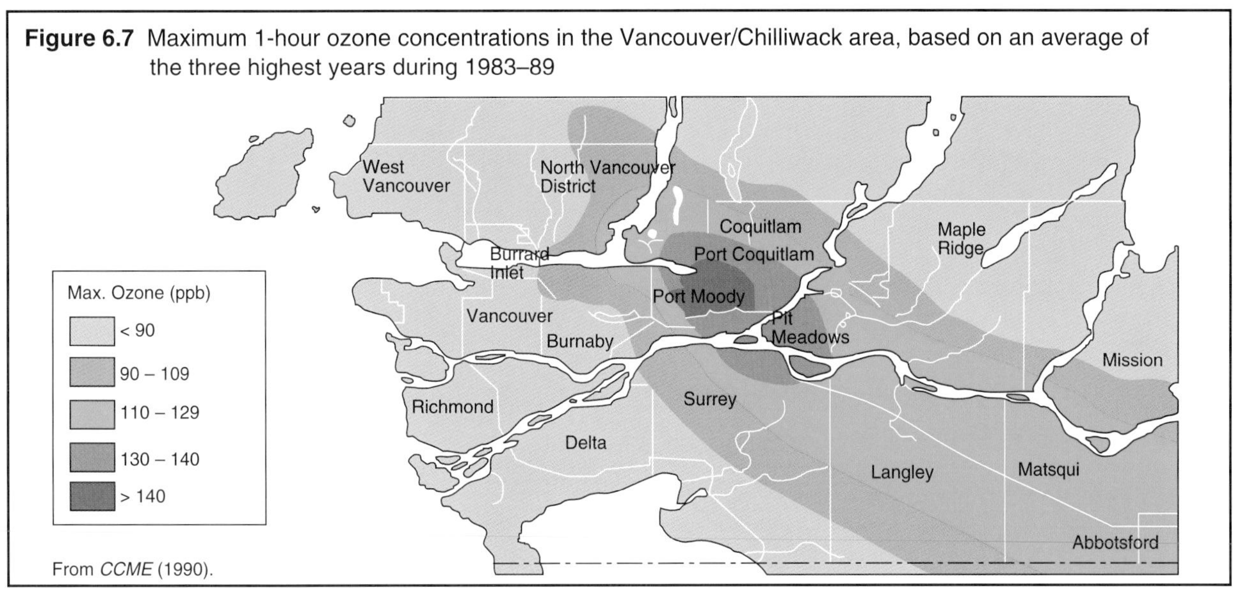

From *CCME* (1990).

Canada/United States acid rain agreement

Because the winds carry acid rain across national boundaries, an international solution to the problem is required. For this reason the Canadian government has placed a high priority on reaching an agreement on acid rain with the United States. A bill revising the Clean Air Act was passed by the US Congress in 1990 to cut sulphur dioxide emissions by 40 percent (from 1980 levels) by the year 2000. The Act allowed states to trade their emissions targets with each other. Canada also had a program of emissions reductions in place dating from February 1985. In 1991 the United States and Canada jointly signed an Air Quality Agreement, in which both countries undertook to reduce sulphur dioxide and nitrogen oxides emissions. They also agreed to set tighter standards for coal burning boilers and for vehicle exhausts.

Photochemical and industrial smog

Smog (smoke + fog) takes two forms. **Industrial smog** occurs when particles and gasses such as SO_2 are emitted by industries and build up in the atmosphere. Before the days of smoke control industrial smog was common in the cities of Europe and North America.

Today western cities are more affected by **photochemical smog.** This form of smog is recognizable by its yellow-brown haze, often forming a "brown dome"over cities in calm weather. It is caused when nitrogen reacts with oxygen to form nitrogen dioxide (NO_2). Sunlight causes a photochemical reaction in which nitrogen oxides combine with hydrocarbons, mainly from car exhaust, to form ozone and a compound called peroxyacetyl nitrate (PAN), as shown in Figure 6.8. Ozone is highly desirable in the upper atmosphere, but at ground level it causes coughing and serious breathing problems. Research shows that healthy young adults exercising in air containing ozone above 82 parts per billion (ppb) may suffer a loss of one-third of their lung capacity.

The Canadian government has placed the maximum acceptable level of ozone at 82 ppb. However, this limit is unenforceable. In 1988 it was surpassed 157 times in north Toronto and 189 times in Windsor. Since then, however, these levels have not been surpassed. Smog is one of the major problems facing many large cities, especially those surrounded by higher land. The problem is at its worst when temperatures are high and the air is calm.

Smog obscures the view of Los Angeles.

Figure 6.8 The causes of photochemical smog. Ozone is formed when hydrocarbons (HC) and nitrogen oxide (NO_x) react to heat and sunlight. Its movement is affected by weather and geography.

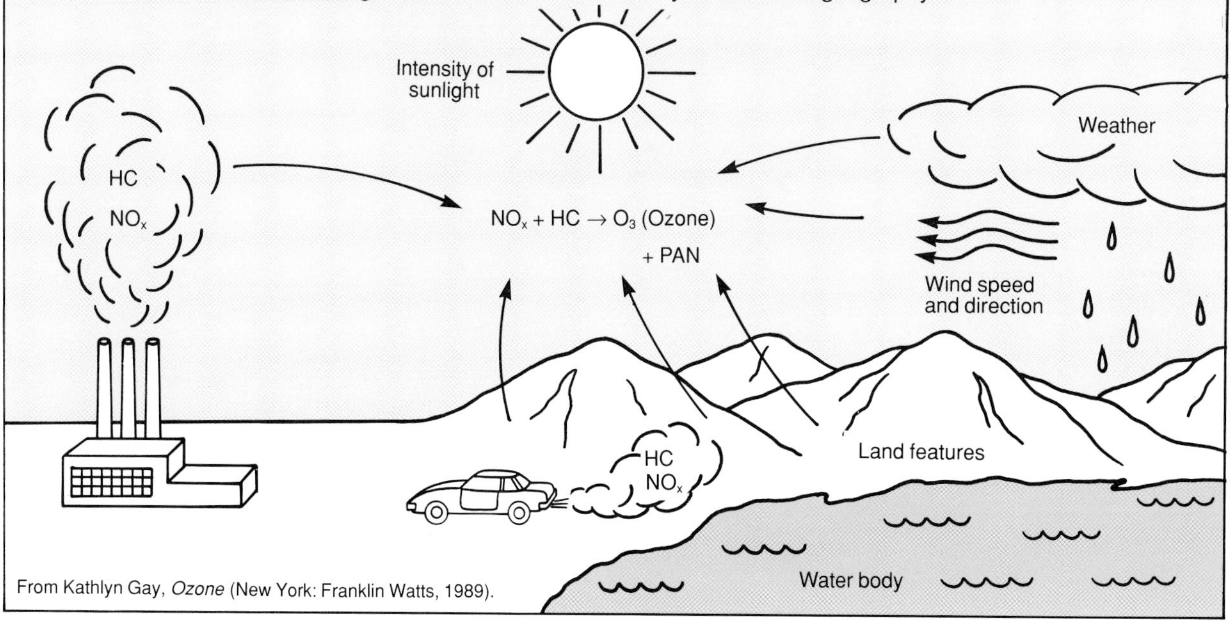

From Kathlyn Gay, *Ozone* (New York: Franklin Watts, 1989).

Figure 6.9 Population and motor vehicles in Los Angeles

	1985	2010 (ESTIMATED)
Population	11 600 000	15 200 000
Motor vehicles	7 700 000	10 400 000
Vehicle km/day	213 900 000	320 000 000

From the California Air Resources Board.

The case of Los Angeles

The greater Los Angeles area faces some of the worst photochemical smog conditions of any large city. The causes of the air pollution problems in Los Angeles are suggested in Figure 6.9.

Los Angeles lies in a basin surrounded by mountains. The air becomes trapped and is not easily replaced. In addition to photochemical smog, the growing economy creates industrial smog from a wide range of industrial and domestic air pollutants.

The pollution problems of the Los Angeles area have been improved in a number of ways, including cleaner-burning fuels, more efficient cars, and a reduction of smoke. Most measures of air pollution, such as sulphur dioxide, lead, and carbon monoxide, have declined since the mid-1970s. However, the ozone concentrations can at times reach 450 ppb, which is

Figure 6.10 Global environment monitoring system report (1989)

		AVERAGE NUMBER OF DAYS PER YEAR ABOVE WHO GUIDELINES	
COUNTRY	CITY	SO_2 LEVELS	SPM/SMOKE LEVELS
Brazil	São Paulo	12	31
Canada	Montréal	10	0
	Toronto	1	1
	Vancouver	0	0
China	Beijing	68	272
	Shanghai	16	133
	Shenyang	146	219
Finland	Helsinki	2	19
India	Bombay	3	100
	Calcutta	25	268
Iran	Tehran	104	174
Japan	Osaka	0	0
	Tokyo	0	2
Philippines	Manila	24	14
Poland	Wroclaw	8	30
Thailand	Bangkok	0	97
United Kingdom	Glasgow	14	6
	London	7	0
United States	New York City	8	0
West Germany	Frankfurt	20	0

From the United Nations Environment Program.

well above the US federal standard of 120 ppb. (It is interesting to note that the acceptable level of ozone in the US is about 50 percent higher than in Canada.)

Increasing attention is being focused on the damage to health and on the economic losses due to smog, such as the lost agricultural production on nearby farms. A more drastic plan aimed at eliminating most smog by 2007 was introduced in 1989. Measures include banning the sale of new gas-powered mowers and making solar power compulsory for new swimming pools. Forty percent of all cars are to be powered by methanol or natural gas by 1998. The average car occupancy must increase from 1.1 to 1.5 persons and every firm with 100 or more employees must have a transport coordinator to ensure that these standards are reached. Since cars create much of the atmospheric smog, improvements in the efficiency of car engines by the use of cleaner-burning fuels would help to reduce the pollution.

While the problems of Los Angeles require radical solutions, air pollution from both transport and industrial sources is even more serious in places like Mexico City, with a possible future population of 30 million. In developing countries the use of fossil fuels in industry and power generation contributes to large volumes of smoke and atmospheric dust as well as to the acid rain gases. Large cities in developing countries seem likely to be the air pollution centres of the future.

Monitoring air quality

Air quality throughout the world is now monitored by the **Global Environment Monitoring System (GEMS)**, sponsored by the United Nations. Figure 6.10 uses 1989 GEMS data. It lists the number of days that sulphur dioxide and suspended particulate matter (SPM) exceeded World Health Organization (WHO) guidelines in selected world cities.

The measurement of air pollution by an **Air Quality Index (AQI)** began in the 1970s. The Index is usually based on five common pollutants (SO_2, NO_x, CO, O_3, and TSP (total suspended particulates), and the length of time that they exceed particular levels. The Index is divided into good (0-24), fair (25-49), poor (50-99), and very poor (100+). Graphs of AQI values for six Canadian cities are shown in Figure 6.11.

Figure 6.11 Air Quality Index values for six Canadian cities

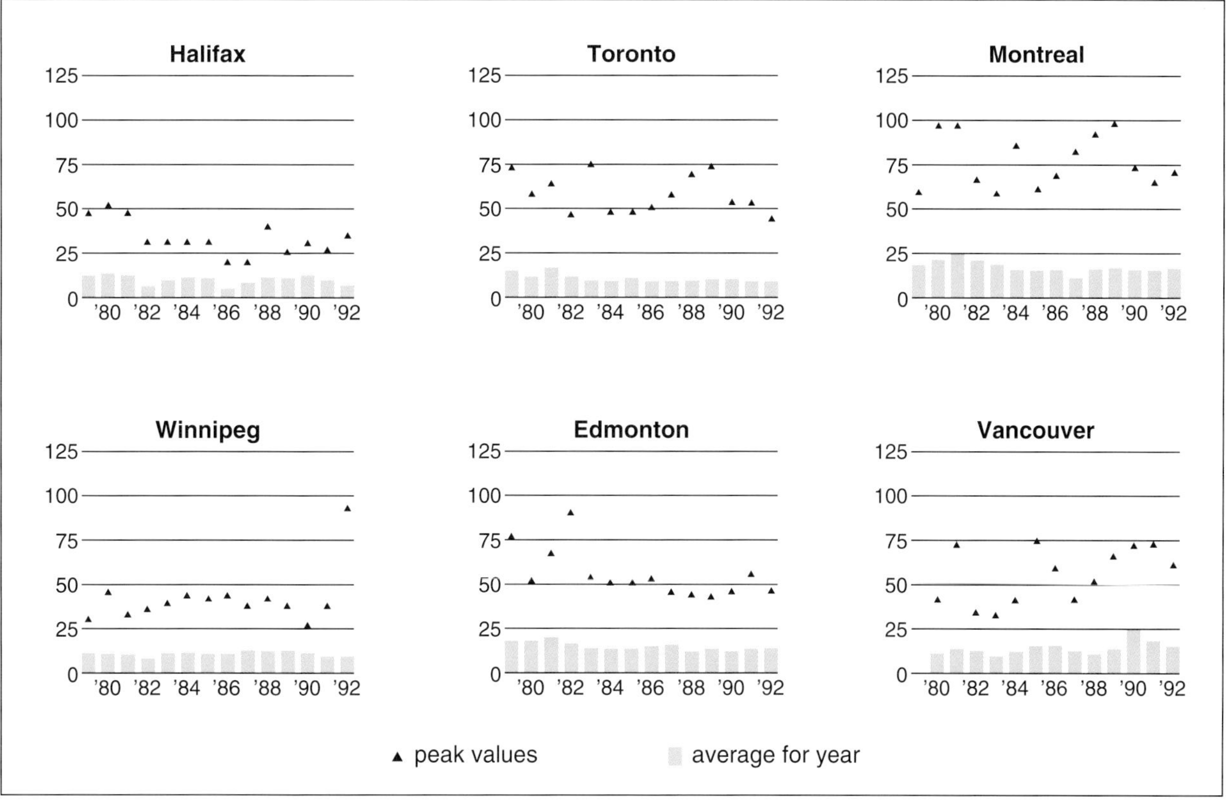

From Environment Canada.

Global warming (the greenhouse effect)

The earth's atmosphere has played the role of a greenhouse for 5 billion years. The **greenhouse effect** is caused by various atmospheric gases, carbon dioxide (CO_2) being the most important. (See Figure 6.12.) Others include methane, nitrous oxide, ozone, and chlorofluorocarbons (CFCs). All these gases do not affect incoming short-wave radiation from the sun, but they trap some of the long-wave heat that radiates from the ground. Any increase in them, might be expected to raise the average temperature of the atmosphere.

This warming trend has been underway for some time. (See Figure 6.13.) The average temperature of the globe has increased by half a degree in the past century. But the rate appears likely to increase. The Food and Agriculture Organization (FAO) has predicted a 1°C increase in average global temperatures by 2010 and a 4.5°C increase by 2050.

Figure 6.12 The greenhouse gases

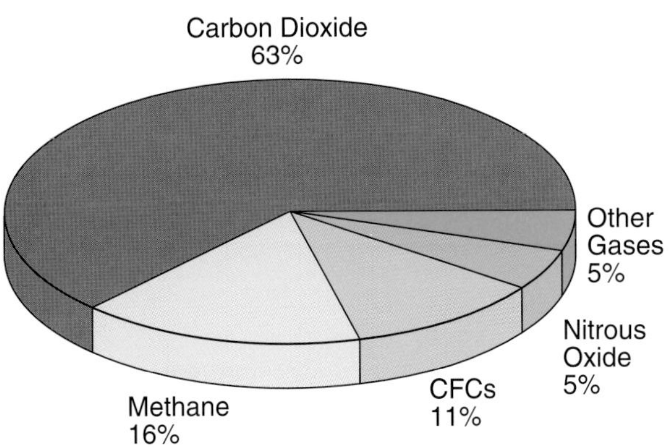

Scientists anticipate a rise in global temperatures of about one degree celsius by the year 2025. The major green-house gases contributing to this warming are expected to be carbon dioxide, methane, and CFCs.

From Environment Canada.

The increase in greenhouse gases

The main reason for this expected warming is our increasing production of greenhouse gases. CO_2 is the main problem, as it rises with the burning of fossil fuels and of the rain forests. Some reductions in fossil-fuel burning took place during the early 1980s as a result of the economic recession, but the burning of rain forests increased. Fossil fuel use will likely increase again, and the output of CO_2 will rise.

Methane is a powerful greenhouse gas becoming more significant in the atmosphere. It is produced in the stomachs of cattle, at the bottom of rice fields, by rotting garbage, and by burning fossil fuels. No decline in the upward trend can be detected. However, the use of CFCs has declined since the early 1970s when their use in aerosol cans was reduced. CFCs contribute to the greenhouse effect and are a threat to the ozone layer.

The effects of global warming

A rise in sea level A rise of 4.5 °C in the average global temperature by the year 2050 would melt large amounts of ice in the Arctic and Antarctic. This extra water, lower atmospheric pressure, and ocean warming would create a rise in **mean sea level** of between 20 to 150 cm. Scientists estimate that sea level could rise by over 4 m by the end of the twenty-first century.

Low-lying coastal areas would be seriously affected by an increase in sea level. If the average sea level rose

Figure 6.13 Increasing CO_2 and global temperature trends

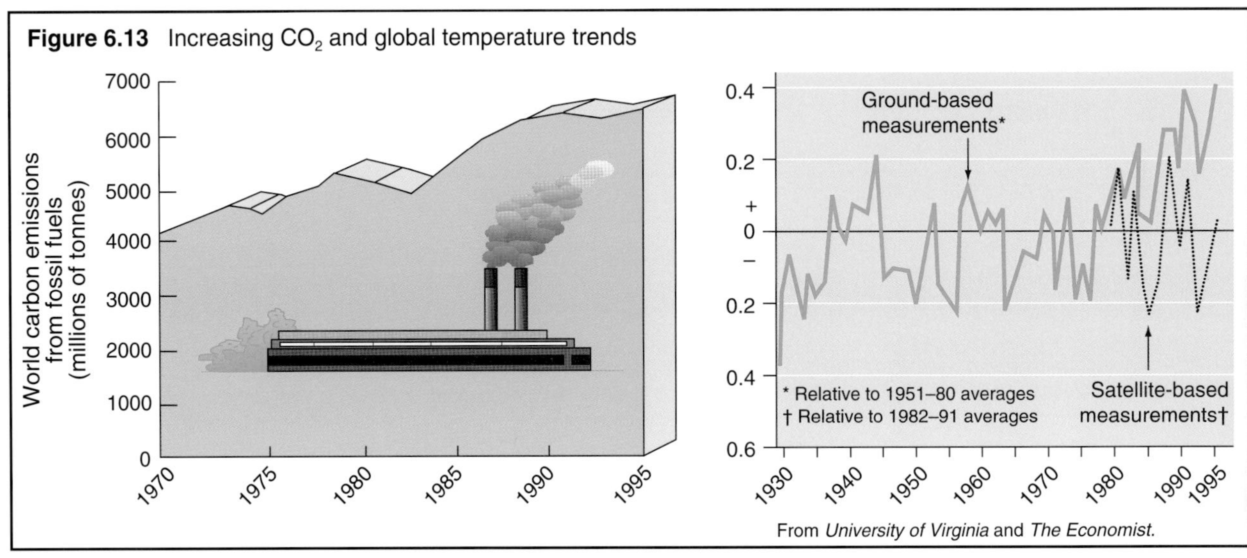

From *University of Virginia* and *The Economist.*

by 1 m, additional storm surges would threaten all land below 5 m. The effects of the loss of land below 5 m could be disastrous. Many of the world's major cities are at sea level, including all seaports.

Assuming the predictions of a rising sea level are correct, several parts of the world would be affected. The Mississippi delta would be flooded and the city of New Orleans threatened. Other deltas, where upstream dams have trapped most of the river silt, would erode and become estuaries. Erosion has already occurred in the Nile delta. Cities like Venice would face enormous costs to stay above water. In the Netherlands, which is one of the countries that would be most seriously affected by a higher sea level, the cost of building more dikes and pumps has been estimated at $6 billion (US) over the next century. A Western country may be able to afford such an expense, but developing countries may not have the resources to protect low-lying coastlines. In Bangladesh and Indonesia much of the recent migration of people has been to just such low-lying coastal areas. Floods in the Bay of Bengal regularly cause widespread loss of life. It is a situation that is likely to get worse.

On a worldwide basis, no less than 5 000 000 km² of low-lying coastal land could be affected. While this is only 3 percent of the world's land area, it accounts for 33 percent of the world's cropland.

Effects on plants Carbon dioxide is essential for plant growth. Some plants, including most of the world's food crops, have a more marked response to CO_2 than others. Scientists at the FAO predict, however, that corn, millet, and sorghum may suffer from competition from weeds. Temperature increases could also cause problems for rice, wheat, and potatoes.

More CO_2 has the effect of increasing carbohydrate growth rather than protein levels in crops. Crops may therefore require more nitrogen fertilizer in an environment rich in CO_2. The manufacturing of nitrate fertilizers uses a great deal of energy, which in turn creates pollution.

Effects on farming belts Global warming would have other adverse effects. The warming trends are expected to be much greater in higher latitudes than toward the equator. Crop belts in temperate regions could be significantly warmed, but they may also dry out as evaporation increases. Warmer temperatures

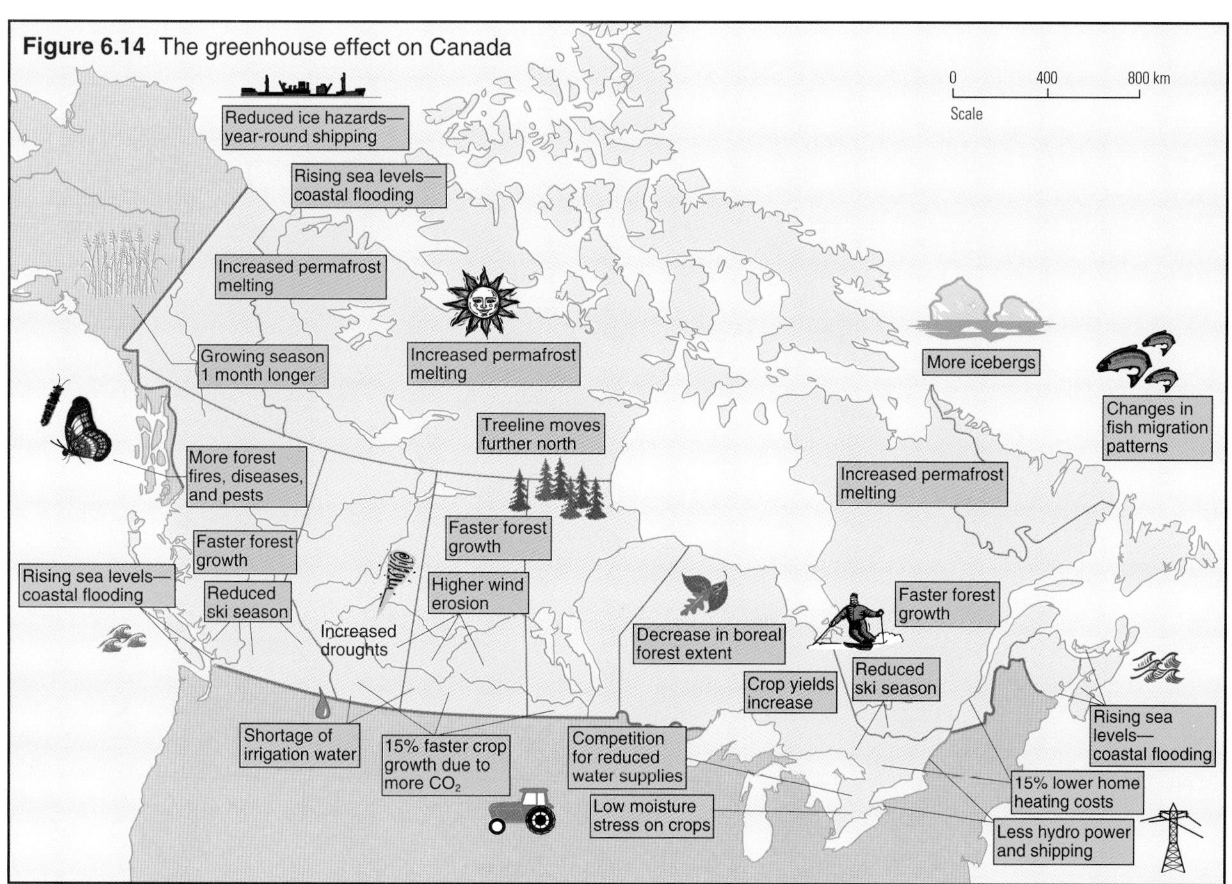

Figure 6.14 The greenhouse effect on Canada

could increase the rate of crop growth but would also lead to the much faster growth of insects and pests. The FAO predicts increased problems from ticks, tsetse flies, and mosquitoes.

Existing agricultural belts would have to make costly adjustments. The United Nations Environment Program (UNEP) calculates that wheat production in the southern Canadian Prairies could decline by 25 percent as a result of drier conditions. On the other hand, warming temperatures could move the farm belts over 200 km northward, increasing production in Canada's northern Prairies and in Russia. Figure 6.14 on page 81 shows some ways in which Canada could be changed by the greenhouse effect.

A shift in climatic belts could also affect forestry, particularly in Canada. Trees in Canada take about 80 to 100 years to mature. In that space of time the climatic belts could move north by 200 or 300 km. Trees are selected for the climatic conditions in which they are planted. Because of possible changes in climate, trees may have to mature in conditions not so well suited to them.

In the world as a whole, UNEP calculates that deserts and grasslands would expand at the expense of forests. Forest fires would increase. River flow patterns would be altered, making some existing hydroelectric plants useless.

Reducing the greenhouse effect

To reduce the greenhouse effect, the roughly 7 billion tonnes of carbon emitted each year into the atmosphere must be reduced. Of this total, the oceans are thought to absorb about 2 billion tonnes. Tree planting has been suggested as a way of absorbing carbon, but very large areas would have to be reforested and current deforestation would have to be reduced or eliminated in many parts of the world. These solutions would require major changes in policy by many countries.

In June 1988 an international conference of climate experts was held in Toronto to discuss the greenhouse effect. They recommended that world carbon dioxide emissions be cut by 20 percent by 2005. To date, however, few countries have adopted this goal. The problem is, as Figure 6.15 shows, that developing countries may use increasing amounts of fossil fuels as they industrialize.

Figure 6.15 World carbon emissions from fossil fuel burning, by economic region, 1950–1994

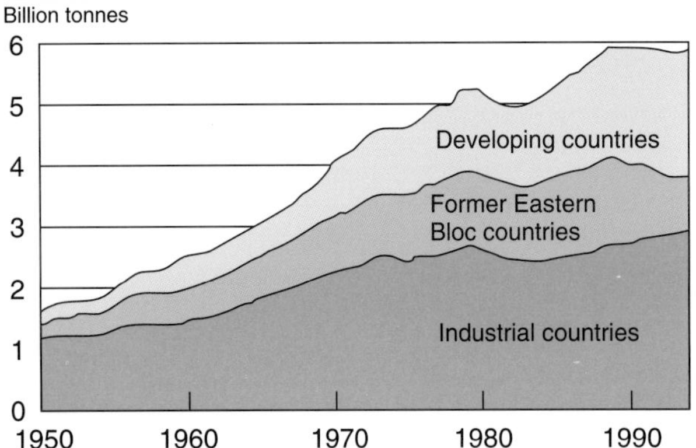

Adapted from Worldwatch Paper #130, *Climate of Hope: New Strategies for Stabilizing the World's Atmosphere*, by permission of Worldwatch Institute.

The scientific uncertainty

It will take time before we can say with certainty that the earth is warming up because of the increase in greenhouse gases. However, the decade of the 1980s included six of the hottest years of the twentieth century. Measurements of the amount of CO_2 and methane in the atmosphere continue to show steady increases, and these trends indicate that future warming is likely.

Those who discount the greenhouse theory claim that a run of warm, dry years is normal and that we may have similar runs of below average temperatures in the future. An interesting point is that cities have warmed more than rural areas because of the heat generated in them. Since many of our climate recording stations are in or near cities, the warming of our climate may have been overstated. It also appears that temperature readings taken from satellites covering the whole earth, and not just the inhabited areas, do not show a warming trend (see Figure 6.13). There is much disagreement in the scientific community about whether or by how much the earth is warming, but there is no doubt that the debate is heating up!

Variations in the amount of volcanic dust can also create changes in temperature at least as great as those caused by changes in greenhouse gases. The explosion at Mount St. Helens in the United States along with erupting volcanoes in Chile and Mexico may have reduced solar radiation in the early 1980s.

Increased cloudiness can also be expected to result from the greenhouse effect. Some experts claim that clouds could reduce the expected warming by as much as half. The clouds would screen more of the incoming solar radiation. Others claim that, although global warming would melt more polar ice, the increase in freshwater would, in turn, lead to more sea ice, which could also counteract the warming trend. Much research needs to be done on the role the oceans play in climatic change on a global scale.

A United Nations conference on climatic change was held in Geneva in 1996. The Intergovernmental Panel on Climatic Change (IPCC) reported that the evidence supporting the human impact on climatic change was becoming stronger. Emissions of CO_2 had risen by 4 percent in developed nations since 1990. As a result, several governments, including the US, demanded stronger action to curb greenhouse gases. Also at the conference, the World Health Organization (WHO) stated that global warming could cause millions of additional deaths as tropical diseases spread to new areas. Malaria, for example, could affect 50 to 80 million extra people, with dengue fever, river blindness, and Lyme disease also spreading.

Many scientists feel that the greenhouse effect is only one factor in a complex series of climatic equations. Some insist that soil erosion or chemicals in the environment present a more immediate threat to our planet than the warming of the atmosphere. But should we risk waiting until the greenhouse effect is proven one way or the other? By then action to prevent its effects will be too late.

The threat to the ozone layer

Ozone is a tiny component of the earth's atmosphere, but it plays a crucial role in filtering out ultraviolet radiation, which in large doses would destroy life on this planet. The so-called **ozone layer** is a band of the stratosphere about 25 km above the earth. Ozone is present in higher than normal quantities in this layer, although it still accounts for only 1 molecule in 100 000. Scientists observed that a "hole" in the protective shield of ozone developed over Antarctica in the mid-1970s. Ice crystals in the upper atmosphere over Antarctica are thought to speed up the destruction of ozone. Since then Canadian scientists have detected a thinning of ozone over the Arctic and even over Toronto.

Causes of the depletion of the ozone layer

Ozone is a rare form of oxygen, with three atoms per molecule instead of the usual two. If all the atmospheric ozone lay directly on the earth's surface, it would create a layer only 3 mm thick. Sunlight produces ozone by the process $O_2 + O \rightarrow O_3$. Ozone is easily destroyed by a number of gases, including several that are produced by industry.

Chlorine and nitric acid in the atmosphere are the greatest threats to ozone. A single chlorine atom can destroy 10 000 molecules of ozone. Much of the chlorine comes from CFCs (chlorofluorocarbons). About 40 percent of CFCs come from aerosol cans, although their use for this purpose is now banned in North America. CFCs are also used in refrigerators and as foam-blowing agents. Other gases that deplete ozone include bromine, halon 1301 (a fire extinguishing agent), and carbon dioxide.

Although these explanations of ozone depletion are widely accepted, not everyone agrees with them. Another theory is that the peak of the sunspot cycle in 1979 and 1980 caused a temporary decline in ozone levels. This theory claims that an increase in solar energy increases the nitrogen dioxide in the upper atmosphere. This in turn can lead to an increase in the compounds that cause a decline in ozone.

As with many other environmental problems, there is a time lag between the activities that release damaging gases into the atmosphere and the actual depletion of the ozone. This time lag may be twenty or thirty years. Even if all the damaging chemicals were banned right away, the ozone layer would continue to deteriorate for many years. This fact underlines the need for prompt action.

The effects of a decrease in the ozone layer

There are three main effects of a reduction in the layer of protective ozone. It is estimated that a 1 percent depletion of ozone would lead to a 4 percent increase in melanoma skin cancer from ultraviolet light. The US Environmental Protection Agency (EPA) has predicted an increase of 153 million cases of skin cancer worldwide by the year 2075 if nothing is done to protect the ozone layer. Increased ultraviolet light can also cause eye problems, both in people and in cattle, and can damage the immune system.

An increase in ultraviolet light may also harm plant growth. Estimates suggest that a 1 percent reduction of ozone would lead to a similar reduction in crop and timber yields. Fish stocks could also decline, since marine algae are easily damaged by ultraviolet light. These micro-organisms are the basis of aquatic food chains. Without them, marine life could not exist.

Protecting the ozone layer

Many scientists share the concern for the ozone layer and they have been pressuring politicians to take action. A twenty-four nation treaty to control the use of most CFCs and other ozone-depleting gases, known as the **Montréal Protocol**, was signed in September 1987. These nations pledged to reduce their 1986 total output of ozone-depleting gases by 50 percent by 1999. In June 1990 the Canadian government announced its intention to stop all CFC production by 1997. At a 1992 international conference in Copenhagen, agreement was reached to accelerate the phasing out of ozone depleting substances by 1996.

Chemical companies are researching new products to replace the CFCs, which were once thought to be safe inert gases. DuPont (Canada) has built a factory in Ontario to produce a new product called HCFC-123. This eliminates 98 percent of the threat to the ozone, but at a cost several times higher than that of CFCs. The replacement of CFCs worldwide has been estimated to cost at least $6 billion (US).

The international agreements described above may be having some success. While reports of increases in the "ozone hole" continue in many parts of the world, measurements of CFCs in the atmosphere seemed to have levelled off in 1996 and may be beginning to decline. If so, there could be an improvement in the overall ozone layer by 2010. A threat to future progress in reducing CFCs, however, is the expected increase in the number of refrigerators in the developing world, especially in China. The resulting increase in the use of CFCs there could more than offset the decline in industrialized countries.

Natural events such as volcanic eruptions can affect the atmosphere, including the ozone layer, in several ways. For example, the El Chichon eruption in Mexico in 1983 sent a large volume of sulphur into the atmosphere in the form of a stratospheric cloud. This led to an increase in acid rain and a decrease in solar radiation reaching the earth. Scientists say the eruption caused the cold winters of 1984 and 1985. The stratospheric clouds created by the El Chichon eruption also led to a sharp decrease in ozone levels, since the destruction of ozone is made easier by the existence of stratospheric clouds.

We have seen that the combined effects of greenhouse gases and ozone depletion present major problems to society. The landscape may be changed, particularly by the rise in sea level. Plant life may be altered, and both humans and animals can be affected. These problems are summarized in Figure 6.16. Overcoming these hazards will be enormously expensive.

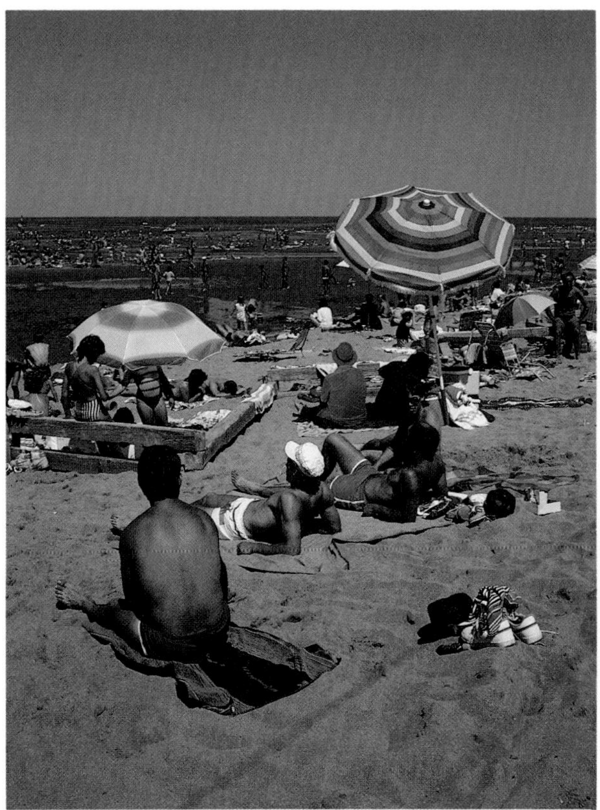

Although it is well known that sunbathing may increase the chances of skin cancer, many people choose to ignore the risk.

Figure 6.16 Social effects of damaging the atmosphere

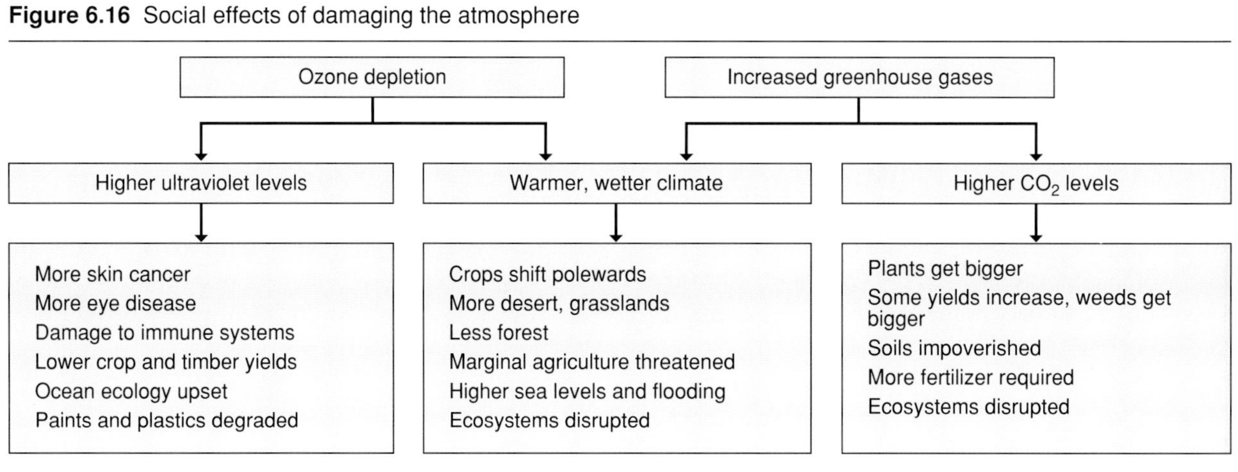

From "Changing the Atmosphere," the United Nations Environment Program.

Modifying the weather

Human actions have damaged, and continue to damage, the atmosphere. However, we can also modify the condition of the air around us to our benefit. Although air modification cannot yet be done on a large scale, local weather conditions may sometimes be altered to benefit urban residents or farmers.

Urban climates

Cities are usually warmer, and certainly more polluted, than the surrounding rural land because of the heat generated within them. Figure 6.17 illustrates the so-called **urban heat island** effect experienced by most cities. Climates also change on a smaller scale, as in the case of a garden protected from winds by a wall.

Another climatic effect in urban areas is **wind tunnelling**. High buildings on each side of a street may channel the wind and increase its speed. For this reason, the corner of Portage and Main Streets in Winnipeg has been described as the coldest street crossing in Canada. This intersection now has underground crossing facilities!

Improving the weather for agriculture and aviation

Figure 6.18 shows how **shelter belts** or **windbreaks** can modify the weather conditions over a small area on their leeward side. Such shelter belts are common in parts of the Prairies.

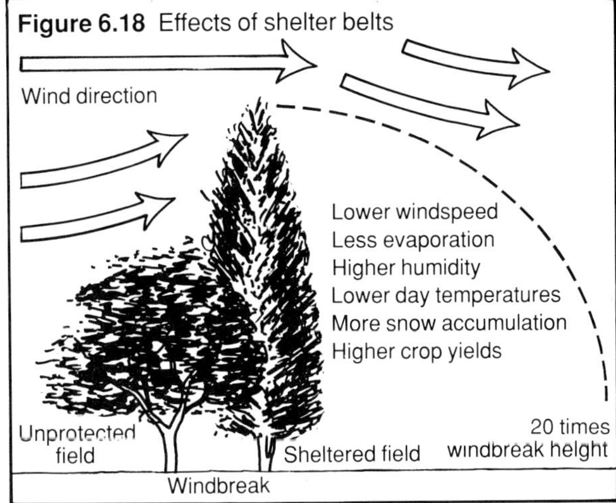

Figure 6.18 Effects of shelter belts

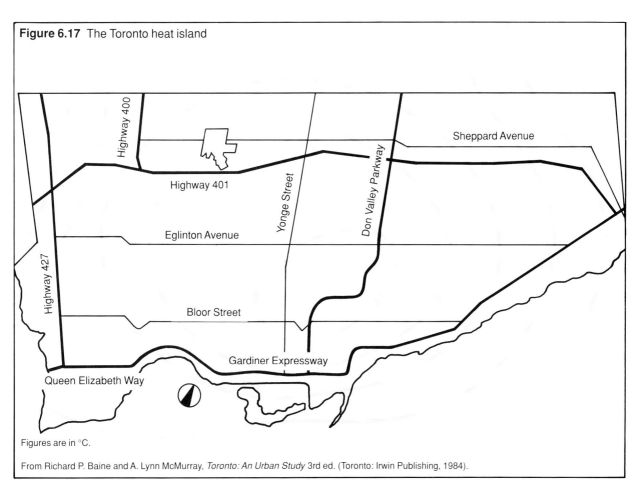

Figure 6.17 The Toronto heat island

Highway 400
Sheppard Avenue
Highway 401
Yonge Street
Don Valley Parkway
Eglinton Avenue
Highway 427
Bloor Street
Gardiner Expressway
Queen Elizabeth Way

Figures are in °C.

From Richard P. Baine and A. Lynn McMurray, *Toronto: An Urban Study* 3rd ed. (Toronto: Irwin Publishing, 1984).

There are other methods of modifying the climate, including preventing frost in citrus groves through the use of oil stoves, fine water sprays, or electric propellers that keep the air circulating. Another means of climate modification is fog dispersal, which is used at some airports. Fog dispersal can be achieved in several ways, including spraying dry ice or liquid propane into the air. This encourages ice crystals to form and precipitate on the ground. The use of jet-powered fans along the runways is another means of fog dispersal, and it has been used successfully at Orly Airport in Paris, France. Finally, hovering helicopters can create "prop wash," mixing ground fog with the drier air above. Needless to say, these methods are expensive.

It has been claimed that the seeding of clouds by spraying fine jets of silver iodide from an airplane can increase precipitation by about 10 percent. The effects of cloud seeding are hard to measure, however, since we cannot say how much precipitation would have fallen naturally. As well, downwind areas may experience a corresponding shortage of precipitation.

Propellers in citrus groves help to reduce the danger of frost.

Figure 6.19 Time spent in indoor and outdoor environments

TOTAL TIME	OUTDOORS (%)	INDOORS (%)
Developed countries		
Urban	11	89
Rural	17	83
Developing countries		
Urban	12	88
Rural	40	60

Adapted from the *World Bank Development Report, 1987* (New York: Oxford University Press, 1987).

The indoor atmosphere

The atmosphere is an important part of our environment. But how much of our time do we spend *outdoors* in direct contact with the atmosphere and its pollutants rather than *indoors*? Think of the environments in which you spend your time, and divide them between indoors and outdoors. An estimate for the world's population is given in Figure 6.19.

Nearly all preventative air pollution measures have attempted to improve the quality of the urban outdoor environment in developed countries. Figure 6.19 shows that city dwellers in the developed world spent only 11 percent of their time outdoors, which is a mere 2 percent of all the time spent, indoors and outdoors, by the world's population.

Based on these figures, a study of the indoor climates and the types of pollution found there should be a priority. We need to know more about the air we actually breathe, whether we are at home, school, or work.

Some common indoor chemicals

Indoor air is partly controlled by the quality of the air outside. But it is also affected by our use of pollutants, such as paints and solvents, spray cans, cigarettes, deodorizers, and dry-cleaned clothes. Paints and plastics also give off toxic gases. The use of lead has been banned from indoor paints for many years, but low levels of lead from old paints can still cause mental problems in children.

Benzene is a pollutant that is thought to cause leukemia. By far the largest amounts of benzene released into the air come from automobiles and industrial emissions. Yet half of the total human exposure to benzene comes from smoking cigarettes or from breathing secondary cigarette smoke. Cigarette smoke becomes highly concentrated in an indoor environment.

Power plants, even with built-in scrubbers, emit twenty-five times as much particulate matter (smoke) as all cigarettes ever smoked. But most power plants emit their dust high into the air while most cigarettes are smoked indoors. Thus the exposure of the average person to cigarette smoke is several times higher than the exposure to smoke from the burning of fossil fuels.

Exposures above recommended limits have been found for other dangerous chemicals, including **trichloroethylene** (TCE), a dry-cleaning agent also used in decaffeinating coffee. Keeping recently dry-cleaned clothes in a bedroom closet can lead to high doses of this possible carcinogen. Dry-cleaned clothes should be well aired away from poorly ventilated living spaces. Yet another possible carcinogen often found indoors is **p-dichlorobenzene** (p-DCB), a deodorant and moth repellent.

Another gas that can be dangerous indoors is **radon**, which is produced by the radioactive decay of uranium 238. This gas occurs naturally in areas where uranium is found, but may build up in poorly ventilated homes. One home in Pennsylvania was found to have radon gas equal to 630 times the maximum permitted dosage of radiation for nuclear power workers. Radon has a half life of only 3.8 days and decays into polonium, lead, and bismuth. However, the particles released by the decay process are associated with lung cancer. The EPA estimates that radon may cause an additional 20 000 cases of lung cancer per year in the United States, making radon second only to cigarette smoking as a cause of this disease.

In our desire to reduce energy consumption by properly insulating our homes, we have often allowed the level of indoor pollutants to build up. Alvin Alm of Science Applications International claims in *Environmental Science and Technology* that the air we breathe indoors poses greater health threats than what we breathe outdoors, and also that the indoor environment was less healthy in 1990 than it had been in 1980.

Indoor pollution in the developing world

Seventy-five percent of the world's people live in developing countries. Because they depend on farming as a way of life, most of these people spend a greater proportion of their time outdoors. But on average two-thirds of their total hours are still spent inside. Most people in poor countries rely on unvented stoves for warmth and cooking. Much of the fuel is dried dung and crop residues. These types of fuel burn with much greater emissions of smoke and chemicals than oil or gas stoves. (See page 153.)

The smoke- and chemical-filled atmosphere in millions of small, unvented homes creates what may well be the world's greatest single health hazard. Millions of infants suffer from respiratory diseases as a result of constantly breathing this choking atmosphere. Up to 4 million children die each year throughout the world from respiratory failure, often in combination with other diseases. None of the atmospheric pollution problems of the Western world create anything like this human death toll. More efficient stoves would help to solve this problem and reduce the enormous demand for fuel wood. Many developing countries are now beginning to use fuel-efficient stoves.

How can you help prevent air pollution?

We all contribute in a minor way to the greenhouse effect merely by breathing out carbon dioxide! Nevertheless, we can help to reduce air pollution in many ways. Most of our contributions to pollution are related to our lifestyles. Changes in our lifestyles can therefore help to solve the problems.

Reducing use of cars

Cars are one symbol of our affluent Western society. Yet the car has been described as an environmental disaster. Making cars requires large volumes of resources, including energy. Running cars contributes both to the greenhouse effect and to acid rain. Few of us are willing to go without cars, but perhaps we should limit our use of them. Public transport creates far fewer pollutants per person than cars do. This topic is dealt with more fully in chapter 13.

Conserving energy

Since so much air pollution comes from the burning of fossil fuels, all forms of energy conservation have an immediate effect on reducing emissions. Turning down the thermostat or insulating your house are effective methods of energy conservation. A couple of minutes less in the shower is another. By conserving energy in the home and at school or work, we not only save resources but help to create a cleaner atmosphere.

Using ozone-friendly products

Using ozone-friendly products means avoiding any aerosols that still use CFCs as well as styrofoam containers and cups blown with CFCs whenever possible. Try not to use disposable articles, since they require more production in order to be replaced. All production requires energy, and the generation of energy is a major cause of air pollution.

Avoiding burning rubbish or leaves

Garden fires contribute not only CO_2 but also traces of other toxic chemicals and heavy metals. When the air is calm, smoke from garden fires can be a major pollutant in our towns and cities as well as being a fire hazard. By not burning leaves and other garden rubbish, the individual householder can make a useful contribution to cleaning up the air we all breathe. Instead of burning garden waste, it is far more useful to use organic material as a source of garden compost.

Looking back

1. (a) Name three regions in North America and Europe where acid rain is particularly serious. In each case suggest where the acidity comes from.
   (b) Describe how acid rain can harm the ecosystem of a lake or river.
2. (a) List the factors that could increase or decrease the amount of fossil fuels burned throughout the world.
   (b) What environmental problems would likely follow an increase in world fossil fuel consumption?
3. Southern Ontario regularly experiences a serious ozone problem.
   (a) What is the main source of this form of pollution?
   (b) How does it affect people and property?
   (c) How can surface ozone be reduced?
4. List ways in which temperature may be modified (a) in the countryside and (b) in towns.
5. What potential air pollution hazards may exist in your own home? In what ways can you protect the indoor environment from these hazards?

Applying your knowledge

1. (a) Collect a sample of rainwater and measure its acidity using litmus paper. Is it more or less acid than "average" rainfall (5.6 on the pH scale)? What are the probable causes of the acidity?
   (b) The costs of cleaning up acid rain are great, but so are the costs of ignoring it. List the people or groups who benefit from acid rain reduction and those who are likely to pay the costs of the cleanup.
   (c) Write a letter to your local newspaper expressing your concern at the slow progress made by governments in dealing with this issue.
2. Obtain AQI data for a city near you. Draw a graph of daily pollution levels and compare the graph with the daily weather conditions. What patterns are evident?
3. Using an atlas and a blank map of the world, locate the cities listed in Figure 6.10. What general observations can you make about air pollution in cities in developing countries compared with Western cities?
4. Using an atlas, find the world's major cities that are located at sea level. Prepare a report that answers the following questions about these cities:
   (a) Approximately how many people live in these cities?
   (b) What problems might the greenhouse effect cause for people in low-lying cities?
   (c) How might people cope with these problems?
5. Figure 6.18 shows six effects of shelter belts or windbreaks. Explain, in a short essay, how each of these may help farmers.

Extending your thinking

1. (a) Sulphur dioxide emissions in 1994 have been listed for twenty US states. On an outline map shade the top ten states. Add arrows showing a typical southwest wind.

Figure 6.20 Sulphur dioxide emissions in eastern US, 1994 (000 tonnes)

State	Emissions	State	Emissions
1. Ohio	1141	11. Alabama	188
2. Indiana	892	12. Maryland	129
3. West Virginia	648	13. New York	80
4. Pennsylvania	568	14. Wisconsin	56
5. Tennessee	548	15. Iowa	42
6. Illinois	543	16. New Hampshire	38
7. Kentucky	410	17. New Jersey	30
8. Georgia	375	18. Michigan	21
9. Missouri	370	19. Kansas	6
10. Florida	196	20. Minnesota	1

From EPA.

   (b) Briefly describe the patterns illustrated by your map.
2. Figure 6.21 gives data for air pollution and per capita income for selected cities throughout the world.
   (a) Draw a graph showing the level of air pollution on the y-axis and per capita income on the x-axis. Each city should be plotted by a dot and named. This type of graph is called a **scatter-graph**.
   (b) Describe the relationship between air pollution and per capita income shown on your graph.
   (c) Are any cities different from the general rule? Suggest reasons why or why not.
3. Make a bar graph comparing the time you spend each week in your house, school, bus, and car. Compare your results with the average data listed in Figure 6.19. Also list pollutants that you think you may be exposed to in each of these places. How can you reduce such exposure to pollution?

Figure 6.21 Air pollution and per capita income for cities in selected countries

COUNTRY	CITY	PER CAPITA INCOME ($US)	OVERALL LEVEL OF AIR POLLUTION (MICROGRAMS PER M³)
United States	New York	26 000	70
Kuwait	Kuwait City	22 300	720
Canada	Montréal	20 000	72
Japan	Tokyo	18 000	70
Denmark	Copenhagen	16 000	42
Germany	Frankfurt	14 000	36
Australia	Sydney	10 200	100
United Kingdom	Birmingham	8 000	110
Venezuela	Caracas	3 400	108
Malaysia	Kuala Lumpur	2 500	150
Portugal	Lisbon	1 850	115
Brazil	Rio de Janeiro	1 500	125
Thailand	Bangkok	750	210
Philippines	Manila	660	110
Indonesia	Jakarta	580	250
Ghana	Accra	510	110
China	Shanghai	420	240
China	Beijing	380	400
India	Bombay	280	200
India	Calcutta	240	410

Adapted from Kirk R. Smith, "Air Pollution: Assessing Total Exposure in Developing Countries," in *Environment*, Vol. 30, No. 10, 1988.

4. Research one of the following topics and prepare a report on your findings:
   - the control of acid rain
   - air pollution in developing countries
   - ground level ozone
   - stratospheric ozone
   - indoor air pollution.

   (a) Collect information on your chosen topic from newspapers, library sources, or the Internet.

   (b) Relate the environmental problem to the ecosystem concepts described in chapter 3.

   (c) Examine the various points of view about the seriousness of the problem and discuss how a lack of agreement may make a solution more difficult.

   (d) Evaluate possible solutions to the problem, keeping in mind the needs of all sectors of society as well as the environment.

7 WATER

Water is the most important commodity on earth and is essential for all forms of life. In the hydrological or water cycle, water circulates from the oceans to the atmosphere, into rivers, lakes, or groundwater, and finally back to the oceans.

From Figure 7.1 you can see that an estimated 496 000 km^3 of water is lifted by evapotranspiration each year, with a similar amount falling as precipitation. The weather systems carry a net amount of about 40 000 km^3 from ocean to land, balanced by a similar amount discharged by the world's river systems.

In this chapter we will focus on two of the four "legs" of that cycle: the flow of water over (or under) the ground to the oceans and the oceans themselves. These aspects of the cycle include virtually all the ways that we use water.

World water resources

There are approximately 1.4 billion km^3 of water on our planet, 97 percent of which is in the oceans. Freshwater accounts for only 3 percent, most of which is in groundwater or frozen in the ice caps. Only 0.33 percent of freshwater is in lakes, with a mere 0.01 percent in rivers and streams.

The world distribution of freshwater

The distribution of freshwater is uneven throughout the world, mostly due to the great differences in climate that exist. Figure 7.3 shows the main areas of water surplus and deficit, which are measured by the difference between the amount of precipitation and evapotranspiration. Note that a water-deficient area

Figure 7.1 The global circulation of water (in thousands of km^3/year)

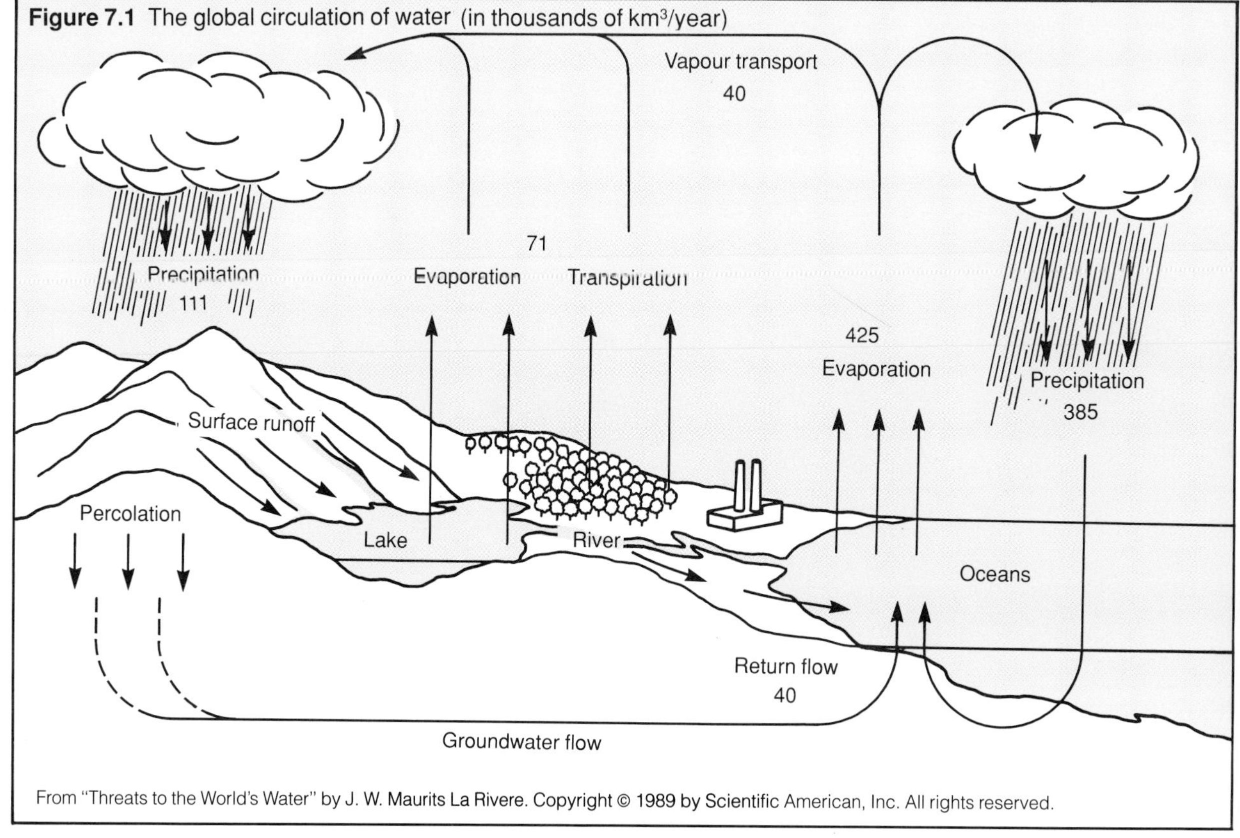

can grow only limited amounts of crops without irrigation.

Precipitation is the main source of water in most parts of the world, but rivers may bring water from wetter to drier areas. Egypt, with a desert climate, has some rich agricultural land fed by the waters of the Nile. Another source of water is found below the earth's surface. Many farmers in the Great Plains of North America use **groundwater** to compensate for the low and irregular precipitation.

We can classify countries as "water rich" and "water poor" on the basis of annual river flow. Brazil leads with the most water flow, followed by Russia and Canada. The world's major rivers can be classified by length, drainage area, and total discharge (water flow at the mouth of the river). While the Nile is the longest river in the world, it is dwarfed by the enormous flow and drainage area of the Amazon. However, river water may not be easily used by people. Most of the Amazon's volume flows unused into the Atlantic Ocean. Several of Russia's rivers flow north into the relatively uninhabited Arctic region. The top ten rivers on the basis of discharge are indicated in Figure 7.2.

Figure 7.2 Main rivers of the world

RIVER	LENGTH (KM)	DRAINAGE AREA (THOUSANDS KM^2)	TOTAL DISCHARGE (KM^3 PER YEAR)
Amazon	6280	6300	3768
Congo	4200	4000	1256
Chang Jiang (Yangtze)	6300	1950	688
Mississippi/ Missouri	6019	3267	556
Mekong	4500	795	538
Orinoco	2736	950	538
Paraná	4500	2800	493
Brahmaputra	2900	580	476
Indus	3180	950	443
Irrawaddy	2293	430	443
ON THE BASIS OF LENGTH, THE TOP TEN RIVERS WOULD INCLUDE THE FOLLOWING:			
Nile	6671	3000	81
Huang Ho	5464	745	104
Niger	4160	1125	224

How we use water

Water use is often divided into consumptive and non-consumptive uses. Hydro power is nonconsumptive in that water passing through the turbines is not used up. Most of the water used by farming, industry, and domestic users is consumptive in the sense that water used for these purposes needs treatment before it can be used again. Most people have no alternative to using water that has already been used, for example, by people farther up the river basin. This is a major reason why water quality is so important.

Agriculture accounts for the largest amount of the water used on a worldwide basis (73 percent). Industry uses 21 percent of world water, with public use (domestic and public water supply) accounting for only 6 percent. The pattern of water use varies widely from country to country. Egypt devotes 98 percent of its water to irrigation, whereas in Canada irrigation accounts for only 10 percent.

The abuse of water

Water is regarded as one of the "commons" or shared interests of the world. We assume it is free, abundant, and renewable. Water is infinitely valuable; we cannot live without it. Yet we often take water for granted and do not expect to have to pay for a glass of water in a restaurant.

For centuries people have regarded rivers as natural disposal systems. Waste products of all kinds, from raw sewage to chemical wastes, have been dumped into rivers, often killing the life that inhabited them. We have now realized, however, the destruction we have caused. Today many previously polluted rivers contain life once again, thanks to water purification efforts.

However, rivers are still abused in many parts of the world. Some of the worst examples are in developing countries, where many cities cannot afford sewage treatment plants. New Delhi in India, for example, pours an estimated 200 000 000 L of untreated sewage every day into the Yamuna River, a tributary of the Ganges. Industry adds a further 20 000 L of chemical waste. Millions of people drink and wash in the waters of the Ganges River downstream from New Delhi. Water that contains bacteria and parasites is a major cause of health problems in developing countries.

Many North American rivers have also been abused. For example, the St. Lawrence River still receives large volumes of untreated sewage, creating health hazards for both the people and wildlife that live along its shores.

Figure 7.3 Global water surplus and deficit

Deficit is the amount by which evapotranspiration exceeds annual precipitation.

Surplus
Over 1000 mm/year
0-1000 mm/year

Deficit
0-1000 mm/year
Over 1000 mm/year

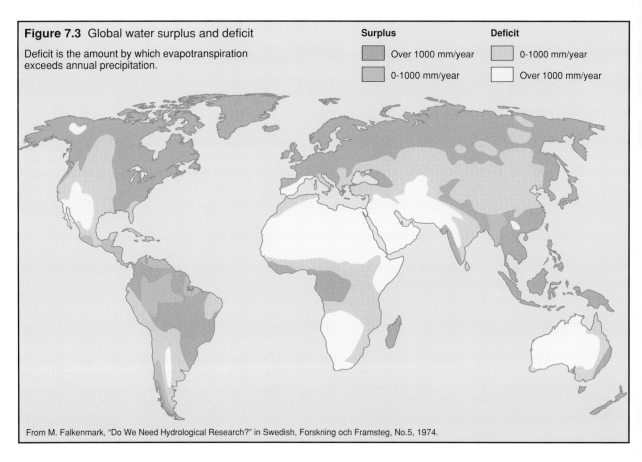

From M. Falkenmark, "Do We Need Hydrological Research?" in Swedish, Forskning och Framsteg, No.5, 1974.

Green algae are a sign of eutrophication in a river or lake.

Eutrophication

Water pollution takes many forms. One is the upsetting of the chemical balance of water by the addition of nutrients such as phosphates and nitrates. These chemicals enter the water cycle in two main ways. First, nitrates and phosphates from fertilizers seep into groundwater under farms, then into rivers. Second, phosphates are disposed of as industrial effluent and domestic waste. Domestic detergents have been a major source of phosphates, though this problem is rapidly being brought under control.

Phosphates and nitrates stimulate the growth of plants and algae in rivers and lakes. This green growth uses up oxygen through **biochemical oxygen demand (BOD)**. When the plant life eventually dies, it sinks and decomposes on the bottom, using up more oxygen. The process of rapid growth of biomass in a river or lake is called **eutrophication**. The water becomes murky and the oxygen content is depleted. Aquatic life changes to forms that need less oxygen, such as sludge worms and carp. The **anaerobic bacteria** that live in a low-oxygen environment give off a smell we often associate with the slimy, green algae on lakes and rivers. Eutrophication also encourages the rapid buildup of sediments, which may cause lakes to silt up.

Toxic chemicals

A second form of water pollution comes from the disposal of toxic chemicals into rivers and lakes. Waste disposal is easier to control than eutrophication, since the sources are at identifiable points. These toxic chemicals include not only heavy metals, such as lead and mercury, but also powerful chemical compounds, including dioxins and polychlorinated biphenyls (PCBs). When mixed with chlorine in drinking water, PCBs may contribute to cancer.

Eutrophication and pollution from waste disposal can also occur as a result of deposition from the atmosphere. Scientists have calculated that up to 20 percent of all the phosphorus entering Lake Michigan is deposited by rain, snow, or dust. Pesticides and metals, such as lead from car exhausts, also reach lakes and rivers through atmospheric deposition.

Heavy metals quickly become concentrated in the food chain. These substances tend to concentrate in the fatty tissues of fish and other creatures. Toxic materials may be up to 1 million times more concentrated in fish than in the water in which they swim. Therefore, eating the fish is much more dangerous than drinking the water.

Organic pesticides have been increasingly used in the past half century. DDT was widely used in the 1940s. It was scattered freely around most North American homes to control bugs. In the developing world, DDT saved millions of lives by helping to control the malaria-carrying **anopheles mosquito**. Soon, however, mosquitoes and other insects became immune to DDT. Its use is now banned in North America, since it is a possible cause of cancer. Many other organo-chlorides are in regular use, however. The dangers of using compounds such as DDT were not fully appreciated at first. Residues of these pesticides continue to exist in birds and other forms of wildlife.

Another source of pollution is the often ignored problem of urban runoff. This mixture of lead, salt, oil, and chemical compounds washes off the roads into the sewers. The Don River in Toronto is badly affected by urban runoff and by industrial and domestic waste. Lake Ontario receives all of this river pollution as well as toxic materials from groundwater and the atmosphere. The high coliform count (bacteria from human and animal faeces) from Toronto's sewage often causes beaches to be closed in the summer. The problems are made worse by the cross connections between sanitary and storm sewers that allow both industrial and domestic waste to flow into rivers. This flow of waste usually occurs after a heavy rainfall.

Reprinted from *The Toronto Star*, 20 July 1987, with permission — The Toronto Star Syndicate.

Thermal pollution

A less obvious form of water pollution is thermal pollution, which means raising the temperature of the water. It occurs when heated waste materials or cooling water from power stations is released into rivers, lakes, or oceans.

A rise in temperature of even a few degrees is enough to interfere with an ecosystem. Heated water stimulates the growth of organisms, which may, in turn, lead to the problems of eutrophication. Warmer water may increase the susceptibility of aquatic life to parasites, diseases, or toxins. It may also interfere with reproduction since fewer eggs survive. A warming of the water will likely have a harmful effect on the fishing industry, although it may extend the fishing season.

Groundwater

Groundwater accounts for over 22 percent of freshwater and for 90 percent of drinkable water worldwide. Its volume is difficult to calculate, since some groundwater occurs at great depths. However, groundwater supplies half of all the drinking water in the United States. It is increasingly used in situations where surface water supplies are scarce or fully utilized.

The occurrence of groundwater

Groundwater is most often found in sedimentary rocks and unconsolidated surface materials, such as sand and gravel. Groundwater fills the cracks and pore spaces in rocks like water in a sponge. Water may flow quite freely through cracks and joints in fractured rock. However, groundwater moves slowly compared with rivers and may remain underground for centuries before being returned to the oceans.

Groundwater may also be trapped underground. This happens when a layer of impermeable rock overlies a layer of rock that carries water, known as an **aquifer**. Sometimes the aquifer brings water from a distance. An **artesian well** occurs when water flows under pressure from an aquifer to the surface of the earth. Groundwater trapped at great depth is sometimes called **fossil groundwater**.

The upper limit at which water occupies pore space in the ground is known as the **water table**. You can check the level of the water table if you have a garden by digging until some freestanding water collects in the bottom of the hole you have dug. You will have less digging to do if you try it after a spell of wet weather.

Problems associated with groundwater

Groundwater quality Groundwater quality may vary. Sometimes the water contains dissolved minerals from rocks. Usually, however, bacteria and sediment are filtered out by percolation as water trickles down through pore spaces and cracks. However, groundwater quality can be damaged by human activities. The seepage of agricultural chemicals into groundwater can raise nitrates to harmful levels. Pesticide and herbicide residues can also enter groundwater. Toxic waste from landfill sites is another source of pollution, as is the disposal of mining waste. In urban areas, toxic materials such as chemicals or the overflow from poorly maintained septic tanks may enter groundwater. (See Figure 7.4.) In addition, the natural percolation of water into the ground is reduced because of the large area of concrete surfaces. As a result, groundwater levels can fall.

The contamination of groundwater is made worse by the fact that the water moves so slowly. Unlike rivers, which flush out quickly, groundwater may remain contaminated for centuries.

Figure 7.4 The effects of urbanization on evaporation, runoff, and groundwater

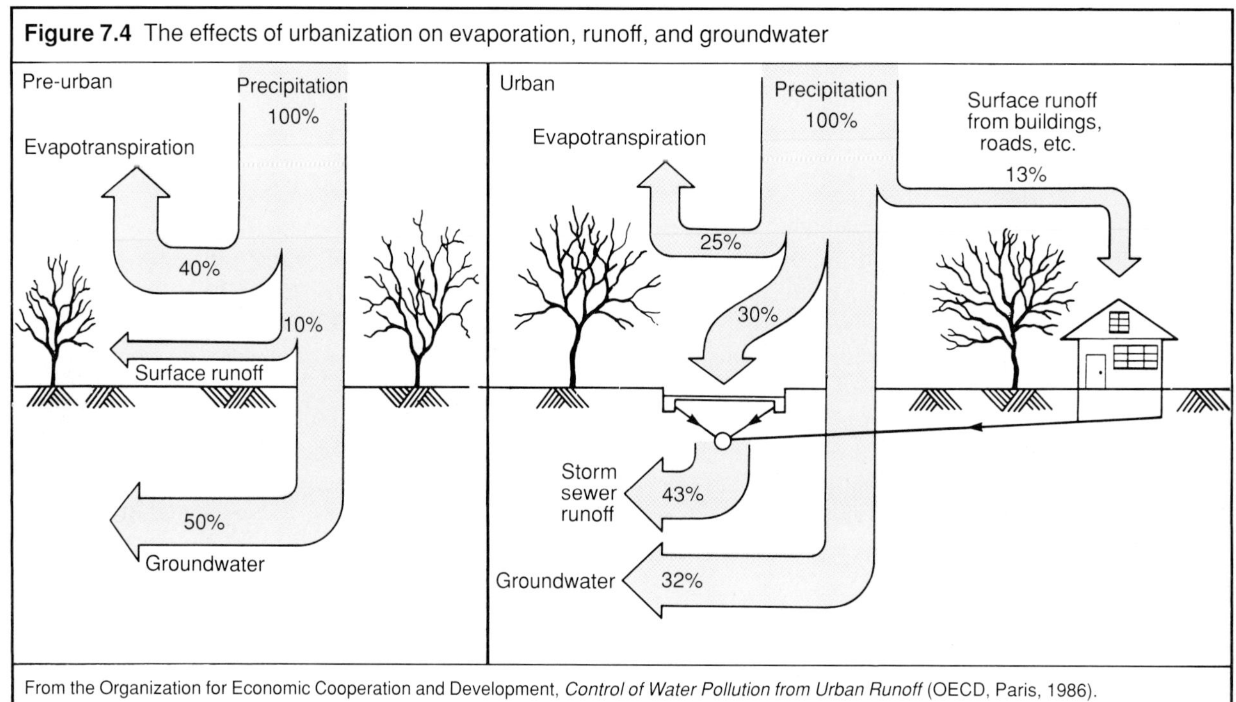

From the Organization for Economic Cooperation and Development, *Control of Water Pollution from Urban Runoff* (OECD, Paris, 1986).

Groundwater overdraft To maintain the flow of groundwater, it should not be used at a faster rate than it is replaced by natural processes. Otherwise a situation known as overdraft occurs. Many irrigation schemes fed by groundwater have lost their water supply for this reason. The famous Ogallala Aquifer in the southern Great Plains of the United States is being lowered by over 1 m each year. Pumping costs have increased and some farmers have run out of irrigation water.

Overuse of groundwater can cause other problems. The surface of the ground may subside if too much groundwater is taken. In southern California the overuse of groundwater has allowed sea water to move into aquifers left empty by pumping.

Groundwater surplus Groundwater can build up so that the ground becomes waterlogged. This has happened in the San Joaquin Valley, southern California's main irrigation area. So much irrigation water has been applied to the soil that slightly salty groundwater threatens to drown the roots of plants. A major drainage channel is needed to get rid of this surplus water, but the costs of construction are high.

Rising groundwater can also be a threat. In some European cities, including London and Liverpool in England, tunnels and basements are flooding due to rising water. This flooding has nothing to do with the rise in sea level predicted by global warming. It is caused by the decreased use of groundwater following the switch from traditional heavy industries to light, technology-based industries.

The Coachella Valley

The Coachella Valley in southern California illustrates the importance of groundwater. The resort town of Palm Springs and the adjacent settlements of Rancho Mirage, Palm Desert, and Indio lie in this arid valley. In the winter the population of the valley increases to almost 1 million people as tourists escape cold weather in other parts of the United States and Canada. Swimming pools, golf courses, and tennis courts are common all over the valley.

The entire built-up area of greater Palm Springs depends upon the use of groundwater. For example, to water a golf course may require up to 4 000 000 L of water a day. Fortunately, the valley is filled with deep, permeable gravel containing billions of litres of groundwater. Present use of water causes the water table to decline by about 1 mm per day, which gives the valley until about the year 2020 before serious shortages may occur.

This golf course in Desert Hot Springs, California, requires huge amounts of water to maintain its greenery.

The water authorities in the Coachella Valley are seeking to replace the groundwater by an ingenious method. Just west of Palm Springs, at the higher end of the valley, water is spread on a series of eighteen ponds. This water comes from the nearby Colorado Aqueduct, which brings water from Colorado to southern California. The water can be absorbed in the spreading ponds at a rate of about 1 m a day within each pond. The groundwater is topped up and gradually seeps down the valley. A number of such spreading sites exist throughout southern California.

Authorities in dry parts of the southwestern US also encourage people to use xerophytic plants in their gardens to reduce the need for watering.

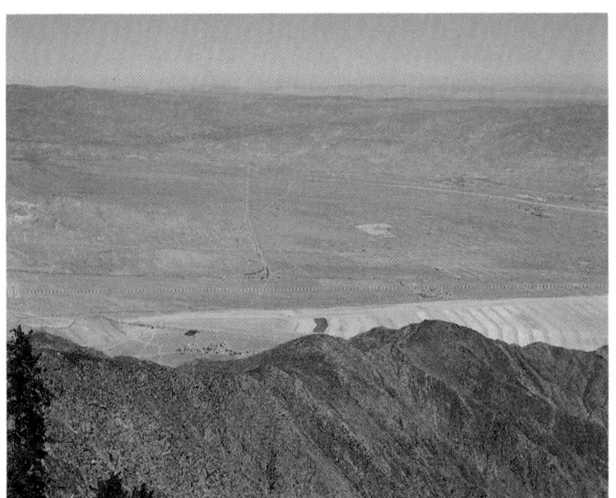

Irrigation

The idea of adding water to crops grown in dry areas is as old as history itself. Early civilizations in the Nile and Tigris/Euphrates valleys depended on irrigation. The Nile did part of the job for the Egyptians. Its annual flood renewed the fertility of the soil by depositing a layer of silt on the land.

Today about 215 000 000 ha of land are irrigated throughout the world. This is about 15 percent of world cropland, with a total production of 40 percent of all crops grown.

Irrigation accounts for about three-quarters of all water used in the world. Therefore it may contribute to water scarcity in many areas. In developing nations irrigation is also responsible for some serious environmental problems that affect both farming and human health.

Methods of irrigation

The most common method of irrigation is **surface irrigation**, which uses systems of ditches and canals to direct water to the fields. The water is allowed to flow over the land through gaps in the small walls, or **bunds**, which surround the fields. Surface irrigation accounts for about 96 percent of all irrigation.

LEFT These spreading ponds near Palm Springs, California, allow groundwater to be recharged.

BELOW This surface irrigation of corn uses siphons from a feeder canal.

Land is irrigated by sprinkler in Libya.

Sprinkler irrigation accounts for nearly all of the remaining 4 percent of irrigated land. The most common method is the use of pipes with sprinkler heads. These pipes are often mounted in large wheels for easier movement. **Pivot irrigation** is another form of sprinkler irrigation. The sprinkler is in the form of a long boom that rotates around a central pivot. This method is efficient, but it irrigates only circular areas. In North America where the land has been divided into squares, pivot irrigation does not easily supply the corners of the squares with water.

Yet another method, which is still uncommon, is **drip irrigation**. Water is dripped from pipes to the roots of the plants at controlled spots. This method is well suited to tree crops, such as those in the Okanagan Valley of British Columbia.

Environmental problems resulting from irrigation

Some serious environmental problems are associated with irrigation mainly in the developing world. An estimated 500 000 ha of irrigated land are turned into desert each year. Irrigation, which should be part of the solution to world hunger, has in some areas become part of the problem. Irrigation is also a major consumer of global water.

Salinization All water contains some dissolved salts, as do most types of soil. The problem is most acute in areas where river water contains a higher than normal amount of salt. A buildup of surface salt can occur if the water first soaks into the soil then comes back to the surface by **capillary action**. As the water evaporates, the salts remain behind, as shown in Figure 7.5 (a). The FAO estimates that about half of the world's 215 000 000 ha of irrigated land suffers some degree of salinization, with 25 000 000 ha no longer suitable for production. The Indus Valley of Pakistan has suffered severe salinization. From the air,

Figure 7.5 The salt problem in irrigation and how it can be solved

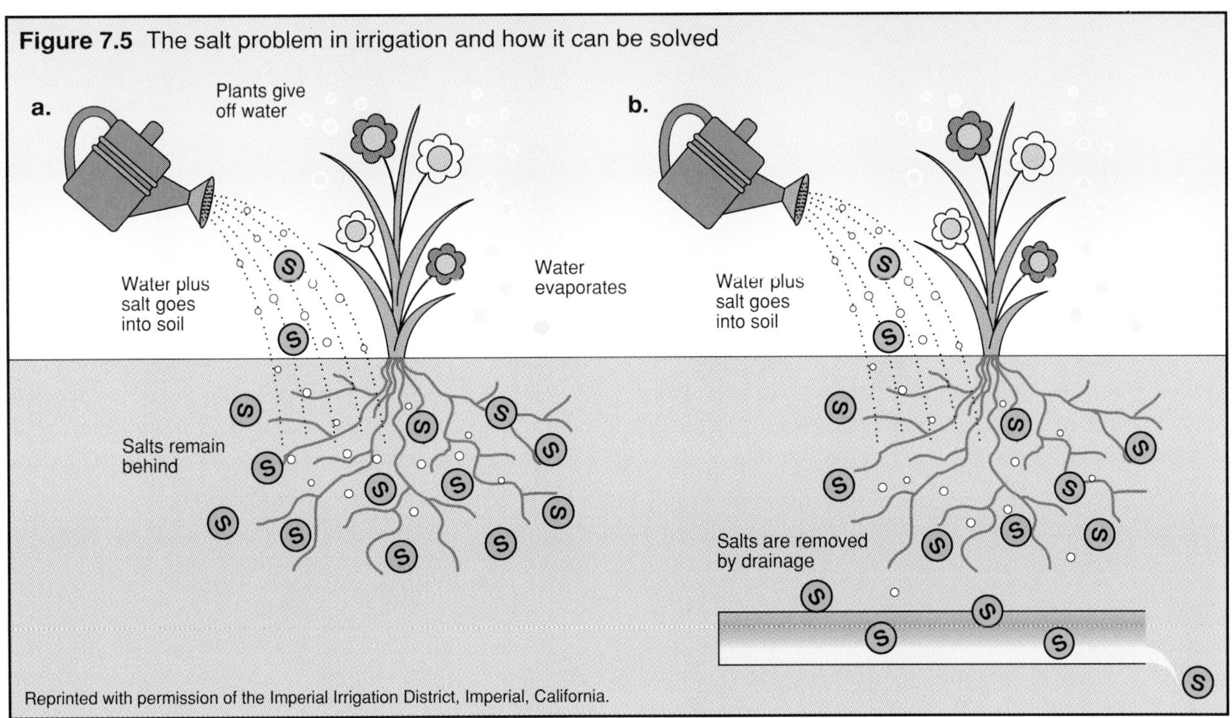
a.
Plants give off water
Water plus salt goes into soil
Water evaporates
Salts remain behind
b.
Water plus salt goes into soil
Salts are removed by drainage

Reprinted with permission of the Imperial Irrigation District, Imperial, California.

large tracts of land appear to be covered with a white crust.

This problem can be corrected by constructing deep tile drains. Figure 7.5(b) shows that salts can be carried away if some of the irrigation water is drained off underground rather than allowed to evaporate from the surface. The Imperial Valley of California is gradually reducing the salt content of its soils by this method.

Damage to fisheries Irrigation can cause damage to fisheries. Irrigation dams tend to trap silt, greatly reducing the flow of plant nutrients downstream. The fisheries in the Sea of Azov in Russia and Ukraine, for example, have been affected by the overuse of water from the Don and Kuban rivers. From 250 000 t a year, the catch in the Sea of Azov has been reduced to almost zero. Fishing near the Nile delta has been hard hit by the loss of nutrients from the silt that is now trapped behind the Aswan Dam.

Overuse of pesticides Irrigation water leads to an increase in insect pests. The warm, stagnant water provides a breeding environment for many kinds of insects, such as mosquitoes, that would not survive in dry climates. An increase in irrigation normally precedes a rise in the use of pesticides, with harmful effects on farmers and consumers.

Health problems Several diseases are closely associated with irrigation in warm climates. The most common is **bilharzia**. This disease is caused by parasites in the human body. These parasites depend on surface water during part of their life cycle. The spread of irrigation has created many dams and other areas of surface water in fields and ditches. As a result, the number of cases of bilharzia has increased in irrigated areas. It is a disease of the poor, who must walk or bathe in slow-moving lakes or canals. The disease can be treated and controlled with medication. Most importantly, however, people must be enabled to build and use sanitation facilities and persuaded not to walk barefoot in irrigated fields or swim in rivers or ponds.

Other parasites, such as the hookworm, live in the surface water provided by irrigation. Water also carries bacteria and viruses as well as parasites.

Malaria is the best known water-related disease. About 150 million cases of malaria, leading to 1 million deaths, are recorded each year. The anopheles mosquito, which acts as the **vector** or carrier, breeds in the shallow, stagnant water found in reservoirs, pools, and badly maintained irrigation canals. Careful irrigation methods that avoid the creation of stagnant water could lead to a reduction of this problem.

River basins

A **river basin** may be defined as the land drained by a single river and its tributaries. River basins are best regarded in terms of river systems and the surrounding land. Like other systems, river basins consist of many elements, most of which are interrelated. For example, the vegetation cover and soils play a vital part in the hydrological cycle.

From Figure 7.6(a) you can see that the actions that people take in the upstream section of a river basin affect people living downstream. For example, if farmers in the upper basin plough the land up and down the slope, soil erosion may be accelerated. This leads to the silting of rivers, causing floods and impeding navigation. Fertilizers from farms may also lead to eutrophication in rivers, and herbicides and pesticides may affect river life.

These problems will only get worse unless measures to control the river basin are introduced. (Some possibilities are shown in Figure 7.6[b]). These improvements may be made by the people themselves if they see that they will receive some of the benefits. However, costly improvements that help only people farther down the river basin will most likely have to be imposed by governments.

Dividing the waters

Some river basins are very large and have waters flowing through several provinces or states. Many flow through two or more countries. The Colorado River, for example, flows through six states of the United States before finishing its course in Mexico.

Several issues arise when rivers cross political boundaries. First, do upstream users have the right to use as much water as they wish? If not, how should the rights to water use be divided? Second, how can upstream users of water be prevented from polluting it for downstream users? The answers to these questions may create complex legal disputes. In the case of the Colorado River, these questions were resolved only in 1963 after half a century of arguments among the six states and Mexico. Still, no one is completely satisfied with the decisions that were made. The Colorado is a river of limited flow in an area of rapid economic development. Its waters will always be at a premium. Therefore the river will likely remain a source of dispute.

The Columbia River flows through both British Columbia and the state of Washington. Its waters are governed by the Columbia River Treaty of 1964. By this treaty the United States received permission to build dams that created lakes extending into Canada.

In return Canada gained financial compensation.

Other examples of actions that affect people farther downstream include the building of the W.A.C. Bennett Dam on the Peace River in British Columbia. When the dam was completed in 1968 the downstream flow pattern of the Peace River was changed. Wildlife habitats in the Athabasca delta have been harmed as a result.

Figure 7.6 River basin management—before and after

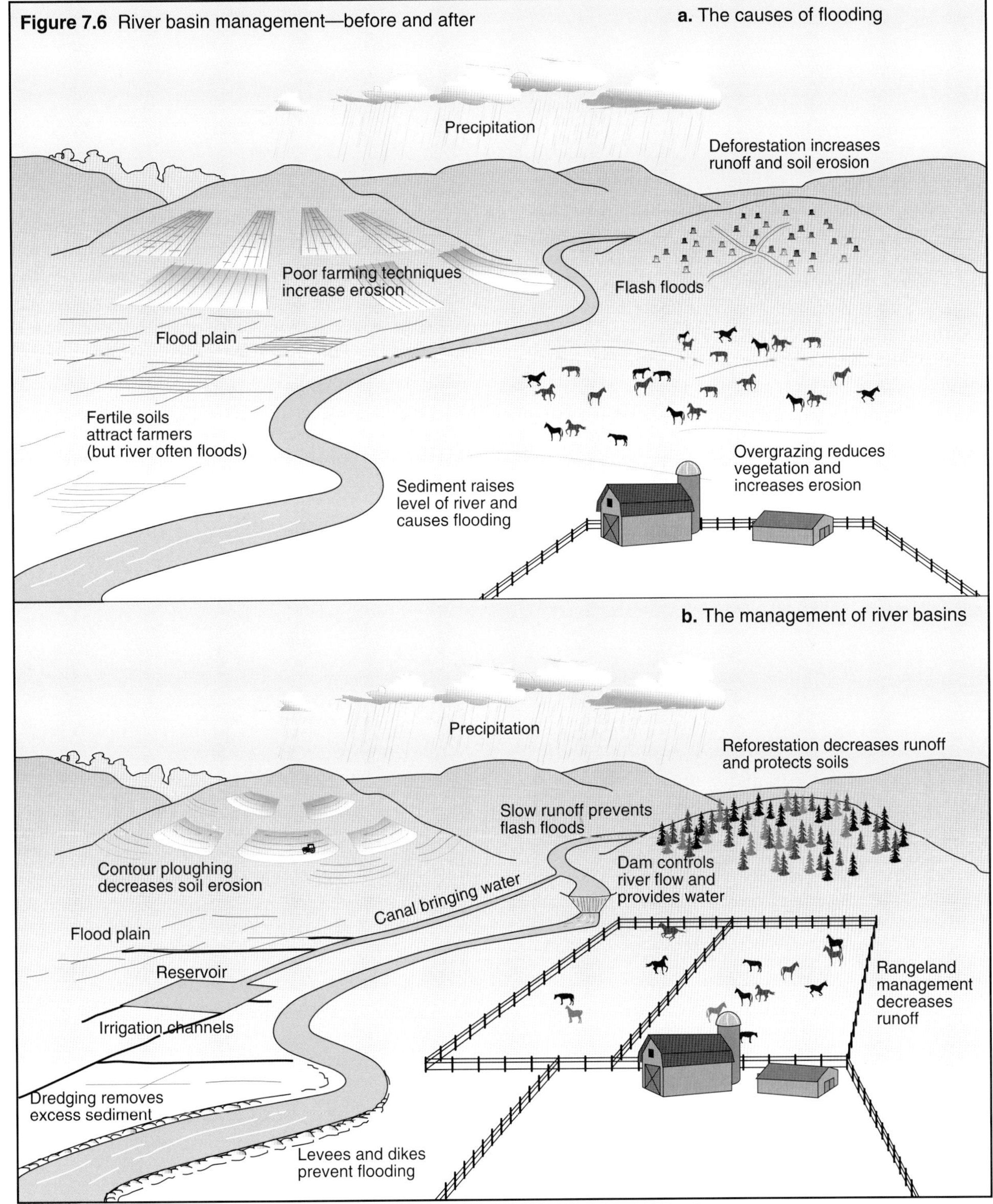
a. The causes of flooding
Precipitation
Deforestation increases runoff and soil erosion
Poor farming techniques increase erosion
Flash floods
Flood plain
Fertile soils attract farmers (but river often floods)
Sediment raises level of river and causes flooding
Overgrazing reduces vegetation and increases erosion
b. The management of river basins
Precipitation
Reforestation decreases runoff and protects soils
Slow runoff prevents flash floods
Contour ploughing decreases soil erosion
Dam controls river flow and provides water
Canal bringing water
Flood plain
Reservoir
Irrigation channels
Rangeland management decreases runoff
Dredging removes excess sediment
Levees and dikes prevent flooding

River diversions

Throughout the world rivers are being diverted from one drainage basin to another. Normally the purpose is to enlarge the flow of a river to increase hydroelectric power or provide extra water for irrigation.

River diversions are costly and raise some serious environmental issues. For example, the diversion of water out of river basins may lead to a loss of water in lakes or in the ground. The transfer of water from one river basin to another may result in the introduction of life forms that can upset the ecosystem.

In Manitoba the upper Churchill River has been diverted into the Nelson River by the construction of a dam and diversion channel. Large-scale diversions are a part of La Grande River scheme for greater water control in Québec. California has two major projects, the Central Valley Project (CVP) and State Water Project (SWP). Both bring surplus water from northern California. The CVP irrigates the arid San Joaquin Valley, while the SWP brings water to southern California.

North American diversion proposals

North America has had its share of large-scale river diversion plans. The now defunct NAWAPA scheme (North America Water and Power Alliance) planned to divert water from northern Canada as far south as California and Mexico. This scheme would have been costly, requiring enormous amounts of energy. It might also have been politically unacceptable in Canada to make a commitment to sell large volumes of water to the United States over a long period of time. Another proposal was the building of a dam across the entrance to James Bay. Water would have been diverted not only to the Great Lakes and St. Lawrence regions but also to the dry southwestern area of the US. The environmental impact of large schemes such as these would be enormous.

Small-scale diversions also create possible environmental issues. In the 1980s Manitoba successfully opposed an extension of the Garrison Dam irrigation scheme in North Dakota, using the provisions of the 1909 Boundary Waters Treaty which governs the quality of water flowing between the United States and Canada. The proposed extension would have caused water from the Missouri River to drain into the Red River system. The danger was that foreign life forms could enter the Red River system, upsetting the ecosystem and, therefore, the fishing industry in Lake Winnipeg.

Figure 7.7 How the Aral Sea has shrunk

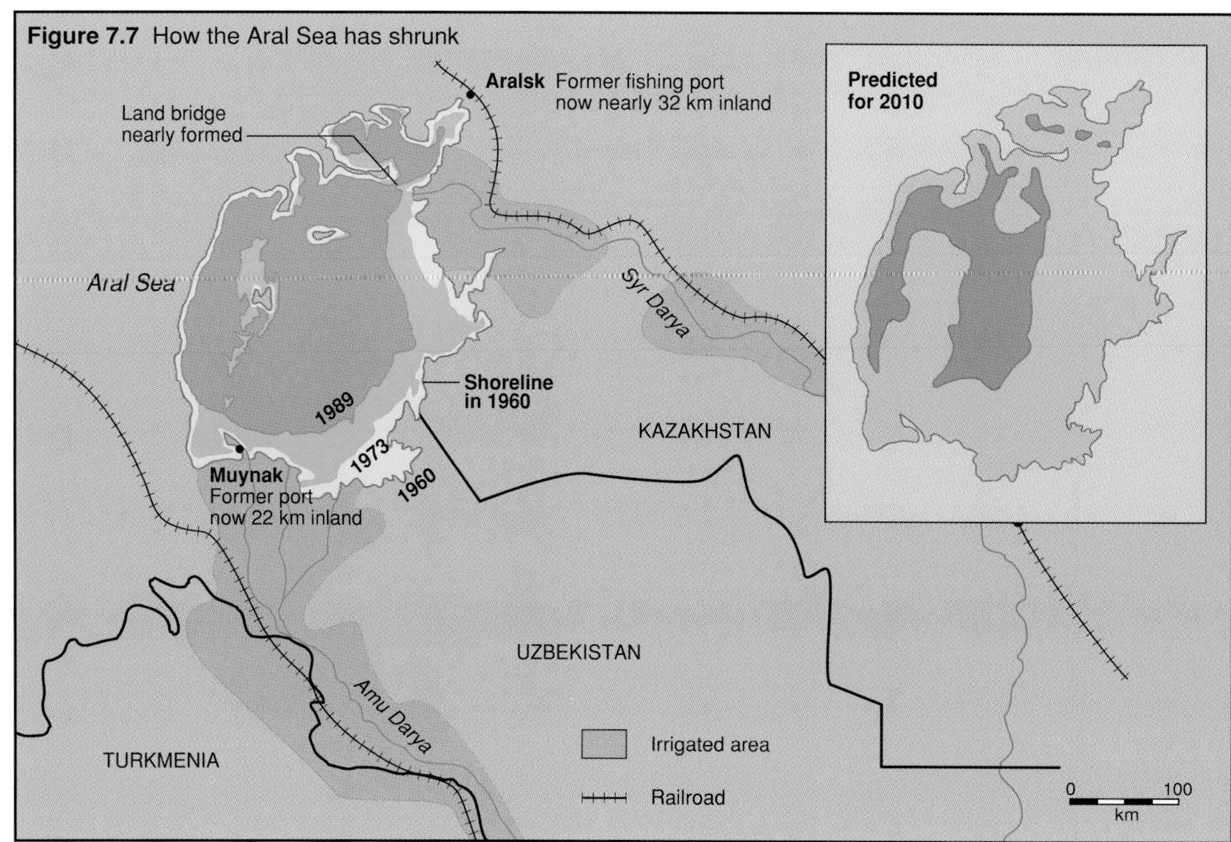

River diversions in the former Soviet Union

The Aral Sea East of the Caspian Sea in the dry lands of central Asia lies the fourth largest lake in the world. (See Figure 7.7.) At least that was true in 1960 when the Aral Sea was a 66 000 km^2 body of freshwater. It was fed by the waters of the Syr Darya and Amu Darya rivers. The Aral Sea supported a fishing industry, providing a good living to people in ports such as Aralsk.

Soviet planners decided to construct the 1300 km Kara Kum Canal from the Amu Darya to irrigate the cotton fields of Uzbekistan. Since the canal was completed in the 1960s, the Amu Darya has dwindled to a trickle. The Syr Darya is also utilized for irrigation. In twenty years the level of the Aral Sea dropped by 13 m. The shoreline has moved as much as 60 km away from the fishing ports, leaving the landscape strewn with rusting hulks. The volume of the Aral Sea has shrunk by about 75 percent.

The environmental effects of the shrinking of the Aral Sea have been devastating. It is rapidly becoming salty and losing its fish life. To keep local workers employed, a local fish canning factory now processes fish from the Pacific coast thousands of kilometres away. An area of 36 000 km^2 around the lake has become an arid, salty wasteland. The climate of the whole region is drying out and becoming colder in winter because the shrunken volume of the Aral Sea can no longer retain as much summer warmth. Above all, the health of the population is suffering. Many people have been poisoned by the overuse of pesticides and other toxic chemicals. Eighty percent of all women suffer from anaemia. Doctors report some of the world's highest rates of disease among children and infant mortality rates as high as those in the poorest regions of Africa. The damage to the Aral Sea region is surely too high a price to pay for the diversion of river waters for irrigation.

Other Soviet proposals Soviet planners proposed a 2500 km canal to divert water from the Ob and Irtysh rivers in the north to the deserts of central Asia. This plan was shelved for economic reasons, although ecologists had long opposed it because it could lead to reduced salinity in the Arctic Ocean and a melting of part of the polar ice cap. Some ecologists fear that global climate patterns would be changed.

Another plan is to divert the Pechora River into the Kama and Volga rivers. The objective would be to provide further irrigation water in the south and to stabilize the Caspian Sea, which has been shrinking rapidly because of irrigation. The environmental costs would be enormous, with 6000 km^2 of farmland flooded.

The Great Lakes system

The five Great Lakes and their connecting rivers make up the greatest inland waterway system in the world. (See Figure 7.8.) They contain no less than 18 percent of the world's freshwater; only the world's ice caps contain more. Thirty-six million people, including 25 percent of all Canadians, live within the Great Lakes drainage basin. Many of them obtain their drinking water from the Great Lakes. Each of the lakes, except Lake Michigan, is shared by the United States and Canada, making an international agreement on their management necessary. The Boundary Waters Treaty of 1909 between the US and Canada set up an **International Joint Commission** to resolve water-related disputes between the two countries.

Each of the Great Lakes has unique properties. For example, Lake Superior is the largest and deepest, containing more water than the other four lakes combined. It is the coldest and the least affected by pollution. Lake Erie, on the other hand, contains the least water. It is the shallowest and warms most quickly in summer. It suffers most from pollution, but has one compensating advantage: its water changes on average every 2.6 years, compared with the 191 years for Lake Superior. Lake Ontario is the smallest lake in area, but its depth gives it over three times the volume of Lake Erie.

Fighting pollution in the Great Lakes

Since the beginning of the twentieth century, economic development in North America has centred on the Great Lakes region, particularly on Lakes Erie, Michigan, and Ontario. Pollution did not become a serious problem until the 1950s when it was found that Lake Erie was suffering from algal blooms and oxygen depletion. DDT residue was also found to be building up in the lake, affecting the reproduction of wildlife. On all of the Great Lakes, floating debris and oil slicks were creating unpleasant conditions. Ships routinely dumped wastes and cleaned their bilges into the lakes, resulting in the closure of many public beaches for health reasons. Although antipollution laws had been in place since the beginning of the century, the fines were trivial and the laws were often not enforced. It was not until the damage to the lakes was fully recognized that ships were banned from their polluting practices.

Concern over the deteriorating water quality in the Great Lakes, and in particular in Lake Erie, led to government action to control pollution. The first **Great Lakes Water Quality Agreement** (GLWQA) between Canada and the United States was reached in

Figure 7.8 Status of Remedial Action Plans for the Great Lakes, 1995

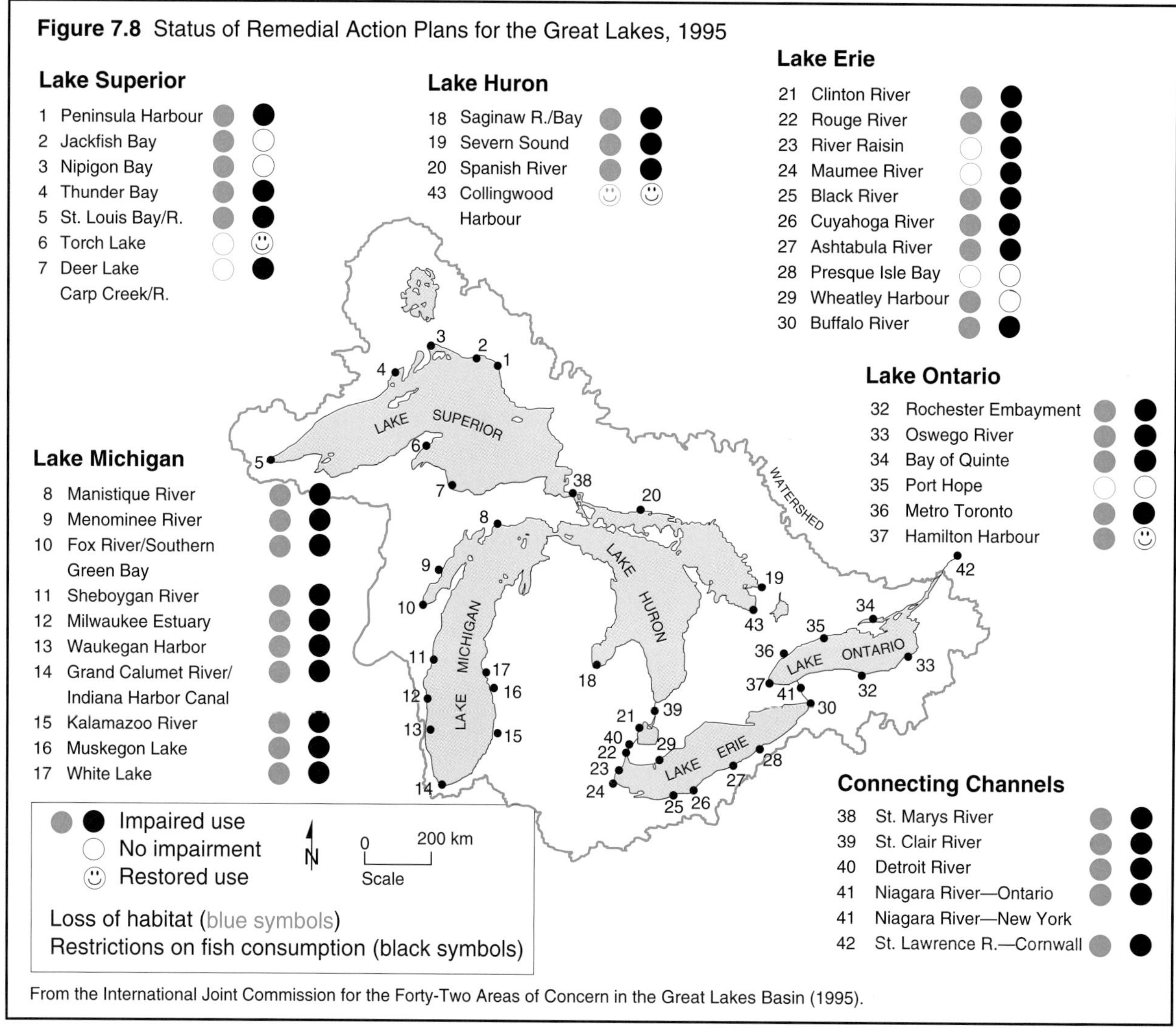

From the International Joint Commission for the Forty-Two Areas of Concern in the Great Lakes Basin (1995).

1972. The emphasis of this agreement was on reducing the visible aspects of pollution.

A major effort was made to reduce the amount of phosphates in the lakes. The volume of phosphates entering and leaving the lakes was studied and target loads were set based on what the lakes' ecosystems could absorb. Since 1972 the volume of phosphates entering the Great Lakes has been reduced by 80 to 90 percent, mainly by upgrading sewage treatment plants. Today more and more household detergents are phosphate free. Some US states have banned phosphates altogether. The problem of eutrophication has improved to the point that phosphate levels are no longer the main problem in any of the Great Lakes. The lakes have become visibly cleaner and some beaches have reopened. Increasing research into the problems of the lakes, however, has proved that some of the more serious aspects of pollution are invisible.

A deadly chemical mix

By the 1980s the Great Lakes contained 460 toxic chemicals, many of which are deadly to humans even in very small quantities. New terms began to appear in newspaper reports and television documentaries—dioxins, furans, mirex, and PCBs. Water from the Great Lakes may look clean, but it often contains potentially dangerous amounts of these chemicals. Moreover, the chemicals build up in food chains, creating a serious threat to wildlife. Research conducted in the 1980s shows an increase in both infertility and birth defects in birds. More young birds are hatching with club feet, eye abnormalities, and missing organs—possibly due to the effects of PCBs. Another chemical, DDT, prevents the intake of calcium, which causes affected birds to lay eggs with brittle shells that may break prematurely.

The chemical mix also creates the serious problem of providing safe drinking water for the millions of people surrounding the Great Lakes. Water obtained from the Great Lakes is treated thoroughly and tests show it to be of high quality and quite safe for drinking. Nevertheless, the fact that tiny quantities of toxic chemicals may still remain in tap water persuades many people to buy bottled water. Ironically, however, many brands of bottled water fare less well in chemical tests than tap water does.

The fishing industry is another casualty of chemical pollution since many species of fish contain toxic substances above safe limits. The *Guide to Eating Ontario Sport Fish* gives details of the condition of the fish found in Ontario's lakes. Fish in many lakes are listed as unsafe for children under fifteen years and women of childbearing age.

A further Great Lakes Water Quality Agreement was signed in 1978 and amended in 1983. Previous efforts to reduce eutrophication were continued, but a new ecosystem approach was applied to the lakes as the best means of counteracting the effects of toxic chemicals. An enormous amount of work remains to be done to clean up the many sources of pollution. The forty-two worst spots for pollution on the Great Lakes system have been identified by the International Joint Commission. (See Figure 7.8.) Remedial Action Plans (RAPs) have been drawn up. Two targeted areas are the St. Clair and Detroit rivers and the Niagara River at the opposite end of Lake Erie. Hamilton Harbour and Toronto Harbourfront also have Remedial Action Plans.

Environmental "hot spots"

The St. Clair and Detroit rivers Many manufacturing industries are located on the St. Clair and Detroit rivers on both sides of the international boundary. Originally, the rivers were noted for sparkling clean water. By the 1950s the Detroit River received increasing volumes of chemicals and sewage. Across the river is the industrialized Canadian city of Windsor. Upstream is Ontario's major oil refining and petrochemical city, Sarnia, in an area known as "Chemical Valley."

In the 1960s, 5 billion litres of industrial waste water and 2 billion litres of sewage were poured into the Detroit River each day. Virtually all kinds of heavy metals and organic chemicals combined with human waste to make the river habitable only to the hardiest forms of wildlife. The industrial effluent also warmed the water, thus upsetting plant and fish life. The river had become an ecological disaster area. *The Detroit News* described the pollution as equivalent to 157 box cars per day dumping their lethal contents into the river. Perhaps the only river in the United States with a worse reputation was the Cuyahoga River in Cleveland, Ohio, where in June 1969 the pollutants on the water actually caught fire.

Most of the pollutants in the Detroit River went directly downstream into Lake Erie, Lake Ontario, and the St. Lawrence River. But some remained as sludge along the banks and in stagnant lagoons and creeks.

Over two decades later the river remains an environmental black spot, but progress has been made. Detroit has spent $345 million (US) to recycle waste. Local industries have spent a further $400 million (US) on waste reduction. Detroit has fourteen incinerators with clean air scrubbers, although residents of Windsor, across the river, experience some smell from the stacks.

Detroit claims to be in the forefront of large cities in the United States in terms of waste disposal and treatment. The city takes pride in the improvements already made to the quality of the Detroit River, although the western end of Lake Erie still suffers from eutrophication. Improvements are also being made along the Ontario side of the St. Clair and Detroit rivers, but a great deal remains to be done. In the mid-1980s a large "chemical blob" was identified on the bottom of the St. Clair River below Sarnia. A major cleanup was necessary. *The Detroit News* pointed out in 1989 that 11 000 Ontario industries were still dumping chemicals into municipal sewage systems.

The Niagara River Rumours had been circulating for some time of a larger than normal number of nervous disorders and birth defects in the Niagara Falls area. In the late 1970s the rumours became reality when several chemical dumps close to the Niagara River were analysed and were found to be dangerous. Figure 7.9 shows the location of a few of the more than 100 dumps.

The most infamous dump is the Love Canal on the American side of the river. This was a 1 km long by 20 m wide abandoned canal site, bought by the Hooker Chemical Company in 1942 to dispose of chemical wastes. It was bought by the Niagara Falls Board of Education for $1 in 1953 and became part of a residential development. A number of birth defects and other unexpected illnesses were observed among the people whose homes were built on or beside the chemical dump. A health emergency was declared in 1978 and 239 homes were evacuated and destroyed. Meanwhile the dump was sealed from the surface. In

1980 the government offered to buy a further 564 homes. Following years of remediation most of these houses have been resold and occupied. However the Love Canal controversy continues.

The dump sites along the Niagara River from Buffalo to below the falls are known to contain dioxins, PCBs, and mirex. The problem is that the chemicals cannot be contained within the dump sites. Rainwater leaches the chemicals into the underlying bedrock. In the Niagara Falls area the rocks are sedimentary, with sandstone, shale, and limestone. The groundwater has become charged with chemicals, which in some places visibly trickle from the sides of the Niagara Gorge into the river. Enough dioxins exist in these dumps to poison Lake Ontario. Chemical residues from farther up the Great Lakes system also pass downstream through the Niagara River into Lake Ontario.

The chemical companies claim that their responsibility is only to line the dumps, which they have done since 1980. Ultimately, the only solution to the problem is the complete removal of the dumps. However, this would cost billions of dollars and governments have been unwilling or unable to pay. As a result, another problem is created, known as the **NIMBY (Not In My Back Yard) syndrome.** Few landowners in North America want toxic chemicals to be disposed of on or near their property. As a result, many dump sites chosen by the Ontario Waste Management Commission have been rejected because of public pressure even though they have been assessed as suitable. Developing countries, which used to accept toxic cargoes for a price, also now reject them for both political and environmental reasons.

Figure 7.9 Toxic waste sites on the Niagara River

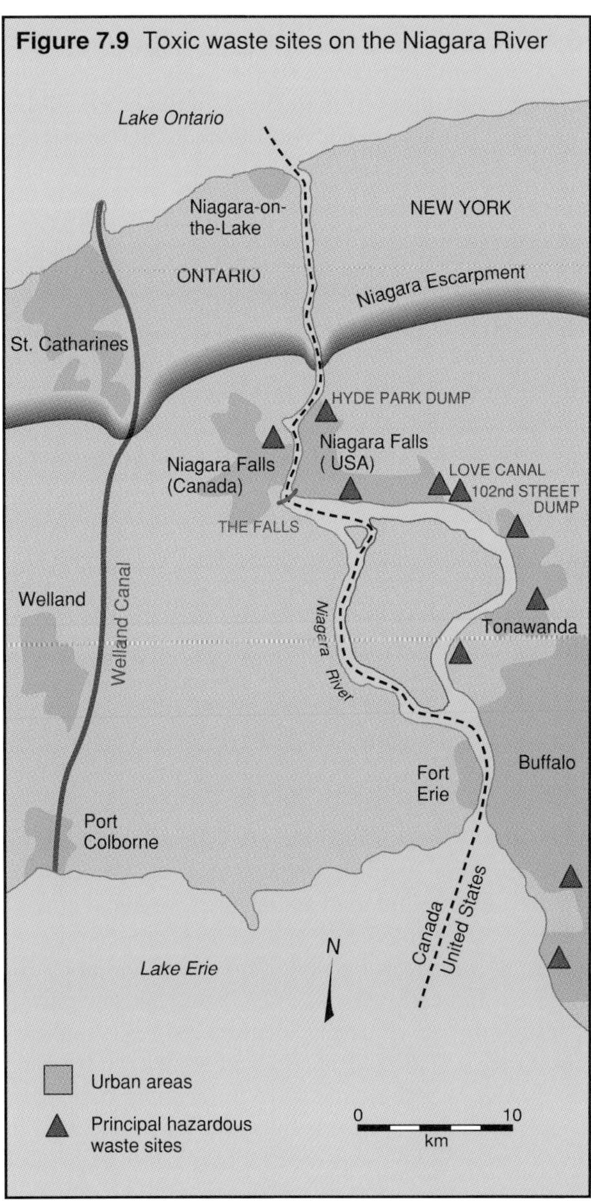

Hamilton Harbour Few water bodies in Canada have experienced greater pollution problems than Hamilton Harbour. The harbour is an almost-enclosed triangular body of water, 494 km^2 in area, at the western end of Lake Ontario. The Burlington Canal provides the only access to the harbour. Hamilton is the site of Canada's two largest steel-producing firms, Dofasco and Stelco. The harbour receives waste from these industries, as well as sewage from over 500 000 people. The steelworks are responsible for high concentrations of ammonia in the harbour, while high levels of phosphorus and nitrogen cause eutrophication.

With such small access to Lake Ontario, the harbour was in urgent need of a cleanup. The treatment of sewage and industrial waste had been under way since 1970, and the water quality had already

These homes were abandoned in the Love Canal residential development in Niagara Falls, USA.

improved by the time a Remedial Action Plan was proposed in 1988. The RAP is being coordinated by Environment Canada and Environment Ontario. Measures being taken include further reducing the volume of ammonia and other chemicals entering the harbour, improving sewage treatment, and creating shoreline habitats for fish and wildlife. Some bird life has already returned to the harbour area.

The St. Lawrence River The St. Lawrence is Canada's most important river. It carries 10 000 ships each year and generates large quantities of hydroelectric power. Millions of Canadians and Americans draw their drinking water from the river.

The St. Lawrence faced a severe environmental crisis in the late 1980s. The river had received little protection through pollution control other than efforts to reduce phosphate levels. Over 2000 companies were pouring effluent into the river from Québec alone. The river was also receiving contaminated run-off from farms and large amounts of untreated sewage. The sediment on the river bottom, like the St. Clair River, is known to be heavily contaminated. The pollutants in the St Lawrence are clearly visible in a satellite photograph.

The St. Lawrence is the home of many kinds of wildlife, including beluga whales. Analysis of dead whales shows that they contain many toxic chemicals at levels several times higher than safety limits. Their bodies are, in fact, toxic waste! Several varieties of birds, fish, and marine mammals in the St. Lawrence are facing extinction.

A St. Lawrence action plan was drawn up in 1988. It aims to reduce by 90 percent the volume of toxic wastes entering the river from the fifty biggest polluting companies by 1993. Sewage treatment has also been made a priority.

Another ever-present threat to the river is the danger of an oil spill or a collision of ships carrying toxic cargoes. Such disasters could have devastating effects on wildlife. In addition, the cleanup after such an accident would be difficult. Current technology works only in slow-moving water and the centre of the St. Lawrence flows at 5 to 7 knots.

The St. Lawrence River enters Lake St. Peter through a delta. Pollutants entering it can be seen on this satellite image.

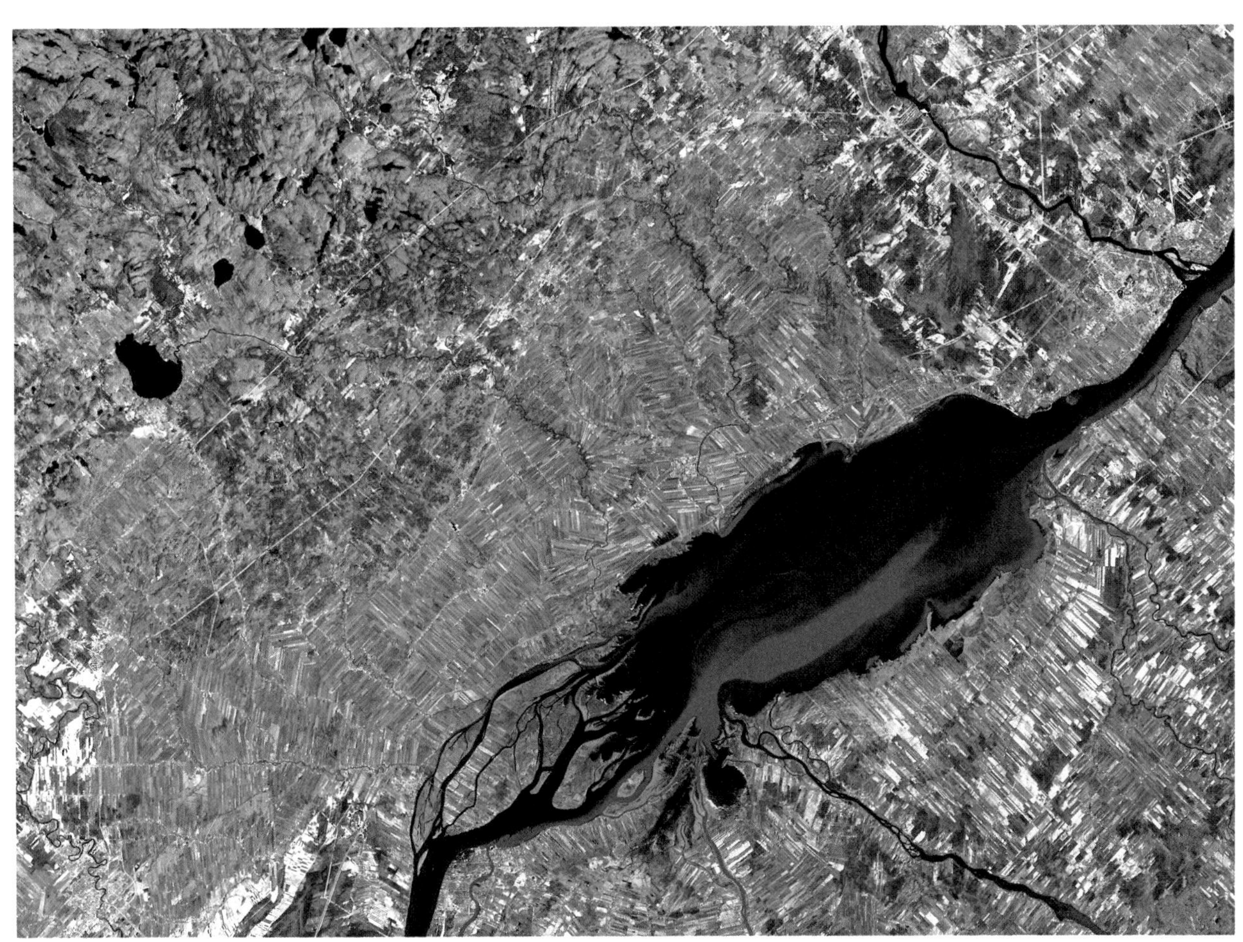

The oceans

The oceans play a vital role in the earth's ecosystem. They regulate world temperatures, provide moisture for the hydrological cycle, and absorb minerals and materials washed down from the land. The oceans also provide a "sink" for carbon dioxide by absorbing it from the air. It is estimated that the **phytoplankton** (microscopic plants) on the surface of ocean waters produce more than one-quarter of all the earth's oxygen. As many as 20 million organisms can live in 1 L of sea water.

Critical parts of the oceans

We should not think of the oceans as one single enormous body of water. Perhaps 90 percent of ocean water lies well under the surface and away from the land. Human beings do not have much contact with this water, except for the passage of ships travelling between continents. Much more important to us are the extremities of the oceans. These include the shallow areas on the **continental shelves**, as well as coastal bays, estuaries, and lagoons. These areas are commonly used for fishing and recreation. The shallow parts of the oceans also receive enormous volumes of waste, particularly sewage and chemical effluent.

The **microlayer** or top millimetre of the entire area of the oceans is of vital importance to the marine environment. It contains many of the eggs, larvae, and adults of tiny marine creatures. They are visible if you look closely at the surface of ocean or lake water on a calm day. With a microscope you can see that the top layer is teeming with life. But the microlayer also receives the entire burden of atmospheric pollutants that settle on the oceans. Half the zinc, cadmium, lead, and mercury that reach the oceans do so through the air. So also do radioactive materials such as plutonium. The microlayer is also vulnerable to oil slicks or other liquids that spread on surface water.

How badly polluted are the oceans?

Some alarming signs show that oceanic pollution is widespread. Surface currents, tides, and winds ensure that pollutants move around. DDT and other pesticides, for example, have been found in Antarctic penguins thousands of kilometres from the source of the pollution. Pollutants may enter the oceans from rivers, from the atmosphere, or by direct discharge from ships and coastal factories.

Although traces of toxic chemicals can be found in the open oceans, scientists feel that pollution problems have not yet seriously affected these areas. The world's oceans as a whole are closely monitored by a United Nations group known as GESAMP (Group of Experts on the Scientific Aspects of Marine Pollution).

Enclosed bodies of water are extremely vulnerable to pollution, however. The Mediterranean and Baltic seas, for example, have more serious pollution problems because they have small links with the open oceans but receive wastes from densely populated areas. About 25 percent of Mediterranean beaches are unfit for bathing at some times during the tourist season. Venice and the northern Adriatic Sea are badly affected by algal blooms. Although algae have been recorded in the northern Adriatic since Roman times, the recent plague of yellowish-brown slime is caused by pollution from the Po River. The Po receives raw sewage from 15 million people plus the waste products of a major part of Italy's farming and industry. The Mediterranean region has had an action plan since 1975, but its pollution problems still pose a serious threat to the environment. Figure 7.10 shows the types of pollution associated with the world's coastal waters and partially enclosed seas.

The North Sea The North Sea is a shallow body of water surrounded by high concentrations of population and industry. Figure 7.11 shows the main sources of pollution affecting the North Sea. Toxic chemicals, sewage, and fertilizers all enter the sea in large quantities, including 1 500 000 t of nitrogen and 100 000 t of phosphorus, mainly from agricultural sources. The toxic chemicals include PCBs, heavy metals, and organic compounds.

A great deal of pollution enters the North Sea from rivers, such as the Rhine and the Thames. West Germany's rivers alone contributed an estimated 1048 t of lead and 1795 t of cadmium in 1986. Chemical wastes are burned at sea in specially designed incinerator ships, and large oil slicks on the surface of the sea are common. It is estimated that almost 500 000 sea birds die each year in the North Sea from contamination by toxic chemicals or oil spills.

In 1987 the North Sea suffered three serious environmental blows. A type of single-celled alga, stimulated by chemical fertilizers from Scandinavia, formed a slick 10 km wide. It washed along the coasts of Sweden and Norway, killing millions of fish. At about the same time a mysterious virus killed thousands of seals on the shores of Denmark and the United Kingdom. Finally, overfishing of the sand eel in northern Europe was blamed for a drastic decline in many species of marine birds, including divers, puffins, and arctic terns. The North Sea also received an estimated 5 t of PCBs from the tragic explosion on the Piper Alpha oil platform in 1988.

Figure 7.10 Sources of marine pollution around the world

POLLUTANTS	NORTH SEA	MEDITERRANEAN SEA	INDIAN OCEAN	SOUTHEAST PACIFIC OCEAN	NORTH ATLANTIC OCEAN	NORTH PACIFIC OCEAN	CARIBBEAN SEA	SOUTH ATLANTIC OCEAN	SOUTH PACIFIC OCEAN
Agricultural pesticides and fertilizers, runoff		■	■	■	■	■			
Food and beverage processing	■	■			■	■	■	■	■
Industries, chemical	■	■			■	■			
Industries, metal	■	■			■	■		■	
Industries, petrochemical	■	■			■	■	■		
Mining		■		■	■	■			■
Petroleum, drilling	■			■	■	■	■	■	■
Petroleum, transportation	■	■	■	■	■	■	■	■	
Pulp and paper manufacturing					■	■			
Radioactive wastes	■	■	■		■	■		■	
Sea-salt extraction			■				■		
Sewage	■	■	■	■	■	■	■	■	■
Sewage sludge, dumping	■				■	■			
Silt from coastal development			■	■			■		
Thermal sources			■		■	■	■	■	

Adapted from *Global Atlas*, Gage Educational Publishing (1993, 1991).

The cleanup of the North Sea will take years. Some progress has been made in reducing the load of contaminants brought in by rivers, especially from Britain. A North Sea conference has been set up to coordinate efforts to reduce pollutants. The conference has urged the International Maritime Organization to make the North Sea a "special area" (like the Baltic and Mediterranean seas). International agreements to improve the world's oceans have been relatively ineffective. The United Nations succeeded in passing the Law of the Sea Convention (LOSC) in 1982, though still without the important signatures of the United States and the United Kingdom.

The 1989 Alaskan oil spill Many of the world's mineral resources, such as oil, are found in remote areas far from the populated centres where they are consumed. As a result, millions of tonnes of crude oil must travel the world's oceans in large supertankers.

When large reserves of oil were found on the north coast of Alaska in 1968, the possibility of using large tankers was considered. An American company successfully navigated the SS *Manhattan* to the icy waters of Prudhoe Bay. However, when the Canadian government, fearful of an oil spill, declared sovereignty over Arctic waters, it eliminated this option.

To bring the Alaskan reserves to the oil-hungry US

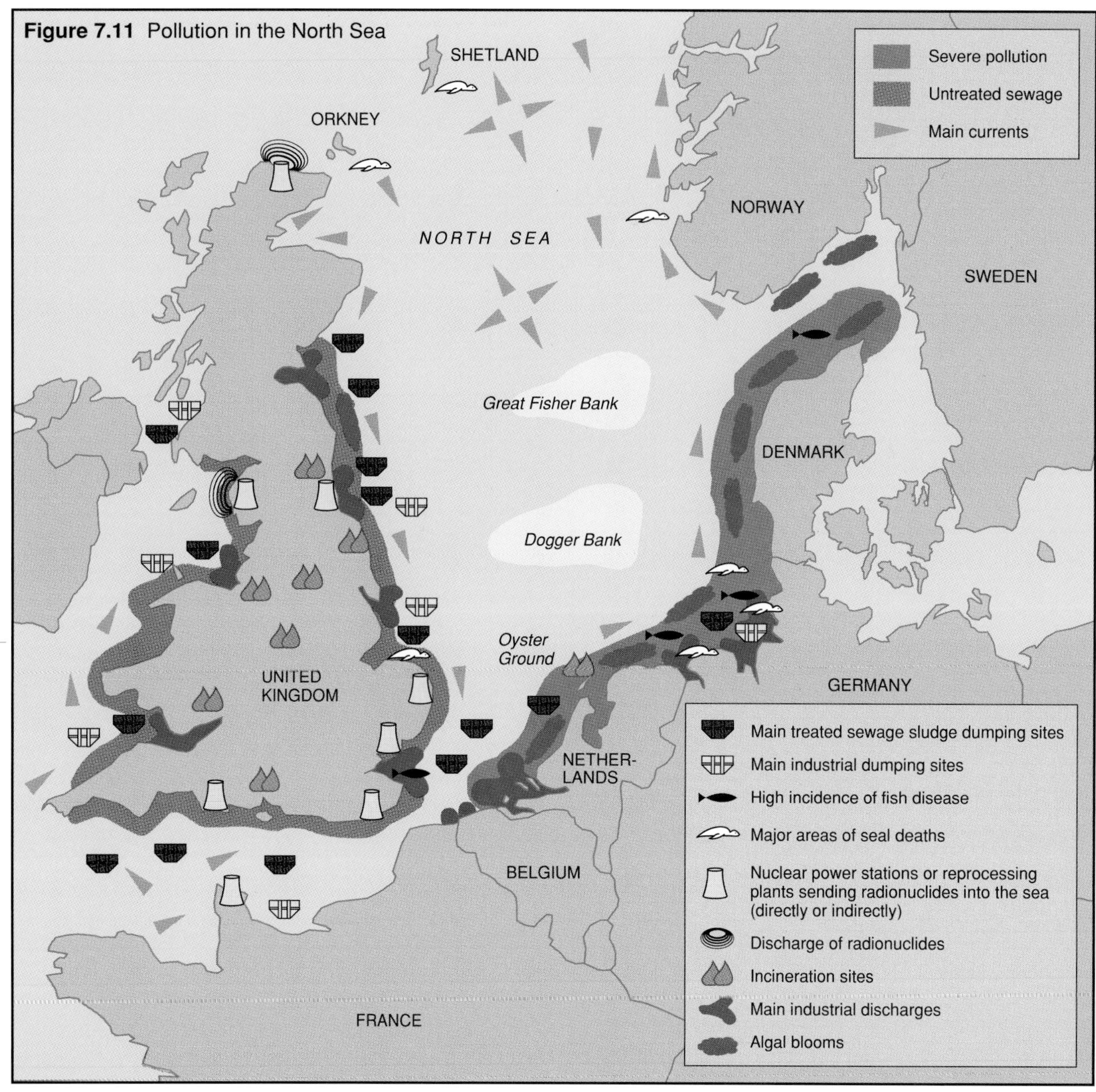

Figure 7.11 Pollution in the North Sea

market, an oil pipeline was constructed across the easily damaged Alaskan tundra to the ice-free port of Valdez in the south. This project, the largest engineering feat achieved to date, took several years of court cases and mountains of reports before permission to build it was granted. From Valdez, tankers carry the oil to the west coast of the United States. For years tankers had docked safely at Valdez, navigating stormy waters filled with fish, whales, and sea birds. On 24 March 1989, however, disaster struck. (See Figure 7.12.) The *Exxon Valdez*, with a full cargo of Alaskan crude oil, ran aground at the entrance to Prince William Sound.

Crude oil floats on the surface of water, at the mercy of winds, tides, and currents. The heavier parts of the oil form a tar-like substance that takes years to break down. Heavy oil from the *Arrow* tanker spill in 1970 at Chedabucto Bay, Nova Scotia, was still visible twenty years later. The wind may also whip oil and water into a brown foam, known in the industry as "chocolate mousse." It is difficult to remove after it comes ashore. Oil spills have a devastating effect on marine life, especially on sea birds. They also affect the local fishing industry and spoil tourist beaches.

Those who appreciate nature inevitably feel upset when they see the effects of oil spills on birds and other creatures. Reporter Richard Nelson, writing for the *Los Angeles Times*, described the scene a few days after the massive oil slick hit the beaches of Alaska.

> And then I found a bird, hiding among the kelp and boulders just above the tide. A western grebe, big as a mallard, long-necked, with a slender needle beak, half submerged in a puddle of mixed oil and water.
>
> She stared up at me, blinking bright red eyes, the one part that still seemed fully alive. Caught in the bird's unwavering gaze, I could not escape my own feelings of guilt.
>
> Each day I am haunted by images of birds setting their wings to land in the morass of crude. And I think of sea otters, those clever and energetic creatures who add such brightness to my days, crawling out to drape themselves on oil-soaked rocks and await a slow death. Prince William Sound has become a killing ground, filled with thousands of animals, each one another story like the doomed grebe.
>
> From "When Civilization Ran Aground Aboard the Oil Tanker in Alaska." Copyright © 1989 by Richard Nelson. First published in *The Los Angeles Times*, "Opinion," 9 April 1989.

In the six months following the *Exxon Valdez* disaster, Exxon spent $1.3 billion (US) on cleanup operations. But it is impossible to remove all the effects of the oil spill. Even the chemicals used in the cleanup persist in the environment, causing problems for marine life.

We all use oil in hundreds of different ways. If we did not, tankers would not need to navigate narrow channels in all kinds of weather to bring it to us. When we ran short of oil in 1979 and 1980, some people behaved as though the end of the world had come. We do not appear ready to give up the economic benefits

Birds and animals were victims of the Alaskan oil slick.

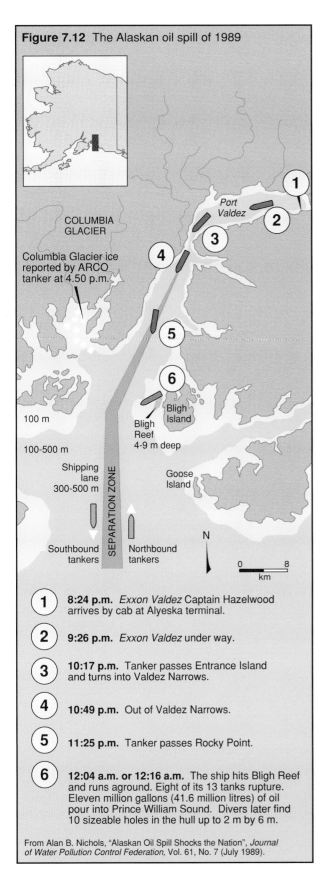

Figure 7.12 The Alaskan oil spill of 1989

1. **8:24 p.m.** *Exxon Valdez* Captain Hazelwood arrives by cab at Alyeska terminal.
2. **9:26 p.m.** *Exxon Valdez* under way.
3. **10:17 p.m.** Tanker passes Entrance Island and turns into Valdez Narrows.
4. **10:49 p.m.** Out of Valdez Narrows.
5. **11:25 p.m.** Tanker passes Rocky Point.
6. **12:04 a.m. or 12:16 a.m.** The ship hits Bligh Reef and runs aground. Eight of its 13 tanks rupture. Eleven million gallons (41.6 million litres) of oil pour into Prince William Sound. Divers later find 10 sizeable holes in the hull up to 2 m by 6 m.

From Alan B. Nichols, "Alaskan Oil Spill Shocks the Nation", *Journal of Water Pollution Control Federation,* Vol. 61, No. 7 (July 1989).

that oil consumption brings, including the thousands of articles made by the petrochemical industry. Richard Nelson says:

> Ultimately, you and I must accept our share of the blame—as members of a society that understood the risks and judged them acceptable. A society that valued convenience and monetary gain above the security of its own environment. A society that placed nature outside the sphere of ethical concern and moral restraint.
>
> And who will pay for the Prince William Sound disaster? You and I. We will cover the cost to government when we pay taxes. We will cover the cost to the oil industry when we buy fuel or anything made with petroleum products. The notion that someone else will pay is an illusion.
>
> From "When Civilization Ran Aground Aboard the Oil Tanker in Alaska." Copyright © 1989 by Richard Nelson. First published in *The Los Angeles Times*, "Opinion," 9 April 1989.

Accidents such as the *Exxon Valdez* are easily blamed on the negligence of a person or company. But is this blame justified? Mistakes are inevitable, and improved procedures can reduce the risks involved. But the environment ends up paying the price for the constant supply of resources we demand.

Hostilities between nations can create even greater disasters. The oil slick released into the Persian Gulf in January 1991 during the Gulf War was estimated to be twelve times the size of the disaster in Prince William Sound.

Harvesting the seas

The coastal zones of the oceans provide about 90 percent of the world's catch of fish. These are the zones that are also most intensively used for recreation and waste disposal. The shallow continental shelves in the northern Atlantic and Pacific oceans provide the largest catches.

The world catch of fish has risen dramatically, as shown in Figure 7.13. According to the FAO, the current total of about 80 000 000 t is the maximum that the earth's oceans can sustain. In some places the catch is well beyond the **sustained yield**, or long-term ability of the ocean to provide fish. The result is that catches are falling in areas such as the Grand Banks off eastern Canada and the "cod basket" near the Lofoten Islands in Norway.

Rising world population puts great pressure on marine resources. In Japan and in developing countries where populations are rising rapidly, over half the population obtains 40 percent of its animal protein from fish. The demand for fish has also increased because of the trend toward eating foods that help to lower cholesterol levels.

Figure 7.13 World fish catch (millions of tonnes)

REGION	1960 – 1964	1970 – 1974	1980 – 1984	1985 – 1988	1989 – 1994
North Atlantic	11.2	15.1	14.2	13.6	13.1
Central Atlantic	2.8	5.6	7.1	7.3	6.9
South Atlantic	1.8	3.6	3.7	4.4	3.5
North Pacific	10.6	16.9	23.0	28.8	28.0
Central Pacific	2.3	5.1	7.0	8.4	9.8
South Pacific	7.1	8.3	8.3	13.4	16.2
Indian Ocean	1.7	2.8	4.4	5.6	7.0
Antarctic	0.0	0.2	0.5	0.4	0.3
Freshwater	4.3	6.4	8.7	12.5	16.4
World total	41.7	64.0	77.0	94.7	101.3

From Food and Agriculture Organization of the United Nations.

The rise in the fish catch throughout the world has been the result of improved fishing techniques, not an increase in the supply of fish. Improved technology, including long-range trawlers and sonar systems for tracking fish, has made finding and catching fish much easier. According to Dr. Leslie Harris, president of Memorial University in Newfoundland, "We have underestimated our own capacity to find, to pursue, and to kill."

Examples of overfishing

The Grand Banks and the Scotian Shelf The Grand Banks and the Scotian Shelf off the coast of eastern Canada are overfished. (See Figure 7.14.) Much of the fishing in the Grand Banks is by offshore draggers that tow a large bag along the ocean bottom. Smaller vessels work the inshore fisheries, catching cod on their annual migration as well as flounder, crabs, scallops, and lobsters.

Before 1977, when Canada declared a 370 km (200 nautical mile) fishing zone, the fishing vessels of about twenty nations had greatly reduced the fish stocks. High interest rates and low catches reduced much of the industry to bankruptcy in the early 1980s. With the help of a quota system and government reorganization, good times returned to the fishing industry in the late 1980s.

In late 1988, however, scientists announced that their estimates of the fish stocks on the Grand Banks had been much too high. The cod quota was cut sharply, as the inset in Figure 7.14 shows. Yet even the quota of 188 000 t for 1991 was too high to allow the fish stocks to recover and the quota was cut to zero in

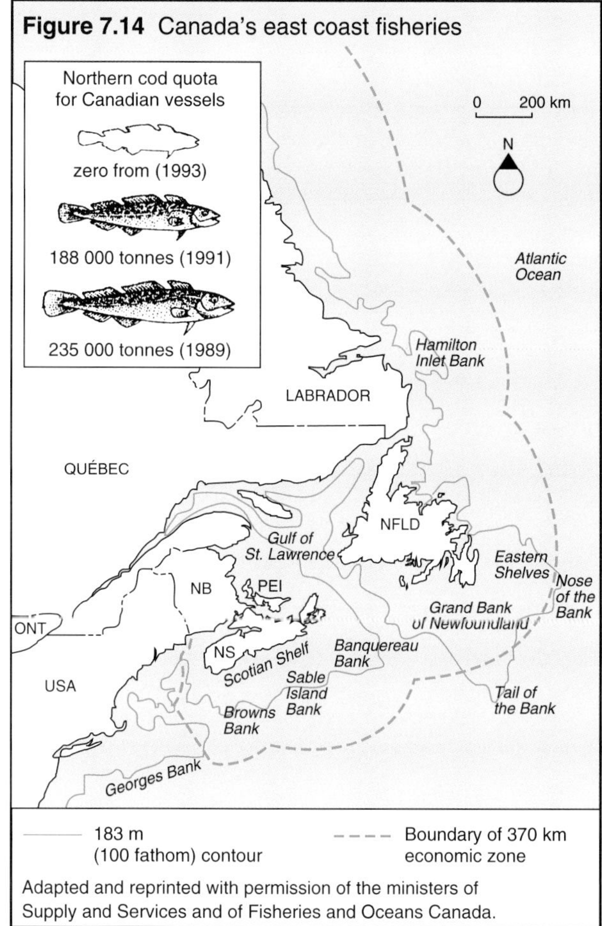

Figure 7.14 Canada's east coast fisheries

Adapted and reprinted with permission of the ministers of Supply and Services and of Fisheries and Oceans Canada.

1993 . The inshore quota for the Scotian Shelf has also been reduced. (See also Figure 11.5.)

The practice of dragging creates the problem of catching fish that are too small to be used. Much of this bycatch of small or unwanted fish has to be thrown back dead. The problem is described in *Canadian Geographic*:

> Draggers perfectly symbolize an unsound and uncaring approach to the fishery — and indeed to the environment at large. Scouring the ocean floor, the dragger indiscriminately captures big fish and small ones, spawning fish and juveniles, plants and lobsters, and rubber boots and tin cans along with the occasional skull or thighbone of a drowned sailor. Like the tree harvester and the dynamite stick, the dragger applies raw force to a complex and sensitive ecological system. The fishery may well be a symbol for the environmental predicaments we face on many fronts.

© Silver Donald Cameron/*Canadian Geographic*. April-May 1990.

Peru A famous case of overfishing was the anchovy fishing industry off the coast of Peru in the early 1970s. Large volumes of anchovy lived off the nutrients in water welling up from the depths of the Pacific. Millions of sea birds, in turn, lived off the anchovy. The birds created thick deposits of **guano** on rocky islands, a resource that was in great demand as a fertilizer. After a few years of frantic fishing, the anchovy stock was almost wiped out. With it went the sea birds and the deposits of guano. The ecosystem lost its productive capacity and many people lost their livelihood. The cause of this disaster was the desire to make a quick profit without regard for the environment.

Driftnet fishing

Driftnet fishing was pioneered by the United Nations to help people in poor countries. But it has turned into the greatest threat facing marine life today. Driftnetting has been described as a marine "wall of death." Nets, up to 50 km long and 8 m deep, are suspended from the surface in the open ocean mainly to catch squid. However, they catch everything in their path, including dolphins (an endangered species), seals, and whales. Sometimes nets are cut adrift, leading to "ghost fishing." The abandoned nets continue to catch fish until they sink under the weight of dead fish. The technique is also used at river mouths to catch fish as they enter the river to spawn.

Driftnetting is widely practised in the Pacific Ocean by people in Japan, Taiwan, and Korea. Many countries, including the United States and Canada, are making great efforts to put an end to the practice. Their opposition is not on purely environmental grounds, however. Driftnetting also threatens North American salmon runs since many salmon are caught during their ocean migration.

Aquaculture

The term aquaculture means "farming the waters" and includes a variety of techniques and products, some of which are shown in Figure 7.15. Aquaculture has been practised for centuries in several parts of the world. Since the mid-1970s it has been growing rapidly in many countries. There are two reasons for the increased production from aquaculture — a larger demand for healthy food and the increasing difficulty of catching wild stocks. Fish farming is one of the most efficient ways of producing protein-rich food.

In freshwater, aquaculture schemes range from small village fishponds, which provide an important protein supplement in many developing countries, to large-scale industrial operations. These may produce trout or catfish for gourmet foods or be used to enhance sport fishing by stocking lakes and rivers.

Fishponds are widely used in south China to supplement agriculture. The elements of a fishpond ecosystem are linked by material and energy flows, as shown in Figure 7.16. The dikes that surround the ponds are used to grow mulberry and sugar cane. Mulberry leaves are used to feed silkworms. In this productive, but artificial, ecosystem all materials are used, including human waste.

Saltwater schemes include the production of salmon and other fish as well as shrimp and lobsters. Also produced are many varieties of shellfish such as abalone, oysters, clams, and mussels. High prices for all of these species can make the considerable investment worthwhile. In some parts of the world, especially in Japan, varieties of seaweed are farmed for food such as nori.

The sheltered **fiord** coasts of Norway, Scotland, and British Columbia provide good sites for aquaculture. A combination of fresh- and saltwater is involved in the operation of salmon hatcheries. Salmon eggs are collected, fertilized, incubated, and hatched. The fry are fed until they are large enough to fend for themselves. The fish then feed in the ocean for two or more years, returning to their birthplace to spawn, when they may be harvested.

The application of genetics to aquaculture may improve the growth rate, taste, and disease resistance of the products. Aquaculture has the potential to be a tremendous food resource, but not without some environmental risks. The high density of fish in most schemes leads to high concentrations of waste products. Another concern is that crowded conditions will lead to an increased risk of diseases, which may then spread to wild fish populations.

Figure 7.15 A model of aquaculture

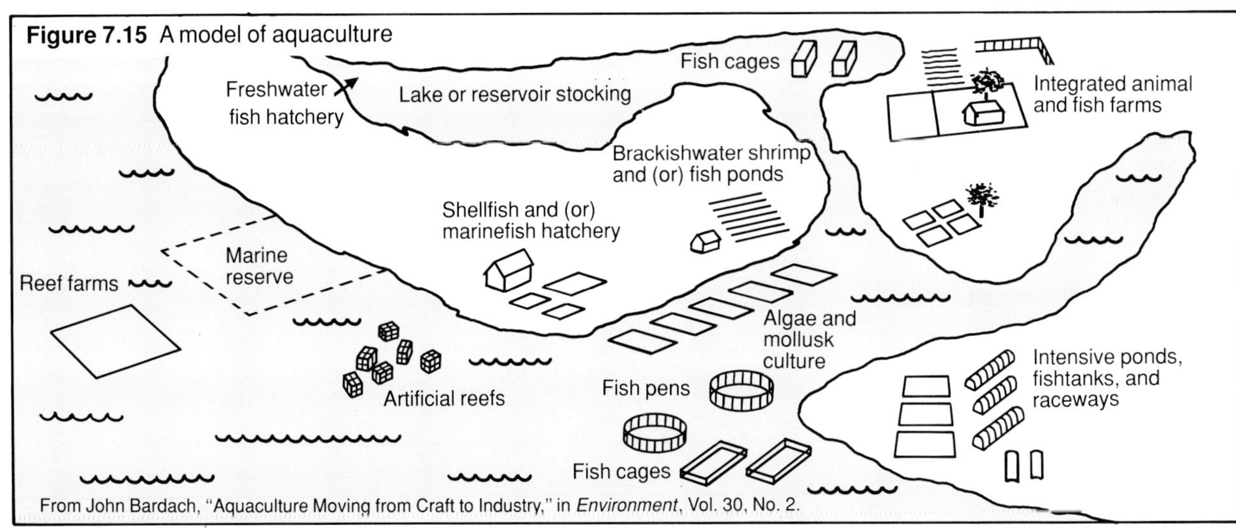

From John Bardach, "Aquaculture Moving from Craft to Industry," in *Environment*, Vol. 30, No. 2.

Figure 7.16 A Chinese fishpond ecosystem

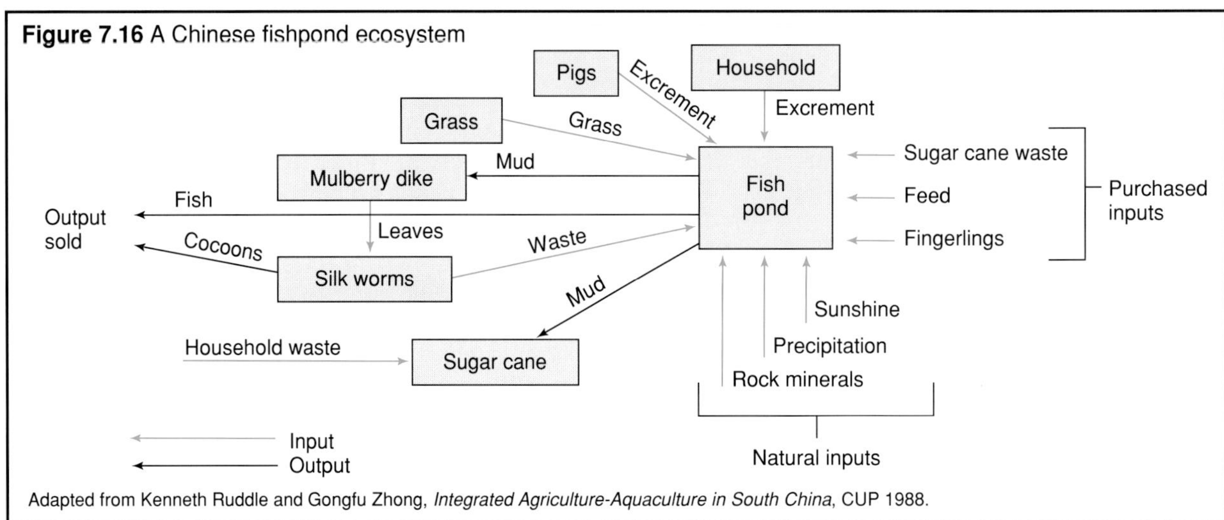

Adapted from Kenneth Ruddle and Gongfu Zhong, *Integrated Agriculture-Aquaculture in South China*, CUP 1988.

Looking back

1. If rivers and streams contain only 0.01 percent of freshwater resources, why are they so important?
2. (a) Describe the importance of groundwater in the hydrological cycle.
   (b) List four ways that groundwater may be polluted by human activity.
3. What special problems arise when determining how to use the water of rivers that cross international boundaries?
4. Explain why drainage is necessary in areas where irrigation water is used.
5. Give reasons why:
   (a) Lake Erie has been the most seriously polluted of the Great Lakes; and
   (b) the cleanup of contaminated areas such as the Niagara River is so difficult.
6. Why is the microlayer of the ocean so important?
7. Which regions have shown the greatest percentage increase in fish caught since the 1950s? (See Figure 7.13.) What problems do these increases cause?

Applying your knowledge

1. Analyse Figures 7.3 and 4.1 to determine in which biomes the greatest water deficiencies are found. Develop a list of the environmental problems that are most likely in areas with low precipitation.
2. Create an organizer that compares the types of river pollution that could come from each of the following: (a) farms, (b) homes, and (c) factories.
3. (a) Using Figure 7.6(a), list the causes and effects of flooding in river basins.
   (b) Using Figure 7.6(b), list the measures taken to control flooding in river basins.
   (c) For both (a) and (b), give Canadian examples.
4. Explain why the St. Lawrence River has the capacity to regenerate itself quickly.
5. Look at Figure 7.10. In a presentation of your own choosing, show which parts of the world's seas and oceans suffer from the greatest range of pollutants and why.
6. Examine Figure 7.16. Write a newspaper article highlighting the following:
   (a) how waste from humans, pigs, and silkworms raises the productivity of the fishpond ecosystem;
   (b) the inputs and outputs the system receives and produces; and
   (c) how nitrogen and carbon move through this ecosystem.

Extending your thinking

1. (a) For each country listed in Figure 7.17, divide the renewable water resources by the total population to get water resources per capita. Note that your answers will be in thousand cubic metres since there are 1 billion m^3 in 1 km^3.
   (b) List your answers in descending order of resources per capita. Divide the column into "water rich" and "water poor" countries.

Figure 7.17 Renewable water resources and population

COUNTRY	RENEWABLE WATER RESOURCES (KM^3 PER YEAR)	POPULATION IN 1993 (MILLIONS)
Brazil	5190	151.5
Former USSR	4384	292.0
Canada	2901	28.8
China	2800	1196.4
Indonesia	2530	189.1
USA	2478	258.2
India	1850	901.5
Bangladesh	1357	115.2
Norway	405	4.3
New Zealand	397	3.5
Australia	343	17.7
Panama	144	2.6
Kenya	14.8	28.1
Egypt	1.8	56.5
Libya	0.7	4.7

From the World Resources Institute and UN data.

2. Use your atlas to find the following:
   (a) two Canadian rivers that flow through more than one province;
   (b) two rivers (excluding the Colorado) that flow through more than one US state;
   (c) two rivers (other than the Columbia) that flow through more than one country.

   In each case, state a possible problem related to the allocation of the water supply.
3. Use a decision-making organizer to determine whether the benefits of transporting oil through coastal waters are worth the risks involved. Be sure to identify clearly the criteria you are using in your evaluation, including the effect they will have on how people receive their energy supplies.
4. The Aral and Caspian seas have been shrinking. Research the environmental results of the loss of these bodies of water. Present your findings from the point of view of people who live in these areas.

8 LAND

We have already looked at air and water as major themes in the environment. Air, water, and land are closely linked, as the hydrological cycle shows. In this chapter we shall deal with issues arising from how the earth's surface is used by the rapidly growing population.

As Mark Twain remarked, land is a good investment because it is not being made any more. The world contains about 131 000 000 km^2 of land. On the other hand, the world's population may well exceed 10 billion within half a century. That means that about 5 billion more people will be using the same area of land.

Land — the basic resource

Land provides us with several basic resources. The first, and most obvious, is the soil. This resource is the basis of both **arable** (crop) and **pastoral** (animal) farming. Soil is therefore an essential part of the system that provides most of the food for the human race.

Surprisingly, only about 11 percent of the world's land is used for growing crops. (See Figure 8.1.) The distribution of arable land can be seen by consulting an atlas. Large parts of the world, such as the tundra or the deserts, are unsuitable for growing crops because the climate is either too cold or too dry. Other parts, such as the world's main mountain ranges, are too rocky or too steeply sloping. Pasture lands occupy more space than crop lands, but these include arid areas, such as the range lands in the American west, where the climate is too dry for growing crops without irrigation.

Timber is another major resource in the modern world. Figure 8.1 shows that about 31 percent of the world's land surface is still forested, in spite of the massive destruction of forests in some parts of the world. The land also provides us with mineral resources, fossil fuels, and living space. Agriculture, forestry, mining, and urban land uses are the main human activities that affect the land.

Our need of space

We use land in a variety of ways. The most obvious use is farming, which provides most of our food. Land is also used by the manufacturing industry and by businesses. Transportation also accounts for more space than you may imagine. Over one-quarter of a North American city is likely to be occupied by roads and parking lots.

Residential land use, including gardens, takes up the greatest amount of space in a modern city. We all make individual demands on land. Each of us, wherever we are at any moment, occupies some of this limited land space. We need space for all our activities, whether at home, at school, or at recreation.

Most of us in Canada also like to have space around us and the chance to enjoy open countryside. Canadians identify with wilderness areas. Wildlife, such as beaver, bears, and moose, is a part of the environment. But some species of Canadian wildlife are threatened by human expansion into their habitat.

Figure 8.1 World land use

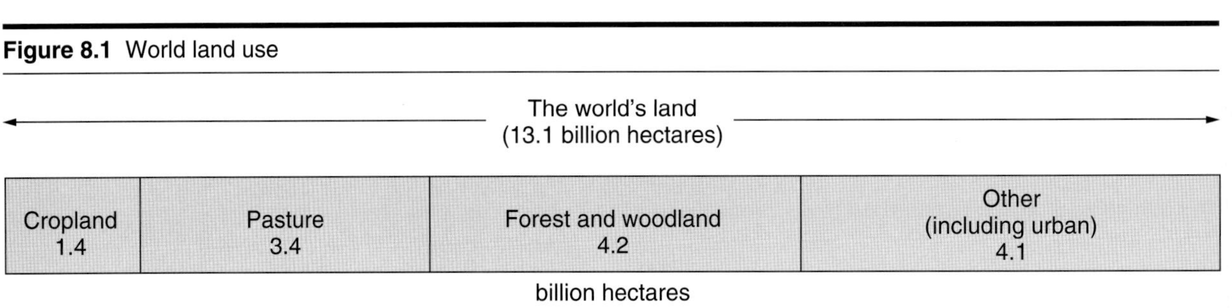

From the Food and Agriculture Organization, 1994.

Pressure on the land

Problems such as lost soil fertility and threatened wildlife are often caused by the demands of a growing population that lives on the land. If there is pressure on the land in Canada, where 30 million people occupy almost 10 000 000 km^2, consider what the pressure must be like in a country such as the Netherlands, where about 15 million people live on only 37 000 km^2. To be fair, of course, we must recognize that most of Canada's 30 million people live on a small proportion of the total land surface along the southern edge of the country.

About 75 percent of all Canadians are concentrated in cities. One-quarter of them live in and around the cities of Toronto and Montréal. Part of western Vancouver has a residential density of 24 000 people per km^2, four times the average population density of Hong Kong. High densities of people mean that large volumes of resources must be brought in to sustain the population. Good waste disposal facilities are also needed to get rid of the enormous amounts of waste.

The world's rising population can be sustained only so long as the soil can be made to produce higher yields of crops each year. In most parts of the world (Africa being a notable exception), the growth of food production has kept pace with population growth. The key question we must answer, however, is "Can farming and forest ecosystems be maintained while we try to gain ever larger amounts of food and resources from the land?"

Sustainable agriculture

Can agriculture meet the demands of a growing population without harming the environment? In this section we will examine the effects of the use of agricultural chemicals on the environment and discuss what alternative farming methods are available.

Chemicals in agriculture

One of the problems with agriculture in Western countries is its dependence on chemicals. This trend has been going on since the Second World War. Large amounts of fertilizers, pesticides, and herbicides are used on farms. The farming industry continues to see chemical products as essential for making profits. Chemical fertilizers can greatly increase crop yields, though they tend to break down the soil and make it more liable to erosion. Weeds can be controlled by selective weedkillers such as 2,4-D, which allows the growth of grain crops but kills weeds other than grasses. This product changed the way grain farming on the Prairies was carried out. Selective weedkillers made controlling weeds on fallow ground easier.

Consumer demand has encouraged farmers to use insecticides in large quantities. Customers want cosmetically attractive products, such as fruit without scabs or marks from insects. The use of pesticides makes the control of the appearance of farming products easier.

Several environmental problems are associated with the intensive use of chemicals in farming. The first is the seepage of nitrates, phosphates, and other materials into the ground. These chemicals enter groundwater and eventually reach rivers and oceans, causing problems of eutrophication and oxygen depletion. Pesticides also leach into groundwater. Residues of at least seventeen pesticides have been found in groundwater in half of the US states.

The second problem relates to the toxic nature of many of the chemicals used. The herbicide 2,4-D is now thought to increase the risk of cancer of the lymphoid glands. Organo-chlorides, such as DDT and dieldrin, also create health problems. They are slow to break down, and they remain in the environment for many years.

Figure 8.2 Pest species resistant to pesticides

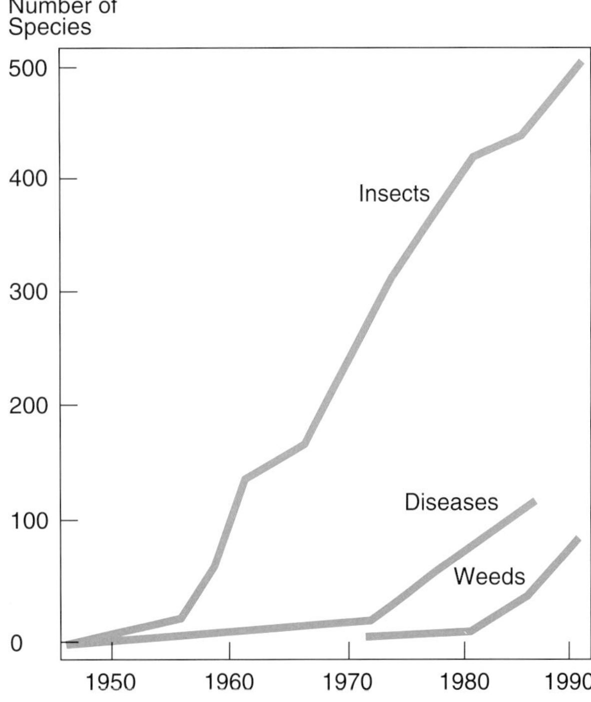

Adapted from "A Place for Pesticides?" by Peter Weber, *World Watch*, May/June 1992. Reprinted by permission of Worldwatch Institute.

The World Health Organization (WHO) estimates that there are 20 000 deaths and 1 million cases of pesticide poisoning every year. While most pesticides are relatively safe if used according to instructions, frequently they are applied carelessly or without proper equipment. In developing countries, for instance, people may not be able to afford protective clothing or the climate may be too hot to wear it.

Third, the use of pesticides and herbicides has serious effects on farming ecosystems. These chemicals are sprayed from tractors or from planes. They affect many species, not only the ones for which they are intended. A pesticide may kill virtually all insects, including those that play a useful role in the ecosystem. Pesticides may also kill the enemies of pests, thus removing a natural check to the growth of the pest population. Many insects are now developing resistance to pesticides. (See Figure 8.2.) This, in turn, leads to the development of new and more powerful chemicals to keep ahead of the pests. This effect is sometimes called the "pesticide treadmill." Evidence also shows that pesticides can change plant metabolism, making them more vulnerable to disease and further pest infestations.

Chemical fertilizers require both fossil fuels and minerals in their manufacture. When farmers use chemical fertilizers to maintain fertility, they are using **nonrenewable resources** (especially fossil fuels) to maintain the system of producing **renewable resources** (crops and animal products). Modern farming thus receives an energy subsidy from our limited reserves of fossil fuels. This subsidy shows that some forms of farming, especially animal farming, are inefficient ways of converting energy into food for people.

Farming can hardly be described as sustainable so long as it depends heavily on the use of fossil fuels and contributes to air pollution.

Integrated Pest Management

Integrated Pest Management is a group of pest control techniques aimed at reducing or eliminating the use of chemicals in farming. With IPM, pesticides are used only to cope with a visible pest outbreak and only when the value of the crop losses is greater than the cost of control. Farmers spray selectively, targeting the affected areas only.

Other IPM techniques, such as **biological control**, avoid the use of pesticides altogether. To control a pest, its natural enemies may be introduced. In Thailand the stink bug is controlled by sticking the eggs of a parasite on to a card and hanging it in the fruit trees affected. Synthetic sex attractants are used to lure male gypsy moths to traps where they can be destroyed. Another example is **irradiation**, which introduces infertility as a means of controlling pest numbers. **Pathogens** (disease-causing organisms) are also used. For example, *Bacillus thuringiensis*, as a component of a bacterial insecticide, is sprayed on the caterpillars of moths and butterflies. Finally, plant breeding may produce varieties of crops that have a built-in resistance to pests.

Organic farming

Public alarm about pesticides and herbicides began after the publication of Rachel Carson's book *Silent Spring* in 1962. Since then public interest in producing crops by **organic** methods has grown. These methods emphasize nonchemical control of weeds and pests and the use of nutrient sources available from the farms, such as manure and legume crops.

To improve the fertility of soils without using commercial fertilizers, farmers may use **crop rotation**, which means growing different types of crops on a piece of land in different years. In addition, the growing of **legume crops**, such as alfalfa, helps to put nitrogen back into the soil. Advances in biotechnology have created varieties of crops that have an improved capacity to fix nitrogen directly from the atmosphere. Organic farmers may also use animal manures. These natural fertilizers have to be stored properly or they may leach into the ground and pollute water just as chemical fertilizers do. The organic residues of crops can be used on fields as mulch. Finally, cultivation techniques, such as **intercropping** (the growing of alternate rows of different crops) may increase the nutrients available to plant roots. Intercropping may also enable the use of plants that repel pests—that is, one crop may repel the pests that attack the other.

In spite of the methods available to organic farmers, their crop yields are normally less than those produced with the use of chemicals. As well, it takes two to seven years to clean the chemicals out of the soil. During that time farmers cannot sell their produce as organic.

On the other hand, organic farming has lower cultivation costs than chemically based farming, and organically grown products command a higher price. In the short term, chemical farming may produce cheaper foods, but this price does not include the costs to society of chemical pollution from farms and health problems from the use of pesticides. It is hard to put a dollar value on these broader costs, but organic farming may offer a safer and cheaper alternative to the chemically based farming practised over the past half century.

Soil erosion and conservation

The desire to make a profit or to meet the demand for food often leads farmers to overuse soils which then lose their ability to produce crops. **Soil erosion** occurs when the soil, weakened by the loss of humus or nutrients, is removed by the action of wind or water.

In order to maintain the soil as a renewable resource, several conditions must be met. First, most soils should not be exposed to heavy rainfall, and in the tropics at least, to intense sunshine. The humus in the soil should be gradually renewed by decaying vegetation. The various nutrients should also be replaced as they are used. If these conditions are not met, soil erosion is likely to take place. Rich, fertile soils may take several hundred years to develop. Yet soils can be destroyed in a matter of a few years — or even days. Any soil system may be destroyed by soil erosion.

Nutrient depletion

Nutrient depletion is an important cause of soil erosion. A soil ecosystem depends upon the decomposition of organic material to return nutrients to the soil. The nutrients can then be used again by plants. When farmers harvest their crops large amounts of vegetable matter in the form of grains, fruits, and leafy material may be removed. The soil is therefore deprived of the nutrients it would have received from these materials. Over a period of time even rich soils, like those of the Canadian Prairies, declined in fertility as successive crops were removed by farmers. After the Second World War prairie soils slowly declined in fertility, and chemical fertilizers were used in increasing amounts to compensate for the loss.

Nutrient depletion also occurs in countries that cannot afford to restore the fertility of the soil by chemical fertilizers. In many parts of Africa and Asia, where soils have been exhausted by continuous cropping, the main available source of fertilizer is cattle manure. Yet because of a shortage of fuel wood, this valuable manure is often dried and burned for fuel rather than used as fertilizer.

When the structure of the soil is destroyed, the soil is then easily eroded. There are two main types of soil erosion — **water erosion** and **wind erosion**. Some of the worst examples of each can be found in North America and Africa, usually as a result of poor management of the land.

Water erosion

Moving water has enormous power to erode material from the land. This power is related to the volume and speed of water flow. The worst soil erosion occurs when vegetation is removed from steeply sloping areas with heavy rainfall. In such areas the exposure of the soil can lead to **gully erosion** in a short time. Gullies are steep, V-shaped gouges that form easily in unprotected soil or clay. Less obvious but equally serious is **sheet erosion**. Sheet erosion is the gradual removal of topsoil on sloping land not adequately protected by vegetation.

Gully erosion and sheet erosion have affected many parts of the world, particularly on sloping land. The southeastern United States has been seriously affected, since that region contains many deforested hillsides. Gully erosion, however, is also common in most of the farmed areas of Canada, including southern Ontario and the Prairies.

Gully erosion can be severe, as shown above in Swaziland, while heavy rains can create sheet erosion, as seen in the lower photograph in Ethiopia.

Ploughing along contour lines helps to prevent the formation of gullies.

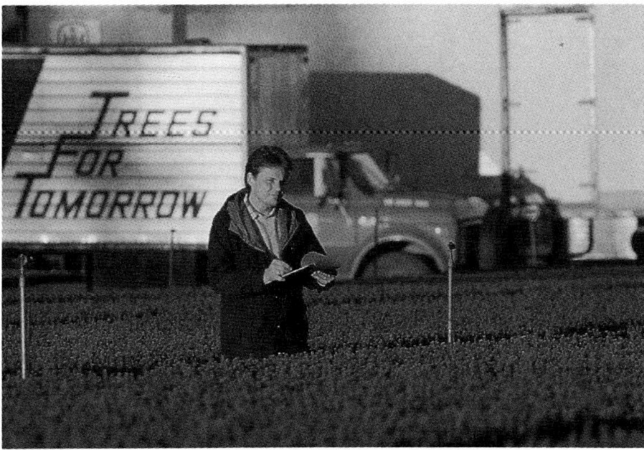

Tree nurseries provide seedlings for reforestation in British Columbia.

Programs to control soil erosion in North America were set up in the 1930s. In Canada these programs were organized under the Prairie Farm Rehabilitation Administration (PFRA), which was formed in 1935. In the United States the responsibility was undertaken by the Soil Conservation Service set up in 1936. Most countries, including developing nations, have set up agencies in recent years to deal with the problems of soil erosion. Some of the solutions include contour ploughing, stream control, gully revegetation, and reforestation.

Contour ploughing means following the natural contour lines of the land to avoid creating sloping furrows that can easily turn into gullies. Stream control is the building of dams, often called **check dams**, to help control river flow. This technique prevents the erosion that can be caused by flood waters. In gully revegetation, vegetation is reintroduced into gullies to prevent the removal of soil during periods of high water flow. Finally, reforestation of the upper parts of river valleys helps to release water into rivers gradually, thus reducing the danger of flooding.

Water erosion by rivers leads to the deposition of the eroded materials farther downstream. This may be beneficial, as when layers of silt supply nutrients to the soils of flood plains. The deposition of silt may also affect the use of rivers for navigation. The Mississippi River, for example, requires constant dredging, since silt deposits clog the river channel. This has caused it to change course several times in recent years.

Wind erosion — the Prairies

The removal of top soil by wind is a continual threat in the more arid parts of the world. Wind erosion mainly occurs in semiarid or arid areas when the vegetation cover is removed or reduced.

Over much of the North American plains, grain farming was adopted as the most profitable use of the land. Saskatchewan, in particular, has specialized in the growing of high-protein spring wheats. To adjust to the semiarid nature of the land, farmers used **dry farming** techniques in the early years of the twentieth century to conserve moisture. This meant that farmers left some fields **fallow** in summer — that is, crops were not planted. The land was then harrowed to break up the earth after rain showers and trap the moisture in the soil. The surface itself was left bare. Unfortunately, many years of cultivation and harrowing, without replacing the humus, gradually broke down the soil structure. The drought of the 1930s quickly turned much of the plains into a dust bowl.

To make matters worse, the drought coincided with a severe worldwide economic depression, which led to a sharp fall in wheat prices. Thousands of farmers, unable to pay their mortgages, went bankrupt and abandoned their farms. To add to the misery of those who remained, an epidemic of a disease called wheat rust and plagues of grasshoppers further devastated their meagre crops.

Both the Canadian and American governments took action to help the areas worst affected. The PFRA and the Soil Conservation Service introduced anti-erosion measures and water storage facilities to farms. The most notable of these techniques was **trash farming**, or **stubble mulching**. In this process the farmer leaves the stubble on the fields after harvest to reduce wind erosion. The growth of weeds on fallow land is controlled by **subsurface cultivators**. These machines are fitted with blades or rods that are dragged through the soil to cut off the weeds at root level. The stubble gets chopped up, creating the messy appearance that gives trash farming its name.

Another anti-erosion technique is **strip farming**. Crops are grown in strips across the line of the prevailing winds. Only narrow strips of soil are exposed to the wind at any one time. **Shelter belts** or **windbreaks** to reduce wind speed also help to limit erosion and preserve moisture in the soil.

Wind erosion in North America has been largely caused by growing crops in areas that would have been better left for grazing. After the drought of the 1930s much of the land that was affected by erosion was taken over by municipalities and turned into pasture.

A combination of water and wind erosion can take place very slowly, even on first-class soils like those of the American Midwest or the **Corn Belt**. Small amounts of top soil, perhaps 1 mm per year, are steadily being removed. A small loss of soil, balanced by the formation of new soil material, is sometimes called the T-value (tolerable value). Much soil in the Corn Belt, as in the Prairies, is being eroded at a rate above the T-value. Farmers, faced with higher costs and lower prices for their crops, are usually not too concerned with small rates of soil loss. However, over long periods of time, even first-class soils may lose some of their productivity. The United States has lost so much soil that its potential to produce food may have been cut by about 10 to 15 percent. This could be a serious threat to the food security of countries that import food from the United States.

This subsurface cultivator in Saskatchewan cuts off weeds at root level.

Strip farming across the line of prevailing winds helps to reduce wind erosion.

Reducing soil erosion in developing countries

Many of the world's poor countries are trying to overcome the problem of soil erosion. However, population pressure and the need to grow cash crops to pay interest on foreign debts has hindered their efforts.

The Canadian government, through the **Canadian International Development Agency (CIDA)**, gives a great deal of help to developing countries with problems such as soil erosion. Many **nongovernmental organizations (NGOs)** also provide practical help. The best solutions must be cheap and require only low levels of technology. They should use local materials and require minimum use of fossil fuels.

Desertification

Desertification, one of the most serious problems facing civilization today, refers to any severe form of land degradation. Human activities are causing the deserts to expand. About 30 000 000 km^2, or over 20 percent, of the earth's land surface containing over 80 million people is threatened by severe degradation. As Figure 8.3 shows, each continent is affected to some degree, with the greatest problems being in North and South America and in Africa.

A United Nations Conference on Desertification (UNCOD) was held in Nairobi, Kenya, in 1977. Ten years later the resolutions on UNCOD had scarcely begun to be implemented. Twenty-one million hectares of once-productive land are still being lost each year throughout the world. This figure is twice the amount of land normally devoted to growing wheat on the Canadian Prairies.

Desertification in the Sahel

Figure 2.6 shows the prolonged drought in the **Sahel** region of Africa. Climatic variability is greatest in the arid areas of the world. So we can expect long dry periods as part of the normal climatic cycle in the Sahel. However, misuse of the land has made the effects of the drought worse. Most of the areas where desertification is occurring have a high rate of population growth. This leads to overcropping and overgrazing as people try to increase the food supply to keep up

Figure 8.3 Desertification throughout the world

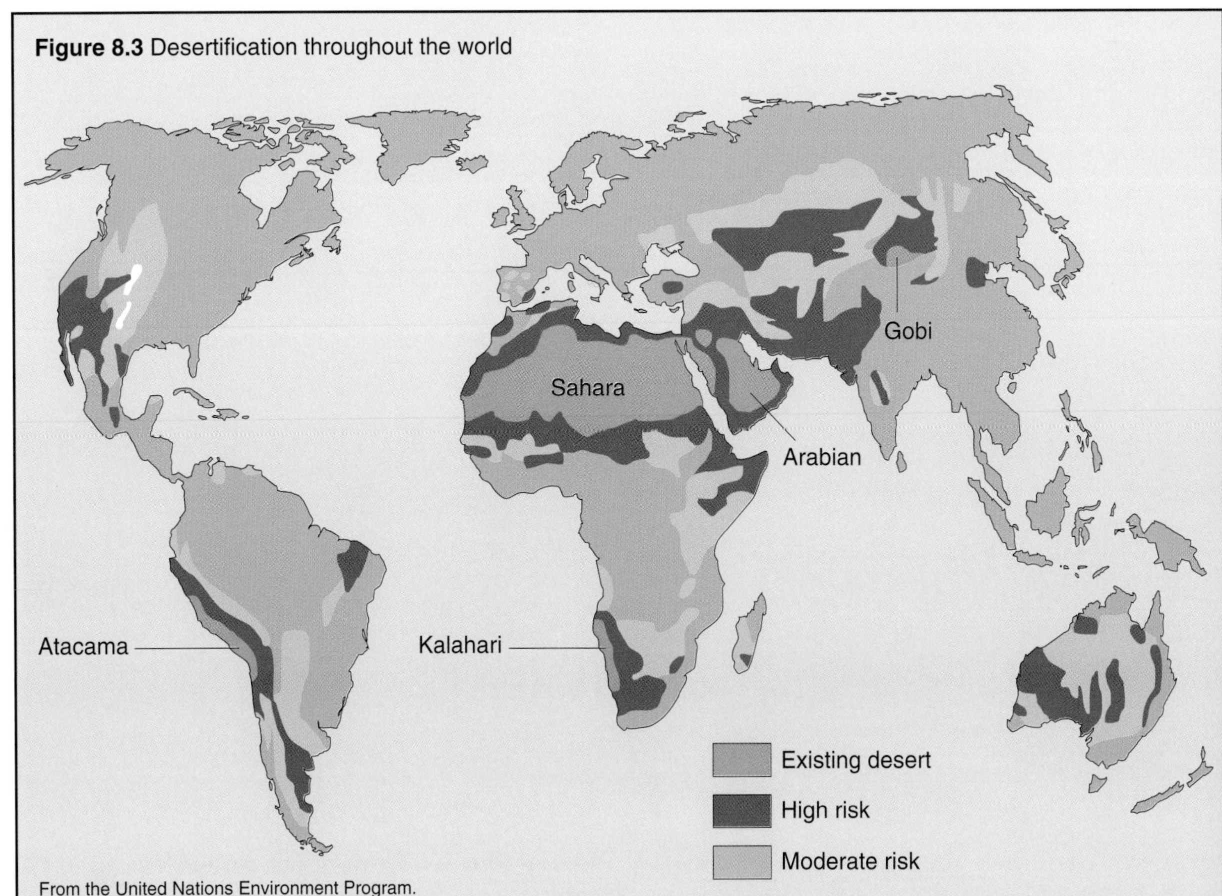

From the United Nations Environment Program.

with population growth. Another possible cause is faulty irrigation. Too little water or inadequate drainage can produce salt crusts on the surface of the ground.

Deforestation also leads to desertification. The removal of trees leaves the soil unprotected and dry. Wind erosion increases, and when rains do occur, the soil cannot absorb the water that runs off, carrying soil with it.

The problem of desertification is difficult to solve. A great deal of money has been spent by development agencies digging deep wells to provide water. But this aid has had an unexpected result. Many nomadic farmers have decided to settle permanently near the watering places, thus increasing the number of animals herded on small areas of land. Such spots are becoming spreading centres of desertification.

Solutions in the Sahel

Desertification is estimated to cost $26 billion (US) in terms of lost agricultural production. The costs of controlling it have been estimated by the United Nations Environment Program (UNEP) at $4.5 billion (US). Why then has the problem not been solved? The answer lies in the difficulty of raising the necessary funds and in persuading governments in developing countries to cooperate with each other. It has usually proved easier to raise short-term emergency funds in response to tragedies in Ethiopia, Rwanda, and Somalia than to raise funds for long-term agricultural improvements. The cost of controlling desertification ($4.5 billion [US]) is about equal to the money spent in 1994 on armaments worldwide in *two days* (4.2 billion [US]).

In spite of the lack of funds, great progress has been made toward restoring parts of the Sahel to stability. Local conservation experts, often assisted by develop-

Bunds help to reduce sheet erosion on fields in Ethiopia.

This check dam in Kenya traps silt after heavy rainfall.

Planting sisal is one way to prevent a small gully from becoming a large one.

Alley cropping in Kenya provides shade and nutrients for the crops.

Figure 8.4 Eight ways to prevent desertification

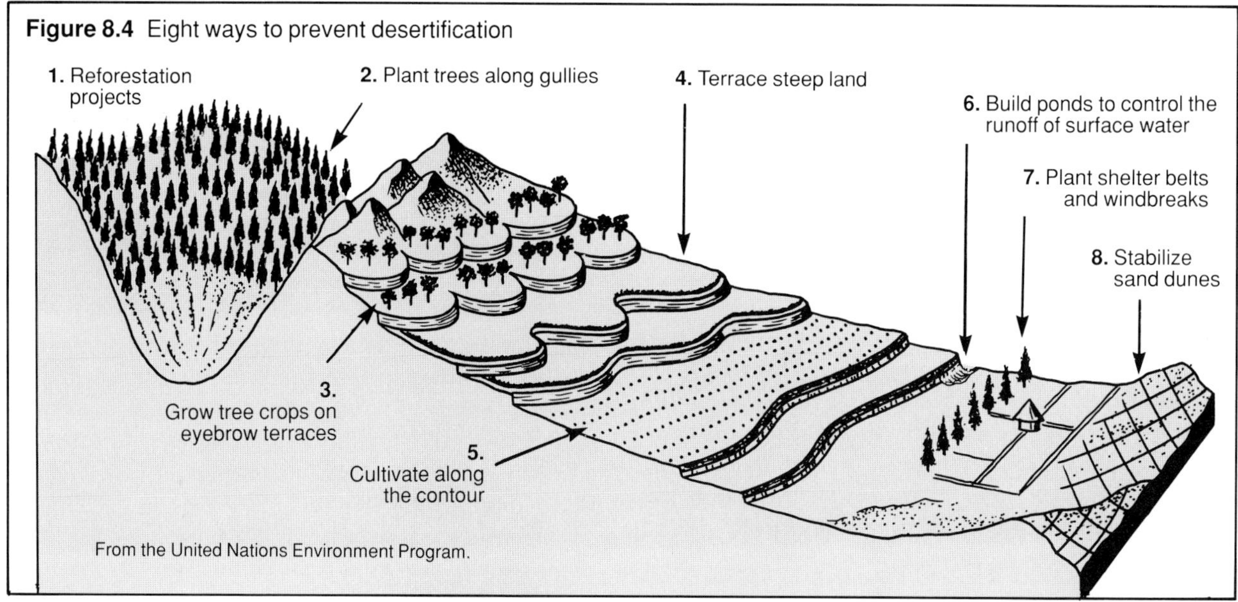
1. Reforestation projects
2. Plant trees along gullies
3. Grow tree crops on eyebrow terraces
4. Terrace steep land
5. Cultivate along the contour
6. Build ponds to control the runoff of surface water
7. Plant shelter belts and windbreaks
8. Stabilize sand dunes

From the United Nations Environment Program.

ment agencies, have introduced many techniques to turn the tide of soil erosion. Figure 8.4 shows a number of ways that desertification can be controlled. The main methods are building **check dams**, practising **gully** protection, constructing **bunds** and **terraces**, and planting trees.

Check dams are built from local stones and are designed to trap the silt that flows down gullies after heavy rain. As the silt is trapped, the dam can be raised by adding more stones. This traps more silt, until the gully is completely filled. Countries like Ethiopia require the construction of hundreds of thousands of check dams.

It is better to prevent new gullies from forming than to have the expense and effort of filling up old ones. Gully prevention can be done by planting shrubs, such as sisal, in any small channel that threatens to turn into a gully. The sisal binds the soil together and helps to prevent the formation of gullies.

Sloping fields can be terraced if the slope is steep. If the slope is gentle, a low terrace or bund can be built. A concave area on the top of the bund traps water and silt after heavy rain. The highlands of Ethiopia are slowly being stabilized by the construction of bunds and terraces.

Trees of all kinds need to be planted in the Sahel and in similar areas where desertification is a threat. However, low-growing, nitrogen-fixing trees can give shade and sustenance for crops and provide fodder for animals. The interplanting of trees and crops is known as **alley cropping**, which is part of the growing science of **agroforestry**.

Figure 8.5 Grass strips to reduce soil erosion

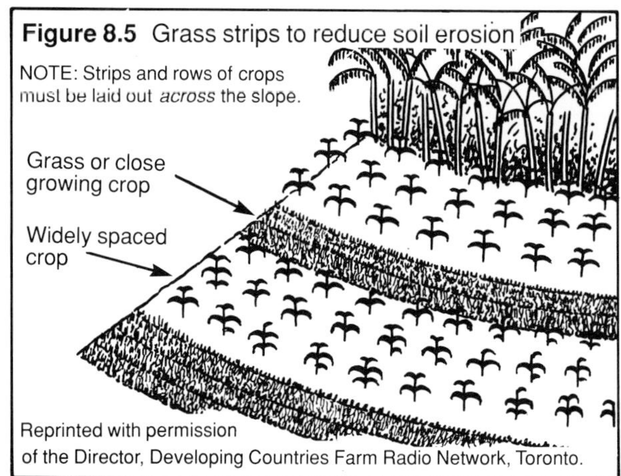
NOTE: Strips and rows of crops must be laid out *across* the slope.
Grass or close growing crop
Widely spaced crop

Reprinted with permission of the Director, Developing Countries Farm Radio Network, Toronto.

THE DEVELOPING COUNTRIES FARM RADIO NETWORK

One Canadian nongovernmental organization that has helped millions of farmers in recent years is the **Developing Countries Farm Radio Network (DCFRN)**. The DCFRN was formed in 1979 by CBC senior farm commentator George Atkins to spread low-cost solutions to farming problems throughout the developing world. It is funded by CIDA. The DCFRN has a monthly radio audience of over 697 million people in about 121 countries and thousands of Canadian subscribers. Broadcasters in these countries receive scripts and interpret the information in local languages. The DCFRN is a grassroots method of sharing effective farming practices among peoples in different parts of the developing world.

The following is one of George Atkins's scripts on soil conservation:

As you know, when it rains, some of the rainwater soaks into the ground and some doesn't — it just runs away and is lost. When this water flows over bare soil, it washes some of that soil away with it.

Now, let's think about the soil where your crops are growing on sloping land. Let's think especially about cultivated crops you've planted in rows — crops like maize or cotton. If there's a lot of bare soil between the rows and between the plants in the row, quite a lot of rainwater will just run away over that bare soil instead of sinking into the ground. As it runs away, it will wash away good topsoil with it.

Of course, you don't want this to happen because you need that good topsoil on your land so you can grow good crops. Also your crops need that water.

How then can you prevent the loss of that water and of that precious soil?

Well, first of all, you must do something to prevent the water from running down the slope so fast — and also give it a chance to soak into the ground better. And you must protect the soil so it won't be washed away.

There are many ways of doing this. You know that if you're planting on a hillside, you must always make your furrows and rows *across* the slope, not up and down. This is very important. Some farmers also make contour bunds or other kinds of barriers across their slopes to stop the water from washing away the soil. And a good ground cover of grasses or other plants close together, or of mulch, will slow down the water moving over the soil and let it soak into the ground better.

Let me tell you about another way to protect your soil and conserve the precious water that falls on it.

Now, I've said that grasses help protect the soil. That's a good thing to remember — so when you are going to cultivate hillside soil, leave narrow strips of land uncultivated across the slope and let grass grow on them. The strips could each be about a metre (3 feet) wide. Then between these grassy strips, you can have cultivated strips of land for the cultivated crops you grow with bare soil between the rows. These strips could be quite a bit wider than the grassy strips.

Remember that all of the strips must be across the slope. Another thing, the steeper the hill is, the narrower the cultivated strips should be, thus giving the grassy strips a better chance to slow down the water that runs down the hill when it rains. If the hill isn't too steep, the grass strips can be farther apart. Strips like this can even be useful on flat land, helping to protect the soil and conserve water.

Reprinted with permission of the Director of the Developing Countries Farm Radio Network.

Tropical rain forests

Almost one-third of the earth's surface is forested. The amount of forest, both hardwood and softwood, in the major world regions is shown in Figure 8.6. The importance of forests to our modern civilization cannot be stressed enough. Forests are a valuable source of timber, the raw material for a variety of manufactured products, recreational areas, and a means of absorbing carbon dioxide to control the greenhouse effect. Deforestation threatens the role of forests in our world.

The tropical rain forest ecosystem is the most productive, varied, and fragile on earth. If trees are cleared, the soils are exposed to the tropical sun and rain. This makes the soil vulnerable to erosion. The humus is quickly burned out or used up. The soil itself, though deep, lacks nutrients and soon becomes infertile.

For centuries, people of the rain forest have practised **shifting agriculture**, also called **slash and burn**. In this system, a small area (1 or 2 ha) is burned, and crops are planted in the fertile ash. The fertility drops off quickly, however, and after three or four years the patch is abandoned for another. Over twenty or thirty years many patches will have been used, but the abandoned land is left to revegetate.

A second type of farming that is widely practised in tropical forests, mainly in Asia, is plantation farming. The land is devoted to cash crops, such as rubber, coffee, or tea. In plantation farming the natural ecosystems are replaced by artificial ones.

Figure 8.6 World forest resources

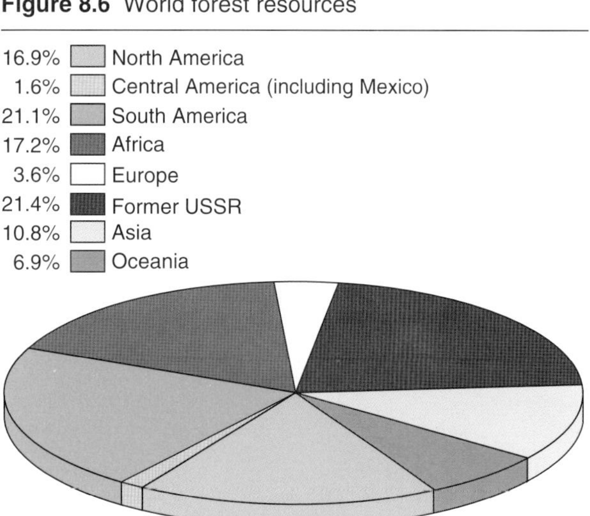

From the United Nations Food and Agriculture Organization.

Why is the rain forest being destroyed?

The rain forest is disappearing at an incredible rate for a variety of reasons. The first is the growing worldwide demand for timber. South America is the most important source of tropical hardwoods. However, Indonesia's forested area, which is only one-third the size of Brazil's forested area, is actually losing its trees at a faster rate. In 1989 Indonesia supplied 40 percent of the tropical hardwoods sold in the Western world.

In Central America two-thirds of the loss of forest have been caused by cattle ranching. The overpopulation of some Latin American countries, such as Costa Rica, has encouraged governments to allow the clearing of the forest for ranching. A small patch of cleared land and a few cattle can give a family an income above bare subsistence level. Some ranching projects have had the support of organizations such as the World Bank. A powerful incentive for the conversion of tropical forests to pasture has been the demand for cheaper sources of beef in Western countries.

Poverty, therefore, has a role in the increased settlement of the rain forests, but poor people cannot be blamed for the major part of the destruction. In Brazil the forest has been lost for a variety of reasons, including large-scale ranching, road development, and the construction of industrial and hydroelectric power projects. The Grande Carajás Program, shown in Figure 8.7, centres around iron ore mining and smelting,

Figure 8.7 Major development projects in Brazilian Amazonia

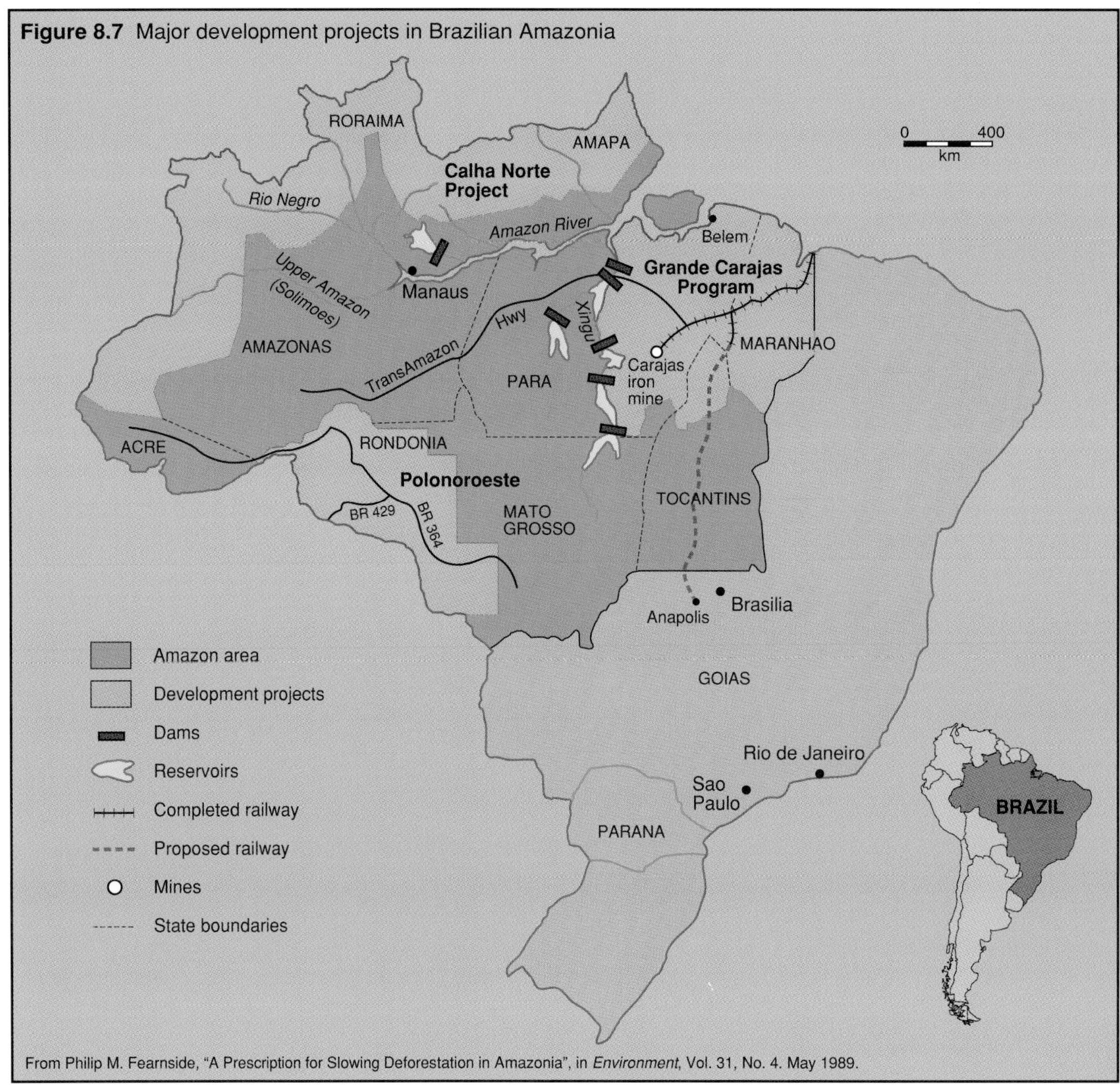

From Philip M. Fearnside, "A Prescription for Slowing Deforestation in Amazonia", in *Environment*, Vol. 31, No. 4. May 1989.

using charcoal from the forest. Loans were provided by the World Bank and the European Economic Community (EEC). The EEC imports a large quantity of ore at bargain prices. The nearby Tucurui Dam has flooded over 200 ha of forest. The Brazilian power authority, Eletronorte, has plans for several additional dams that will flood much more land and alter the Amazon River system.

In the western Amazon state of Rondonia the situation is almost as bad. The opening of the BR-364 Highway into the region in 1987 has accelerated the process of clearing. In a few years this area will have little forest left.

Violence also threatens those who would stand in the way of the developers in Brazil. For example, a leading Brazilian conservationist, Chico Mendes, was murdered in December 1988.

NASA satellite studies show that about 15 000 km^2 has been lost each year in Brazil since 1978. This is less than is sometimes claimed, but NASA also reports serious "edge effects" (the destruction of habitats on forest boundaries). The FAO claims that as much as 50 000 to 80 000 km^2 was being lost by 1990.

Consequences of the destruction of the rain forest

The destruction of tropical rain forests means that a stable ecosystem is replaced by a very unstable one. Ranching in the hot, wet tropics quickly exhausts the soil. The production of meat is only about 50 kg/ha compared with about 600 kg in Western countries. After three or four years the soil may support no more than coarse grass and scrub. In its natural condition, the rain forest ecosystem can produce ten times as much from nuts, fruit, rubber, and fish. There are also several other serious side effects of the destruction of the rain forests.

Possible climatic changes The burning of tropical forests adds possibly 2 or 3 billion tonnes of carbon per year to the atmosphere in the form of carbon dioxide (CO_2). This is about half the amount released by the burning of fossil fuels throughout the world (almost 5 billion tonnes). The increase of CO_2 is the main cause of the greenhouse effect and global warming.

Deforestation also causes an increase in methane, which is twenty-five times more powerful as a greenhouse gas than CO_2. Methane is produced by cattle and by the billions of termites that live in rotting timber. Over one-third of global methane emissions are thought to result from tropical deforestation.

The climate of the Amazon basin will become hotter and dryer if the forests are destroyed on a large scale. As much as half of the moisture that falls near the coast is evaporated and transpired to be carried inland. The forest recycles the moisture between the atmosphere and the ground. Without the forest most of the rainfall will run off into the rivers and be lost to the land.

The loss of plant and animal species Tropical rain forests throughout the world contain over half of all species of living things. They house between 3 and 4 million species of plants and animals, only a small proportion of which have been studied in detail. The Amazon basin alone may contain over 1 million species of plants and animals. This diversity is by far the world's largest **gene pool**. This resource has enormous potential for the human race. Already the tropical forests provide drugs such as L-dopa (used in the treatment of Parkinson's disease) and could provide many more. The potential for using genes to increase crop yields is equally great. Continued clearing of the rain forest could result in the extinction of over half of all the species of plants, animals, and insects alive today.

The loss of winter habitats Millions of birds migrate in winter from Canada and the United States to Central and South America. The loss of their forest habitat results in a decline in the numbers of migrating birds, perhaps as much as 4 percent a year according to the Smithsonian Institution. This loss of birds has an environmental effect in North America. Since song birds consume millions of insects, farmers are having to rely increasingly on pesticides to control insects.

The effects on Native peoples Many Native peoples live in the Amazon basin and to a lesser extent in other tropical rain forest areas. They hunt, fish, and live in harmony with the forest. From it they derive their

Native peoples are threatened by development in the Amazon basin.

building materials, clothes, medicines, and implements. Since they occupy land desired by the incomers to the forest, many Native peoples have been killed. This can only be described as a major human tragedy.

Contrasting views in developing countries How do people and governments in developing countries feel about the destruction of their own natural forests? In Brazil the government's view has been that people are better off carving out a living for themselves in the forests than living in squalor in an urban slum. The Indonesian government appears to have similar views. It set up a Transmigration Program that has already moved several million people to less populated, but densely forested, parts of the country.

Many people in countries such as Brazil point out that, although Westerners insist the rain forest be preserved, the world's air pollution problem is mainly due to the burning of fossil fuels by Western countries for 200 years. Didn't Western countries cut down their own forests to expand their economies? Why then are they trying to prevent people in developing nations from using their resources to improve themselves, just as Westerners have done? Recently, however, Brazil has been more open to the idea of conserving rain forests in return for economic help in dealing with its large foreign debt. Several **"debt for nature" swaps** have been arranged with Latin American countries. By this arrangement some foreign debt is cancelled in return for the protection of areas of tropical forest.

The forest cover of Thailand had been reduced from 53 percent in 1961 to 10 percent in 1994. The export of hardwoods helped Thailand to pay for economic development. However, severe deforestation led to a series of mudslides in the 1980s that buried villages and farmland. Villagers put pressure on the government to take action to protect the forests. Finally, in 1989, the government of Thailand banned all logging throughout the nation. However, it has not stopped Thai logging companies from exploiting forests in nearby Laos and Cambodia. It remains to be seen whether other nations threatened by deforestation will also take positive action.

Overall, the clearing of the tropical rain forest has been described as the greatest natural calamity since the Ice Age. At the present rate of clearing, most of the forest will be gone by the year 2020. By then, the consequences of this destruction on the atmosphere and the soils should be all too clear. But we will not be able to turn back the clock. This great ecosystem, and its abundant genetic resources, could well be lost for all time.

Northern coniferous forests

Canada has about 436 000 000 ha of forest. Most of it is classified as northern coniferous (boreal) forest. Two other forest ecosystems may be distinguished. They are the mixed forests of the Great Lakes region, St. Lawrence Valley, and the Atlantic provinces, and the coastal rain forest of British Columbia.

Climate plays a large part in the distribution of Canada's forest types. The warmer southern fringes of the coniferous forest produce larger trees. The main species in the forests of Ontario and Québec are pine, spruce, and balsam fir. Still farther south, the remaining mixed forests of the Great Lakes region and the St. Lawrence Valley contain maple, beech, and oak. On the coast of British Columbia the long growing season and heavier precipitation permit more rapid tree growth. Western hemlock, Douglas fir, western red cedar, and Sitka spruce are the main species of trees, some of which grow to almost 100 m in height. Overall, Canada possesses about 40 percent of the world's northern forests.

The forest industry has played a significant role in the history of virtually all regions of Canada. Until the Second World War lumber companies did little reforestation. With such a large area of uncut forest, they left reforestation to nature.

At the beginning of this century, some people called for the systematic replanting of trees. The 1929 Pulpwood Act in Ontario established the principle of **sustained yield**, though it was not effectively practised for many years. Not until the Second World War was the first official policy established to manage forests on a sustained yield basis. By then, the valuable white pine forests of eastern Canada had been almost completely cut.

Sustained yield involves cutting timber at a rate not

Figure 8.8 The growth of timber in relation to age

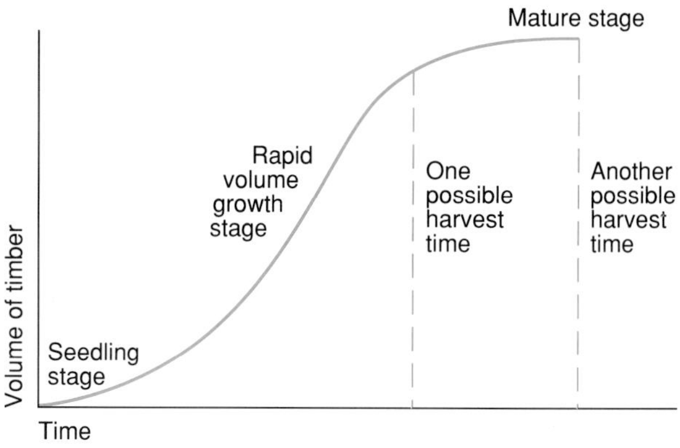

greater than the rate of growth, after allowing for losses from causes such as fire and disease. To do this, it is necessary to define the **annual allowable cut (AAC)**. We can understand the AAC by looking at a graph of tree growth. (See Figure 8.8.) The annual rate of growth speeds up as trees develop past the seedling stage and then slows down as trees reach maturity. The best time to cut trees is at the mature stage (after about eighty years). However, **old growth forests** contain trees that are much larger than would be produced after eighty to one hundred years. The volume of a second growth forest harvested after a rotation age of eighty or one hundred years would therefore be less than for an old growth forest.

The forests of Canada grow mainly on crown (government) land. They belong to all of us, and we should take an interest in how they are managed. We should also note that according to the Canada Forest Act of 1978, the forests of Canada provide a variety of resource uses, with water management, fishing, and recreation co-existing with forestry. The same act reaffirmed that the forests are a permanent resource to be managed on a sustained yield basis.

Are the forests being replaced?

Since the 1960s the AAC and timber production have risen in Canada. One reason is because many species of timber that used to be regarded as "weeds" are now utilized, including aspen, hemlock, and lodgepole pine. Another reason is the greater use made of each tree, for example by cutting stumps lower and by using smaller diameter timber. Thus more timber can be extracted from a given area of forest.

However, in British Columbia at least, the AAC will likely be reduced when the present period of cutting old growth forests is over. Some say the supply of old growth timber will run out soon after 2010. On the other hand, 1994 statistics for BC's forests show an inventory of 4.4 billion cubic metres of old growth timber (over 140 years), of which about 50 million cubic metres is cut in one year.

On reforestation, Figure 8.9 suggests that an attempt is being made in British Columbia to make up for a historic shortfall in replanting. Critics of the reforestation program point to the amount of so-called "junk forest" that replanting has created in all parts of Canada. This is reforested land where the new growth has failed to become properly established, either because of soil erosion or poor planting. Many people within the forest industry admit to this problem, but they maintain that forests are planted much more effectively today. For example, the survival rate of seedlings in British Columbia is now 73 percent.

Figure 8.9 Timber harvesting and reforestation in British Columbia

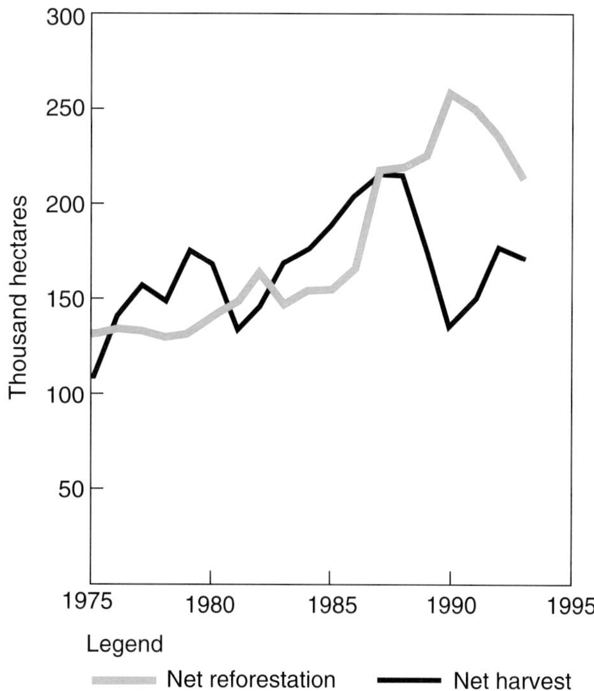

From the British Columbia Ministry of Forests.

Is the ecosystem being preserved?

One hectare of forest contains many types of wildlife and millions of organisms woven together into the delicate balance of an ecosystem. Cutting down timber may have devastating short-term effects on the soils of hilly areas, exposing them to the weather and to the scarring impact of heavy machinery. This, in turn, affects the whole forest ecosystem.

Evidence shows that soil productivity is being reduced, especially on steeply sloping land. If forests are satisfactorily regrown on a logged area, the rotation age of, say, eighty years may be enough to produce a usable stand of timber. But that time period will not replace the old growth ecosystem. Second growth forests are more uniform and regimented. You seldom hear a woodpecker or see a deer. Sustained yield management, in other words, can replace the volume of timber, but not the forest ecosystem.

Some scientists point out that the long-term fertility of forest soils is being threatened not only by erosion but also by the loss of fungi, known as mycorrhizae, that play a part in the release of nutrients to the trees. The loss of these fungi is blamed by some for the decline in productivity of Scandinavian and German forests, which have been managed for a longer period.

Clearcutting or selective logging?

If you visit areas where deforestation has recently taken place, you may find areas where the saleable timber has been completely removed, leaving only "rubbish" on the ground. This is **clearcutting**, meaning the complete cutting of all useable timber in a relatively small area. Clearcutting is distinguished from **selective logging**, where only particular trees are taken out. Selective logging may not be suitable in areas with very large trees.

Figure 8.10 Clearcutting and selective logging

CLEARCUTTING	SELECTIVE LOGGING
Leaves unsightly open area	Leaves forest largely intact
Increases speed of runoff	Leaves river flow unchanged
More danger of river silting	Less danger of river silting
Disrupts wildlife	Less damaging to wildlife
Less dangerous for loggers	More dangerous for loggers
Large trees easily extracted	Large trees hard to extract
Less attractive for tourists	More attractive for tourists
More economical method in areas of large trees	Less economical method for large trees

Protesters blockade the construction of a logging road in Clayoquot Sound in 1993.

Clearcutting probably cannot be avoided altogether, especially for the large trees in the forests on British Columbia's coast. However, the public is increasingly aware of the ugliness of clearcutting, especially in tourist areas. Better planning may help to screen clearcuts more effectively from the roads. Some critics also claim that the size of clearcuts is too large. Some are over 50 ha in area, compared with under 10 ha in other logging countries, such as Sweden. Smaller clearcuts, while more expensive to operate, could also help to control soil erosion.

Should old growth forests be preserved?

The Clayoquot Sound in British Columbia Situated on the west coast of Vancouver Island, the Clayoquot Sound is an area of outstanding natural beauty. However, forestry, fishing, and mining activities have for many years earned millions of dollars for the regional

Old growth forest in Clayoquot Sound, British Columbia, is destroyed by clearcutting.

economy ($162 million in 1991). In the late 1980s a movement to protect the forests of Clayoquot Sound from further logging gained momentum and public support. A four year study produced a compromise land use plan in 1993. The plan, which had the backing of 11 local interest groups, doubled the area of protected old growth forest by cutting the commercially forested area in half. The AAC was cut by one third, with an expected loss of 1000 jobs. Environmentalists, however, did not agree to the compromise plan and started an international campaign to have logging banned altogether in Clayoquot Sound.

A compromise, it seems, rarely satisfies all parties. Few dispute the needs of society for timber products, but many claim that areas of great natural beauty should be preserved and argue that a greater percentage of the province's forests should be protected. In every case that arises, the choice lies between preserving jobs and revenue on the one hand, and protecting the old growth ecosystem on the other.

The Temagami Forest in Ontario The Temagami Forest Reserve was formed in 1901 to create a sustained yield from the valuable pine forests of this part of Ontario. Temagami contains one of the last remnants of the old growth pine forest in eastern Canada. The area contains some of Ontario's best scenery and canoeing rivers, as well as Native peoples' trails up to 3000 years old. The ecosystem contains the endangered golden eagle and the nearly extinct aurora trout.

To protect some of the best land, the Lady Evelyn Smoothwater Park was created in 1983 removing 7200 ha of timber from the threat of logging. The forest industry is seeking access to the remaining timber resources and claims that without logging Temagami will lose its economic base.

In 1989 the Ontario Supreme Court ruled in favour of an extension of the Goulard and Red Squirrel logging roads in the Temagami forest (See Figure 8.11.) The expansions to these roads threatened the remaining old growth pine forest. In response, the Temagami Wilderness Society claimed that logging in these areas would provide income and jobs for only a few years, whereas the ecosystem would be destroyed forever.

After several years of consultations, the Ontario government released a report in 1996 allowing mining and expanded logging in certain areas of Temagami under strict conditions. This predictably upset environmentalists. Dan McDermott of the Earthroots Coalition claimed that logging of old-growth pine forests would destroy an important part of Canadian life.

Figure 8.11 The Temagami forests of Ontario

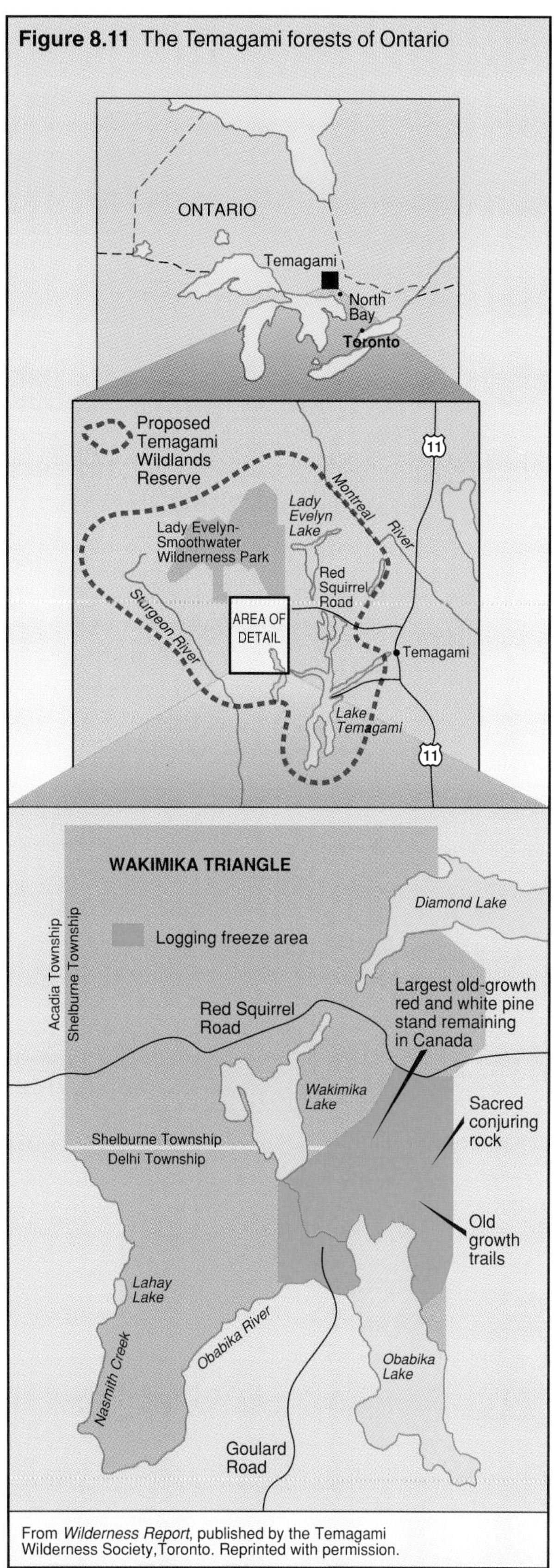

From *Wilderness Report*, published by the Temagami Wilderness Society, Toronto. Reprinted with permission.

The role of silviculture

Silviculture is the science of growing trees. Canada is beginning to spend more money and time on silviculture. Science offers the prospects of genetically improved trees, which will grow faster and be more resistant to pests and diseases. At the present time insects are the main threat to timber in Canada, although fire causes more spectacular losses. Canada spends on silviculture only about one-fifth of the amount spent in Sweden for an equivalent area of forest.

Forest fires such as this one in British Columbia cause great losses to the timber industry.

The economic importance of forestry in Canada

Before coming to any conclusions about the role of the forestry industry, we have to ask how important it is to the economy of the country and to our standard of living. Forest products account for 15 percent of Canada's exports and 780 000 jobs. If we include those who serve the forest industry, for example, shopkeepers and teachers in logging towns, a much higher number of people depend on the forest industries for their livelihood. The Council of Forest Industries in British Columbia estimates about forty cents out of every dollar earned in the province comes directly or indirectly from forestry.

However, we cannot rely on overcutting to boost our economy in the short term while reducing the capacity of the forests to produce for the long term. In the words of a well known environmentalist saying: "We do not inherit the forest from our [parents]; we borrow it from our children." If so, Canadians have to clarify their priorities in relation to the long-term protection of the forest environment.

● | Mining and urban land uses

Farming and forestry are the main economic uses of land by area throughout the world. In Canada the renewable resources of farming and forestry use the greatest amounts of land, while mining and urban uses occupy seemingly small areas. But these mining and urban activities can encroach upon the amount of land available for renewable resource production. These two land uses may also seriously reduce the quality of the land. The mining industry can harm rural land by disturbing the surface or discharging toxic wastes into rivers and groundwater. The growth of cities is responsible for converting increasing amounts of land from rural to urban uses. This problem affects not only Canada but virtually all countries. Both mining and urbanization greatly affect the limited amount of land available to us.

Mining

Mining is the extraction of mineral ores or fossil fuels from the ground. It usually involves serious disruption of the land surface. Mining has played a large role in the development of countries, such as Canada, that are rich in natural resources. There are two main types of mining: **underground mining** and **open pit** or **strip mining.**

Underground mining Underground mining is practised wherever the mineral to be mined is far enough underground to require a shaft and a system of tunnels to be dug. (See Figure 8.12.) Underground mining was extremely dangerous in the past because of the hazards of inflammable gases (especially in coal fields) and the collapse of tunnels. Even today, these problems can create mining disasters. Mining was also dangerous to the miners' overall health as working underground in a dusty atmosphere could cause lung disease. The risk of lung disease still exists, although most modern mines have elaborate health safeguards.

Underground mining can affect the surface of the ground in two ways. First, the slow collapse of tunnels can cause the surface of the ground to sink. Buildings may sink as the ground slowly settles. Many coal-mining sites can be recognized by the presence of derelict land and subsidence ponds.

Second, the accumulation of waste from deep mining can create unsightly dumps and tip heaps on the surface of the ground. These, too, can be dangerous. In 1966 at Aberfan in Wales, a tip heap, swollen by rainfall, collapsed and engulfed a school, killing 26 adults and 116 children.

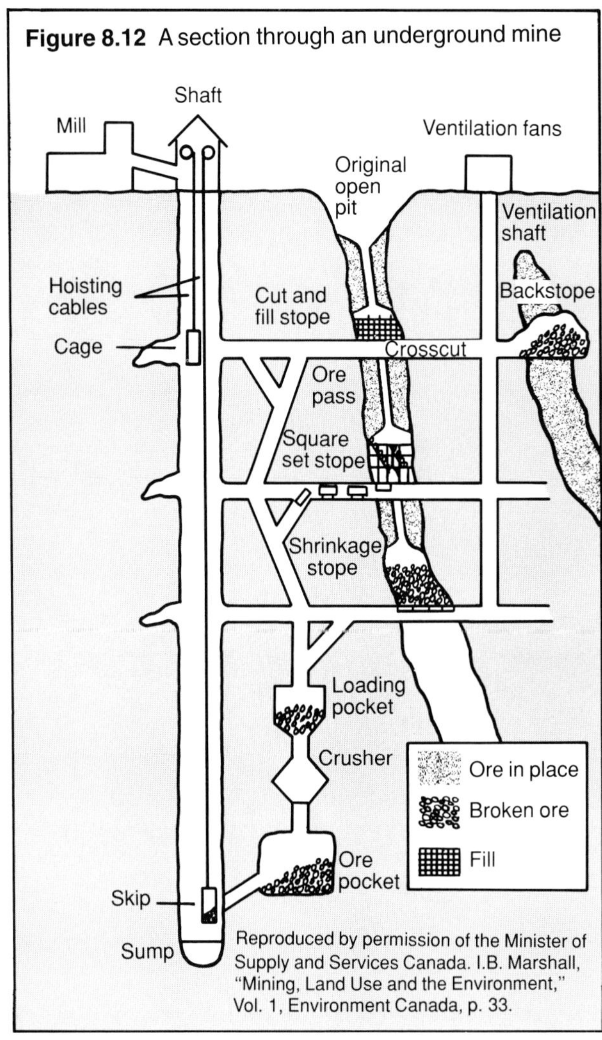

Figure 8.12 A section through an underground mine

Reproduced by permission of the Minister of Supply and Services Canada. I.B. Marshall, "Mining, Land Use and the Environment," Vol. 1, Environment Canada, p. 33.

Open pit (strip) mining Open pit mining has a much more obvious effect on the surface of the ground, since the minerals are obtained by digging a large surface pit. (See Figure 8.13.) Some mines may be over 2 km long and 0.5 km deep. Open pit mining is less dangerous than underground mining, but it creates dust and noise, which can be a nuisance to local residents. The mine may conflict with adjacent land uses, such as tourism. In some cases mining may be restricted or prohibited by the greater needs of the environment, as in the case of national parks.

Open pit mining is usually on a large scale, with millions of tonnes of rock being moved about. Some machines can scoop out over 100 t at a time, replacing the work of many miners and reducing the costs of production. Open pit mining enables low grade ores to be mined. In the case of a **base metal** like copper, the metal content of the ore may be less than 1 percent. This means that over 99 t of waste are created in order to obtain 1 t of pure copper. A great deal of water is used in the recovery and concentrating of ores. Mining operations therefore have large waste tips and **tailings ponds** — water reservoirs that allow mining wastes to settle.

Mine wastes often contain toxic materials. Other toxic chemicals, such as cyanide, may be used in the recovery process. Therefore, great care must be taken to ensure that contaminated water does not leak into river systems or groundwater. In spite of these efforts, spills do occur. The smelting of metals can create further environmental problems, especially air pollution. Figure 8.14 summarizes the many kinds of contamination that mining can cause.

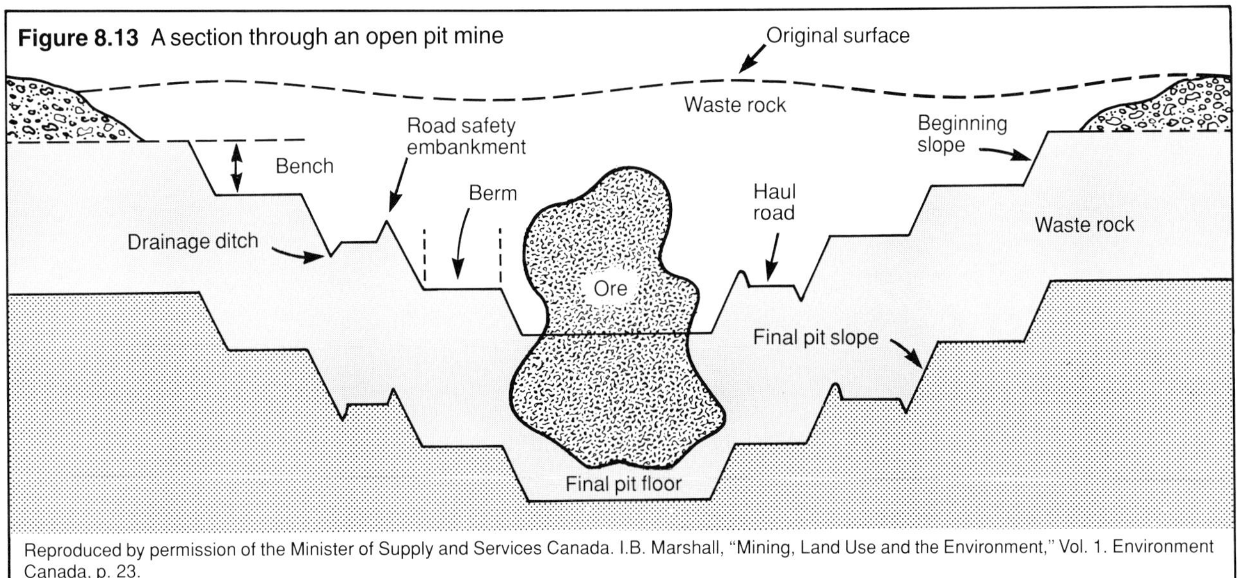

Figure 8.13 A section through an open pit mine

Reproduced by permission of the Minister of Supply and Services Canada. I.B. Marshall, "Mining, Land Use and the Environment," Vol. 1. Environment Canada, p. 23.

Figure 8.14 Environmental damage caused by mining

Waste rock
Tailings
Slag
Sediment in river channels
Soils from air pollution
Floodplain sediment/soil
Ground water at open pits
Reservoir sediment
Ground water beneath ponds
Groundwater from contaminated reservoir sediment
River sediment reworked from floodplain

PRIMARY
SECONDARY
TERTIARY

Reprinted with permission from *Environmental Science and Technology*, Vol. 24, No. 9. Copyright 1990 American Chemical Society.

We all make use of mineral products, so taking the extreme view that mining should be stopped altogether is impractical. We can insist, however, that waste be put back in the mine pit when mining is finished, although this has not always been done. Land that has been carefully restored can become productive again.

Urbanization

Towns and cities have been growing rapidly, both in population and area. Most of the land converted to urban uses was previously farmland, much of it high quality agricultural land. Ontario and the Prairie provinces have most of the top-quality land in Canada. The rapid growth of the Golden Horseshoe around the western end of Lake Ontario has resulted in much of this prime land being swallowed up by houses, factories, and roads. The problem is particularly acute in the Niagara Peninsula between Hamilton and St. Catharines.

The problem is that more money can be made from land used for industry or residential development than from farming. If no restrictions are in place, many farmers may be offered much more money for their land than they could ever make by farming. Not surprisingly, many have sold out to developers. Good laws and careful planning can help to prevent the further loss of good farmland in Canada.

British Columbia, with its pleasant climate and diverse landscapes, is not surprisingly the destination for large scale migration. The Fraser River Action Plan (FRAP) points out that, if present trends continue, the population of Vancouver and the lower Fraser Valley will increase by about 1.5 million people by 2020. To reduce the loss of farmland, the BC government has put in place a land use policy known as the **Agricultural Land Reserve**, which limits the transfer of land from farming to urban or industrial uses.

Environmental pressures from urbanization in BC have also increased the pollution of the Fraser river and its tributaries. This causes hazards to human health, and is disastrous for salmon runs. The sources of pollution include industrial wastes, sewage, and urban run-off. In the light of rapid population growth, FRAP raises the questions as to whether we can continue to afford the luxuries of two car families and sprawling suburban development in an area already so congested.

Urbanization encroaches upon prime farmland in the lower Fraser Valley of British Columbia.

Looking back

1. (a) List the land uses that could be classified as human.
   (b) List the land use with the greatest number of people (urban) first and the fewest last.
   (c) What type of land best suits each of the following: urban development, agriculture, industry, and transportation?
   (d) Examine Figure 8.1. Why is only 11 percent of the world's land suitable for growing crops?
2. (a) How do agricultural chemicals get into the food chain?
   (b) Explain why the following statement is true: "The consumer is partly responsible for the use of chemicals in agriculture."
3. (a) List three farming practices that contribute to desertification.
   (b) Why are these practices becoming more common in some parts of the world?
   (c) Explain why low technology solutions, such as the ones suggested by the Developing Countries Farm Radio Network, are appropriate for developing nations. (See pages 122 to 123.)
4. How can new wells in the Sahel indirectly create further soil erosion problems?
5. Explain what is meant by sustained yield harvesting.
6. (a) Why has open pit mining become more widely practised recently?
   (b) List the problems that result from this practice.

Applying your knowledge

1. Suggest ways in which urban growth can continue without the loss of the best farm land.
2. For each of the photographs on pages 119 and 121 explain whether the technique shown is one of prevention or cure.
3. Create a three-column organizer entitled "Chemicals in Agriculture." In the first column list the chemicals used in agriculture and identify them as fertilizers, herbicides, or pesticides. In the second column describe the advantages of using each chemical. In the third column describe the disadvantages.
4. Analyse the arguments for and against the logging of areas of old growth forest. Is a compromise solution possible?

5. Explain how trash farming, or stubble mulching, is an improved method of fallowing compared with earlier forms of dry farming on the Canadian Prairies.

6. Write a magazine article explaining how each of the techniques of controlling desertification shown in Figure 8.4 can help to restore the stability of the Sahel.

7. (a) Prepare a presentation in which you (i) outline the arguments used to justify the exploitation of the tropical rain forests and (ii) explain whether or not these arguments are valid.

   (b) Suggest ways in which Canadians can help to save tropical rain forests.

8. (a) How does a managed second growth forest differ from an old growth forest ecosystem?

   (b) What are the advantages and disadvantages of old growth and second growth forest from the points of view of (i) naturalists and (ii) foresters?

9. Using the information in Figure 8.14, prepare a written or an oral explanation of how mining can interfere with the atmosphere and the hydrosphere and how this, in turn, can affect farming and forestry.

Extending your thinking

1. Refer to your organizer in question 2 in Applying Your Knowledge. Write an essay either in favour of or against the use of chemicals in agriculture in terms of the cost to the environment.

2. Figure 8.15 gives population and land use data for several countries that experience some form of pressure on the land. Canada is included for comparison.

   (a) Calculate the arable land in hectares per person for each country. To do this, convert the arable area into hectares by multiplying it by 100 and divide by the population.

   (b) Draw proportional squares, as in Figure 8.16, to show the arable land per person for each country. Give reasons for the wide variations.

Figure 8.15 People in relation to cropland (mid 1993)

COUNTRY	POPULATION (MILLIONS)	AREA (1000 KM²)	DENSITY (PEOPLE PER KM²)	ARABLE AREA (1000 KM²)
Canada	28.8	10 000	2.9	400
China	1 196.4	9 450	126.6	1 040
Egypt	56.5	986	57.3	30
Ethiopia	51.9	1 209	42.9	121
India	901.5	3 168	284.6	1 584
Indonesia	189.1	1 903	99.4	228
Italy	57.1	301	189.7	151
Netherlands	15.3	34	441.2	23

From the United Nations Food and Agriculture Organization.

Figure 8.16 Arable land per person in Canada and China

To draw a proportional square, find the square root of the hectares per person figure calculated in (a). This gives the length of the side of the square as a decimal of 100 m (e.g., Canada: $\sqrt{1.4}$ hectares per person = 1.18 or 118 m.

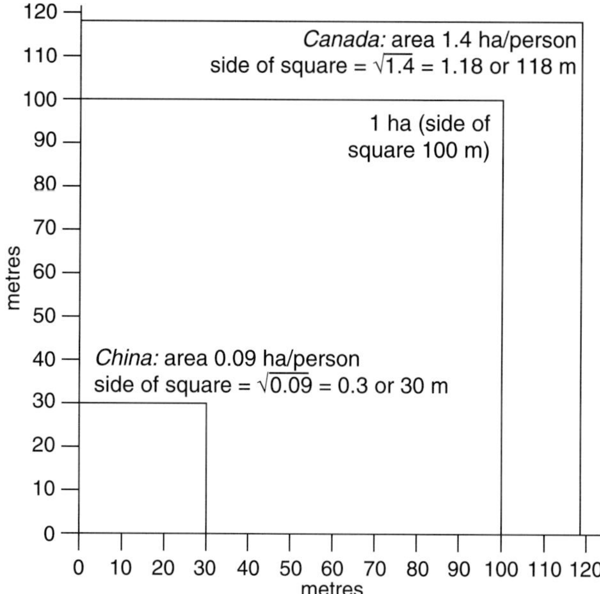

3. (a) Visit a protected forest area in your community. Take a camera and photograph as many species of trees and wildlife as you can find. Identify each species in a poster or scrapbook presentation.

   (b) How does this protected forest improve your environment?

4. Compose a letter to a government in a country with a tropical rain forest environment in which you explain your arguments against the destruction of the rain forest.

5. Debate the following statement: "The Clayoquot Sound (or the Temagami) should be entirely preserved."

9 ENERGY

Every action requires the use of energy. The history of the world's economic growth is closely related to the increasing use of energy, especially since the Industrial Revolution. Coal was first widely used in the nineteenth century, followed by oil and gas in the twentieth century. Population growth and an improved standard of living have been the main factors contributing to more energy use throughout the world.

Few topics today raise as many questions as energy use. Will an oil shortage in the future mean a comeback for coal? Does the emission of carbon dioxide (CO_2) mean that the use of fossil fuels should be decreased in favour of nuclear power? Is hydroelectric power the ultimate "clean" source of power, or are hydro dams an environmental liability? Can solar power and other renewable sources of energy meet the growing demand for energy worldwide? Is nuclear fusion a practical possibility within the foreseeable future?

In this chapter we will explore the effects of the growing use of energy throughout the world. We will also consider some alternative energy sources that may prove less damaging to the environment and how to use energy more efficiently.

Changing energy use

Primary sources of energy are sources that are directly available from nature, such as coal, oil, natural gas, hydroelectric power, and nuclear power. (See Figure 9.1.) Electricity, other than hydroelectricity, is a secondary source of energy, since it is produced from primary sources of energy, particularly fossil fuels.

All forms of energy use affect the environment, especially the burning of fossil fuels, coal, oil, and natural gas. People debate endlessly on the relative merits of fossil fuels as compared with nuclear or hydroelectric power. Previously, such debates concentrated on the economic aspects of each energy type. Today, however, the focus has shifted to the impact that each source of energy has on the environment. Reducing the pollutants released by burning fuels is now one of the most important issues. Energy conservation has become necessary, not only because of the shortage of some fuels, but as a means of saving the environment.

As we have seen, nearly all energy comes from the sun in the form of photosynthesis. Carbon is absorbed by vegetation as carbon dioxide (CO_2). As the vegeta-

Figure 9.1 Commercial energy consumption by region, 1992.

REGION	POPULATION (MILLIONS)	OIL	COAL	NATURAL GAS	HYDRO	TOTAL
		(MILLIONS OF TONNES OF OIL EQUIVALENT)				
Africa	689	96	75	37	8	216
North America	287	990	531	656	273	2 450
South America	465	131	18	60	37	246
Asia	3 350	850	1 039	331	143	2 363
Europe	726	911	711	841	366	2 829
Oceania	27	43	45	22	6	116
World	5 544	3 021	2 419	1 947	833	8 220

Note that energy use is expressed in terms of oil equivalent tonnes. For example, if 2 t of coal gives the same amount of energy as 1.5 t of oil, then 4 000 000 t of coal consumption would be 3 000 000 t of oil equivalent.

Adapted to oil equivalent from UN figures.

tion dies and is consumed or burned, the carbon is released again. However, the use of atmospheric CO_2 is not always balanced by the creation of it. Large amounts of carbon have been stored in vegetation or animal life, which was fossilized 300 million years ago to become fossil fuel before being consumed and returned to the air.

These fossil fuel deposits take millions of years to accumulate. They are being used thousands of times more quickly than they were created by solar energy. For example, we have used nearly half of all the oil on this planet in less than a century, releasing large quantities of carbon dioxide into the atmosphere in the process. This rapid use of fossil fuels has a great impact on the environment and future energy sources.

The availability of energy sources affects the pattern of energy use. The Soviet Union, Eastern European countries, and China have economies that for many years were planned in detail by their governments. Each of these countries relied heavily on coal as its main energy source. The economies of North America and Western Europe switched much more quickly to oil after the Second World War. Canada is fortunate in that it has more hydroelectric power potential than most other countries, as well as a full range of fossil fuels. For the majority of people in the world, however, wood is the main source of energy. Most people in the developing world depend on wood for heating and cooking.

Figure 9.2 Per capita energy use and income in selected countries, 1992

COUNTRY	PER CAPITA ENERGY USE (OIL EQUIVALENT TONNES)	PER CAPITA INCOME ($US)
Australia	7 464	16 715
Canada	10 534	20 660
China	836	378
France	5 618	23 149
India	344	306
Japan	4 743	29 387
Mexico	1 882	3 736
Nigeria	234	256
Poland	3 484	2 356
South Africa	2 631	2 882
former USSR	6 632	5 306
United Kingdom	5 403	18 182
United States	10 736	23 332
Germany	5 865	24 157

Adapted from United Nations and World Bank data.

Canada consumes up to forty times as much energy per capita as a poor country, as shown in Figure 9.2. Since the production and use of energy has an impact on the environment, Canada, with its relatively small population of 30 million, may well have as much impact on the environment as a poor nation with several hundred million people.

Estimates of future world energy use vary from 9.5 to 12 billion tonnes of oil equivalent by the year 2000. Some forecasters have predicted a rise in world energy use of up to 39 billion tonnes of oil equivalent by 2050. Can fossil fuels be supplied on this scale, and if so, what impact will burning these fuels have on the environment?

Fossil fuels

Coal

Coal was the main fuel of the Industrial Revolution. The mining of coal has left its mark on many older industrialized countries, such as Britain and Germany. It led to sinking of the land and the creation of large heaps of waste. Mining is also hazardous to people, especially before the days of safety lamps and properly ventilated mines. Accidents in coal mines still occur today, and many miners suffer various forms of lung disease.

Coal has one great advantage over other fossil fuels. It is much more abundant. Supplies of coal will last longer than supplies of other fossil fuels. Today coal may have been surpassed by oil as an energy source, but it is still being mined at near record levels.

In Western countries, many of the markets for coal have been overtaken by the oil industry. No longer are trains and ships powered by coal, and few people burn it in their homes. The steel industry still uses coal as a fuel but in smaller quantities. By far the main market for coal is power generation. In the United States about two-thirds of all the coal burned is used to generate electrical power. Nearly all of Alberta's electrical energy is generated by coal-fired stations even though it is the province with the most oil.

Environmental effects of coal

There are many types of coal, ranging from the highest quality **anthracite**, which is about 90 percent carbon, to low-quality **lignite**, containing about 35 percent carbon. Most of the world's coal is **bituminous**, with about 60 to 70 percent carbon.

Burning lower quality coal creates much more gas, steam, and ash than burning high-quality coal. All coal

Figure 9.3 Production of coal (all types) in millions of tonnes

	1980	1982	1984	1986	1988	1990	1992
China	435	463	554	638	699	771	797
USA	626	624	668	672	723	772	747
former USSR	562	489	479	509	587	487	470
Poland	166	165	167	172	174	133	125
Australia	69	109	95	119	123	143	157
Germany	205	212	206	208	198	188	140
World	2 661	2 703	2 801	3 056	2 804	3 261	3 210

From United Nations data.

The Sundance generating station in Alberta burns low-sulphur coal for fuel.

burning creates carbon dioxide in the combustion process and therefore contributes to the greenhouse effect. Some coals contain large amounts of sulphur, which is a major cause of acid rain. Much of the sulphur can be trapped by **scrubbers** in the chimneys of coal-burning facilities. Scrubbers are extremely expensive, however, and are not totally efficient. Developing countries cannot usually afford such technology.

The large volume of ash created from burning coal is up to 20 percent of the original volume of the coal. It usually contains small amounts of toxic metals. New techniques of combustion are helping somewhat, but the disposal of millions of tonnes of ash is a major problem for the coal industry. Burning coal also releases small amounts of **radionuclides**, or radioactive particles, into the atmosphere. Since so much coal is burned, this release of radioactivity is a significant problem.

More use has been made of high-quality, low-sulphur coals in recent years. In the United States the first Clean Air Act of 1970 led to the use of some low-sulphur coal from the western states in place of high-sulphur Appalachian coal. However, the problem is not entirely solved. Western coal has to be shipped farther, and the unsightly strip mining in the western states does not help the tourist industry. Coal from western Canada is relatively low in sulphur.

Oil and natural gas

Oil or petroleum is a liquid mixture of organic hydrocarbons that may vary in type. Larger molecules form heavy hydrocarbons that may be as thick as tar. From them we obtain waxes and heavy fuel oil. Lighter hydrocarbons are refined into heating oil and gasoline.

Natural gas is a mixture of lighter hydrocarbons, in particular methane, propane, and butane. It is found either in association with oil deposits or on its own. Natural gas is often called sweet or sour, depending on the amount of hydrogen sulphide it contains. The sulphur in natural gas can be separated before the gas is used as a fuel or as a petrochemical feedstock.

Although it is a nonrenewable resource, natural gas has an environmental advantage over oil and particularly over coal. When it is burned it gives off only carbon dioxide and water. Although it contributes to the greenhouse effect, it does not contribute to other forms of atmospheric pollution.

Environmental effects of oil and gas

Nearly 60 percent of world oil reserves lie in the Persian Gulf area, with other reserves in remote or offshore places, such as Alaska and the Beaufort Sea. The location of these reserves creates a serious potential environmental problem. Millions of tonnes of oil are transported every year by giant oil tankers from producing to consuming centres. The results of an oil spill from a tanker can be disastrous.

The exploration for offshore oil is also hazardous. New technology has enabled oil to be drilled in waters up to 200 m deep on the continental shelves. Stormy weather is a major danger. In the North Sea the waves can be 30 m high. Oil platforms and rigs off Canada's east coast are also plagued by icebergs. (See Figure 9.4.) Since 1980 several tragic accidents involving offshore oil rigs have resulted in lost lives, such as the *Ocean Ranger* disaster off Newfoundland in 1982. Several other accidents have released large amounts of oil or gas into the ocean, with disastrous effects on aquatic life. Oil spills in the Arctic are more serious than in warmer climates, since the bacteria that break down the oil work much more slowly.

Oil is used in many ways, but the most environmentally damaging use of oil is for transportation. Automobiles emit over half of the nitrogen oxides that contribute both to acid rain and ozone depletion. Exhaust fumes also include carbon monoxide (CO), hydrocarbons, and small amounts of trace metals. The move to lead-free gasoline and the use of catalytic converters have greatly reduced emissions in recent years. Good engine maintenance also reduces the volume of nitrogen oxides that cars spew into the air, as does the use of propane as a fuel.

Large reserves of oil exist in the form of oil sands, mainly in Canada and Venezuela. Two plants extract heavy oil from the Athabasca oil sands in Alberta. However, further development of this resource will be expensive and will require large volumes of water.

Figure 9.4 Canada's east coast oil and gas fields

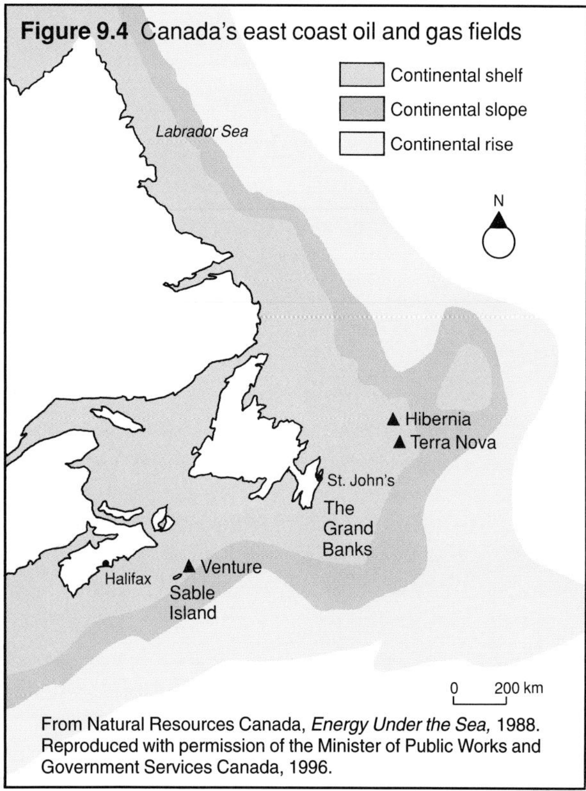

From Natural Resources Canada, *Energy Under the Sea,* 1988. Reproduced with permission of the Minister of Public Works and Government Services Canada, 1996.

Water power

The use of falling water to generate power is the best-known form of renewable energy. Rivers that have a large volume, relatively constant flow, and fall from a considerable height have great potential energy.

Water power is the oldest form of mechanical energy. In 1000 B.C., water wheels were used to help lift irrigation water on to fields. In the thirteenth century, water power was harnessed for use in the English woollen industry. More recently, water wheels were used in eastern Canada to mill grain. The first use of water for generating electricity came in the late nineteenth century. Hydroelectric power was first generated in Canada on the Winnipeg River in 1906. In 1992 water power provided 12 percent of all the energy and 61 percent of the electricity used in Canada.

The advantages of hydroelectric power

Power generated from falling water has been regarded as the ultimate "clean" source of power. It creates no emissions of carbon dioxide, so it does not contribute to the greenhouse effect. Neither does it produce the sulphur dioxide and nitrogen oxides that create acid rain. The construction of dams is necessary to create a sufficient supply of water to cope with variations in river flow. Dams also create a "head of water," which means the drop from the level of water in the dam to the river below. Dams are expensive to construct but cheap to operate.

Hydro dams have benefits other than the generation of electricity. They create a reservoir of water that, in drier areas, can be used for irrigation. Many of the world's major dams were constructed for irrigation as much as for power. The Aswan Dam in Egypt and the dams on the Murray River system in Australia are examples.

A major benefit of river dams is flood control. Some rivers flood periodically, causing great havoc. Deforestation in upper valleys tends to make such floods more frequent and devastating. Dams allow for a steadier release of water downstream, which greatly benefits the people who live on flood plains. The Columbia River Treaty (1964) was aimed at achieving flood control in rivers in both the United States and Canada.

Dams also provide recreation sites. Many beaches and marinas are on artificial lakes, such as Lake Diefenbaker in Saskatchewan and Lake Shasta in California. Furthermore, lakes created by dams provide an assured water supply for nearby towns and cities. If hydro schemes have several purposes other than power generation, they are referred to as multipurpose projects.

Created by a dam, Lake Diefenbaker, Saskatchewan, provides opportunities for recreation, as well as an assured water supply.

Environmental effects of hydro dams

In recent years the environmental hazards of hydro dams, in spite of their numerous benefits, have become obvious. In the first place, dam construction involves flooding the land, some of which may be high-quality farmland. Many people may be displaced as a result. For example, the construction of the Aswan Dam resulted in the forced relocation of over 50 000 people in Egypt plus another 50 000 in Sudan. This dam is a breeding ground for insects. In China dams may flood ancestral graveyards, which are of great spiritual significance to the Chinese people.

Flooding forested land can release mercury from the soil into the water. This was discovered in Manitoba after the diversion of the Churchill River into the Nelson River to enlarge the flow for the Kettle Rapids Dam.

Although the generation of hydro power is clean, the construction of dams is not. Enormous quantities of concrete, steel, and other materials are required. Producing these materials disturbs the environment at the mining and manufacturing stages. The construction of dams may also be disruptive for rural communities. Therefore hydroelectric power does contribute to environmental pollution.

Dams may also interfere with groundwater. The large Glen Canyon Dam on the Colorado River has allowed groundwater to seep through the sandstone walls of the canyon. Landslips may occur since the water lubricates joints and faults in the rock. In the case of large reservoirs, the weight of the water may cause geological instability and earth tremors. Occasionally, dam failures occur, often leading to great loss of life in the land immediately below the dam.

The flow of water downstream from a dam is more regulated than it was in its natural condition. This may benefit flood control, but wildlife habitats are disturbed. Sometimes wetland breeding grounds are reduced for many kinds of birds and other wildlife. For example, in the Athabasca delta, where the Peace River enters the Slave River at the western end of Lake Athabasca, the wetlands have been greatly reduced.

Finally, dams have limited lives. Lakes created by dams act as settling ponds for the silt and nutrients in the water. Dams such as Aswan will silt up sooner or later, though the process may take hundreds of years.

La Grande River Scheme La Grande is Québec's third largest river, flowing into James Bay about 1000 km north of Montréal. (See Figure 9.5.) La Grande flows through a natural wilderness area of stunted forests inhabited by caribou and small mammals such as fox and beaver.

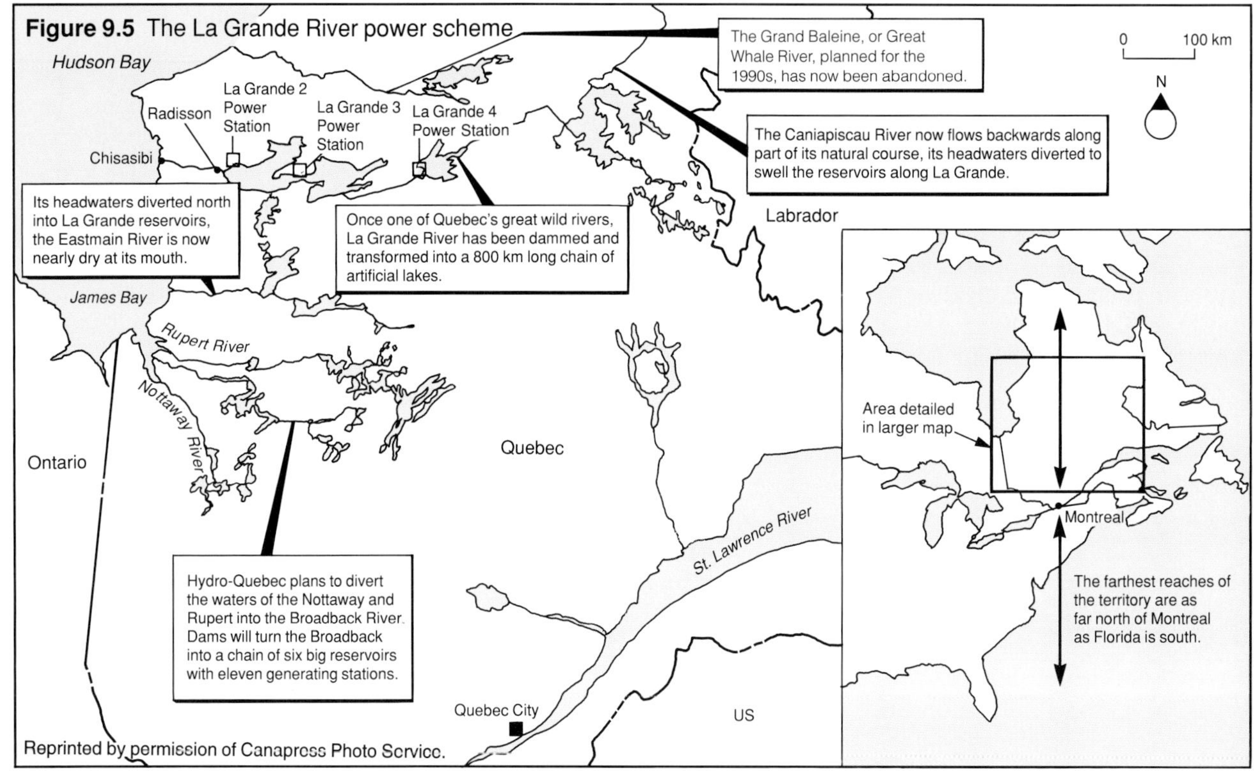
Hudson Bay
La Grande 2 Power Station
Radisson
La Grande 3 Power Station
La Grande 4 Power Station
Chisasibi
The Grand Baleine, or Great Whale River, planned for the 1990s, has now been abandoned.
The Caniapiscau River now flows backwards along part of its natural course, its headwaters diverted to swell the reservoirs along La Grande.
0 100 km
N
Its headwaters diverted north into La Grande reservoirs, the Eastmain River is now nearly dry at its mouth.
Once one of Quebec's great wild rivers, La Grande River has been dammed and transformed into a 800 km long chain of artificial lakes.
Labrador
James Bay
Rupert River
Nottaway River
Ontario
Quebec
Area detailed in larger map
Montreal
St. Lawrence River
Hydro-Quebec plans to divert the waters of the Nottaway and Rupert into the Broadback River. Dams will turn the Broadback into a chain of six big reservoirs with eleven generating stations.
The farthest reaches of the territory are as far north of Montreal as Florida is south.
Quebec City
US
Figure 9.5 The La Grande River power scheme

Reprinted by permission of Canapress Photo Service.

Since 1971 La Grande River has been turned into a series of lakes by the construction of dams, known as La Grande 2, 3, and 4. Six rivers have been diverted to enlarge the flow of water, flooding over 12 000 km^2. The largest dam is La Grande 2, which is 150 m in height. Together, all three dams have a power capacity of 10 281 megawatts (MW), sufficient for a city of 4 million people.

> 1 kilowatt (kW) = 1000 watts (10^3 W)
> 1 megawatt (MW) = 1000 kilowatts (10^6 W)
> 1 gigawatt (GW) = 1000 megawatts (10^9 W)

Further work is required to finish the La Grande scheme. La Grande 1 is under construction, and a 1900 MW expansion is planned for La Grande 2. The Great Whale complex to the north was abandoned in 1995 after a long campaign by environmentalists and Native peoples to stop it. At that time, a decision had not been made about the future of the Nottaway-Rupert Broadback complex to the south. With greater efficiencies in power use, it is likely that Quebec Hydro could not find adequate markets, in Canada or the US, for the additional power.

Interestingly, the importing US states appear to be more concerned about the environmental effects of La Grande than Québec itself is. No mandatory public enquiry is required before northern projects are begun in Canada, although schemes such as La Grande have to be approved by a committee that includes Native peoples. The Native communities agreed to the construction of La Grande only after receiving compensation payments of $174 million (CDN) and hunting rights. New England states, on the other hand, cannot even import power without setting up an environmental impact study.

When a river system is turned into a series of connected dams, environmental problems are inevitable. For example, fish populations are affected. River species have declined in the area of La Grande, while lake species are on the increase. The problem of mercury contamination, first observed in Manitoba, has had an impact on fishing in La Grande. This is a serious threat to the diet of the Cree, a band of Native peoples living in the area. The changing volume of freshwater entering James Bay is predicted to have drastic consequences on fish and wildlife, including polar bears and ringed seals. Other wildlife can also be affected. For example, in 1984 an estimated 10 000 caribou drowned as they tried to cross La Grande at a time when surplus water was being diverted downstream.

Many caribou drowned while trying to cross the La Grande River in 1984.

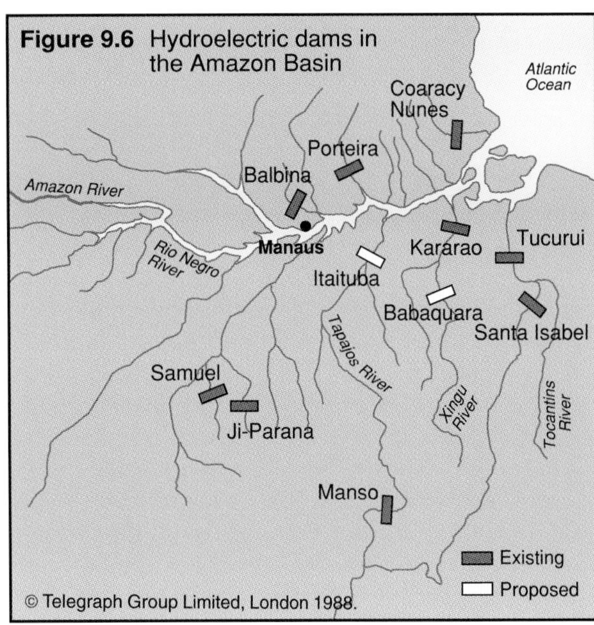

Hydro-Québec has spent $180 million (CDN) on repairing the environment, in particular in planting alder and willow trees along the waterlines to encourage the return of mammals. This sum is relatively small compared with the total sum of $11 billion (CDN) spent on La Grande by 1989.

Dams in the Amazon Basin In 1988 there were nine dams on tributaries of the Amazon River, all of them in Brazil. (See Figure 9.6.) The Brazilian government power company, Eletronorte, has plans for four more before the end of the century. Brazil also has dams in other areas of the country. The most notable is the world's largest hydro power project at Itaipu on the Paraná River in the south.

Some of the dams in the Amazon basin were built without serious problems, but two may be singled out as environmental disasters. The Balbina Dam, costing nearly $1 billion (US), is not filling as planned because of high evaporation and smaller than expected river flow. Although 1500 km^2 in area, it averages only 8 m in depth and generates little power. Since it is only partially filled, the Balbina scheme can generate just over 100 MW, less than half of the needs of the nearby city of Manaus.

The dam created problems in the area as well. Many Natives had to be resettled before construction took place. The lake was flooded without proper clearing of the trees. Rotting underwater vegetation has created acids in the lake water which threaten the health of 300 000 people living downstream from the dam. However, tens of thousands of animals were rescued before the slowly rising waters flooded their habitats.

The Tucurui Dam on the Tocantins River has a much higher generating capacity (5000 MW). It provides power at discount rates to the steel and aluminum industries in the Carajás region of the country. (See Figure 9.6.) However, the dam has stopped the natural renewal of the land by silt during the rainy season. This has hurt the cacao, rubber, and palm industries. Rotting vegetation has acidified the lake and killed most of the fish. The local people were not consulted before the dam was built, and only a few were offered any compensation.

Not all hydroelectric dams have these problems. However, the bigger the dam, the greater the potential damage to the environment. The biggest dam proposed anywhere to date is the Three Gorges project on the Chang Jiang (Yangtze River). When dammed, the Chang Jiang will have a potential capacity of 18 200 MW. However, this project will flood 660 km of river valley, including dozens of towns. Over 1.2 million people will have to be relocated, and China will lose a precious 400 000 ha of farmland.

Florentin Krause, a critic of hydro projects in developing countries, claims that they "often end up drowning tribal cultures, ancestral lands and irreplaceable genetic resources alike, and all this for the purpose of supporting affluent urban elites or foreign-owned aluminum plants, which ensure a steady supply of throwaway beer cans...." Several other proposed large-scale hydro projects in developing countries have also been criticized for providing benefits for Western industrialized countries while damaging the local environment. Examples include the proposed Nam Choan Dam in Thailand and the Narmada Dam in India.

Small-scale hydroelectric power

A great deal of research has gone into the possible use of small-scale hydroelectric power units. These generate less than 1 MW. The term **microhydro** refers to units of less than 100 kW of power capacity. The capital costs of such schemes are low and very little land is flooded.

An example of a microhydro scheme is located at Strathcona Park Lodge and Outdoor Education Centre on Vancouver Island. A 75 kW hydro installation was completed in 1989. The scheme includes a dam 2 m high and 15 m long. The water from the dam drops 141 m to the powerhouse, where it drives the turbines and is discharged into Buttle Lake. Since water flow in Strathcona Park is low during August and September, a diesel generator is on hand to provide power during these two months or whenever it is needed. The project was built at a total cost of about $221 000. Some of the labour was donated by volunteers. A loan of $100 000 was provided by Energy, Mines, and Resources Canada. The hydro scheme replaces the burning of fossil fuels and creates no emissions into the atmosphere. The project has resulted in savings of about $35 000 per year for the centre.

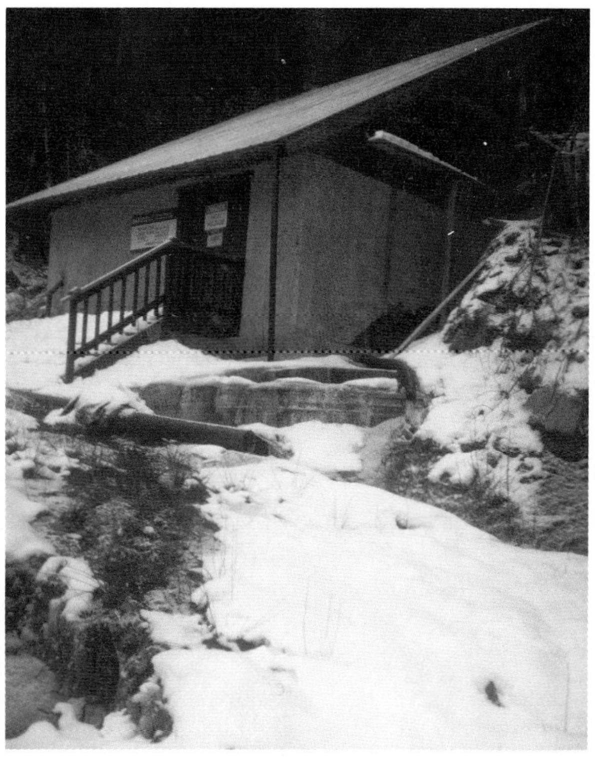

The microhydro project at Strathcona Park Lodge, British Columbia, generates 75 kW of energy at low cost.

Nuclear power

On a world scale nuclear power accounts for only 4 percent of all the energy used. But countries such as France and Taiwan are heavily committed to it, generating more than 50 percent of their electricity from nuclear sources. In Canada, the comparable figure is 11 percent.

Nuclear power is highly controversial and affects the environment in a number of ways. Issues involving nuclear power need to be examined not just on their own, but in relation to the problems of other sources of power.

Nuclear power comes from the splitting of the uranium atom, as shown in Figure 9.7. One attraction of nuclear power is the small quantity of raw materials required to generate large amounts of electricity. One kilogram of uranium can be used to generate as much electricity as 3000 t of coal. In addition, nuclear fission does not create carbon dioxide or other gases that pollute the atmosphere. However, it does create by-products that are highly radioactive, including caesium 137, strontium 90, and plutonium.

Nuclear power was first used commercially in the 1950s, but grew rapidly in the early 1970s after the dramatic rise in the price of oil. Several different nuclear technologies are used, depending on the cooling mechanism in the reactor. The most common is the pressurized water reactor (PWR), which accounts for about 60 percent of the approximately 400 nuclear stations existing in 1989. Canada has pioneered a reactor cooled with heavy water, known as CANDU, recognized technically as the world's best system.

Figure 9.7 The fission of one atom of uranium (U-235)

Fission means splitting apart. Nuclear fission involves the splitting of the nucleus of an atom into smaller, lighter parts. When nuclear fission occurs, energy is released which can be used to do work. For example, the potential energy in a kilogram of uranium is roughly equal to the energy in 3 million kilograms of coal or 2 million litres of fuel oil.

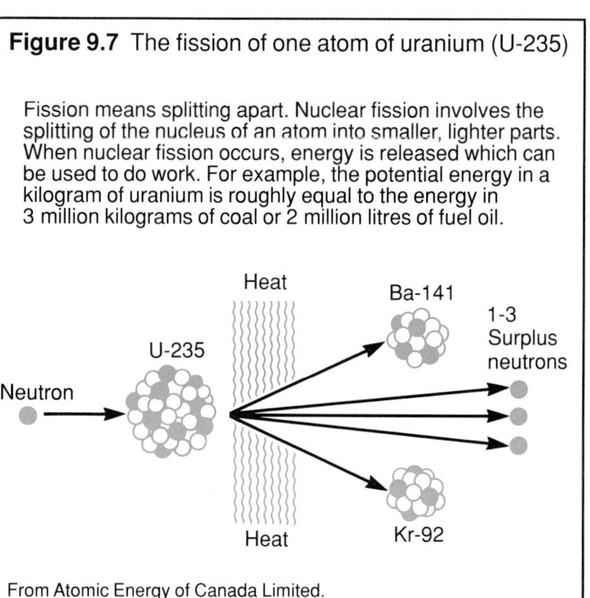

From Atomic Energy of Canada Limited.

The hazards of nuclear power

Radiation Radiation is the main hazard that most of us associate with nuclear power. Radiation refers to electromagnetic waves. This energy may be non-ionizing, as in the case of radio waves or microwaves. Nuclear radiation is ionizing, which means that it creates charged ions that have the capacity to damage living cells and possibly cause cancer.

Radiation is measured by **rads** (radiation absorbed dose) or **rems** (roentgen equivalent in man). These units are broadly similar, except that the rem allows for a correction factor for different types of radiation. One rad or rem is a significant dose of radiation. Smaller doses are measured in thousandth parts—that is, millirads and millirems.

Not many people realize that we live in an environment of constant radiation. The average amount of radiation received per person in a year from the atmosphere and from rocks such as granite is 53 millirems. Another 25 millirems comes from materials within our own bodies and from the food we eat. If you live at a high altitude, as in Denver, Colorado, you receive 104 millirems from cosmic and terrestial sources each year, plus 25 millirems from within your body. A chest X-ray will give you up to 15 millirems, and a six-hour flight at 10 000 m will add another 3 millirems. A nuclear power station, operating normally, will emit only tiny doses of radiation, certainly much less than we get from the radionuclides emitted by burning fossil fuels.

In 1996 at Chernobyl in Ukraine an explosion occurred in a nuclear reactor, blowing off the roof and releasing large quantities of radioactive material into the air. An accident such as this one can create an exposure of 50 to 100 rems. Fifty rems will normally cause radiation sickness, but exposure to 10 rems may damage the lymph nodes and bone marrow, greatly increasing the risk of cancer. Ten years after the accident, low level radiation still affected soil, vegetation, and buildings over large areas of the Ukraine. The effects on the health of the population continue to rise. Many new cases of leukemia and thyroid cancer are occurring, especially among children. It is predicted that this upsurge will continue for up to 20 years. Another group affected are the so-called "liquidators" who conducted cleanup operations after the explosion. The Ukrainian government has promised to close Chernobyl in the year 2000.

The worst nuclear accident in North America took place in 1979 at Three Mile Island in Harrisburg, Pennsylvania. In this incident, human error led to overheating in a reactor. A small amount of radiation was released. According to official sources no health effects were caused by the accident, but researchers claim that some increase in cancer and birth defects has occurred.

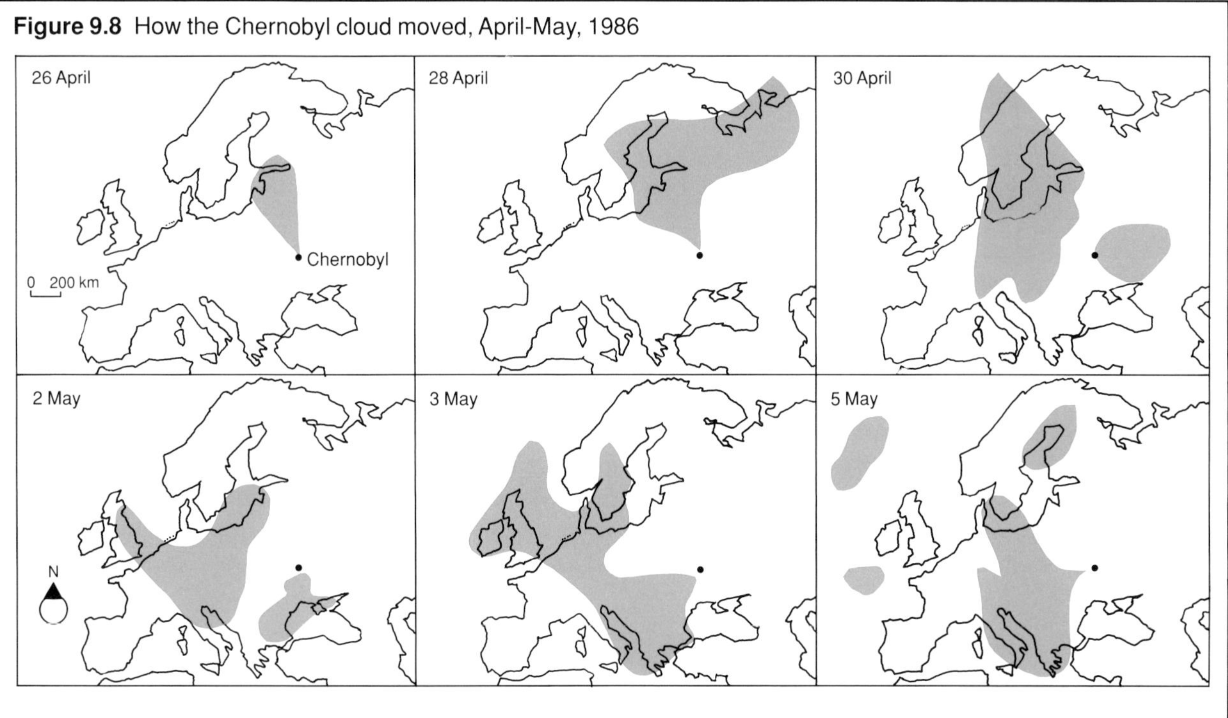

Figure 9.8 How the Chernobyl cloud moved, April-May, 1986

The problems of nuclear waste disposal More discussion centres on the issue of nuclear waste disposal than any other related to nuclear power. The by-products created by nuclear fission, such as caesium, strontium, and plutonium, have "half-lives" of thousands or even millions of years. After that length of time they will have lost half of their radioactivity. Although it is hard to believe, nuclear wastes were once dumped at sea in concrete drums. These drums will never last as long as their radioactive contents.

About 90 percent of nuclear waste is low-level or medium-level waste, which presents a relatively short-lived hazard. The nuclear industry claims that concrete vault storage is appropriate for this waste. The remaining 10 percent is high-level waste, coming mainly from the chemical reprocessing of spent fuel. This waste generates heat and intense radioactivity. Today this waste is usually stored at nuclear sites, awaiting a more permanent solution. This problem is being intensely studied in countries that use nuclear power.

Many nuclear waste disposal techniques have been suggested. Shooting waste into space is often mentioned, but it is too dangerous and costly to be considered practical. Burying waste deep in geologically stable rock is one possible method. The use of deep undersea shafts is another. The main problem is that no municipality or province wants to have these wastes dumped in their territory. The voters would have something to say at the next election. (Remember the NIMBY syndrome!) Some people fear that highly radioactive materials could be used as a form of terrorism if they fell into the wrong hands. This fear also applies to plutonium, which is a raw material in the nuclear weapons industry.

Finally, there is the problem of how to get nuclear waste from the reactor site to an eventual dumping ground. Roads and railways pass through many settlements. Carrying nuclear waste invites the possibility of serious accidents that could expose people to high doses of radiation.

Not surprisingly, many people fear the nuclear industry and do not want to have it located anywhere near their homes, especially after the accident at Chernobyl. In Sweden, for example, the government has decided to phase out its nuclear reactors at the end of their planned lives and to replace them with other types of power stations.

The nuclear power debate

A complicated issue such as nuclear power tends to divide people along sharply opposing lines. Our opinions are shaped by what we read or see on television. Newspaper articles and TV reports that influence our views often combine fact with opinion. Fact is something known to be true; opinion is a firmly held belief, but it is not necessarily supported by facts. You should bear this in mind when you read the opposing two arguments on pages 145 and 146. The first article is by naturalist Russell Peterson, written for the *Los Angeles Times*. The second article is by engineer Andrew Kenny who has worked in both the coal and nuclear power industries. His article first appeared in *The Spectator* magazine.

The issue of nuclear power cannot be considered in isolation. If we do not use nuclear power, other sources of power have to be developed. Renewable sources of energy, as we will see, will not meet our energy needs in the near future. Oil and natural gas are increasingly scarce resources and are better used for other purposes. This leaves coal as the most abundant available resource for the generation of power. China, for example, plans to build 200 coal-fired stations over the next thirty years. This has serious consequences for the state of the global atmosphere.

The arguments in favour of nuclear power have been strengthened recently by the growing concern over the greenhouse effect and other results of the burning of fossil fuels. The supporters of nuclear power also point out that research into nuclear power may one day lead to **nuclear fusion**, with the prospect of generating enormous quantities of power by combining rather than splitting atoms. The main problem standing in the way of nuclear fusion is the need to contain the enormous temperatures involved. The gain is a much lower production of radioactive waste than from nuclear fission.

In isolation nuclear power seems a very dangerous way of generating electricity. If, however, we must have electricity, we can only make a valid decision about how to generate it if we carefully examine the advantages and disadvantages of each method.

Small-scale nuclear power

Nuclear power can be generated on a small scale using the Slowpoke technology, originally invented in Canada in 1970. It is small-scale, safe, and self-regulating. The fuel core of a Slowpoke unit is equivalent in size to a 4 L can of paint and lasts twenty-five years. It has been used in medical research at the University of Toronto since 1970.

A newer version of the Slowpoke, called the Slowpoke Energy System (SES), is being developed. This version requires a fuel core equivalent to 120 L, lasting five years. Heat is carried by circulating water to a heat exchanger. (See Figure 9.9.) A unit of this system should be able to generate 10 MW of electricity or could be used to heat water in smaller communities.

Figure 9.9 How the Slowpoke nuclear furnace works

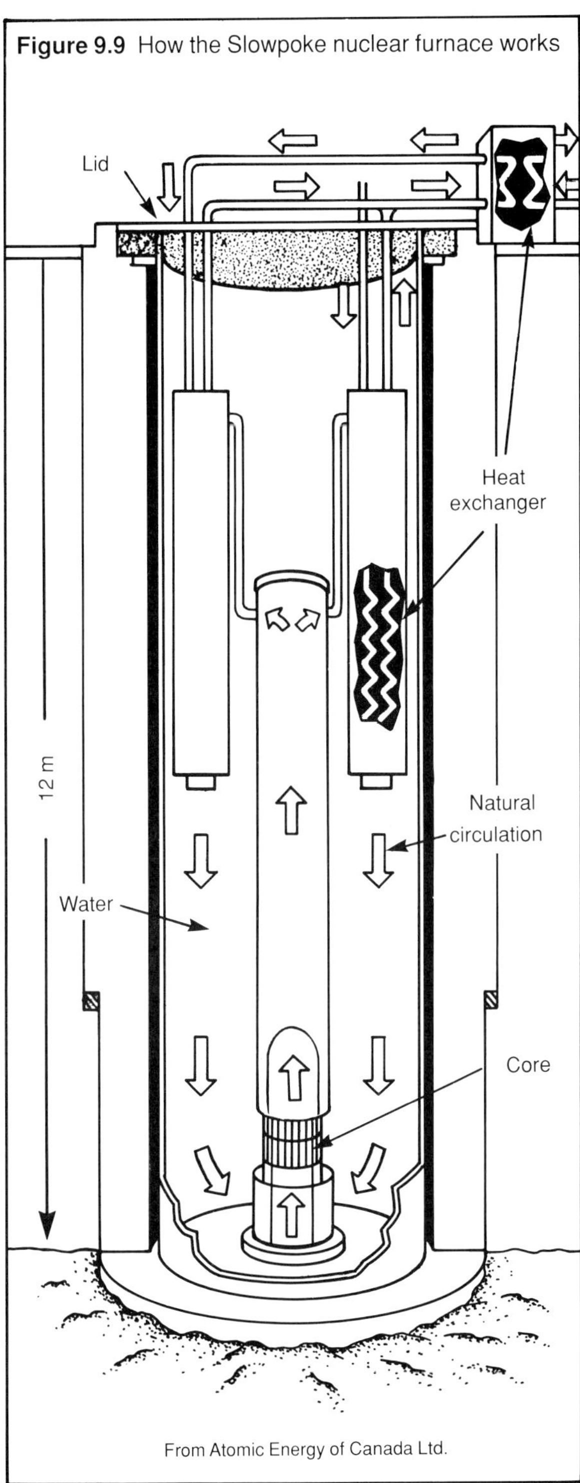

From Atomic Energy of Canada Ltd.

MELTDOWN HASTENS SEARCH FOR SAFER ENERGY SOURCES

The nuclear reactor disaster in the Soviet Union should awaken world leadership to the need to expand research and development on alternative sources of energy.

Not only Chernobyl, but the fiasco at Three Mile Island in 1979 and the recent tragic failure of the space shuttle *Challenger* should warn us all how fallible we humans are.

Nuclear energy is super-dangerous and we must face up to this fact.

Why else would we spend a billion or more dollars for safety devices for a single reactor? Why else would we install a containment building with metre-thick steel reinforced walls around the reactor? Why do insurance companies refuse to cover the nuclear industry's potential liability? And why did the industry refuse to go ahead with the construction of nuclear plants until the federal government drastically limited the amount of damages that the utilities would have to pay out in the event of an accident? Why, after seven years and the expenditure of hundreds of millions of dollars, is the damaged reactor at Three Mile Island still not cleaned up? Why do the news media and government leaders cry out hour-by-hour about the great hazards of the Chernobyl accident? Is it because nuclear energy is safe?

The Soviet disaster, which may have killed thousands and incapacitated many more, and which will probably make a substantial part of the Ukraine uninhabitable for decades, is just the current debacle. More will certainly follow.

The world now has 361 nuclear power reactors in operation, with another 144 under construction or on order. Many of the older ones are increasingly susceptible to failure. The serious financial problems of the nuclear industry and the waning interest in technical careers in this field bode ill for adequate staffing and management of the reactors in the future.

Forty years into the nuclear era, the world still does not have the means to dispose of the highly radioactive waste accumulating at nuclear plants. Each year about one-third of the used fuel loaded with highly dangerous fission products is placed in pools of water outside the protection of the containment buildings, waiting for a decision as to what to do with it — or for some accident or terrorist act to spread it around the countryside.

The most serious threat from nuclear energy plants — one far beyond another Chernobyl-type disaster — is their production of plutonium, the ingredient of nuclear bombs. It is now becoming an article of international commerce. Little imagination is required to picture a terrorist with a homemade bomb holed up in a rooming house on Capitol Hill in Washington.

It appears essential, then, to provide humanity with alternative sources of energy supply.

THE CLEAN ANSWER TO KING COAL'S POISONOUS REIGN

By every measure the death rate from coal power is much larger than the death rate from nuclear power. Per unit of energy extracted, coal mining claims more than ten times as many deaths as uranium mining. Far worse are the civilian casualties. Study after study into the deaths caused by coal pollution agree that the figure is about fifty deaths per medium-sized coal station per year. This figure is necessarily tentative [because the effects of coal pollution are widespread but not always observed. It translates into 25 000 deaths per year in America and 1700 deaths per year in Britain].

The World Health Organization estimates that the Chernobyl accident may cause 1600 premature deaths over the next thirty years. Thus coal in the United Kingdom will kill more civilians in one year than Chernobyl will kill in thirty. And Chernobyl is the only civilian nuclear accident ever to claim a life. Three Mile Island killed nobody, and exposed the nearest civilians to radiation less than one-tenth of one dental X-ray.

The direct human casualties from coal power, although far larger than from nuclear power, are dwarfed by the devastation coal causes to the environment. Acid rain, caused by sulphur dioxides and nitrogen oxides from coal stations and other burning of fossil fuel, has already caused vast damage to the planet's lakes and forests and the damage is spreading.

Even more ominous are the future consequences of the millions of tonnes of carbon dioxide that coal stations pour into the atmosphere. The "greenhouse effect" has been much in the news recently. ...The global weather system is very complicated and very finely poised, and it is difficult to make short-term assessments. The human race is threatened by several rising trends...but of all the graphs of doom none gives such apocalyptic warning as the rising levels of carbon dioxide. Nuclear stations produce not one drop of acid rain, nor one breath of carbon dioxide.

There is no such thing as a clean coal power station. A "clean stack" simply means that the visible pollution has been removed. But most coal pollution is invisible. Only a minority of advanced coal stations have chemical scrubbing and even these only attempt to remove the SO_2 and the NO_x. None tries to remove the heavy metals. It is impossible to remove the carbon dioxide.

The best argument for nuclear power is simply a comparison between its dangers and the dangers of all competitors, including the renewable resources, but mainly coal. ...The dangers of coal are much greater than those of nuclear power but much less well publicized. ...Some people suspect that the power utilities are covering up a big secret about nuclear power. They are right. The big secret is that nuclear power is very much safer than coal.

Published by permission of *The Spectator*.

Alternative energy sources

This term applies to all methods, other than hydroelectric power, that attempt to harness power from renewable sources of energy. Hydroelectric power has been in existence long enough to be considered a conventional energy source. All forms of energy that use renewable resources are sometimes known as **soft energy**, since they do not create as much pollution as the burning of fossil fuels. They do affect the environment, however. Solar energy, for example, uses great quantities of materials, such as silicon, glass, or aluminum, per unit of electricity generated. Soft energy is usually decentralized and produced in smaller units than conventional large-scale power stations.

Solar power

The harnessing of solar energy has been an attractive goal since the rise in energy costs in 1973. Sunlight brings to the earth the equivalent of 170 billion MW of power. Half an hour's sunlight could, in theory, provide the energy used by the whole world in one year. Unfortunately, solar energy is not concentrated but is spread over the earth's surface.

Solar energy may be used in construction in two ways. With **passive solar energy**, buildings are designed to make the best use of sunshine. Design features may be as simple as the placement of windows or the use of insulating materials. **Active solar energy** involves the use of devices to heat water or space within buildings. Many homes and swimming pools in Canada are heated by solar systems. Techniques have also been developed to store excess summer heat to be used in the winter, as in the government of Canada building in Scarborough, Ontario, where heat is stored in an underground aquifer. (See Figure 9.10.) The initial cost of installing a system is high, but the running cost is low and maintenance is easy. However, many people may not want to wait the fourteen years or so that it takes to recover the costs of solar heating.

Generating electricity from solar power is another matter. There are two methods used. One is the use of **photovoltaic cells**, which means using high-grade silicon to harness solar energy waves. Some 3000 systems are in use across Canada, mainly to operate remote beacons or meteorological stations.

Several photovoltaic power stations existed in southern California in 1990, but some were dismantled and the silicon panels sold for domestic use. The reason was the high capital cost of constructing the stations. The cost of generating electricity was twelve cents per kilowatt-hour, yet the power was being sold to utilities for only four cents per kilowatt-hour. The

Figure 9.10 The government of Canada building, Scarborough, Ontario

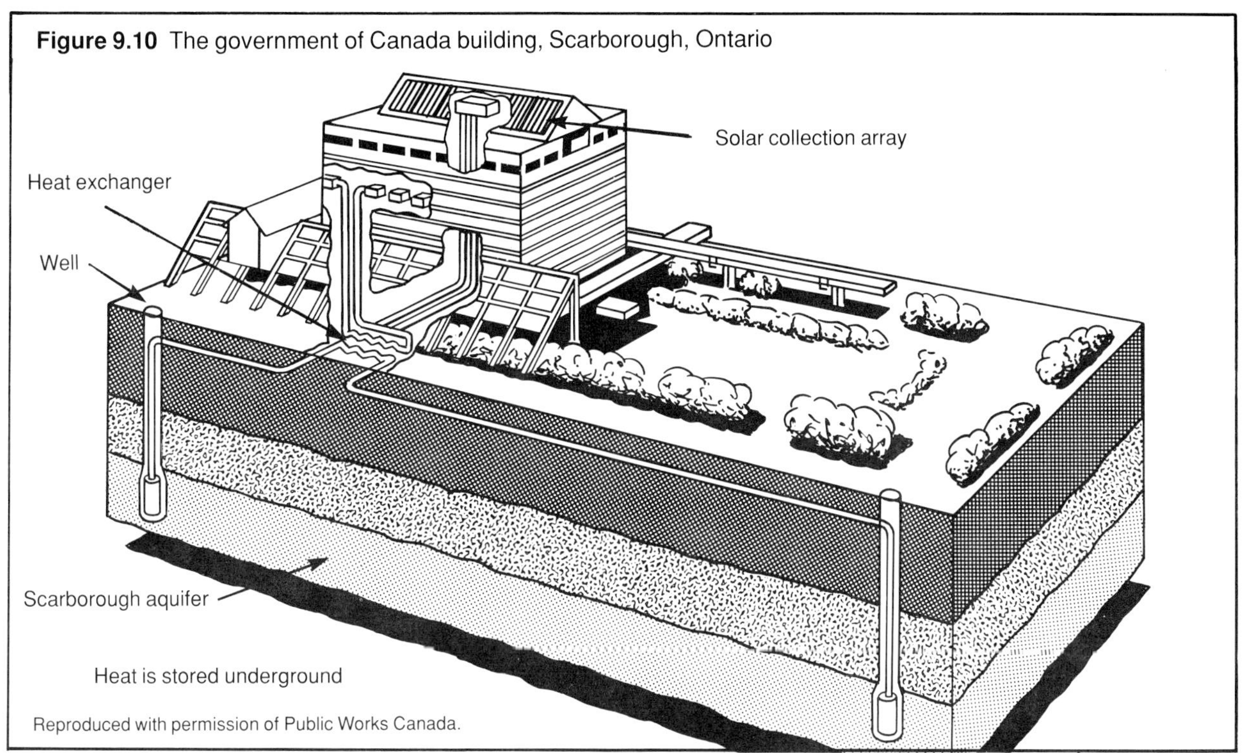

Reproduced with permission of Public Works Canada.

operators of photovoltaic projects claim that solar power will become economical only when the price of oil rises to over $40 (US) a barrel and when the government stops subsidizing the costs of electricity generated by fossil fuels.

A less costly method of generating power from the sun is the use of solar mirrors to create **solar thermal energy**. Mirrors track the sun and focus solar energy on pipes filled with synthetic oil. The oil is heated to nearly 400°C and then used to convert water to steam, which drives the turbines. The largest power stations of this type are operated by Luz International (now Solel) in southern California with a total capacity of 354 MW of electricity, enough for 170 000 homes. The costs of this type of solar generation are around eight cents per kilowatt-hour and are still falling.

There are many predictions as to how much solar electricity can be generated in the world by 2000, but the highest prediction is only 0.5 percent of all electrical energy needs. The future of solar energy as a source of water and space heating is more promising than as a source of electricity.

The photovoltaic solar station in southern California (top) and the Luz International thermal solar station at Kramer Junction, near Barstow, California, are two alternative sources of energy.

Wind power

Wind power is one of the least damaging forms of energy. Windmills were first known to be used in Persia before A.D.1000. Later the Dutch used windmills to grind corn and to drain low-lying land.

Today the Worldwatch Institute estimates that about 1 million small windmills pump water for livestock, irrigation, and domestic use throughout the world. In addition, nearly 20 000 wind generators produced over 3 000 MW of electricity in places as far apart as Denmark and California in 1994.

As in solar energy, the costs of constructing wind turbines is high. A 150 kW turbine costs about $165 (US) to build. The cost of wind-generated electricity is about 5 to 7 cents per kWh, only slightly higher than energy produced by conventional means. This cost comparison may change for a number of reasons. Fossil fuels may rise in price, or the power utilities may be forced to pay for the environmental damage they cause. Apart from the cost of the materials used to make wind generators, they are a clean source of energy. Some people, however, object to wind farms on account of their appearance.

Tidal power

Another potential source of power lies in the movement of the tides. Twice a day, enormous volumes of water move in and out of bays and estuaries. The world's first tidal power project was built on the La Rance estuary in Brittany, France, in 1967. The Bay of Fundy, between Nova Scotia and New Brunswick, has one of the world's most favourable potential tidal power sites. Here the tidal range is up to 16 m. A barrage across the bay, with built-in reversing turbines, could produce over 4000 MW of electricity. A small (20 MW) pilot project was built in 1984 at Annapolis Royal in Nova Scotia.

Tidal power has the advantage of not creating acid rain or greenhouse gases. However, there are concerns about the environmental effects of a barrage across the Bay of Fundy. The fishing industry strongly opposes the scheme. So do environmentalists on the grounds that wildlife would suffer. A Bay of Fundy barrage would affect large-scale water movements, possibly raising sea level by as much as 13 cm as far south as Boston. Much debate will occur before a decision is made to build this $10 billion (CDN) project.

Wind farms such as this one in Hawaii cause minimal environmental damage.

The Annapolis Royal pilot tidal power project in Nova Scotia has caused concern among environmentalists.

Geothermal power

Geothermal energy comes from the heat contained in the earth's crust. Geysers and hot springs are examples of geothermal energy released on the surface of the earth. Iceland, Mexico, and New Zealand have generated power from geothermal sources for many years. However, only 7000 MW of electrical capacity from geothermal sources existed in the world in 1993.

The temperature under the surface of the ground normally increases by about 25°C for every 1000 m. In certain locations hot rocks lie close to the surface and the rise in temperature is much greater than 25°C per 1000 m. This can happen in both volcanic and sedimentary areas.

There are two methods of obtaining energy from geothermal sources. (See Figure 9.11.) The first uses hot water or steam reservoirs. The hot water or steam can be tapped from the underground source and used to drive steam turbines. An alternative method, still at the experimental stage, is to pump water into an area with hot rocks by using an injection well. Steam could then be tapped from a second well and used to drive turbines or heat homes.

Geothermal power has some advantages over other forms of energy. In places such as Iceland, where fossil fuels are not locally available, geothermal energy is the cheapest source of heat. In Canada this is not yet the case. A good potential site exists, however, at Mount Meager in British Columbia. Surface drilling by BC Hydro has found temperatures as high as 280°C at a depth of 3000 m. Another Canadian location where hot water is found is in the sedimentary rock under Regina. The University of Regina heats a building from this source.

Geothermal power has some environmental disadvantages, although not on the scale of those caused by fossil fuel burning. Undesirable gases, especially hydrogen sulphide, may be given off. The underground water that brings the heat may also contain salts and heavy metals. Ideally this water should be re-injected into the rocks from which it came. Geothermal power sites can be noisy and release large amounts of heat into the atmosphere. Finally, geothermal power may not be truly renewable since the rocks that provide the hot water may cool down faster than they heat up again.

Figure 9.11 Methods of obtaining geothermal power

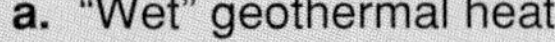

a. "Wet" geothermal heat

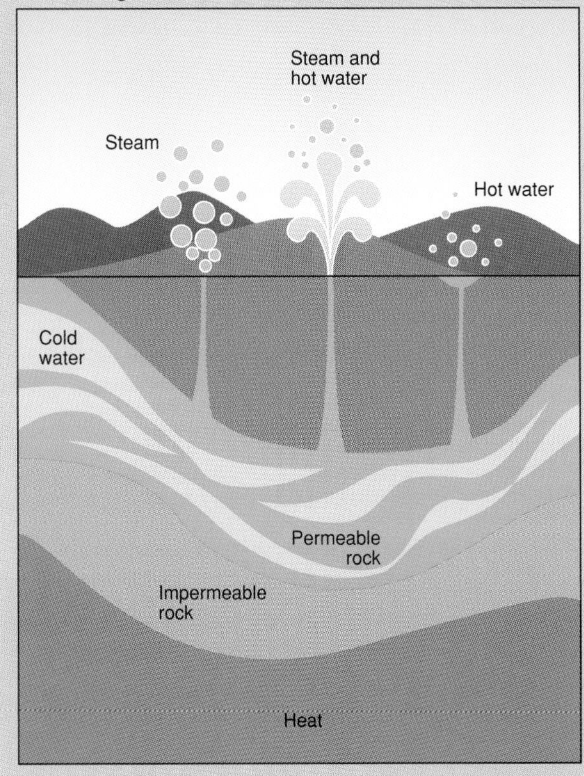

b. "Dry" geothermal heat

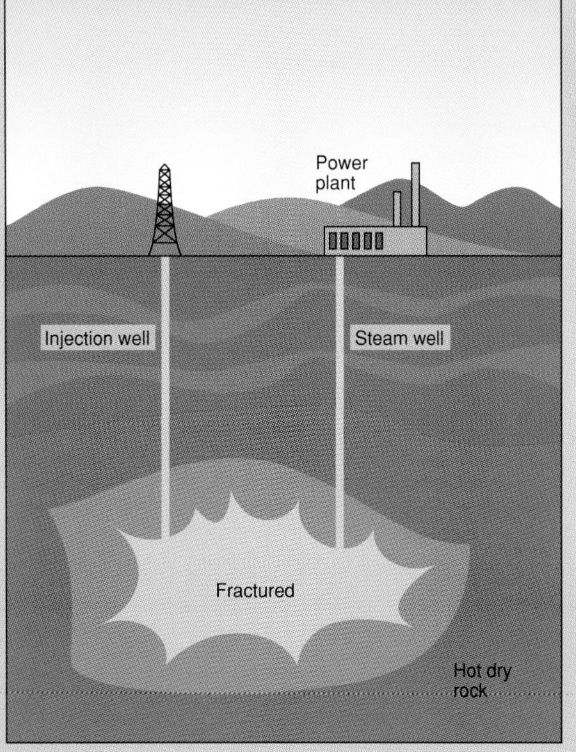

From Environment Canada, *Exploring Energy 3: Geothermal Energy*. Reproduced with permission of the Minister of Supply and Services Canada.

Biomass energy

Solar energy creates biomass, or living matter, by the process of photosynthesis. Photosynthesis is a far more efficient means of gathering energy from the sun than all the methods used by people.

A great deal of energy is available in the form of wood wastes. Canada now generates 3 percent of its energy from these wastes. Sawmills and pulp mills are increasingly using "hog fuel" (wood wastes) to generate power for their own operations instead of burning the wastes in "beehive" type burners. On the domestic front, 2 million Canadians heat their homes by burning wood, although they create some "log smog" in the process.

Much of the 2 kg of garbage that each of us creates each day is organic. In some Canadian cities this garbage is burned to provide heat. In Charlottetown, Prince Edward Island, this source of heat is used in a local hospital. In Québec City garbage incineration provides steam for a pulp and paper mill. It is better, however, to recycle rather than burn garbage.

Gas from biological sources is another form of energy generated from organic sources. Organic wastes can be harnessed, particularly dung from farms and methane from landfills, and turned into gas that can be used to provide heat or generate electricity. Some farms in Ontario already use biogas.

Biogas from dung is also used in some parts of China and India to generate power on a local scale providing lighting and pumped water. The left-over sludge is rich in nutrients and is returned to the fields as fertilizer.

Bioenergy research is still at an early stage and will not likely lead to more than small reductions in the use of fossil fuels.

McMillan Bloedel generates power from wood waste.

Using energy more efficiently

In North America we have become used to cheap, abundant energy. Our use of power and consumption of energy have been regarded as symbols of progress. But the creation of energy places stress on the environment, and fossil fuel reserves will not last forever. Our present attitude toward energy spells nothing but trouble in the future. Energy has to be used more sparingly and with greater concern for the environment. We should look at some ways to make our existing energy sources go further.

Saving electricity

Our use of energy is inefficient in many ways. Electricity contains only 35 to 40 percent of the heat value of the coal or oil from which it is generated. Yet we turn this electricity back into heat to warm our homes. This is a great waste of the heat that nature has stored for millions of years.

By the year 1989, an estimated $20 billion was being spent annually on new generating plants throughout the world. Most used fossil fuels to produce power at a cost of 4 to 6 cents per kWh. However, if the demand for power could be reduced by conservation measures (**demand-side management**), the amount spent on new capacity could be reduced. The cost of reducing the demand for electricity is only about 2 cents per kWh.

Ontario Hydro, Hydro Quebec and BC Hydro all had demand-side management programs in place by 1994. As a by-product, carbon emissions could be cut by 20 percent by 2005. Savings in energy use could be achieved by:

- requiring cars to get better gasoline mileage;
- increasing the use of mass transit;
- increasing the use of more efficient lighting in homes and office buildings;
- better insulating and/or solar heating our homes and office buildings;
- recycling more waste or using it to generate electrical power.

Much of this saving depends on the actions of individuals and families. By not overheating our homes in the winter or overcooling them in the summer, much power can be saved. Home insulation and the reduced use of home appliances also helps to cut bills. For example, washing clothes in cold or cool water and drying them on a line instead of in a dryer helps to reduce the total demand for electricity.

Planning future power demand — Ontario Hydro

The expansion of Ontario's economy in the middle and late 1980s was expected to lead to a shortage of electricity in the 1990s and beyond. In 1989 Ontario Hydro used a major publicity scheme to encourage consumers to reduce their energy demands (**demand-side management**). Conservation is the best way of reducing the large sums spent on new generating facilities. Because of reduced demand, Ontario Hydro has abandoned its ambitious expansion plans.

BC Hydro also has a demand-side management scheme, called *Power Smart*. Figure 9.12 shows the cumulative savings in power use since 1989.

Figure 9.12 Total *Power Smart* impact (including on-going savings)

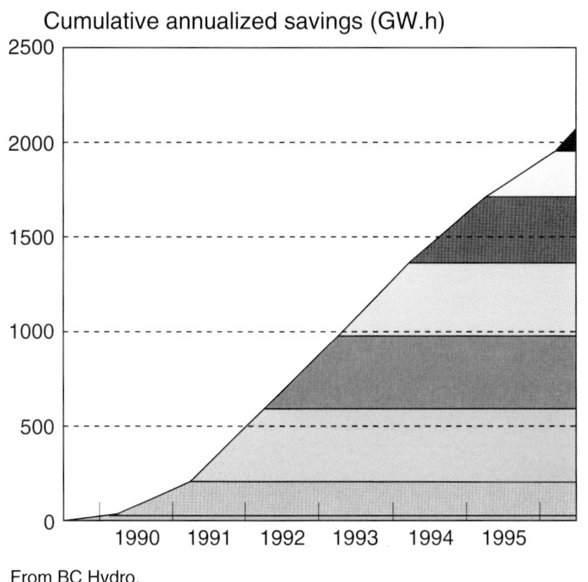

From BC Hydro.

Combined Heat and Power (CHP)

Much of the heat that power stations waste is lost to the atmosphere through cooling towers. One way of saving this energy is to circulate heat from power stations to homes and other buildings in the area. Such schemes are known as **combined heat and power (CHP)** or **cogeneration** and can operate at efficiencies of 80 percent or more compared with 35 or 40 percent for fossil fuel power stations. CHP gas turbines could reduce the energy costs of heating buildings by an estimated 80 percent. These turbines use small power stations that are centrally located with respect to population. CHP schemes are well suited to run on natural gas, which is the least polluting and most readily available fossil fuel. The Netherlands has led the way in introducing CHP, with Germany not far behind. Many such schemes are being introduced in the United States and Canada.

Other possibilities for saving energy

Technology offers many possibilities for saving energy, as Figure 9.14 shows. Savings of up to 75 percent of present fuel consumption may be possible for cars. Some car makers have already produced engines that use less than half the amount of fuel. New fuels, such as hydrogen, may offer cleaner and more efficient energy. Furthermore, home appliances could be designed to use about 50 percent less energy, and more efficient air transport could save over 25 percent of the energy now used. Many of these improvements could be introduced now, but the costs of the products would be considerably higher.

Savings of this size would require strong government leadership and probably high taxes on the use of energy. Leaving energy conservation to the individual does not always achieve enough. For example, the

Figure 9.13 The cogeneration plant at the Ottawa Health Sciences Centre

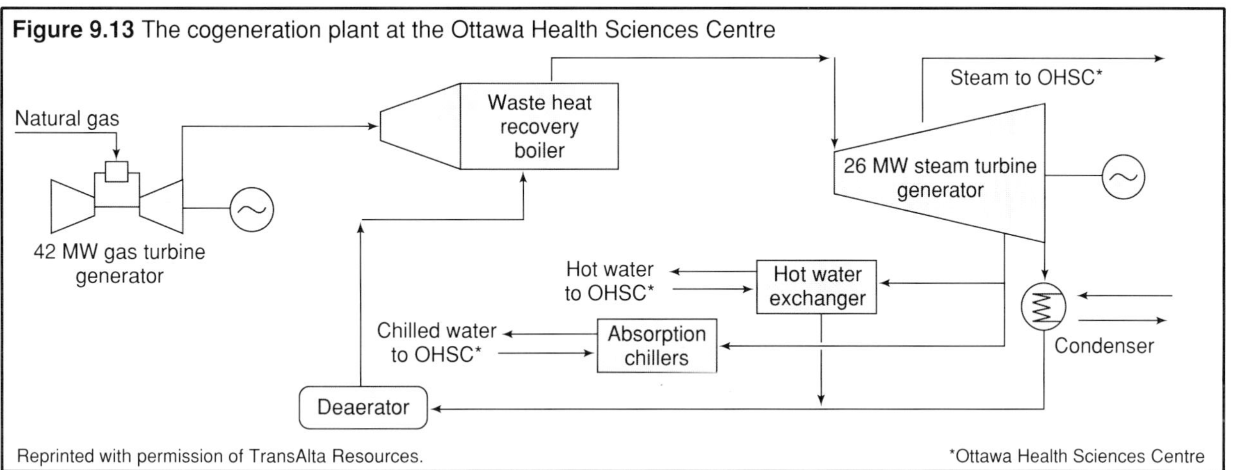

Reprinted with permission of TransAlta Resources.

*Ottawa Health Sciences Centre

lower oil prices of 1986 set in motion a renewed demand for gas-guzzling cars. To lead the move to energy conservation, governments would have to invest large sums of money in alternative energy sources. They can set a good example by saving energy in their own buildings and operations.

Figure 9.14 Opportunities for efficiency in the use of energy

	MODEL AVERAGE	NEW MODEL AVERAGE	BEST MODEL	BEST PROTOTYPE
Car (kilometres per litre)	7.6	11.4	21.1	32.5
Home (thousand joules per square metre)	190	110	68	11
Refrigerator (kilowatt-hours per day)	4	3	2	1
Gas furnace (million joules per day)	210	180	140	110
Air conditioner (kilowatt hours per day)	10	7	5	3

From "Strategies for Energy Use," by John H. Gibbons, Peter D. Blair, and Holly L. Gwin.

Saving energy in developing countries

Biomass plays a vital role in the lives of people in developing countries. The burning of wood, crop wastes, and dung provides most of their energy. India may be the tenth largest industrial country, but cooking accounts for half its energy needs. In Western countries, cooking uses less than one-tenth of all energy consumed.

There are two possible answers to the fuel shortages of developing countries.

The first is to concentrate on growing trees specifically to provide a regular harvest of fuel wood. The community would plant and manage these forests. **Community forestry schemes** would reduce the random collecting of firewood that has caused so much deforestation and soil erosion, especially in Africa. The availability of wood would take an enormous burden off women in the developing world who may spend as many as six hours per day collecting wood and water. In both Africa and Asia women lead the way in the provision of new forests for both fuel and fodder. In Kenya several hundred women's organizations are planting trees for fuel wood and soil conservation. The Chipko Movement in India is another women-led force for reforestation.

The second method of saving energy in developing countries is to introduce more energy- efficient stoves. This would also help to protect the forests. The traditional African stove is three large stones with a fire underneath and a pot on top. Such stoves are only

Ethiopian women plant trees by the roadside.

about 30 percent efficient. Much research has taken place, some of it by aid agencies, into providing low-cost energy-efficient stoves that could reduce the demand for fuel wood in developing countries by as much as half. These methods will help to reduce one of the most serious threats to the world environment — a surge in the energy demands of developing countries.

Cooking on a traditional African three-stone hearth consumes a considerable amount of fuel wood.

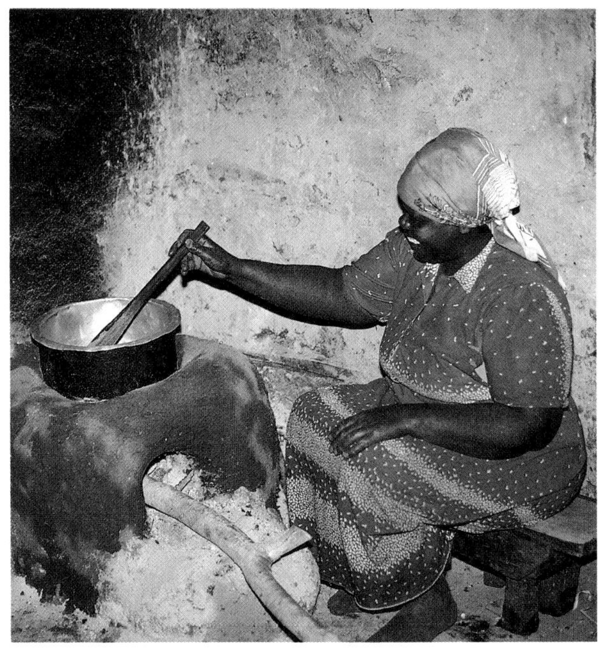

Energy efficient "jiko" stoves, such as this one in Kenya, can help to reduce energy demands in developing countries.

Looking back

1. Which of the countries in Figure 9.3 have increased their coal output and which have shown a decline? Can you suggest reasons for the changes?
2. (a) List the questions about energy use that are raised in the text.
   (b) Add at least three of your own questions about energy use.
3. In what sense is the burning of fossil fuels an inefficient way to generate electricity?
4. Why is it difficult for alternative energy sources to replace fossil fuels as the main sources of energy?
5. Explain the advantages of CHP schemes.
6. Describe two ways that the fuel wood crisis in the developing countries might be solved.

Applying your knowledge

1. In small groups, choose one of the following methods of generating electricity and create an organizer to show its environmental advantages and disadvantages.
   - hydroelectric dams
   - nuclear power plants
   - fossil fuel plants
   - alternate sources of energy.

   Share your group's findings with the rest of the class.
2. Examine Figure 9.1.
   (a) Draw a pie graph to show world energy consumption based on the data. (To find the number of degrees for each sector of the graph, take the total energy figure for each region, divide by the world total of 8220, and multiply by 360.)
   (b) Is there any correlation between the size of the population of a region and the amount of energy it consumes?
   (c) Describe how you arrived at your answer to (b).
   (d) What reasons can you give for this relationship?
3. Research the fossil fuels burned to produce usable energy. (This could be done in groups, with each group working on one fuel.) Your investigations should include:
   (a) the characteristics of the fuel (that is, is it plentiful? costly? easily transported? etc.);
   (b) how the fuel is converted into electricity (include a diagram);
   (c) the damage to the environment the extraction of the fuel causes;
   (d) the pollution the burning of the fuel causes; and

(e) how much of our total energy is produced from this source.

Present your findings to the class. When all of the presentations have been made, brainstorm to reach some conclusions about fossil fuels.

4. (a) Prepare a table listing the advantages and disadvantages of hydroelectric power from an environmental point of view. Do you consider hydro power to be a sound energy alternative?
   (b) La Grande River scheme has been hailed as the greatest power project in Canada. Do you agree with this assessment? Give reasons for your answer.
5. Safety and waste disposal are the two major problems of nuclear generation of power. Write a short essay in which you predict the future of nuclear power. Include the reasons behind your prediction.
6. Arrange a field trip to the nearest power-generating plant in your area. After the trip, prepare a report outlining the type of plant visited, its contributions to the local area, and the environmental problems it creates.
7. (a) Draw an organizer to show how each of solar, wind, tidal, geothermal, and biomass power affects (i) the atmosphere, (ii) the hydrosphere, and (iii) the biosphere.
   (b) Briefly explain which of these alternative energy sources you think has the greatest potential to generate environmentally safe power.

Figure 9.15 Canada's energy sources (by percentage share)

1973

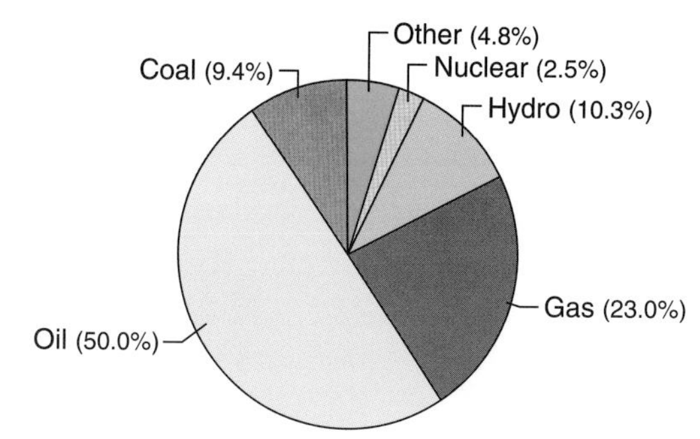

1993

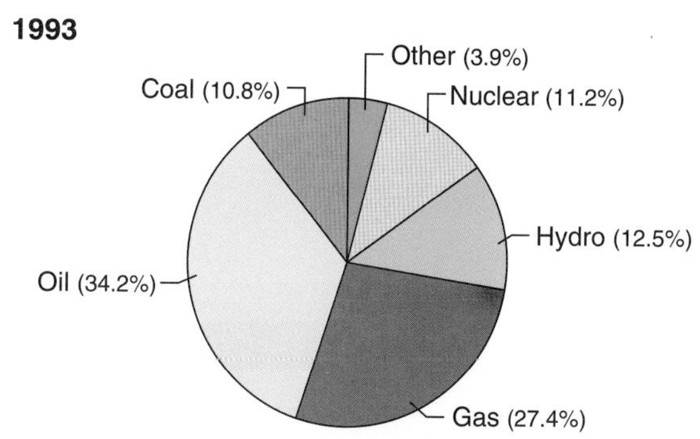

From International Energy Agency, OECD.

Extending your thinking

1. Use Figure 9.2 to complete the following activities:
   (a) Draw the outline for a **scattergraph** with per capita energy use on the y axis and per capita income on the x axis. Use a scale of 1 cm per tonne on the y axis and 1 cm per $1000 (US) on the x axis.
   (b) Plot each country from Figure 9.2. Add the names of the countries to your graph.
   (c) From your graph describe the relationship between per capita energy use and income. Identify any countries that do not fit the general pattern. Why do you think they are different?
   (d) Suggest reasons why Canada is near the top of the per capita energy use list.

2. Construct bar graphs of energy use in Canada in 1973 and 1993 using Figure 9.15. Explain the changes in the sources of energy used in Canada between 1973 and 1993.
3. (a) Survey your family's use of energy. What type of heating do you have? How fuel efficient are the cars? Check the appliances' Energuide labels and the type of light bulbs you use. List ways you and your family consume energy.
   (b) As a class, brainstorm ways you might reduce your energy consumption. Produce a personal energy conservation plan.
4. (a) Debate the resolution: "Nuclear power should play a major role in Canada's energy plans."
   (b) Do you find the arguments for or against nuclear power more convincing? Why? Which points raised do you consider to be fact and which ones opinion?
5. A major energy shortage is about to occur and you are to advise an emergency council on energy conservation. Produce a plan to reduce energy consumption in your community.
6. Prepare bulletin board displays depicting the following topics: "Alternative Energy Sources" and "Efficient Use of Energy." Try to place your displays in prominent positions in the school.

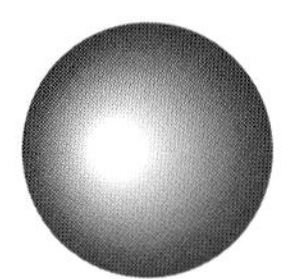

10 WASTE DISPOSAL

Canadians are among the most wasteful people on earth. We have the world's highest per capita energy consumption, creating a great amount of air pollution. We throw out enormous volumes of garbage, and we have one of the poorest records in the business of recycling, as Figure 10.1 shows.

The creation and disposal of garbage raises some important issues. Our dumps and **landfills** are rapidly filling up. New sites are both expensive and scarce.

Figure 10.1 Waste generation and management in selected countries

Per capita domestic waste generation per day in kilograms, 1989

Canada	1.7
United States	1.6
West Germany	1.4
Netherlands	1.1
United Kingdom	0.9
Japan	0.9
Sweden	0.8
China	0.5

How waste is managed in selected countries, 1989

	Disposal	Recycled or converted into energy
Canada	82%	18%
United States	76%	24%
West Germany	55%	45%
Japan	27%	73%

From the *Royal Bank Reporter*, Spring 1990, Environment Issue — To Conserve and Protect.

Yet the garbage issue is much more than finding places for our so-called waste products. Our wastes contain large volumes of potential resources, such as metals, organic nutrients, and paper. If these could be recycled, rather than added to the waste stream, we could reduce the pressure on the world's limited resources. We would also save much of the energy needed to make things from new raw materials. This would solve at least some of the atmospheric problems we are now facing. Fortunately, people are beginning to take the problem of waste disposal much more seriously.

Canadians generate about 1.7 kg of domestic **solid waste** per person per day (Figure 10.1). The largest single component of this waste is paper, as Figure 10.2 shows. The Canadian Council of Ministers of the Environment (CCME) aims to cut the amount of waste by 50% from 1988 levels by the year 2000.

If we include all forms of waste, including **sewage** and the waste products of mines, mills, and factories, the Canadian total is an alarming 6.2 kg per capita. The United States has a similar total, but Japan and most of the countries of Europe produce lower amounts of waste material and recycle a larger percentage of it.

Figure 10.2 What we throw away

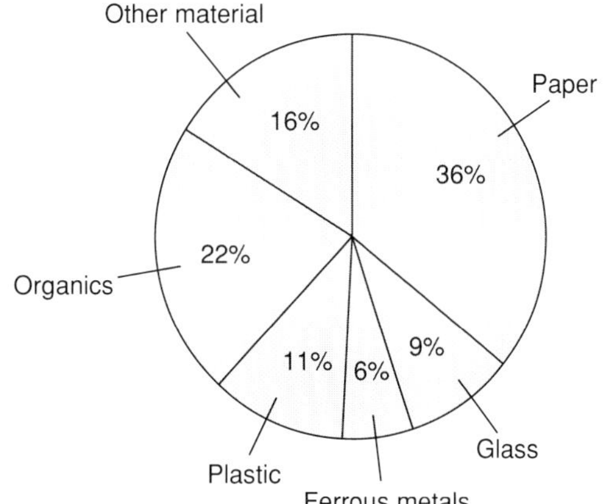

From the Recycling brochure, the Victoria Capital Region District Engineering Department, 524 Yates Street, Victoria, B.C.

Figure 10.3 How long does litter take to decompose?

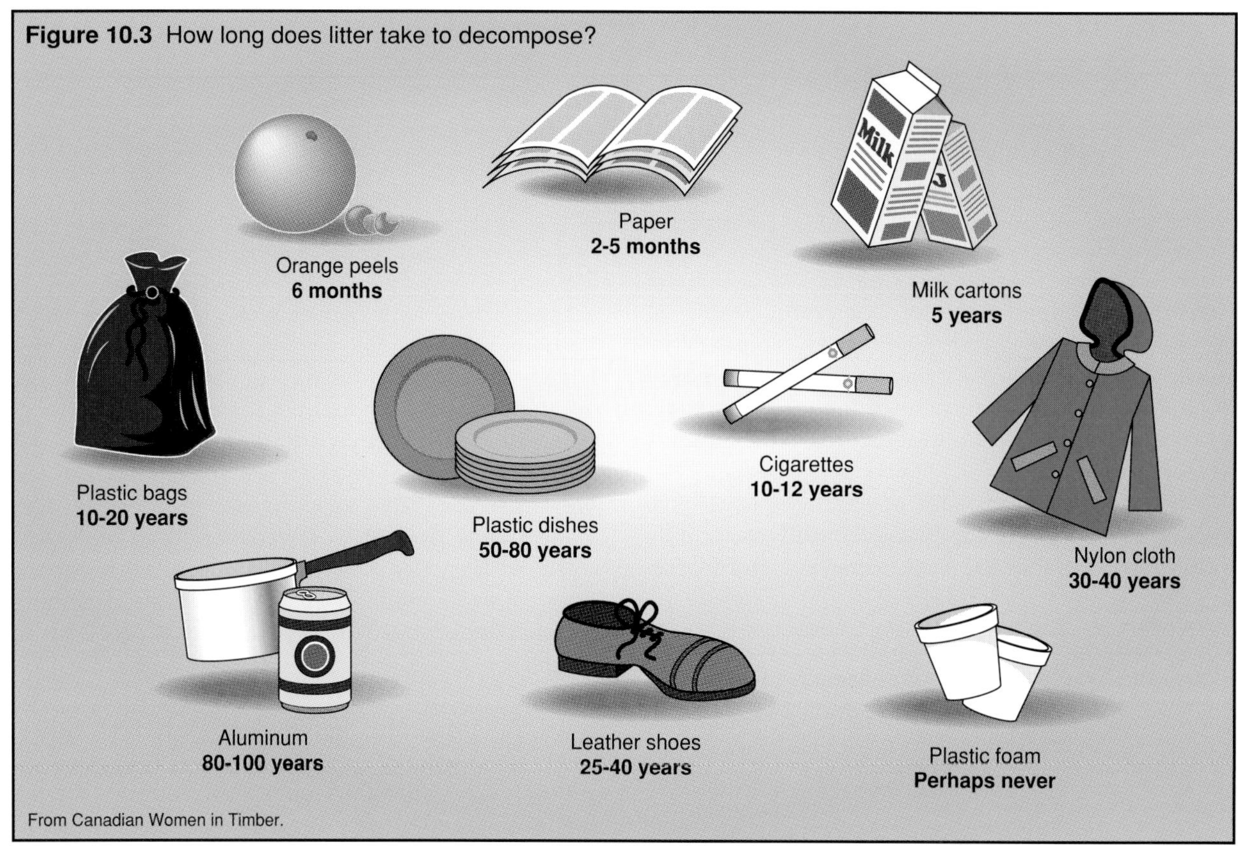

From Canadian Women in Timber.

Our garbage actually takes a surprisingly long time to decompose, especially in landfill sites where it is compressed before storage. Styrofoam, for example, may never decompose. (See Figure 10.3.)

Why so much waste?

There are several reasons why we create so much waste. The first is population growth. Even if the world's population maintains a steady rate of waste creation, its continued growth will be almost enough to generate a 2 percent increase in waste each year.

The second reason reflects our increased material standard of living. A two-income family has become the norm in most of the Western world. Many busy families believe they do not have time to reuse products, preferring to throw them away in favour of new replacements. Therefore they buy large amounts of disposable products, using paper plates and disposable diapers rather than buying products that can be washed and reused. Manufacturers have contributed to this trend by designing products with a limited lifespan. This is known as planned obsolescence. For example, cars that do not rust or wear out reduce future sales for car makers.

A third reason for the volume of waste is the packaging of our food and other products. Packaging alone accounts for 30 to 35 percent of what we throw out. Think of the moulded plastic containers in which many cheap articles are packaged and the use of plastic film to keep products supposedly clean. About 50 percent of the volume and 30 percent of the weight of domestic garbage consists of packaging of various kinds. The packaging industry in the United States has sales of $30 billion (US) per year.

Industry also contributes to the increased volume of waste. Increasingly complex industrial processes and the use of low-grade raw materials help to create much of the waste materials in our landfill sites.

The main problem is that we use so many articles only once, or a small number of times, before discarding them as garbage. This places a strain on the energy resources of our planet and on the limited supplies of minerals and other raw materials. The average Canadian consumes 18 000 kg of energy sources (coal, oil, natural gas, and uranium) every year through the production of consumer goods and the heating of our homes. Not surprisingly, both fossil fuels and minerals are likely to become scarce in the relatively near future. The large volume of materials used in North America also poses serious pollution problems.

Sewage

Sewage is the form of waste that we create most frequently. It contains not only human wastes, but the volumes of water that we use every day in our homes and places of work. In Canada we create about 750 L of sewage per capita each day.

Sewage removes, in liquid form, human wastes and other effluent from our homes and commercial buildings. Human waste is organic and degradable in the sense that decomposing bacteria reduce it to inorganic nutrients. The Chinese have recognized this, and they use human waste as **night soil** to fertilize their fields. In so doing they help to maintain the nutrient cycles. In most countries, especially in the West, these nutrients are not recycled into the ecosystem but are dumped into rivers, lakes, and oceans. Many Canadian cities located on bodies of water do just that, often without any treatment of the sewage beyond breaking up solids through a screening process known as **primary treatment.** **Secondary treatment** of sewage degrades the wastes to their inorganic elements. **Tertiary treatment** recovers these elements for future use. Only rarely is treated sewage effluent or sludge returned to the ecosystem through its application to farmland.

In the 1990s each Canadian family pours an average of 40 L of toxic wastes down the drain. For example, we carelessly dispose of solvents, paint thinners, pesticides, and engine oil into domestic sewage, thus contributing to the buildup of toxic chemicals in rivers, lakes, and oceans.

Many of the toxic contaminants in sewage do not degrade easily. If urban runoff is allowed to mix with sewage, then a whole range of heavy metals and oil residues will be mixed with sewage effluent. We also flush into sewage solid materials that will not degrade.

Sewage as a resource

The volume of potential nutrients in sewage makes it necessary to look at ways of recycling the nutrients back into the soil. Sewage contains many nutrients, as Figure 10.4 shows. The treatment of sewage results in two products for disposal, **sewage effluent**, which is a liquid, and **sludge**, which is semisolid.

If sewage is dumped in large quantities into water bodies, it can cause **eutrophication.** It may also create a major health hazard. For example, in the mid-nineteenth century the Thames River in England was virtually an open sewer. The smell became so bad that shields had to be fixed on the windows of the Houses of Parliament. During a cholera epidemic in the nineteenth century, research on the problems of the Thames River led to the discovery that cholera was a disease that was transmitted by drinking infected water. London's problem was solved in part by the construction of sewage interceptors that diverted sewage downstream from the city.

Even today, outbreaks of cholera may be linked to the pollution of drinking water from spills of untreated sewage. In less developed countries, river and groundwater pollution from untreated sewage is a major health hazard.

Figure 10.4 Nutrients in typical sewage

Biodegradable organic matter	15 to 100 mg/L
Suspended solids	15 to 100 mg/L
Total nitrogen	10 to 30 mg/L
Total phosphorus	4 to 10 mg/L
Potassium	5 to 40 mg/L

From Alberta Environment.

The problem of toxins in sewage

With time or treatment, human waste reverts to inorganic nutrients without creating great health hazards. At least this is true in a country such as Canada, which has a high standard of public sanitation and a chlorinated water supply. More serious are the chemicals that we use in our homes. Ironically, we use many of these chemicals in our efforts to keep clean. We use large quantities of laundry and dish-washing detergents, bleach, and other cleaning agents. Until the 1970s nearly all detergents contained phosphates. When released into lakes and rivers, these phosphates contributed to eutrophication. Most detergents no longer contain phosphates, although they do contain other cleaning agents that are toxic to some degree.

The alternative to using sewage nutrients for agricultural purposes is to continue to use chemical fertilizers in large quantities. The production of fertilizers requires the heavy use of fossil fuels, contributing to problems such as increased levels of carbon dioxide in the air. Chemical fertilizers are also too expensive for most farmers in developing countries.

The use of sewage effluent

The use of sewage effluent in farming appears to offer a solution to at least some of these problems. Some parts of Canada have experimented with sewage effluent. For example, since 1969 sewage effluent projects have been successfully introduced in Alberta. Figure 10.6 shows one way that the effluent is applied. Solid material is allowed to settle in the lagoon before the liquid is applied to the fields.

Several factors limit the technique shown in Figure 10.6. The fields have to be flat to prevent effluent running off into rivers or streams. Careful monitoring of the soil is necessary to ensure that sewage effluent does not contaminate groundwater, which is also true for the use of chemical fertilizers. Another problem is that large sources of sewage require expensive distribution facilities. The harmful micro-organisms associated with sewage are usually killed by exposure to strong sunlight. Alberta Environment summarizes the sewage effluent schemes in Figure 10.5.

Figure 10.5 The use of sewage effluent

ADVANTAGES	COST ITEMS
Increased crop production	Storage facilities
Reduction in fertilizer costs	Transmission facilities
Reuse of nutrients and water	Pumping facilities
Elimination of effluent discharge to surface waters	Purchasing or leasing of land
Conservation of surface water sources	Irrigation equipment
DISADVANTAGES	Runoff collection facilities
Potential for disease transmission	Monitoring facilities
Potential adverse effects on the soil and groundwater	Roads and fences
	Operation and maintenance

The use of sludge The composition of the more solid sludge is varied. It contains organic material and water but also varying quantities of heavy metals, salts, and sand. Sludge must be analysed to ensure that it is appropriate for application to the land. However, sludge is usually rich in nutrients and is therefore a good fertilizer. It may contain as much as 70 percent organic matter, which is good for building up the quality of the soil. In some places sludge is used to breed earthworms.

Sludge also involves health risks from micro-organisms. Therefore sludge should not be used on grazing land or on crops that will be eaten raw. Because of the amount of lead, chromium, and other heavy metals in sludge, great care must be taken not to pollute groundwater.

If the use of sludge on fields seems to have more disadvantages than sewage effluent, remember that it is a low-cost means of disposal. If sludge is not used in this way, it must be disposed of in landfill sites or incinerated. This can be expensive and is environmentally hazardous.

Figure 10.6 Applying sewage effluent to agriculture

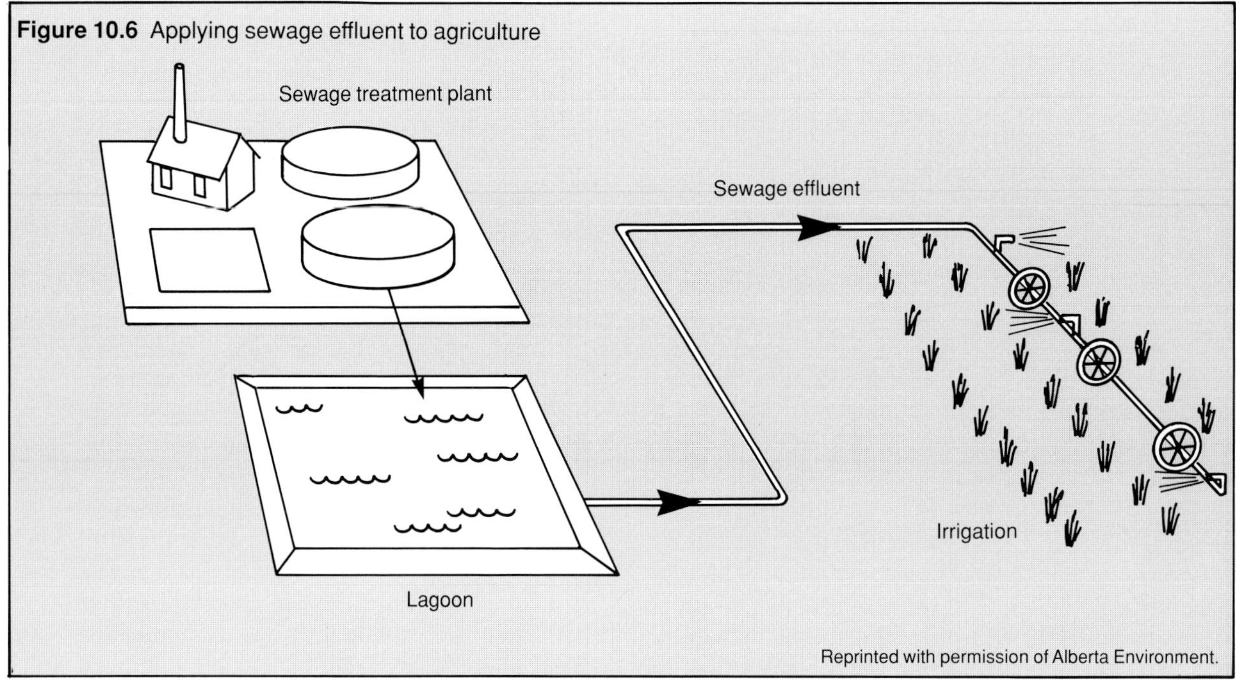

Reprinted with permission of Alberta Environment.

Solid waste disposal

Enormous quantities of solid wastes are created each year, not only in Canada, but throughout the world. This waste may be disposed of in two main ways: **landfill** and **incineration**. Prior to either of these methods of disposal, the volume of garbage can be greatly reduced by **resource recovery** or **recycling**.

Landfill

Most of our garbage ends up in landfill sites, which vary from open dumps to engineered **sanitary landfills**. Old quarries were often used as dumps since they could be obtained cheaply. Open dumps present a threat to the environment. Gases such as methane may escape from the decomposing garbage, toxic wastes may leach into groundwater, and flies and rats may spread disease. Other health hazards come from the 1.7 billion disposable diapers added to landfill sites each year in Canada. Their contents not only create odours but also provide breeding grounds for bacteria that transmit diseases.

On the other hand, an engineered landfill compacts the waste and seals it above and below. The bottom is lined to prevent seepage, and trenches collect toxic fluids. (See Figure 10.7.) Without these provisions, toxic liquids may leach from landfill sites into groundwater, posing health hazards.

Canada's landfill sites are rapidly filling up with wastes and new sites are hard to come by. In fact, a severe crisis is emerging. Many municipalities must now look beyond their boundaries for new sites. Vancouver, for example, trucks some of its solid waste to Cache Creek, near Kamloops. Toronto's dump at Pickering has reached capacity. The city is seeking new sites, which local residents oppose vigorously.

Many badly engineered landfills are at risk from explosions caused by methane. This flammable gas is produced when organic wastes decompose in the absence of oxygen. However, some places, such as the Fresh Kills landfill on Staten Island, New York, collect methane for use in gas utilities. Gas recovery at Fresh Kills reaches 200 000 m^3 per day, enough to heat 50 000 homes, according to the Worldwatch Institute.

Landfill was the preferred method of solid waste disposal because it was relatively cheap. The average cost of collecting garbage and disposing of it in landfill sites was about $30 per tonne (CDN) in 1986. Most municipalities are now required to engineer their landfills to a high standard, and with tipping fees the costs of landfill have soared to as much as $75 per tonne (CDN). Incineration, may also cost up to $75 per tonne (CDN).

Figure 10.7 An engineered landfill

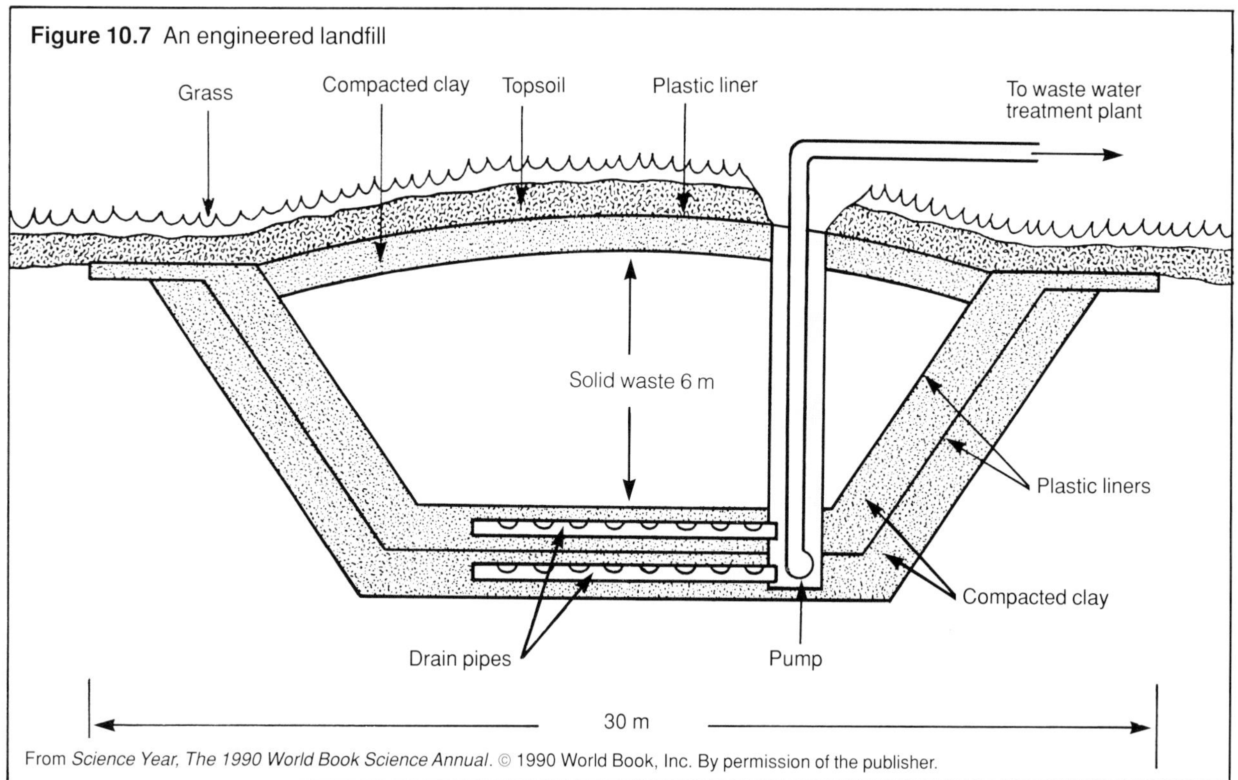

From *Science Year, The 1990 World Book Science Annual*. © 1990 World Book, Inc. By permission of the publisher.

Incineration

Burning garbage has some obvious advantages. First, it gets rid of up to 90 percent of the bulk that would otherwise occupy landfill sites. Second, steam or electricity can possibly be generated from the incineration process. Before combustion, screening may remove most of the glass and plastics. Magnets are used to remove ferrous metals. What remains for combustion is called **refuse derived fuel** (**RDF**). The installation of **scrubbers** removes most of the emissions of acidic gases.

The United States now has over 100 incinerators, many of which also generate steam energy. Ontario operates three incinerators, handling 5 percent of the province's solid waste. The only incinerator in Ontario that uses RDF is in Hamilton. Toronto's incinerator is purely for waste disposal. Energy is recovered at the London Victoria Hospital incinerator.

Some Canadian provinces are giving financial assistance to municipalities that generate electricity or other forms of energy from municipal waste. Ontario's Ministry of Energy has a budget to assist such projects. The federal government also provides grants for projects, such as the steam-producing Burnaby incinerator in British Columbia. The energy sold from schemes like these helps to cover the costs of the disposal of the waste.

Recently, the incineration of municipal waste has been questioned. Incineration contributes to the increase of carbon dioxide in the atmosphere. CO_2 is emitted from all incinerators, even those equipped with scrubbers to remove the materials that cause acid rain. The ash may also contain heavy metals and traces of dioxins caused by incomplete combustion. This ash itself has to be disposed of in a specially designed landfill at a cost of over $200 per tonne (CDN).

The three Rs

To try to reduce the volumes of waste that we dispose of, and to help reduce the demands that we make on resources, we should practice the three Rs — *reduce*, *reuse*, and *recycle*.

First, we should reduce the amount of garbage that we create. We can do this in many ways. The general principle is to use a minimum of throwaway articles. This means buying products with less packaging, which accounts for so much garbage. If customers say they prefer articles with less packaging, producers are likely to respond to their wishes. Reducing waste also means using both sides of a sheet of paper and buying food in bulk instead of in single servings.

Many articles can be reused or have new uses found for them. Consider the wasted material and energy that goes into the production of even a single article such as a soft drink bottle. It may be used only one time before occupying space for centuries in a landfill site. Clearly, such bottles and similar containers should be reused. They could be used about thirty times. When their useful life is over they should then be recycled rather than thrown away. Reuse means selling or giving away old clothes and furniture and using reusable cloth bags instead of plastic bags.

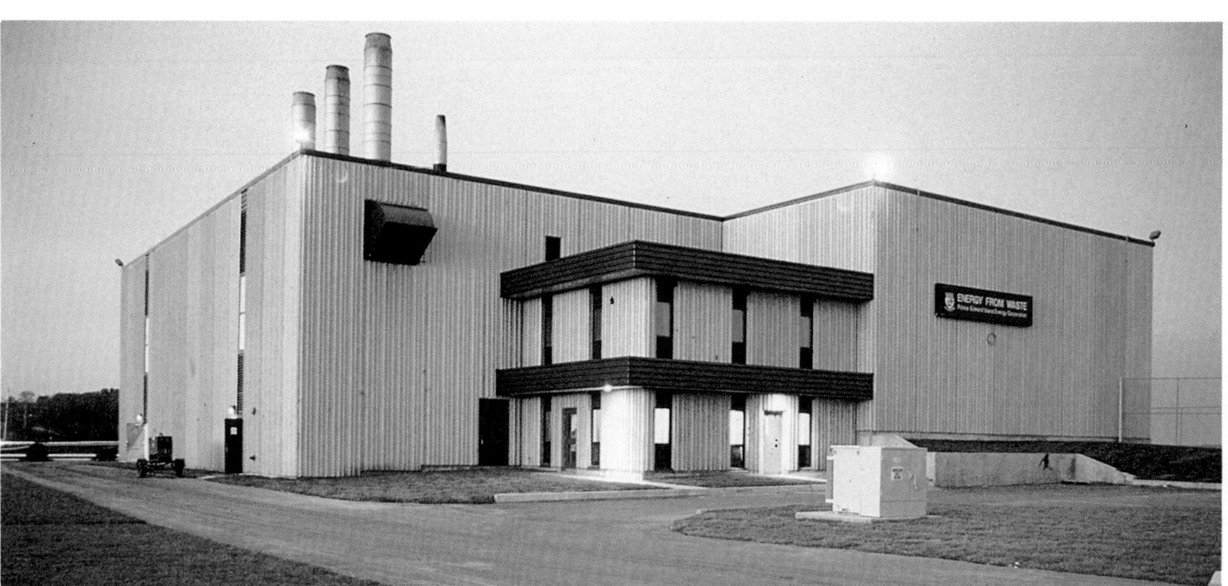

An incinerator generates power in Prince Edward Island.

Recycling

Recycling involves separating the different elements of our garbage so that useful materials can be collected and prepared for reuse, either in their original form or in a new one. Figure 10.8 is a simple diagram of recycling processes.

According to William Chandler, writing in *The Futurist*, throwing away an aluminum can wastes not just the aluminum but an amount of energy equal to the same can half-filled with gasoline. This is the amount of energy required to make the can. Recycling conserves energy, fights pollution, saves jobs, and improves the future supply of materials. But adapting our throwaway society to recycling is difficult. Not only do we have to change people's attitudes, which is hard enough, we also have to build recycling plants for large amounts of waste paper and scrap metals. For this reason, a market for recycled material should exist before collection begins. Otherwise, unwanted materials that cannot be used or sold may pile up.

The real way to increase the efficiency of recycling is to stop the waste before it starts. For example, refunding bottles and cans motivates customers to return these products before they ever get into the garbage stream. British Columbia's legal requirements for refunds on beverage containers were the first in Canada. The practice is spreading in both the United States and Canada. Some countries, including Canada, Sweden, and the United States, use reverse vending machines as a method of recycling cans. These machines take in cans and give out money.

Reverse vending machines allow people to return their used cans and bottles.

Figure 10.8 The recycling process

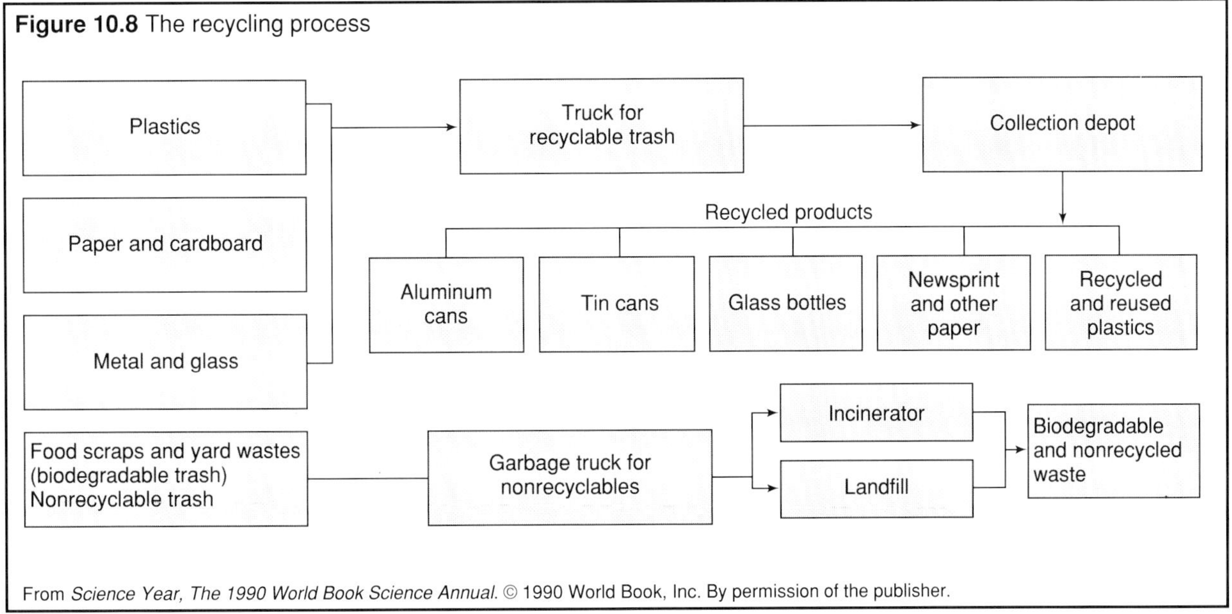

From *Science Year, The 1990 World Book Science Annual.* © 1990 World Book, Inc. By permission of the publisher.

The benefits of recycling

Recycling makes sense, not only because raw materials are scarce, but because the energy used to manufacture products is also scarce. Environment Ontario calculates that an average family can save as much as 407 kWh of electricity every year by recycling as much of their paper, steel, glass, and plastic soft drink bottles as possible.

Taking this example further, if each family saved 407 kWh of electricity each year by recycling, each would contribute to a reduction of 5 kg in the emissions of sulphur dioxide and nitrogen oxides. If 1 million Ontario families were to achieve this level of energy saving by recycling, the reduction of 5000 t of SO_2 and NO_x emissions would make a significant contribution to reducing acid rain in the eastern part of North America. The families would also reduce the amount of landfill space by 300 000 m^3 every year. This is equal to the amount used by a city the size of Kitchener, Ontario, (1991 population of 356 421) in a year. Additionally, deforestation in Canada would be reduced by 1.5 million trees a year. Demands for freshwater would also be greatly reduced.

More recycling would help to maintain ecosystems. At the present time, we take too many materials from their natural places, use them, and discard the residue as garbage. The result is that one day the world will be short of raw materials but overflowing with garbage.

Recycling domestic garbage

Domestic garbage accounts for almost half the volume of all waste products. Analysis of typical domestic garbage shows that about 50 percent of the contents are suitable for recycling. An additional 30 percent of the contents could be composted, allowing the nutrients to be recycled back into the soil. The techniques of recovering these usable waste materials are available. The main obstacles are a lack of awareness of the problem, the availability of markets for recycled materials, and financial support.

The "blue box" schemes

Ontario has led the way among Canadian provinces in the recycling of domestic garbage. Curbside collection of materials for recycling began in Ontario in 1981. Since 1987, the program has become much more comprehensive. Blue boxes are issued to householders as a means of **source separation**. Different materials must be separated early in the process before they become contaminated, as in the case of food wastes and paper. Households separate recyclable waste into separate categories, such as newspapers, cans, and glass. Having separate bins for separate products helps. When unsorted garbage arrives at depots, it may be sorted by hand. In newer depots, machines have been installed to separate different kinds of waste.

Blue box schemes are now in use in many centres across North America. Rates of participation have increased to as much as 70 percent of households. The use of blue boxes has helped to increase participation, since the sight of the boxes reminds neighbours to put out their recyclable materials. However, some blue box schemes have been much less successful in actually recycling the materials collected. In Metro Toronto in 1989 only about 4 percent of garbage collected for recycling was actually recycled. The rest was simply put in warehouses or disposed of.

Businesses are also being targeted for source separation schemes. Offices provide a great deal of used paper, while bars and restaurants provide bottles. Service stations are the source of used lubricating oil, which can be refined and reused.

These items are separated for recycling.

Blue box curbside collection exists in most Canadian cities, like Victoria, British Columbia.

In Toronto 400 000 t of glass bottles were rejected as unsuitable for recycling.

The costs of recycling

Unfortunately, recycling is not always economic. High costs are involved in starting up a program, such as the blue box scheme. The boxes themselves cost $8 to $10, with high costs for labour, vehicles, and other facilities. Often, the revenue from selling recyclable materials is not enough to cover the costs of collecting them. It may even appear to be cheaper to send all solid waste to landfill sites, as before.

Initially, the success of the blue box recycling schemes led to a glut of newsprint, aluminum, and glass, leading to a fall in prices. Some municipalities took large losses to dispose of materials overseas. Much of the glass collected from blue boxes in Ontario was rejected by purchasers as contaminated. This problem can be resolved only by further source separation into different colours of glass and by removing metal collars from discarded bottles. Rising prices for paper products have lessened the problem.

However, to compare the costs of recycling garbage with the costs of operating landfill sites, we have to include *all* the costs in each case. Most municipalities do not fully account for the costs of their landfill sites. These sites have to be bought, maintained, and eventually sealed when full. The costs of such sites are rising sharply. The environmental costs of landfills are high, making recycling a desirable alternative. An increase in recycling will mean that less material will be sent to landfill sites, which will, in turn, have a longer lifespan.

As disposal costs rise, recycling should become more economical. However, recycling costs may not always decrease. Imagine that the price paid by a company for 1 t of recycled newspaper is $40, and that this is below the cost of collecting it. If, however, the cost of disposing of that paper as waste came to $100 (CDN), it would be worthwhile for the city to pay some of the difference between $40 and $100 to the recycling company. It would then be more profitable for the company and the city would also save money on its landfill costs. A shared savings system like this can help to make recycling a wiser and more profitable way to use the resources of our planet.

Businesses would be encouraged to recycle if our governments stopped subsidizing production from new raw materials. For example, subsidies are paid to some steel makers and to the forest industry. Water is also available at below its true cost. All of these subsidies make it harder for recycled products to compete with new products. In effect, we are subsidizing the throwaway society.

Other problems of recycling

We have seen that recycling depends on the existence of a market for the materials to be recovered. This has proved to be a problem in the past because of the low value of recycled material per unit of weight. In some cases the market for recycled material is limited by the lack of processing facilities. As well, reuse would be increased by the standardizing of products such as glass bottles. Much energy would be saved if bottles did not have to be separated and returned to specific producers, often at great distances. Recycling would then become more economical in small or remote communities.

Both energy and materials are required to organize and carry out recycling programs. In some areas of the country these costs are so high that recycling is not a practical possibility. But such areas can still reduce the volume of their garbage and recycle any materials that have a local market.

Plastics, a product of the petrochemical industry, create a problem for recycling. They do not degrade easily. They are light in relation to their bulk and take up much space in landfills. Our use of plastics has grown to the point where more plastic is produced than all metals (other than iron) combined. Forty-six different plastic substances or resins are used in everyday articles. If these are mixed during recycling, the result is a lower grade plastic. This mix can be used for articles where quality is not of great importance, such as fencing materials and seats. Research into other uses for plastics made from mixed resins is continuing.

Case studies of recycling

Paper More than one-third of all the timber cut throughout the world is for paper making. In many countries timber is harvested at a rate greater than the capacity of nature to replace it. Recycling paper helps to secure the supply of timber in the future. The recycling of paper also leads to energy savings and space in landfills. Telephone directories alone take up much landfill space.

About 25 percent of paper is now recycled, but this amount could probably be doubled if effective recycling schemes are introduced. Not only would energy be saved, but about 8 000 000 ha of forest would be preserved each year in Canada. In the United States the recycling of a single issue of the weekend edition of *The New York Times* would save about 75 000 trees!

Newspaper is the main type of paper that is recycled. However, the demand for quality paper, such as the paper used in photocopying machines, is increasing. Paper that is unfit for recycling can still be used as insulating material or as animal bedding.

A serious problem has emerged for Canada due to the rapid change in recycling legislation in the United States. Many states legally require a proportion of newspapers, and even telephone directories, to be printed on recycled paper. The state governments of California and Connecticut, for example, have passed legislation requiring that 50 percent of newsprint must come from recycled sources by the year 2001. Non-compliance with this legislation will incur fines. The move to use recycled newsprint came at a time

Paper is ready for recycling at this plant in Thorold, Ontario.

when Canadian forest product companies had built many new pulp mills to process new pulpwood, not recycled paper. In British Columbia, for example, newsprint mills in 1990 could only handle new pulp, and newspapers to be recycled were exported to Oregon state. However, by 1996, 23 mills existed across Canada that could de-ink recycled newsprint, and many more used recycled content.

Japan and the Netherlands have led the way in paper recycling. Other countries with good recycling records are Mexico, South Korea, and Portugal. All of these countries are small, densely populated, and short of timber resources. They have recycled because of necessity. If Canada could achieve a record of paper recycling equal to Japan's, 80 million trees would be saved a year, an amount equal to the annual cut in Ontario.

Iron and steel Steel has been one of the most commonly used industrial materials for over a century. The raw material from which it is made is abundant, which does not encourage us to recycle steel products. However, the volume of used steel products creates an enormous resource of scrap steel. Junked automobiles in one year in the United States alone contain an amount of scrap steel equal to 4 percent of world annual production. Even if all this steel could be recycled, the energy originally consumed to make the steel could never be recovered. Every tonne of steel that is recycled saves over 1.5 t of iron ore plus energy equal to three barrels of oil.

The leading countries in the recycling of steel recycle between 30 and 40 percent of their steel. Belgium, the United Kingdom, the United States, and Japan are among the countries that attain this level of reuse. One trend that is helping to increase the use of scrap steel is the growing number of mini-mills. These are smaller production units that normally rely completely on supplies of scrap steel. Mini-mills are common in several European countries, including Spain and Sweden. According to the Worldwatch Institute, scrap steel and scrap paper together account for about 40 percent of exports from the port of New York. Steel made from scrap uses much less energy than steel made from iron ore in integrated plants.

More scrap steel could be recycled if the market for recycled steel were free of all restrictions. However, steel-making companies in large steel-producing countries have continually tried to restrict the export of scrap steel, particularly to developing countries. Their purpose is to keep the price of steel high. Today a drop in the price of steel could seriously affect the major steel-producing countries.

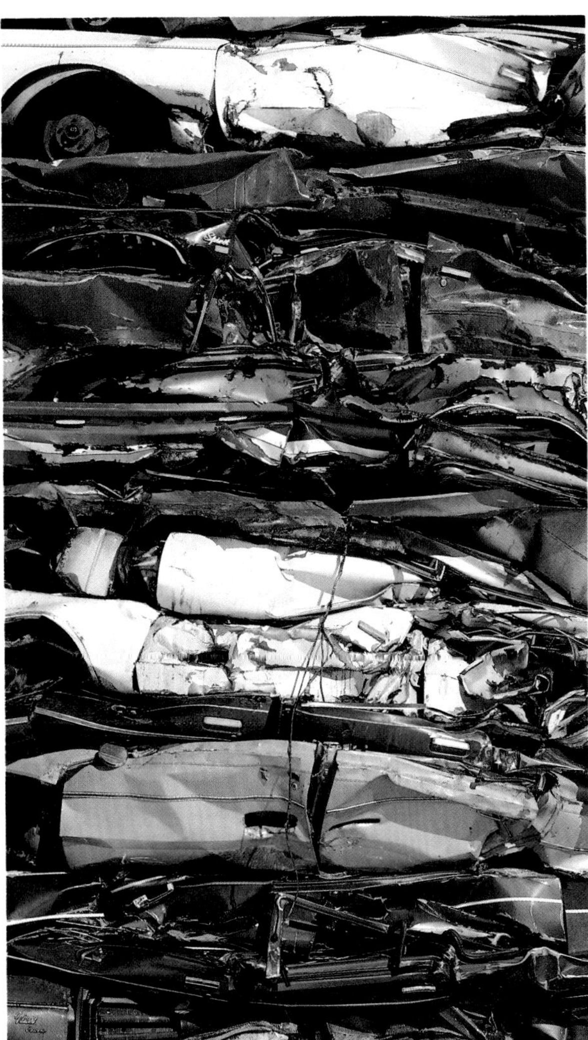

Junked automobiles can provide large amounts of scrap metal.

Recycling beverage cans saves large amounts of energy.

Aluminum Of all recyclable commodities, there is most to be gained from recycling aluminum. This is because aluminum requires more energy to make than any other material, several times as much as steel. The recycling of aluminum cans and other aluminum products uses as little as 5 percent of the energy that would be required to smelt new aluminum from bauxite, its raw material. The recycling of aluminum also reduces the environmental problems created by bauxite mining, though it hurts the economies of producing nations such as Jamaica and Guyana.

Aluminum beverage cans first came on the market in 1963. Now aluminum is used for all but 6 percent of the 70 billion or so cans used each year. The recycling of aluminum cans on a large scale could eliminate over 1 million tonnes of air pollutants worldwide.

Composting Two components of our garbage, food wastes and garden refuse, consist almost entirely of degradable organic wastes. High water and organic content make these "wastes" a valuable raw material for domestic gardens and for agriculture. First, the material has to be digested over a period of time by bacteria. It can then be spread on gardens and fields. (See Figure 10.9.) The compost is rich in nutrients, and the organic material helps the soil hold moisture and avoid erosion. Composting is the ideal antidote to the worldwide problem of the loss of topsoil. It is much more common in Europe than in North America.

Figure 10.9 How to build a garden compost

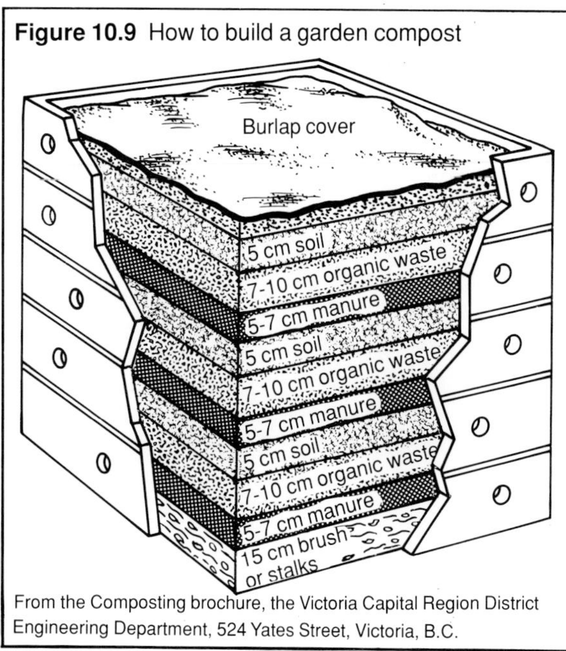

From the Composting brochure, the Victoria Capital Region District Engineering Department, 524 Yates Street, Victoria, B.C.

Industrial wastes

Industrial waste accounted for over half the total volume of waste in Canada in the early 1990s. Like domestic waste, much of this waste is preventable and much can be recycled.

Some companies, such as Minnesota Mining and Manufacturing (3M), have set the pace in behaving responsibly toward the environment. Other companies have been much slower. 3M set up a "3Ps" program (Pollution Prevention Pays), which has been copied by other companies. By 1989 3M had saved $400 million (US) in disposal costs by using water, energy, and other materials more efficiently. The emphasis has been on *preventing* rather than *curing* pollution. Today companies are afraid that their public image will suffer if they do not seem environmentally responsible. Waste disposal has become a sensitive issue with the public. The setting up of waste exchanges has made it easier for companies to reduce their waste disposals.

The Canadian Waste Materials Exchange (CWME)

The Canadian Waste Materials Exchange, operated by Ortech Corporation, was set up in 1978 to encourage the exchange of waste materials. Many such materials are one company's waste but another's raw material. Such exchanges have two main benefits. First, the pressure on limited supplies of raw materials is reduced. Second, less industrial waste has to be disposed of in chemical dumps or burned in incinerators. Similar waste exchanges now exist in Ontario, Manitoba, Alberta, British Columbia, the United States and other parts of the world.

Spills of industrial waste cause pollution.

The CWME operates a bimonthly bulletin that may list as many as 1000 materials of various kinds. These are listed as either "wastes available" or "wastes wanted." Each is listed in code to protect company privacy.

The CWME believes that waste management should be thought of as a series of objectives. In order of importance, they are as follows:

Waste Abatement	Don't make it.
Waste Minimization	If you have to make it, minimize its volume and toxicity.
Waste Reuse	See if someone else can use it.
Waste Recycle	If it can't be used as is, reclaim as much as possible.
Waste Treatment	Treat what can't be reclaimed to render it safe.
Waste Disposal	Dispose of residues to air, water, or land.

From Ortech International, "Is There a Market for Your Recycled Industrial Material?" by Mary Jane Hanley, Ontario Waste Exchange 20 September 1989.

In the first seventeen years of the CWME's existence (1978-1995), 1212 exchanges of waste were recorded, about one-fifth of the total wastes listed. While the value of such wastes is difficult to estimate, the purchase of alternative materials would have cost over $12 million (CDN) each year. Further benefits have come from the fact that the materials exchanged have not had to be disposed of. In the long run, both companies and the environment benefit.

Disposing of old tires

Every year 26 million tires are discarded in Canada, one for every person in the country. In tire dumps across North America, there are as many as 6 billion tires. To increase safety on the roads, the technology of making tires has improved steadily. Unfortunately, that same technology has made tires almost indestructible. In dumps they become a breeding ground for rats and are a serious fire hazard.

In early 1990 the worst fire ever to occur in a tire dump in Canada broke out at Hagersville, 35 km southwest of Hamilton, Ontario. The fire, fed by millions of tires, burned for more than two weeks. The fear was that the millions of litres of water put on the fire would carry toxic materials from the burning rubber into groundwater, polluting well-water over a large area. The other danger was toxic poisoning, possibly including dioxins, from the heavy black smoke that spread from the fire site. Hagersville had the makings of a major disaster, although the groundwater was not, after all, seriously contaminated. Later in 1990, a similar fire in Quebec was extinguished much more quickly by dumping wet sand on it.

The Hagersville fire raised the question of whether tires should be incinerated or disposed of in a better way. One possibility is to shred tires and burn them in the furnaces used for making cement. The danger is the creation of atmospheric pollutants, including greenhouse gases. Several provinces now levy a tax on new tires to contribute to the costs of disposal.

The fast-food business

Much attention has been focused on fast-food restaurants as creators of waste. In the United States environmentalists campaigned against fast-food chains because of the volume of waste they created and the fact that CFCs from styrofoam containers were damaging the ozone layer.

The largest fast-food chain, McDonald's, at first responded by replacing the chemical CFC-12 by HCFC-22 in its foam containers. HCFC-22 causes only 5 percent of the damage to the ozone layer of CFCs. However, the problem of disposing of its foam containers still remained. Public pressure finally convinced McDonald's to eliminate its use of foam containers, but some research claims that on balance paper products are more damaging to the environment than styrofoam.

It was believed that the tire fire at Hagersville, Ontario, in 1990 would severely pollute the groundwater, although the worst fears did not materialize.

Hazardous wastes

A waste is described as hazardous if it poses a particular threat to health or the environment. Such wastes require special disposal techniques to reduce the hazards involved. Hazardous wastes include toxic wastes but also those materials with dangerous properties. Some materials, for example, are highly flammable, while others are corrosive or radioactive. Not surprisingly, the volume of chemical waste has risen in proportion to our use of chemicals. Organic chemicals (i.e., those containing carbon) are particularly hazardous. (See page 13.) The production of organic chemicals in the United States alone rose fifteenfold between 1945 and 1985.

The main sources of hazardous waste are industrial and domestic toxins and wastes from laboratories and hospitals. They include acids from metal smelting processes, dioxins from the bleaching of paper products, and a wide variety of pesticides and herbicides. Ontario produces almost half of the hazardous waste in Canada.

The danger of disposing of these wastes in normal landfill sites is that they will leach into groundwater and get into domestic water supplies. Alternatively, they may enter rivers, lakes, or oceans and get into the food chain. If this happens, toxic wastes may have the capacity to alter the cell structure and reproduction of the species concerned.

As in the case of the recycling of garbage, the best way to solve this problem is prevention — that is, to try to avoid creating the waste in the first place. Companies may be able to create ways of using materials that they might otherwise discard as toxic waste. Or they may be able to use organizations such as the Canadian Waste Materials Exchange to find a user for their waste products.

Disposing of hazardous wastes

There are four main methods of getting rid of hazardous wastes: **incineration, detoxification, biological degradation**, and waste exchange. Some of these methods may be unsuitable for each of the many kinds of toxic materials disposed of throughout the country.

Incineration, as discussed earlier in this chapter, is an effective method of oxidizing materials to remove their toxic qualities. Carbon dioxide is created, as when anything containing carbon is burned, but the burning of some toxic materials may emit small quantities of dioxins into the air or leave traces in the ash. Very high temperatures usually solve this problem.

Some chemicals may be detoxified by neutralizing them with others. Cyanide, for example, may be made safe by a process known as **alkaline chlorination.** In this process chlorine is added to a sodium hydroxide solution, which can then be used to neutralize the cyanide.

Many toxic materials may be biologically degraded by the action of micro-organisms. Some bacteria live on oil products and will, in time, eliminate the results of oil pollution. On the other hand, mercury can be changed into the more lethal form **methyl-mercury** by the action of micro-organisms.

Since one company's waste can be another's raw material, an information service is needed to enable the disposers of toxic waste to link up with those who can make use of it. The Canadian Waste Materials Exchange is one of the largest of these services.

The transport of hazardous wastes

On-site disposal of toxic wastes is obviously the best method, but it may not be possible. Dangerous materials, therefore, may have to travel on Canada's road and rail systems. The transport of these goods requires careful control.

The **Transportation of Dangerous Goods Act** was passed in 1980 and came into force in 1985. All hazardous cargoes are labelled, recorded, and tracked. Under the same act, all import and export of dangerous goods must receive the approval of the federal government.

The 1979 train derailment in Mississauga, Ontario, underlined the dangers of transporting flammable materials.

Developing countries — a dumping ground?

Before 1988 several African countries were paid to have toxic wastes disposed of in their territories. Usually the waste was not carefully sealed but merely dumped on some unused piece of land. No care was taken to keep it away from people or to prevent it from leaching into groundwater. Pesticides that are banned in North America have also been exported to developing countries under the guise of "aid."

Some of these deals were very lucrative for the countries involved. Guinea-Bissau, a small African country, stood to receive $600 million (US) for receiving 15 million tonnes of waste over a five- year period. This figure is nearly four times the country's annual Gross National Product.

In July 1988 this state of affairs became widely publicized. Some African countries, particularly Nigeria, took the lead in persuading the Organization of African Unity to condemn the dumping of industrial waste in Africa, describing it as "a crime against Africa and the African peoples." These African countries wanted to have nothing to do with what they called "toxic colonialism."

In March 1989 an important agreement was reached in Switzerland. The Basel Convention was supported by 105 nations. The agreement controls the transport and disposal of the most toxic chemicals created by industry. But the export of toxic materials is not banned outright. For this reason African countries were slow to ratify the treaty.

Cleaning up industrial wastes

No industry has made a greater visual impact on the landscape since the Industrial Revolution than the iron and steel industry. At an iron and steel plant large amounts of iron ore and coal must first be stockpiled, which means the building up of a reserve supply. The furnaces in which steel is made create air pollution. Finally, large volumes of wastes remain from the steel-making process. These wastes were originally piled up as heaps of slag. Iron and steel sites are usually large and ugly.

The Sydney Steel Corporation (SYSCO) in Nova Scotia

The steel industry has existed in Sydney, Nova Scotia, since 1899. The industry was highly profitable at first. However, with the growth of a modern steel industry in Hamilton, Ontario, Sydney steel became less economical. After a series of financial losses, the company was purchased by the Nova Scotia government in 1967 and became the Sydney Steel Corporation (SYSCO).

The SYSCO plant used imported iron ore and local coal. The coal was converted to coke in coking ovens, which released smoke and gases into the air. Coking creates sludge and tar as by-products. Untreated effluent from the coke ovens was released into the adjacent Muggah Creek. Over the years the creek sediments became contaminated. The oily black deposits were known as the Tar Ponds, and most forms of wildlife disappeared from them.

In 1983, studies showed that Muggah Creek contained large volumes of **polynuclear aromatic hydrocarbons (PAHs)**, some of which are known to be carcinogenic. These same chemicals formerly caused cancerous tumours in eighteenth-century chimney sweeps. Other environmental sources of PAHs include forest fires, the burning of tires, and cigarette smoke.

Evidence proved that the residents in the areas near the coke ovens had a higher than average incidence of cancer. In 1982 the commercial lobster plant in nearby South Arm was closed down. The federal Department of Health and Welfare recommended closure of the coke ovens in 1985. This did not happen right away, however. The coke ovens and the blast furnace were not closed until 1988.

This aerial view shows the Sydney Steel Corporation plant.

The Sydney Tar Ponds cleanup operation

Plans to clean up Muggah Creek, the largest hazardous waste site in Canada, have been under consideration since 1986. The original plan was to remove and incinerate the wastes at an efficiency of 99.99 percent. However, no action was taken until a provincial crown corporation, Sydney Tar Pond Clean-Up Incorporated (STPCUI), was formed in 1995. Estimates to remove and incinerate the wastes were obtained, but the expected costs were around $120 million. A compromise plan was adopted to contain, fill, and landscape the site at a cost of only $20.4 million, including the removal of PCBs. Critics of the plan are concerned that most of the toxic wastes will remain on the site. Work on the project began in 1996.

Looking back

1. List four reasons for the large volume of waste created by Canadians.
2. (a) How does the use of sewage for fertilizer help to maintain balance in an ecosystem?
   (b) Explain the advantages and disadvantages of using sewage effluent in farming.
3. (a) List the air pollution problems that can be caused by the incineration of solid waste.
   (b) What are the objections to the use of tires as fuel in the cement industry?
4. (a) List the environmental advantages of recycling.
   (b) List five products that you use regularly that could be recycled.
   (c) Explain why it is important to have a market for recycled materials.
   (d) Why is it particularly important to recycle aluminum?
5. (a) Why are some wastes identified as hazardous or toxic?
   (b) What is meant by **toxic colonialism**? Why have developing countries taken a stand against it?

Applying your knowledge

1. Working with a partner, create a diagram illustrating the average Canadian family's waste products and how they should be disposed of to ensure the least damage to the environment.
2. If possible, visit a sewage treatment facility in your area. Take notes and make sketches during your visit. Afterwards, draw a diagram showing the collection of raw sewage and the path it takes through primary, secondary, and tertiary treatments. Indicate on the diagram what happens at each stage as well as what happens to the products of each stage.
3. The average Canadian family (3.1 persons in 1991) can save 407 kWh of electricity each year by recycling everything they can. Consider this information and relate it to the current population of Canada. Write a newspaper editorial entitled "Recycle and Save Electricity" in which you use this information to encourage people to recycle.
4. Develop a presentation based on the waste management objectives of the CWME. Be sure to highlight the order of the objectives and the reasons for this order. Give examples of instances where the waste products from one company could be the raw materials for another.
5. (a) Look at the photograph of the Sydney Steel plant on page 169. What features of the site can you identify? What problems are the nearby residents likely to experience?
   (b) Examine the report on SYSCO on page 169. Why do you think it took so long before the health problems of Muggah Creek were recognized?
   (c) Find examples of other industrial sites that have had to be cleaned up. Develop a comparison organizer of the similarities and differences of these sites compared with SYSCO.

Extending your thinking

1. Examine newspapers and magazines over a two-week period. Cut out all the articles that relate to waste disposal. Divide a scrapbook into sections with titles such as Sewage; Landfill; Hazardous Waste; Recycling; etc. Paste the clippings in the appropriate sections. Highlight the important facts in each article. Write one or two sentences under each clipping stating how the ecosystem is affected (either positively or negatively) by the event.
2. Prepare a case for or against the following statement: "In spite of emissions of carbon dioxide, incinerators are a better means of waste disposal than landfill sites."
3. In groups of four or five, act as a committee formed to draw up an action plan to reduce waste disposal in your community. Prepare an outline of a plan that would achieve the following:
   (a) reduce the volume of landfill;
   (b) encourage recycling;
   (c) safely dispose of hazardous wastes; and
   (d) reduce or stabilize the costs of waste disposal to taxpayers.

   Present your plan to the class. Which plan do you think would be the most effective *and* the most realistic?
4. Debate the following topic: "The export of hazardous waste should be banned."
5. Write a short essay in which you either (a) justify the amount of resource consumption and waste production by North Americans or (b) propose alternatives to our high-consumption lifestyle.

UNIT 3

MANAGEMENT AND CONSERVATION

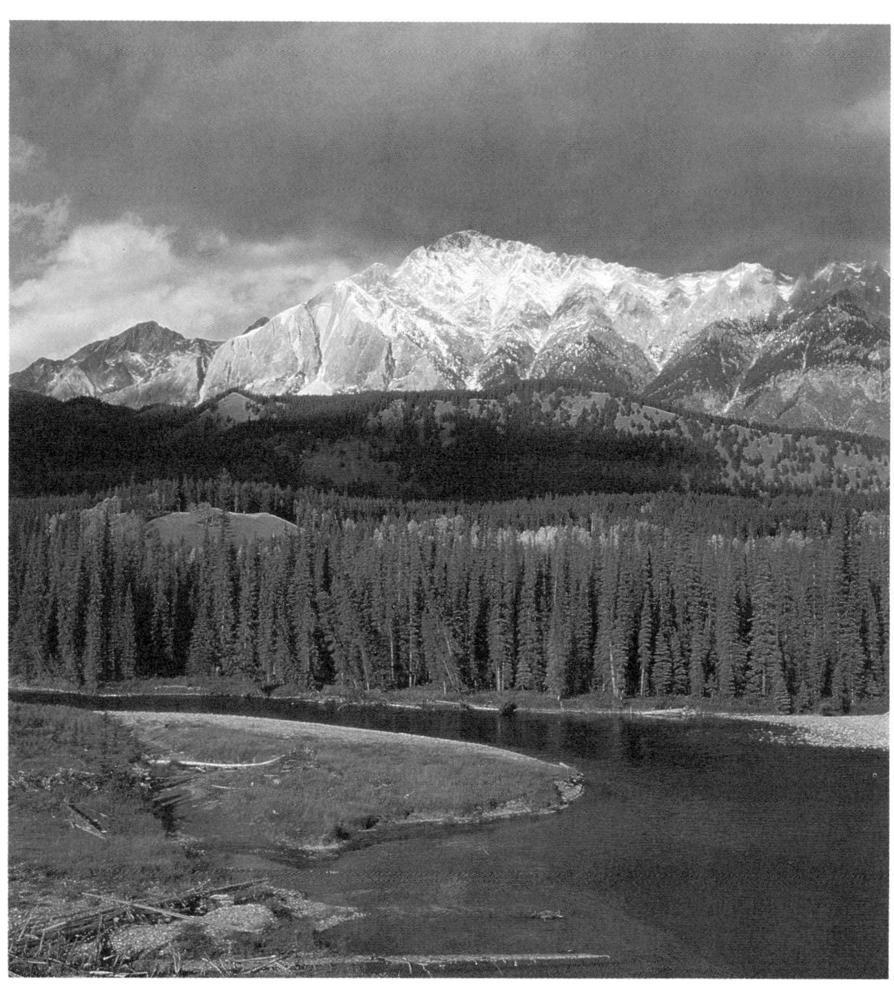

The Bow River flows through Banff National Park in Alberta.

11 THE ENVIRONMENT AND POLITICS

All forms of pollution can create health hazards. In Canada the federal government has the responsibility of setting standards with regard to public health and the environment. If governments are not willing to undertake this responsibility, then probably no one else will. In this chapter we will examine environmental health issues and the role of governments in environmental management. We will also look at the question of who should pay for cleaning up environmental pollution and the problem of the effects of conservation on the economy.

Environmental health

Our actions with regard to the environment can influence our health in many ways. On days that you feel unwell you may have wondered if some form of pollution in your environment is affecting you. For example, can a headache come from chemical residues in a breakfast of bacon and eggs? Are contaminants in the water supply causing you to feel nauseous? Are the fluorescent lights releasing PCBs or causing eye strain? Is your health affected by insecticides? We cannot avoid some of the harmful effects of our mismanaged environment. The way the environment physically affects us is called environmental health.

Changing health risks

Over the past century the patterns of disease in Western countries have changed significantly. The shift has been away from **infectious diseases**, such as tuberculosis, to **noninfectious diseases**, such as heart disease and cancer. Medical science has been able to control, or even eliminate, some of the infectious diseases that were once major causes of death. A clean water supply and good sanitation have helped to reduce the spread of infectious diseases.

Types of health risks

Risks from the natural environment Clearly, potential health dangers exist in the natural environment. We now realize that water supply and even the conditions of underlying rocks may have a bearing on diseases such as cancer.

Many substances found in the natural world are poisonous, such as insect bites. Natural foods also contain some poisons that are designed to keep animals and insects away. For example, many vegetables, from cauliflowers to potatoes, contain naturally toxic substances. Rhubarb and poinsettia leaves are extremely poisonous. According to Californian biochemist Dr. Bruce Ames, we are over 500 times as

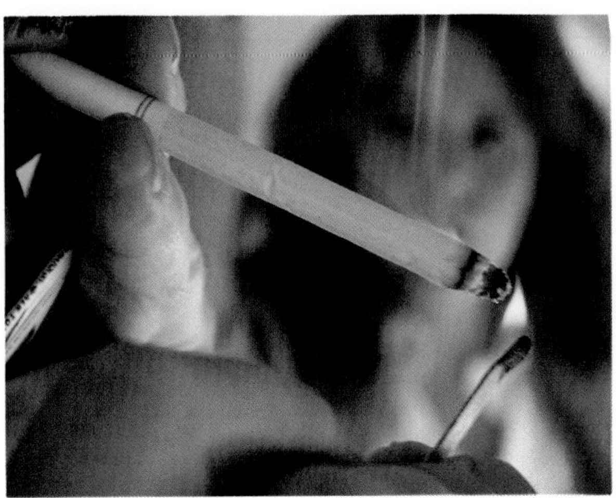

Smoking is one of the leading health issues.

Rhubarb leaves are extremely poisonous.

likely to get cancer from eating mushrooms than from apples sprayed with Alar. (Alar brings a shine to apples and is banned in Canada and the United States.) Not everything natural is pure, while not everything manufactured is dangerous.

Risks from the "manufactured" environment Recently, the number of manufactured pollutants in the environment has greatly increased. For example, some products of the chemical industry are dangerous substances. Many of the chemicals in regular production are now known to produce harmful effects on life. Most environmentalists believe that the environment is chemically overloaded. The abundance of chemicals is often blamed for the growing number of people with allergies and asthma.

It is claimed that buildings can cause persistent illness for some of the people that work in them. This is called sick building syndrome (SBS). It takes the form of nausea, headaches, or acute tiredness. SBS is usually caused by the air conditioning system, which fails to allow enough fresh air to enter the building. Indoor pollutants, such as chemicals and carpet glue, can also easily accumulate. Infections can spread quickly among the people who work in a building.

Risks associated with lifestyles Finally, health risks are associated with the lifestyles we choose. Obvious examples include smoking, using drugs, and drinking too much alcohol. Taking part in dangerous sports or even living in crowded cities can be hazardous to our health. A sedentary or stressful occupation can also lead to a greater risk of heart disease.

Cancer — an environmental disease?

The term "cancer" includes at least sixty-five different diseases that most frequently affect the lungs, bowels, pancreas, and stomach. Although the diagnosis of disease was not as thorough in the last century as it is today, increased instances of cancer seem to reflect our misuse of the environment. According to the World Health Organization, 90 percent of all cancers may be caused by pollutants in the environment. A study done in 1990 by Statistics Canada and the Canadian Cancer Society blames smoking, too much sunshine, and a poor diet for many cases of cancer. All cancers have increased by 1 percent a year in Canada since 1970. The overall rise in cancer relates to the fact that people live longer and are less likely to die of other diseases at an earlier age. Cancer now exceeds heart disease as the leading cause of death in Toronto, as Figure 11.1 shows. The decline in heart disease may be caused by an overall improvement in physical fitness.

Figure 11.1 Deaths from heart disease and cancer for the City of Toronto, 1983–1993

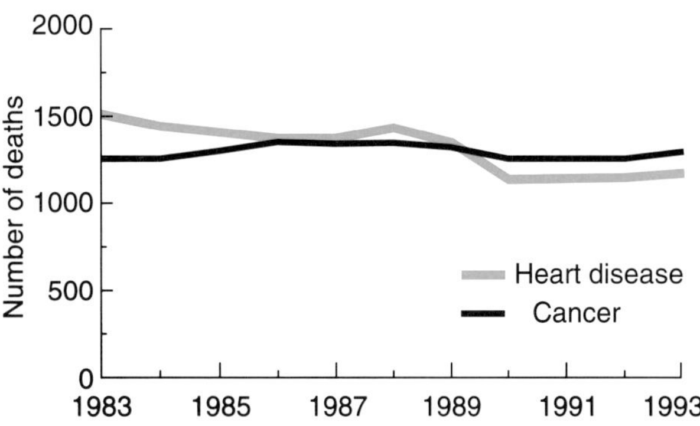

From the Department of Public Health, City of Toronto.

COST OF CANCER DOUBLES SINCE 1986
The Canadian Press

TORONTO

The cost of treating Canadians with cancer has nearly doubled in the past seven years — to at least $3.5 billion a year, according to statistics released yesterday.

The 1996 Canadian Cancer Statistics booklet, a sweeping survey compiled by Health Canada, Statistics Canada, and cancer groups, says the direct cost of treating cancer patients was at least $3.5 billion in 1993 (the latest year figures were available).

That's up from about $1.9 billion in 1986.

"That's a lot of money and the sad thing about it is a third of this could be prevented if we could get better control of tobacco," said Elizabeth Kaegi, of the National Cancer Institute of Canada and the Canadian Cancer Society.

"We're facing health-care cuts and that's why it's important to prevent cancers where we can, so we can have some resources left for treating cancers that we can prevent."

Kaegi said smoking remains one of the major sources of cancers, accounting for 30 percent of the total cancer burden and 85 percent of all cases of lung cancer.

She urged the federal government to introduce tougher laws to control the sale of tobacco, combat smoking and eventually reduce the rate of lung cancer.

"The community has to create an environment where smoking is clearly unacceptable," she said. "I speak as a mother of a child that smokes."

The booklet says there were 116 200 cancer patients and 56 144 cancer deaths in 1993.

In 1996, it estimates 129 200 new cases of cancer will be diagnosed and 61 800 will die of cancer.

It also says lung cancer remains the leading cause of cancer death among both Canadian men and women. This year, the booklet projects that 12 400 men and 7 600 women will be diagnosed with lung cancer and 11 000 men and 6 000 women will die from the disease.

Lung cancer deaths now exceed breast cancer deaths in women older than 50.

Lung cancer also remains the leading cause of cancer deaths for men older than 40, although prostate cancer is becoming a greater threat.

For 1996, it is estimated at least 124 men per 100 000 will be diagnosed with prostate cancer, more than double the 1969 rate of 54 men per 100 000.

Prostate cancer is now the most commonly diagnosed cancer in Canadian men," said Kaegi.

One spot of good news in the booklet is death rates for men are coming down.

The overall cancer death rates for Canadian men have gradually declined from a peak of 253 per 100 000 in 1988 to an estimated 241 per 100 000 in 1996.

But since 1984 there has been little change in overall cancer mortality rates for women — mostly because of rising lung cancer deaths.

Figure 11.2 shows that cancer mortality was relatively high in parts of eastern Canada. The highest rates are usually linked with hazards such as air pollution from the manufacturing industry or asbestos mining. Asbestos residues in older buildings likely increase the risk of cancer. Water supply has also been linked with cancer. Digestive cancers are more common in areas with soft water, especially if the soils are saline.

Figure 11.2 Male cancer mortality in Canada

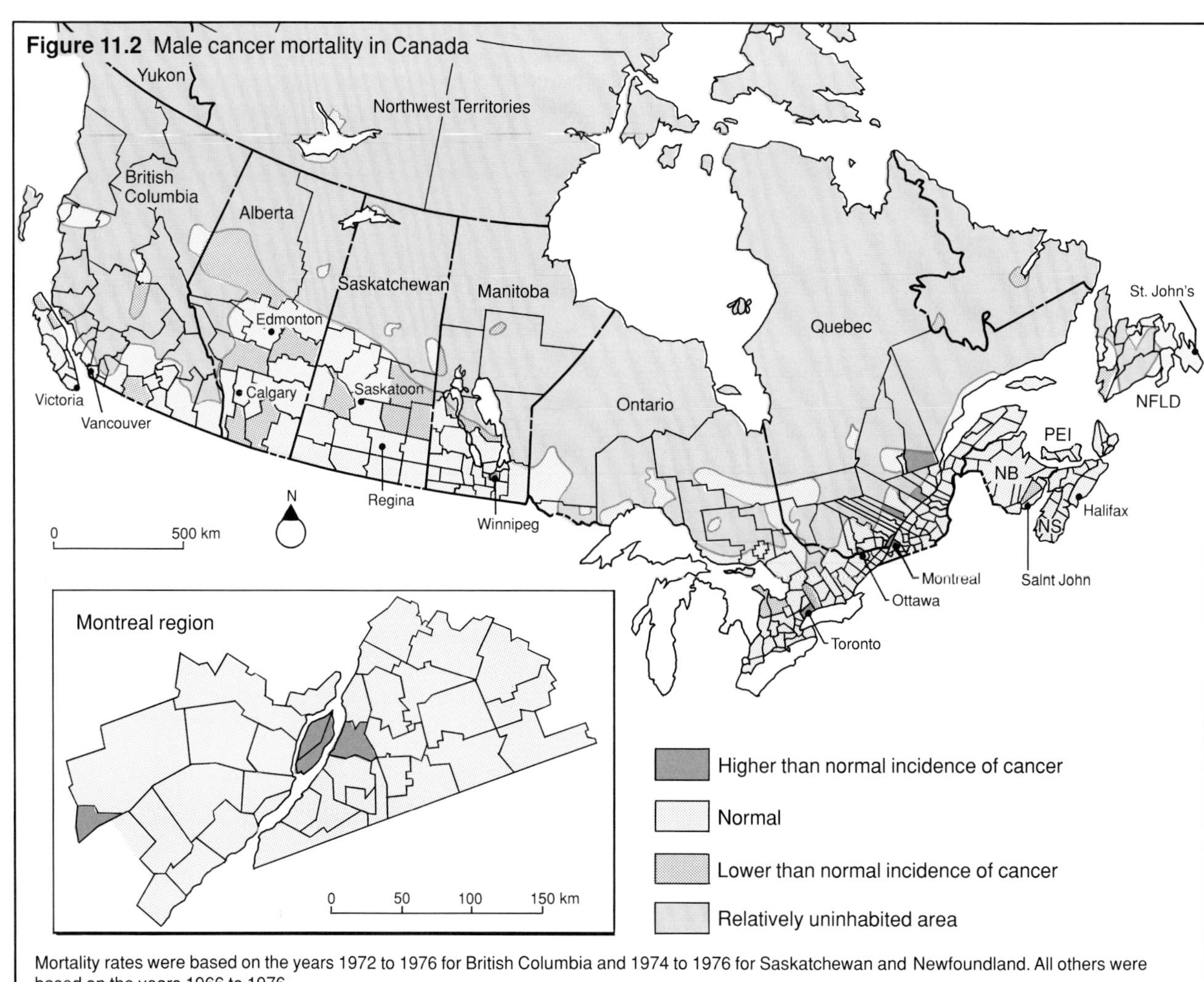

Mortality rates were based on the years 1972 to 1976 for British Columbia and 1974 to 1976 for Saskatchewan and Newfoundland. All others were based on the years 1966 to 1976.

From Health and Welfare Canada, *The Mortality Atlas of Canada* (1980). Reprinted with permission of the Minister of Supply and Services Canada.

Living with risk

The use of technology has given us a high standard of living, but it has also added an element of risk. The chemical industry, for example, has given us many benefits, including lower costs and increased convenience. This industry has also provided many important drugs for the control and cure of diseases. But the benefits of anything should be weighed against the risks.

The risks of using chemicals almost always involve the health of the people who use them and the public in general. Comparing the benefits of chemicals against the risks involved is difficult. Some people claim that no risks of any kind should be accepted. Others claim that risks are inevitable, but they should be minimized according to clearly established safety standards. If we insist that absolutely no risks should be taken, then virtually no modern technology (including planes and cars) would be accepted as safe. Most foods would also be regarded as unsafe.

Measuring risks

Risk is usually measured by the increased chance of catching a disease or dying when exposed to a hazard, as opposed to nonexposure. Figure 11.3 shows how much risk is involved in a variety of situations, including radiation risks. The risk factor has been converted into the number of days that the life of an average person might be shortened if exposed to each situation.

For many chemicals there are no clearly defined standards for safe levels of exposure. Toxic chemicals may not be entirely safe at any level. Even the smallest quantities of a certain toxic chemical may be enough to cause cancer in a few individuals. If you turned out to be one of those people, you would certainly not believe that the use of the chemical was justified. The US Food and Drug Administration (FDA) regards the risk of one death per 100 million people from carcinogenic (cancer causing) traces in foods as "virtually safe."

Even more important is the **synergy effect**, which happens when the combined effect of two or more chemicals is greater than the sum of their individual effects. Millions of potential synergy effects would have to be studied to assess all possible risks.

The main problem in assessing the effects of chemicals on human beings rises from the fact that we cannot, morally or legally, experiment on people. Many of the safety standards that are used today are based on the results of laboratory experiments on animals, a practice that is under much protest today. If a chemical causes tumours in rats, then it may cause similar effects in humans. But this cannot easily be proved.

Responding to risks

Since we cannot live in a risk-free environment, we have to consider how much risk we are willing to accept. For example, if the risk of contracting a fatal disease amounts to one person in one hundred, it is considered serious enough to build hospitals to treat the disease. On the other hand, if the risk of being killed in a plane crash is one in 1 million, it is considered an acceptable risk. The government would not ban flying on the basis of that amount of risk.

We are not very rational when it comes to taking risks. Consider the following example: the use of Alar on apples is thought to produce an additional 100 cases of cancer every year in North America. This has caused Alar to be banned in the United States and Canada. Yet automobile accidents cause 90 000 deaths every year in North America and nothing much

Figure 11.3 Life expectancy lost in certain situations

Situation	Life expectancy lost
Fallout from atomic weapons tests	–1 day
Cosmic rays at sea level	–22 days
Cosmic rays at 1500 m	–33 days
Living on sedimentary rock	–50 days
Living on granitic rock	–94 days
Living in brick or concrete home	-about 150 days
Being 25 percent overweight	–1300 days
Living in a city	–1800 days
Sedentary lifestyle	-about 1800 days
Smoking (1 pack per day)	–3300 days

From The American Heart Association and the US Department of Health, Education and Welfare.

Most of us accept the risks of driving automobiles.

is done about it. Why is there so much concern about the one risk, but not about the other?

Usually, we are tolerant of risks that we impose upon ourselves, but not of risks that other people impose upon us. We willingly take part in risky activities, such as driving on a highway during rush hour. Many of us love to sunbathe, in spite of the proven risk of malignant melanoma (skin cancer). Even sports such as skiing present a greater chance of injury or death than our exposure to most chemicals in the environment. Yet because the risky activity has been chosen by us, we accept it as a reasonable risk to take. But when a chemical company imposes a risk on us, by dumping toxic waste into Lake Ontario, for example, we demand government action — even though the risk it creates may be many times lower than sunbathing or driving on a crowded highway. It seems to depend on whether we create the risk for ourselves or someone else imposes it on us.

Lifestyle risks

Some health risks are caused by atmospheric problems such as urban smog. Lifestyle habits, such as smoking, can also cause the pollution of the air we breathe. Cigarette smoke consists of 4700 compounds, including 43 carcinogens, according to the EPA. Not surprisingly, regular smokers take upon themselves greater health risks than nonsmokers. On average they die younger and miss work more often.

Nonsmokers often breathe in much second-hand or passive tobacco smoke. Sidestream smoke consists of smaller particles than mainstream smoke, reaching deeper into the lungs. According to Dr. Stanton Glantz of the University of California, passive smoke kills 50 000 Americans a year, most of whom die of heart disease. Passive smoking ranks as the third-highest preventable cause of death, after direct smoking and alcohol consumption.

The problem of air pollution caused by smokers is complex, since smoking was an acceptable social habit for many years. Only since the Second World War have its health hazards become known. Smoking, however, does impose costs on society, including lost work time due to illness and medical costs to treat smoking-related diseases. These costs are borne by society as a whole, not just by smokers. However, smokers do pay a heavy tax on cigarettes.

The costs of medical treatment in Canada are paid through medical premiums, which are subsidized by our taxes. Most Canadians approve of health insurance. However, if environmental problems increase the number of people who are sick, the effects will be higher medical premiums and greater taxation.

Who do we believe?

Many environmental health issues are controversial. For example, some people may feel that automobiles are not worth the environmental risks involved, while others strongly disagree. How do we decide which viewpoint we agree with?

Controversial environmental problems are often the focus of media attention. Many sides of an issue may be presented. Facts and opinions are easily confused. Consider the following two articles about the dangers of PCBs. Each one offers a very different point of view. To become environmentally aware, we must be able to evaluate the information presented in the media and form our own opinions. Remember that most issues are not clear cut.

NOT AT ALL

by Pascal Dennis

What would happen if you sat in a bathtub full of polychlorinated biphenyls? Answer — Nothing serious would happen; at worst you would get a mild case of acne.

As toxic chemicals go, PCBs are small potatoes. They simply aren't that toxic. This was demonstrated recently at an investigation of the tragic Yusho incident in Japan in 1968. About 1000 people had used cooking oil heavily contaminated with PCBs. In analyzing the PCB samples the researchers found they were contaminated with high levels of far more toxic dioxins. Subsequent tests on animals led the researchers to the conclusion that the dioxins, rather than the PCBs, were responsible for the Yusho incident, and that PCBs reduce dioxin toxicity.

Yet it is "common knowledge" that PCBs are deadly. We spend a great deal of money and energy studying them, disposing of them, worrying about them. Meanwhile the real needs of our environment go unattended.

...For the media, PCBs make great stories. Lazy reporters can use monster-movie clichés (Ports Refuse to Accept Soviet Ship of Death's PCB Cargo!) and the stories practically write themselves.

Of 285 PCB articles printed in *The Globe and Mail* and *The Toronto Star* in the past two years, only six described the hazards accurately. In the rest, PCBs were usually described as "deadly," "cancer-causing," or "causing infant mortality." No wonder the public is terrified.

Every dollar devoured by the PCB hoax is a dollar taken from our real problems: the destruction of rain forests, the hole in the ozone layer, health conditions in factories, the air quality in cities.

There is also the "boy who cried wolf" syndrome. When the

public at last discovers the truth about PCBs, will it take chemical threats seriously?

We need journalists who can educate the public and focus attention on the real issues, who can keep politicians and demagogues honest. The environmental beat is no longer a part-time job. The stakes are just too high.

FULL RESULTS AREN'T KNOWN

by Stephen Shrybman

Some commentators have suggested that public concern about PCBs is entirely out of proportion to the actual risk. Well. . .yes, and no.

Yes, because mere proximity to securely contained PCBs presents little if any risk. Exposure is primarily through ingestion. It's the fish on your plate, not the transformer on your block, that should be of the greatest concern.

We don't know all the implications of PCBs for human health, or how they affect other aspects of the ecosystem, such as fish and wildlife. But we do know that governments have failed miserably to respond to the challenge of proper management and disposal.

PCBs may not be the most toxic of substances, but they are pervasive and persistent. The very qualities which make them valuable to industry — their stability and ability to mix with organic materials — have made them environmental contaminants of the first order. A particular species of fish can accumulate concentrations of PCBs several thousand times greater than those in the food it consumes.

This is why some creatures have levels that are truly staggering. Autopsies on beluga whales have found more than 500 parts per million in tissue, and more than 1700 in breast milk. In effect, this makes the belugas hazardous waste in Canada (the official figure is 50 parts per million).

PCB concentrations of 0.76 parts per million have been found in the breast milk of women living in Ontario. This is nearly four times the federal guidelines for dairy products.

Those who eat a lot of fish can have even higher levels. A 1988 survey of Inuit women on the east coast of Hudson Bay found an average of 3.6 parts per million in breast milk — among the highest levels ever reported.

Think of our species as something akin to a biological magnet for the PCBs in the environment, and of our children as guinea pigs in a massive experiment that will expose them to PCBs and other toxic substances. Now think about how little is known about what this exposure will do. In this light, it's hard to consider public concern about PCBs overblown.

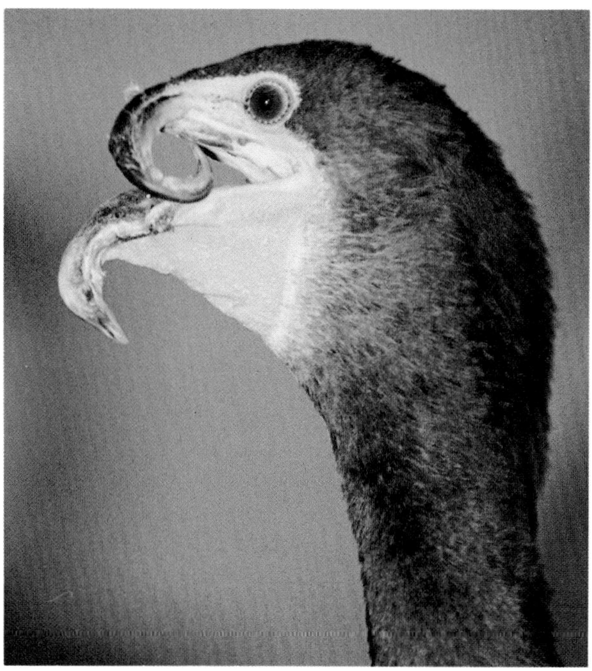

This cross-beaked condition was probably caused by exposure to PCBs.

Environmental protection

No one really knows what is dangerous to us in the environment. Is the air we breathe and the food we eat safe? Are birth defects merely occasional genetic quirks? Do we really know whether birth defects are rising or falling?

Many people have been living in dangerous situations without knowing it. For example, people living near the Sellafield nuclear station in England in the 1950s were unaware of a serious radiation leak. In 1976 people living near a chemical factory in Séveso, Italy, did not know of the emission of dioxins. The worst ever chemical disaster killed more than 3300 people in Bhopal, India, in 1984, when methyl isocyanate leaked from a tank at a Union Carbide plant. In all these cases, local people were unaware of the dangers posed by the local factories or plants. They had no means of protecting themselves against the hazards.

Today, however, action groups insist that the public has the right to be informed about potential environmental hazards. Governments have responded by creating laws to that effect. The United States created the **Environmental Protection Agency (EPA)** in 1970. Its role is to evaluate environmental hazards and to create laws that would reduce them. Canadian environ-

The gas leak in Bhopal, India, caused many deaths and injuries, including loss of eyesight.

mental regulations have existed for many years. The **Canadian Environmental Protection Act (CEPA)** of 1988 emphasizes the right of Canadians to be aware of possible threats to their environment.

The World Health Organization recognizes that individual countries must decide what safety standards should be applied. However, this has led to an extraordinary range of values (up to a factor of fifty times) in the maximum acceptable level of some chemicals in different countries.

A poll taken in 1991 showed that many Canadians support laws to protect the environment. (See Figure 11.4). Most Canadians want to see firm action taken to control pollution created by corporations. However, support on individual issues is not uniform across Canada. A 1989 poll showed that banning garden pesticides was most popular in Québec but least acceptable on the Prairies where grasshoppers have caused much damage. An increase in nuclear power was approved by the majority of people in Ontario and Québec but was opposed by most people in British Columbia.

The Canadian Environmental Protection Act

A number of acts relating to Canada's environment have been in force for several years. The most comprehensive act — the Canadian Environmental Protection Act (CEPA) — was developed between 1982 and 1988. The full name of this act is "An Act Respecting the Protection of the Environment and of Human Life and Health."

CEPA incorporates previous acts, such as the Clean Air Act and the Environmental Contaminants Act, which already covered the use of such materials as dioxins, PCBs, mirex, asbestos, mercury, and lead. The act gives the federal government broad powers to manage toxic chemicals and protect the environment. Industry must now show that a new chemical is safe rather than let the government prove that it is dangerous.

Environment Canada and Health and Welfare Canada administer CEPA together. The penalties for breaches of CEPA are more severe than those of previous acts. Fines range from $200 000 to $1 million

Figure 11.4 Public support for selected environmental protection policy measures, 1991 (Percent)

ACTION	COMPLETELY IN FAVOUR	SOMEWHAT IN FAVOUR	AMBIVALENT	SOMEWHAT OPPOSED	COMPLETELY OPPOSED	DON'T KNOW
Government sharply curtailing resource companies' access to wilderness lands	28	36	15	10	7	4
Ban on logging in old growth forests	16	27	19	21	13	4
Requiring industry to pay out of own profits for disposal of toxic wastes	51	31	9	4	3	2
Charging households a direct fee for each can or bag of garbage	19	29	11	16	23	2

From Angus Reid Group, *Canadians and the Environment,* Toronto, 1991.

(CDN), with jail terms of from six months to five years. Breaches are assessed daily, which means that polluters can be fined for offenses on consecutive days. This gives the act considerable extra power.

CEPA adopts an ecosystem approach to the environment, which integrates air, water, soil, and wildlife control. It is concerned with the effects of toxic wastes, possibly the main threat facing the country in the future. Some specific areas covered are:

- controlling trade in toxic substances, such as CFCs and other chemicals that damage the atmosphere;
- developing guidelines on the level of risk attached to the use of toxic substances;
- ensuring that industry knows how to control substances and takes all reasonable measures to prevent spills and accidents;
- setting specific standards for the use of substances, such as lead in gasoline; and
- informing the Canadian public of their rights under the act.

It is important to know whether or not federal acts take priority over provincial laws. In the case of CEPA much effort has gone into making sure that the standards of the federal and provincial governments are similar. Charges can be laid under provincial law only if the provincial standards are as high as the federal standards. The act states that penalties for breaking federal and provincial laws should be the same.

CEPA also commits the government to report regularly on the state of the environment. Several other countries, such as France, Japan, and the United States, make similar reports regularly. Canada's first report appeared in 1986; further reports were issued in 1992 and 1996.

A number of new government initiatives regarding the environment have taken place since 1990. The **Federal Environmental Stewardship** initiative was established in 1992 to co-ordinate the adoption of good environmental practices among government agencies. The position of **Commissioner for the Environment and Sustainable Development** (1995) was created to assess how well departments are doing in creating "greener government." The Commissioner is answerable to the Auditor General, a move designed to increase accountability in government.

Sustainable development has been defined as "development that meets the needs of the present without compromising the ability of future generations to meet their own needs." This statement from the Brundtland Commission was developed at the Earth Summit in Rio de Janeiro in 1992. Canada, along with most participating nations, accepted the need for global partnership to solve environmental problems. Among the items emphasized are waste reduction, with a target of reducing waste by 50 percent from 1988 levels by 2000, and continued work on atmospheric issues and Great Lakes water quality.

The green approach to government also focuses on strict observance of the pollution prevention legislation in CEPA, for example in the areas of discharges into fishing waters, preserving wildlife habitats and curtailing the transportation of dangerous goods. Finally, the government stated its commitment to work closely with Canada's provinces and territories.

Environmental assessment

Most development projects, such as the construction of coal-fired power stations, hydro dams, and pulp mills, raise environmental issues. At the federal level, the Environmental Assessment Review Process is concerned with projects that receive federal funding. A process known as Environmental Assessment (EA) exists in most Canadian provinces. When a new project is planned the provincial environmental ministry examines it to see whether it considers an Environmental Assessment necessary. If so, the process is begun and public hearings may take place.

The process is designed to give everyone the right to be heard. The result should be better planned projects that are environmentally sound. However, it does not always work out that way in practice. The Environmental Assessment process is illustrated in these examples.

The Rafferty and Alameda Dams in Saskatchewan

In 1985 the Saskatchewan Water Corporation drew up plans to construct the Rafferty and Alameda dams in the Souris River basin. The purpose was to store water to cool a coal-fired power plant and to end a serious flooding problem. Water would also be provided for irrigation and recreation.

With the approval of the federal government, work on the Rafferty dam started in 1988. A year later, the federal minister of the environment ordered a reassessment, which resulted in a court order in April 1989 to stop the work. Later, work on the scheme was restarted after further restrictions were imposed. The structures were completed in 1992.

The Rafferty-Alameda scheme has been opposed on environmental grounds. The Souris River flows from Saskatchewan into North Dakota and back into Manitoba. People objecting to the scheme claim that North Dakota would get the major flood control benefit, while Saskatchewan would be more affected by the loss of wildlife habitats. The flood control aspects of the scheme proved successful in 1996 when the US city of Minot was spared serious flooding. However the two dams have the effect of reducing wildlife habitats for birds and mammals. The waters of the Rafferty and Alameda dams have not yet been used for industry or for irrigation.

Pulp mills in Alberta In the late 1980s the Alberta government gave approval in principle to several companies to build pulp mills in the province, using previously unused aspen hardwoods as a timber source. Several mills received planning permission and were completed or under construction by the end of 1990. One pulp mill, proposed by Alberta-Pacific Forest Industries Inc. (Al-Pac), remained stuck in the environmental review process.

Public hearings were held in many Alberta centres, including Edmonton. The company claimed that its state-of-the-art mill would release virtually no contaminants into the Athabasca-Peace river system. Environmentalists claimed that the rivers were already overloaded with effluent from existing pulp mills. Reports presented to the review panel showed that small quantities of dioxins and furans could be found in the Athabasca River below the existing pulp mills. The company was also unable to satisfy the panel that its effluent would not cause oxygen depletion in the river. Finally, in December 1990, the Al-Pac project received environmental approval.

The Point Aconi power plant in Nova Scotia A large coal-fired power station was completed in 1995 at Point Aconi, 50 km north of Sydney. Public hearings had taken place early in 1990 under the provisions of Nova Scotia's Environmental Assessment Act. However, the time made available for public hearings was limited and the provincial government awarded the main contract to construct the Point Aconi plant several months before the hearings took place. As a result, many found it hard to believe that Environmental Assessment is a serious process.

Construction of the station provided over 1000 jobs, and the 400 000 t of coal burned each year helps the Cape Breton coal industry. The plant exceeds sulphur dioxide reduction targets. Critics say that the power needs of Nova Scotia could have been met by smaller plants and improved energy conservation.

International laws

Several international treaties exist to protect the environment. The OILPOL Convention of 1954, the MARPOL Convention of 1973, and the United Nations Law of the Sea Convention (LOSC) of 1982 are examples of treaties to protect the world's oceans.

All international conventions of this type have two basic defects. First, some important nations may fail to sign the latest convention. For example, the United Kingdom and the United States did not sign LOSC. Second, all international regulations are difficult to enforce. For example, tanker captains often clean out their tanks at some distance offshore without paying fines for creating an oil slick.

Many international groups seek to protect aspects of the environment by informal agreement, without the support of international treaties. One of these is the **Pesticide Action Network (PAN)**. PAN unites over 300 organizations in 50 countries in its efforts to raise awareness of the dangers of pesticides. It seeks to promote alternatives to pesticides and lobbies for the introduction of strict codes governing their use.

Several pulp mills have been constructed in the Athabasca region of Alberta.

Who pays for pollution?

Logically, pollution should be paid for by those who cause it. Until now, this has seldom happened. Polluters have paid nothing or very little for discharging their wastes into the air, rivers, and oceans. These global "commons" have been misused, and society as a whole has had to bear the costs of the environmental damage. These costs are known as **external costs**, meaning that the costs have been borne by the environment rather than by companies or individuals.

Air pollution by industry, for example, has caused countless deaths and millions of hours of lost production. Yet industrial companies have not been asked to pay for it. The utilities that contribute to acid rain have, until now, paid nothing toward the costs of restoring acidified lakes, dying forests, and eroding buildings. Municipalities and industries have not had to pay for the harmful effects of their effluent on aquatic life. Those of us who drive cars also do not have to pay for our contribution to air pollution. Even the high costs of providing roads and parking spaces are met through general taxation rather than by a specific tax on the use of cars.

Often, factories and utilities that pollute are subsidized by governments. They may receive grants or subsidies in return for employing people or creating power to allow other companies to employ people. Subsidies for utilities that burn fossil fuel are a stumbling block in the way of solar energy research. This is just one example of how the spending of our tax dollars may actually harm rather than help the environment.

The polluter pays principle

The polluter pays principle maintains that polluters should pay for the external costs of pollution — that is, the costs to society and to the environment. In many countries, especially in Europe, polluters are charged for their harmful acts. The aim is to change their behaviour. Financial penalties may encourage them to invest in pollution control equipment. One of the objectives of charging polluters is to provide a fund for authorities to finance pollution control measures.

Several types of penalties are used. Effluent charges are the most common; France, Germany, the Netherlands, and Australia make great use of these. Noise pollution, especially from aircraft, is also charged in several European countries and in Japan. In the case of the Niagara River, American companies pay for some of their effluent that is dumped into the river, but Canada, which bears the brunt of the pollution, does not receive any of the funds that are raised.

Charges may also be laid on products that pollute, usually in the form of taxes. For example, many countries place higher taxes on leaded gasoline. Scandinavian countries tax the purchase of nonreturnable containers and mercury and cadmium batteries. In the United Kingdom and Sweden some products such as pesticides are taxed when they are introduced.

Many people feel that cash penalties should be used to make those who legally pollute pay for their actions. This is in addition to normal regulations on emissions and discharges that are designed to make it illegal for companies to pollute.

Ontario's Spills Bill

Part IX of the Ontario Environmental Protection Act is commonly known as the **Spills Bill**. It deals with spills that occur during manufacture or transport. This bill came into force in 1985 and is supported by a province-wide emergency response program. The Spills Action Centre tries to establish the source of a spill so the polluter can clean it up. If the spill is on a provincially controlled highway, the Ministry of Transport may undertake the cleanup and bill the company or person responsible.

The Spills Bill provides some compensation for damages as a result of spills. The Spills Action Centre also informs the public about spills that may endanger health or safety.

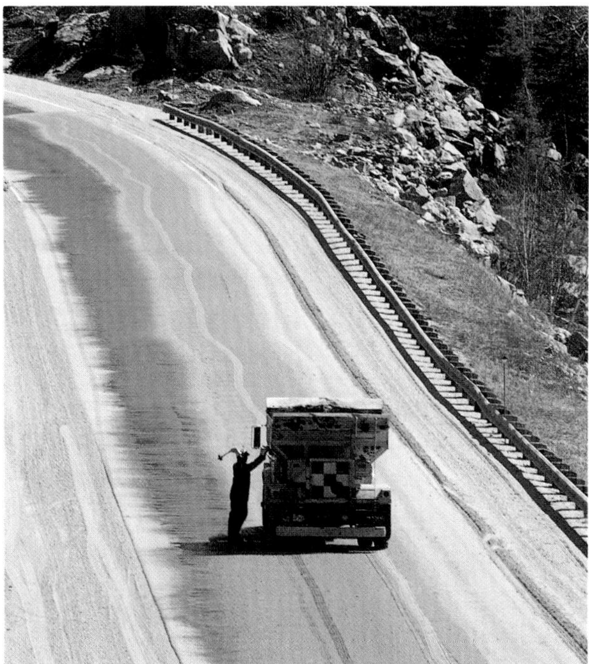

Ontario now has legislation to deal with spills such as the PCB spill near Kenora in 1985.

Environmental issues and the economy

The growing importance of environmental issues will have an impact on the economies of most countries. Initially, the costs of cleaning up and managing the environment will be high. The main problem is that these costs will likely put some jobs at risk.

Clearly, short-term costs of preventing pollution and cleaning up the environment will be enormous. According to the research group Informetrica, the bill to clean up the Canadian environment could amount to at least $1400 (CDN) per family per year by the turn of the century. The majority of people polled in the Informetrica study consider the disposal of chemical waste the leading problem to be faced in the next few years. This ranked ahead of ozone depletion, oil spills, and the contamination of water supplies.

How will cleanup costs be met?

Some financial assistance from the government is given to industrial firms to help them meet the costs of cleanup. Such help may come from taxes levied on polluters and from general taxation. Taxes will probably go up because of the increased costs of waste disposal and because most governments spend a lot of money trying to solve environmental problems. Industry will likely pay its own cleanup costs and pass these costs on to the consumer in the form of higher prices. Some factories may be unable to meet these higher costs, resulting in closures and a loss of jobs.

Many products in everyday use are going to become more expensive because of the higher environmental standards that will be required. Metal prices will rise because of the need to control emissions. Farm produce may go up in price, since a reduction in the use of fertilizer and pesticides is likely to lower crop yields. The price of energy may increase dramatically because of the high costs of preventing atmospheric pollution. If so, most things will rise in price, since energy is used in the manufacture and transport of almost all we use.

The environment or the economy?

Sometimes the conflict between protecting the environment and saving the jobs of people can sharply divide a community. This is especially true when the economy of a town or region depends heavily on a single industry. The problem arises when an environmental issue threatens to curtail, or even close down, that industry. The Atlantic fishing industry and the fate of the spotted owls in the northwest of the United States are examples of issues that can divide communities.

The Atlantic fishing industry What happens when the supply of fish runs out? This kind of question is asked by people working in the Atlantic fishing industry. As we learned in chapter 7, the supply of fish on the Grand Banks has been declining. In 1993 when the government cut the northern cod quota to zero, thousands of people in the fishing industry were laid off and several fish processing plants were closed. In many cases these plants were the economic mainstay of the communities where they were located. The effects on the Atlantic provinces and Newfoundland in particular can be seen in Figure 11.5.

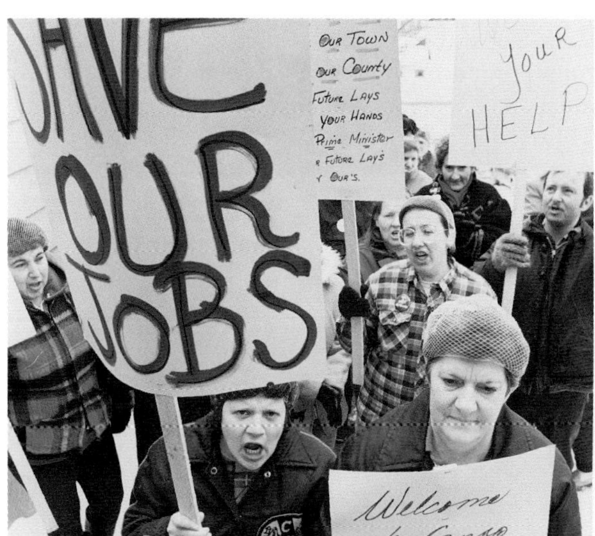

Protestors demonstrate outside a fish processing plant in Nova Scotia.

Figure 11.5 Number of registered commercial fishers and total catch in eastern Canada, 1988 and 1994

	NEWFOUNDLAND	PEI	NOVA SCOTIA	NEW BRUNSWICK	ATLANTIC PROVINCES
Fishers 1988	29 830	4 929	16 321	7 903	58 983
Fishers 1994	22 011	5 795	16 945	8 887	53 638
Catch 1988 (000 tonnes)	561	58	520	157	1 296
Catch 1994 (000 tonnes)	138	48	340	142	668

From Statistics Canada.

Newfoundland and Nova Scotia were hard hit, since their economies have a greater dependence on fishing. Prince Edward Island and New Brunswick rely more on inshore fishing for scallops and lobsters, so they were not as badly affected. The suddenness of the economic decline left many people in hardship. Many more were bitter toward the federal government, whom they accused of mismanaging the situation.

Owls and logging In June 1990 the United States government declared the northern spotted owl a threatened species. By law its habitat became protected. Some 5000 pairs of spotted owls live mainly in old growth forests from northern California to the Canadian border. If a ban on logging is carried out, the forest industries of the northwest states will be devastated. About 28 000 jobs could be lost, many of them in one-industry communities. Protecting the owls, like the Atlantic fisheries, can be done, but at the price of some economic progress.

Figure 11.6 The northern spotted owl

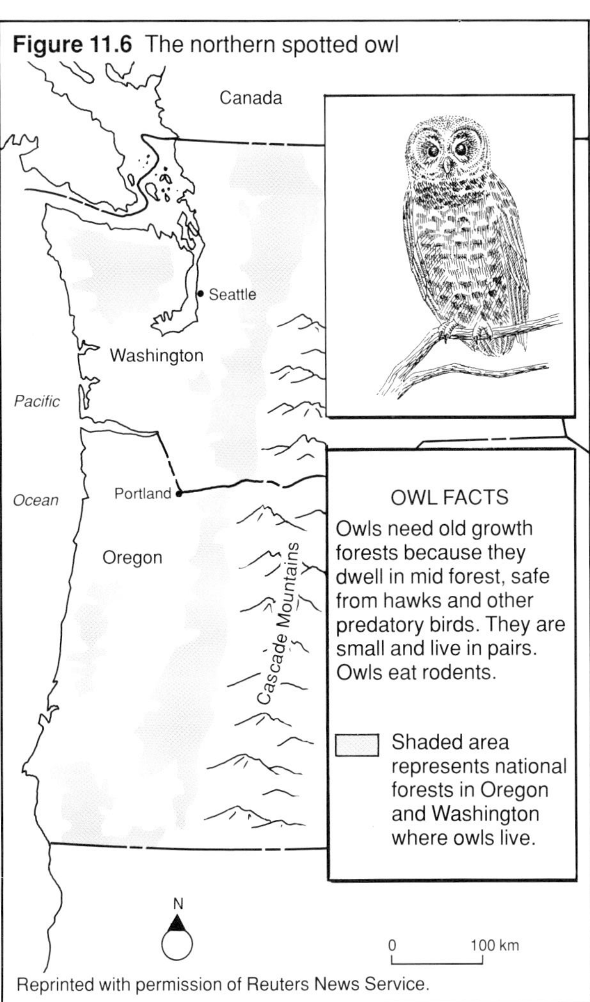
Canada
Seattle
Washington
Pacific
Ocean
Portland
Oregon
Cascade Mountains
OWL FACTS
Owls need old growth forests because they dwell in mid forest, safe from hawks and other predatory birds. They are small and live in pairs. Owls eat rodents.
Shaded area represents national forests in Oregon and Washington where owls live.
N
0
100 km

Reprinted with permission of Reuters News Service.

Are we willing to pay the price?

Most people are willing to pay the price to protect and clean up the environment. Figures 11.4 and 11.7 show that environmental action is popular. They also show that Canadians are willing to make some sacrifices to protect the environment. However, in return Canadians want to see tougher laws and more decisive actions from our political leaders.

In spite of the support shown in polls for tough environmental measures, we sometimes do not support them when it comes to voting for proposals that would increase our taxes. For example, in November 1992 voters in Victoria, British Columbia, rejected a proposal to install sewage treatment facilities. In the United States many proposals that will cost a lot of money are voted down. The Clean Air Act of 1990 was passed only after years of efforts to defeat it, because some taxes had to be raised to pay for the proposed measures.

Chrysler chairperson Lee Iaccoca once said, "Clean air or cheap fuel; you can't have them both." Suppose that the cost of gasoline were to rise to cover the pollution costs of the automobile. The price of gas would be an estimated $1.50 to $2.00 per L. Would we be prepared to pay that much to drive our cars? If we did have to pay that much for gas, would we use our cars more sparingly and walk or use public transport more often? If so, the higher price of gasoline would help to prolong the life of one of the earth's most scarce resources.

A sharp rise in the price of gasoline would, however, cause a serious problem in rural areas. People living well away from public transport would be penalized by the high cost of gasoline. They need to use their cars to get to essential services, which may be some distance away. Gasoline may need to be subsidized

Figure 11.7 Are we willing to pay more to protect the environment?

	PERCENTAGE		
	YES	NO	UNSURE
Buy unbleached paper products	86	10	4
Pay 50% more for garbage collection	67	25	8
Pay 10% more for safe packaging	66	29	5
Pay 5 cents more for gasoline	63	31	6
Pay $1000 (CDN) more for a car	63	29	8
Pay $250 (CDN) more/year for sewage cleanup	58	32	10
Pay 10% tax on energy	57	37	6

Margaret Munro, *The Vancouver Sun*.

in remote rural areas. As well, inflation would increase as a result of high energy costs. Industrial costs would be higher, and we would have to get used to paying more for most items we buy.

The environmental protection industry

The higher costs of producing goods without polluting the environment will likely cause some problems for Canadian industries. They may not be able to compete with companies in countries with lower wages and less strict environmental standards.

However, the protection of the environment has already created a rapidly growing new industry. In 1989 a report prepared for Environment Ontario showed that the importance of prevention and clean-up is creating a whole range of new activities and providing many new jobs. Approximately 2200 companies were engaged in making and servicing antipollution equipment in 1995. Others worked in the fields of environmental monitoring and surveys.

Some of the products made by the environment industry are scrubbers and flow measurement devices used in the measurement and control of air pollution. Water purifiers, filters, and pumps are used to control water quality, while incinerators and compactors are manufactured for the waste disposal industry.

The environmental protection industries in Ontario employed about 35 000 people in 1995. This is roughly equal to the employment provided by the clothing or wood industries. The sales of environmental protection industries in Ontario were estimated at between $1.5 and $2 billion (CDN). This would indicate a possible total output of at least $6 billion (CDN) for the whole country, more than 1 percent of the Gross National Product.

The production of pollution control devices has the further advantage of being a growth industry, since environmental standards are likely to be strengthened in the future. This growth should help to offset declines caused by pollution control.

Demand for equipment for monitoring the environment is creating economic opportunities.

Risk/benefit analysis

In this book we have seen that very few environmental issues have simple and obvious solutions. For example, cloth diapers have the advantage over disposable diapers in that they can be reused many times, thus reducing the pressure of demand for the world's timber resources. Using cloth diapers is therefore beneficial to the environment. However, this benefit cannot be achieved without some cost. In this case, the washing of diapers uses water and detergent, as well as energy to heat the water.

This example shows that in order to form an opinion about an environmental issue we have to include not only the benefits but also the costs involved. The costs are not merely economic costs, measured in dollars and cents. We also include risks to the environment or to our health, such as the effects of water and air pollution. What we have to do is to try to weigh the benefits of our actions against these costs. This process is known as cost/benefit analysis or risk/benefit analysis. Cost/benefit analysis is used where the pros and cons can be measured mainly in terms of money. If we are dealing with risks to our health or to the environment, which may be difficult to measure in terms of money, the process is better described as risk/benefit analysis.

Examples of cost/benefit or risk/benefit analysis

Recycling is a good example of an environmental issue which cannot be decided without cost/benefit analysis. We saw in chapter 10 that recycling saves both resources and the use of energy. It economizes on the use of space in landfills. But recycling also involves the use of additional resources and energy. Think of the need for building recycling facilities and trucks to collect recyclable materials. Energy is also used in collecting materials and in the recycling process.

Recycling is an issue that most of us take for granted. But it is clear that it will only work effectively if the benefits outweigh the costs. There is a danger that recycling projects could be abandoned because local governments fail to consider all of the benefits as well as all of the costs. Often, environmental benefits are forgotten because they are not easily measured in dollars.

We can see the benefits in relation to costs and risks more clearly if we construct an organizer. The following example is a risk/benefit analysis of nuclear power, using some of the points mentioned in chapter 9. You may wish to add others. Remember that physical, social, economic, and environmental aspects of the issue are all important.

Risk/Benefit Analysis of Nuclear Power

RISKS/COSTS	BENEFITS
Nuclear reactors are costly to build	Nuclear reactors are relatively cheap to operate
Accidents can be deadly (e.g., Chernobyl) with great loss of life	Accidents are extremely rare; coal mining and burning cause many more deaths than nuclear power
Fossil fuels are used in the construction phase of nuclear power plants	No fossils fuels are used in operating plants; no SO_2 or CO_2 is created
Uranium mining causes some health hazards and low-level wastes	Tiny amounts of fuel are required; coal stations need large amounts
High-level wastes are extremely radioactive; disposal causes social and political problems; transport is dangerous	High-level wastes are low in total volume; technical solutions are possible. Coal wastes contain toxic materials
Nuclear fission can be used for military or terrorist purposes	Nuclear fission research may lead to a safer technology — nuclear fusion

Looking back

1. List examples of ways in which the environment can affect your health.
2. (a) Which forms of cancer have increased most in Canada? Which have decreased most? Can you suggest any reasons for these trends?
   (b) Look at the map of male cancer fatalities in Canada (Figure 11.2). Why do you think that urban cancer rates are higher than rural rates?
3. Create an organizer that shows how the chemical industry contributes to both the "good life" and to the creation of a harmful environment.
4. Why should federal and provincial governments have similar environmental laws?
5. Why can we not have both cheap fuel and clean air?

Applying your knowledge

1. Brainstorm to create a list of (a) infectious diseases that have decreased in Canada and other developed countries and (b) noninfectious diseases that have increased in these same countries. Using data bases and library indexes, find information to explain why noninfectious diseases have increased while infectious diseases have decreased.
2. Write an editorial that explains why we tolerate so many deaths from road accidents each year yet show great concern over the possibility of a few deaths from a chemical used in farming.
3. Discuss whether Pascal Dennis's or Stephen Shrybman's views of the threat from PCBs is more valid.
4. Survey your local area for violations of environmental laws. Determine what action has been taken and whether or not the problem has been solved. Prepare a report of your findings.
5. Write a short essay explaining external costs and how our costs have been lowered in the short term because we have freely polluted the environment.
6. Develop a chart outlining:
   (a) reasons why it is sometimes difficult to make polluters pay for their actions;
   (b) examples of types of pollution for which there are no penalties.
   (c) suggestions for legislation that would help make polluters responsible for their actions.

Extending your thinking

1. (a) Working in groups, list the risks to our personal health that we *choose* to take. Your list could include activities such as driving a car or skiing down a mountain as well as lifestyle risks such as smoking. Rank the risks in decreasing order of harm or danger.
   (b) Suggest ways in which each of these risks could be reduced or eliminated.
2. "The environmental assessment process can both create problems and solve them." Give examples to support this statement.
3. In groups of four or five, construct your own opinion poll based on Figures 11.4 and 11.7. Organize the distribution of the questionnaire to ensure that it is answered by at least 100 adults. Make sure that the same people do not receive more than one questionnaire. Compare the results with those in Figures 11.4 and 11.7.
4. Use the Internet or library sources to prepare cases for and against one of the following statements:
   (a) Smoking should be banned in public places.
   (b) The use of toxic chemicals in homes and gardens should be prohibited.
   (c) The government should do more to stop industries from polluting our environment.

   Do you agree or disagree with the statement you chose? Give reasons for your answer.
5. Find out if any pollution control devices are manufactured in your area (or in the industrial area closest to your community). What products are made? What are they used for? How successful are these products in reducing pollution? Report your findings to the class.
6. Complete a risk/benefit analysis of an environmental issue other than nuclear power. For instance, you might want to analyse the environmental effects of the construction of a hydro dam in Québec or British Columbia; the impact of an environmental tax on gasoline; or a plan to make pulp mills fully accountable for the pollution they create.

12 RURAL MANAGEMENT AND CONSERVATION

Human beings have often exploited the resources of ecosystems for selfish reasons. We have tried to make the environment adapt to us instead of adapting to it. For example, several species of whales will soon be extinct unless actions are taken to protect them. Many species have already been lost. Forest resources, especially in the tropics, could also be destroyed soon. In this chapter we will focus on the ways in which rural and wilderness areas of the world can be conserved.

Conservation and preservation

Today we hear a great deal about conserving the environment. First of all, we must ask what **conservation** means. At one extreme, it can mean preservation, or maintaining the natural world with no additional use of resources. As our world population steadily increases, this objective is very difficult. In most areas preserving a truly natural environment is not possible, since the environment has already been influenced by people. In such areas it is more realistic to practise conservation, or the creation of an environment in which existing species and their habitats can be sustained. This is no easy task. Many groups want to use the physical world in different ways. As a society we have to define our priorities and make decisions. This is what we mean by the management of the environment.

Management may be the responsibility of the federal, provincial, and/or municipal governments. The cooperation of private landowners and businesses is also needed. Effective management usually involves the coordination of different levels of government together with private interests.

A protected area has special provisions to shield the natural environment. In many cases plants and wildlife are protected by law. Scenic features or locations of special interest may also be protected, such as Dinosaur Provincial Park in Alberta, which protects fossil sites. Other protected areas include national marine parks and heritage areas.

The Badlands near Dinosaur Provincial Park in Alberta are a protected area.

Wilderness areas

Wilderness areas may be defined as "undeveloped land still primarily shaped by the forces of nature." According to the **International Union for Conservation of Nature and Natural Resources** (IUCN) a wilderness area should not be developed in any way that would destroy the plant and animal species that live there. It should be available for recreation, but only to those who travel in ways that are not harmful, such as by canoe or snowshoe instead of by motorboat or skidoo. Areas should be without roads, improved trails, and developed campgrounds. Many people are concerned that on a daily basis the world's wilderness areas are being eroded by human activities.

Figure 12.1 shows the areas of wilderness in selected countries. Canada has one of the largest wilderness areas. Much of this wilderness is in the Northwest and Yukon territories, as well as in the northern parts of Québec, Ontario, and the western provinces.

Large though it is, Canada's wilderness has been greatly reduced. Since the days of the fur trade the exploitation of natural resources has increasingly enveloped wilderness areas. The spread of farming, forestry, and mining across southern Canada has left little natural landscape.

Figure 12.1 Wilderness areas in selected countries

COUNTRY	WILDERNESS AREA (KM²)	PERCENTAGE OF TOTAL AREA
Former Soviet Union	7 520 000	34
Canada	6 406 000	65
Australia	2 294 000	30
China	2 108 000	22
Brazil	2 021 000	24
United States	441 000	5

Why protect wilderness areas?

There are a number of reasons why we need to give special protection to wilderness areas. The reasons may be natural, cultural, or scientific. Natural reasons include the fact that the wilderness is part of our natural heritage. If we allow it to be lost, we will lose many forms of life. Creating wilderness parks also helps to preserve forest cover on watersheds, reducing the risk of erosion and flooding.

Wilderness areas also have a special place in the lives of Native peoples, whose culture shows a much greater appreciation for the unity of the earth and all forms of life. Many wilderness areas are sacred to Native peoples. The use of wilderness for logging and the construction of hydro dams are serious threats to Native cultures. In general, the wilderness has a relaxing effect upon people who visit it. It is an antidote to the stress of today's busy life.

Scientifically, the wilderness is an essential part of monitoring the global environment. Air and water quality and the rate of biomass production can be measured. Soils can be studied in a way that helps the farmlands of Canada. For example, the study of the protected soils of Riding Mountain National Park in Manitoba has been used to set the standard for measuring the loss by erosion of other nearby soils.

Canada's national and provincial parks

Canada's first national park was at Banff, Alberta. Land was set aside in 1885 and approved by an act of Parliament in 1887. The park was at first a spa centred on the hot springs: a tourist venture, similar to parks, mainly in the Alps in Europe, with a large hotel and later a golf course. Soon the park began to attract visitors who wanted to enjoy the more energetic pursuits of hiking, canoeing, and camping.

In 1930 Canada had fourteen national parks. By 1981 the number had risen to twenty-nine, with the addition of Grasslands National Park in Saskatchewan. Ellesmere Island National Park Reserve was added in 1987. Additions in 1988 included Gwaii Haanas (Queen Charlotte Islands) in BC, and the Bruce Peninsula in Ontario. By 1996 several more parks, mainly in the Yukon and the Northwest Territories (Aulavik, Auyuittuq, Ivvavik, Vuntut, and Tuktut Nogait) brought the total to thirty-eight.

The purposes of Canada's national parks

A National Parks Act was passed in 1930. This act outlined the purposes of national parks and made the following commitment:

> The Parks are hereby dedicated to the people of Canada for their benefit, education and enjoyment, subject to the provisions of this Act and the Regulations, and such Parks shall be maintained and made use of so as to leave them unimpaired for the enjoyment of future generations.

From the beginning the commercial pressures to generate revenue from park resources proved too strong. In 1960 these pressures prompted Alvin Hamilton, the minister responsible for national parks, to ask for help:

> It is my feeling, as minister in charge of parks, that it is about time all those millions of people in Canada who use the parks and love them should band together and form themselves into a national parks association. How can a minister stand up against the pressures of commercial interests who want to use the parks for mining, forestry, for every kind of honky-tonk recreational device known to man, unless the people who love these parks are prepared to band together and support the minister by getting the facts out across the country?
>
> From Monte Hummel, *Endangered Spaces* (Toronto: Key Porter Books, 1989).

Lake Louise lies in Banff National Park.

This call did not go unheeded. Within a few years the organization now called the **Canadian Parks and Wilderness Society** was created to voice the concerns of Canadians about their parks.

There has always been a conflict of aims with regard to national parks. Should the parks allow access to as many visitors as possible, or should the emphasis be on preserving them as natural wilderness areas for the benefit of all creatures in the ecosystem?

Since the 1960s the Canadian public has moved toward the latter view of its parks. Yet our increased mobility has made it possible for millions of people to drive into national and provincial parks to view the wilderness that they long to protect. Some people say that we may be in danger of "loving our parks to death."

The Canadian Parks Service, in managing the national parks, has to balance the opposing views in the best way possible. The National Parks Act requires the Canadian Parks Service to produce management plans for each park. These must be tabled in Parliament and reviewed every five years.

Figure 12.2 Land use zones in Banff National Park

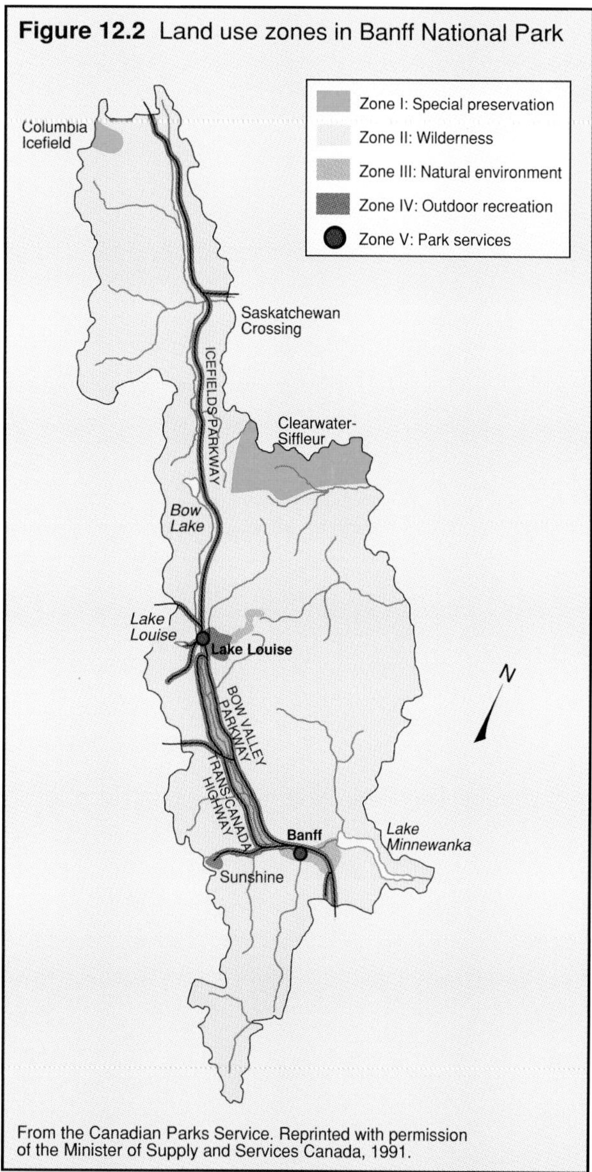

From the Canadian Parks Service. Reprinted with permission of the Minister of Supply and Services Canada, 1991.

Banff National Park

Banff National Park in Alberta is not only the oldest, but also the largest and best-known national park in Canada. It adjoins Jasper, Yoho, and Kootenay national parks to form the Four Mountain Parks. These four parks contain such a diversity of magnificent scenery and wildlife resources that they have been designated by UNESCO as a World Heritage Site. (See page 195.)

As in most of the national and provincial parks, the park area in Banff is divided into several types of land use. (See Figure 12.2.) Most visitors to the parks use the **frontcountry**, or the sections of the parks that are accessible by road. Only about 5 percent travel to the less accessible **backcountry**.

The backcountry is divided into three zones. The more heavily used "semi-primitive" areas provide some facilities, such as campsites. On the other hand, only random camping is permitted in the "primitive" and "wildland" areas.

Each year approximately 10 million people visit the Four Mountain Parks. In fact, most visitors pass straight through the park on the TransCanada highway. (The Banff and Jasper parks lie across the two main transcontinental road and rail routes.) The park is heavily used for skiing in winter and for hiking in summer. The largest single use is passive viewing of scenery and wildlife from cars. Banff National Park is the only park in North America that has not lost animal species during its existence.

Two specific objectives for the Four Mountain Parks are as follows:

1. The major objective for the parks is to preserve and protect their natural resources and processes.
2. The highest level of attention, however, will be given to resources and processes which are:
   (i) nationally significant;
   (ii) unique, rare or endangered;
   (iii) good examples of the natural resources of the Canadian Rocky Mountains; and
   (iv) important for the retention of the parks' wildland character.

As noted earlier, a park management plan is required for each national park. These contain guidelines for the protection, development, and use of parks. The different views on how the park should be used have to be reconciled in the plan.

For example, there may be some conflict of opinion between those who want increased access for the public in national parks and those who want to restrict access. Politicians are among those who favour heavy use of the parks. On the other hand, environmentalists may wish to limit its use to ensure the conservation of the natural environment.

Figure 12.3 Land use zones in Algonquin Provincial Park

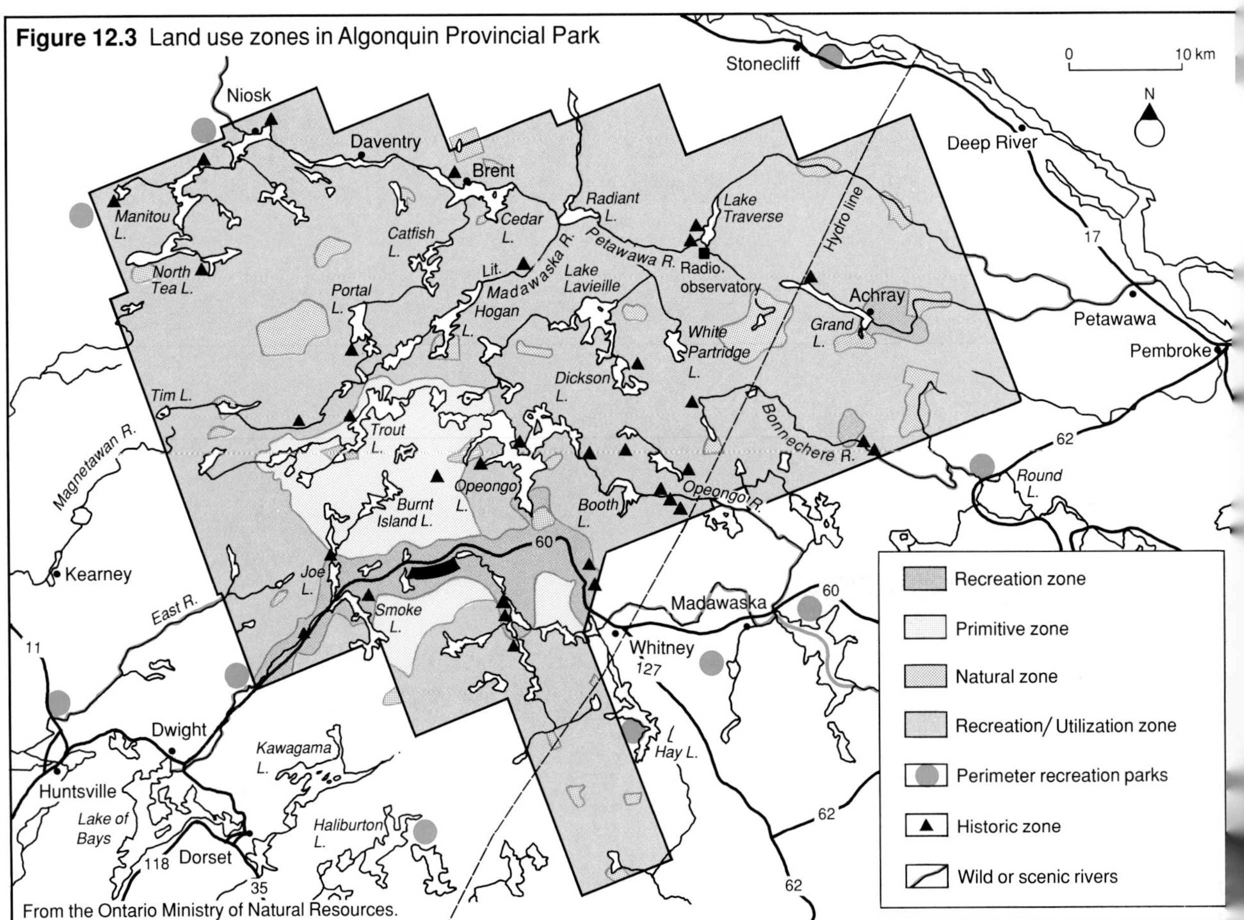

From the Ontario Ministry of Natural Resources.

Algonquin Provincial Park

Algonquin Provincial Park in Ontario was the first provincial park to be established in Canada in 1893. The park lies on the southern edge of the **Canadian Shield** between Georgian Bay and the Ottawa River. Algonquin Park contains some excellent scenery created by the ice sheets that scoured this area of Canada. Much of the park consists of rocky hills, sand and gravel deposits, and thousands of lakes. It contains some of the few remaining areas of old growth white pine forest in Ontario.

Algonquin Park is administered according to a master plan approved in 1974. The plan designates land use zones, as shown in Figures 12.3 and 12.4.

Figure 12.4 Land use zones in Algonquin Provincial Park

ZONE TYPE	PERCENTAGE OF PARK AREA
Natural and historic	4.7
Primitive	8.9
Recreation and access	4.4
Recreational reserves and deer yards	7.1
Recreation/utilization	74.9

Seventy small nature reserves protect points of particular natural and historic interest. Minimum access is permitted in the wilderness area of the park. As in Banff National Park, there is a high-use frontcountry corridor (along Highway 60). Most visitors to Algonquin see only this section of the park. However, about 75 percent of the park is a "Recreation/Utilization" zone. Logging takes place in this zone in spite of strong opposition from people concerned about the long-term survival of Ontario's forest ecosystems.

The logging in Algonquin Park illustrates one contrast between provincial and national parks. Provincial governments are much more likely to allow resource use in their parks. For example, mining activities take place in Strathcona Provincial Park in British Columbia. Land use in national parks is much more strictly controlled by Parks Canada.

The province of Ontario is one of the provinces that has established a long-term plan for its parks. Six classes of parks are recognized: wildlife, natural resource, natural environment, waterway, historical, and recreational. The natural resources of Ontario's parks have been carefully studied. This helps both the government and conservationists to be informed about ecological issues in Ontario's most scenic areas.

Endangered areas

Some rural areas have outstanding scenic beauty. If these areas are situated close to expanding urban centres, they may be in danger of being swallowed up by the spread of housing or industry. Another threat to areas of natural beauty is air or water pollution from acid rain or the discharge of industrial wastes. Two examples of scenic areas that are threatened in these ways are the Niagara Escarpment in Ontario and Howe Sound in British Columbia.

The Niagara Escarpment

A rugged limestone cliff known as the Niagara Escarpment extends from the Niagara River to the Bruce Peninsula (now a National Park) on Lake Huron and onward across Lake Michigan. Its best-known feature is Niagara Falls, where the Niagara River crosses the escarpment. The Niagara Escarpment creates some of the finest scenery in Ontario along its 700 km length. Unfortunately, the impact on human activities on the escarpment has threatened to destroy much of its beauty.

There are several causes of this pressure on the landscape. The southeastern portion of the Niagara Escarpment is located in the highly urbanized belt on the western end of Lake Ontario. Fruit farming is located on the fertile low-lying land north of the escarpment along the Niagara Peninsula. Locations on the crest of the escarpment have been sought after for residential lots. Many industries are nearby, particularly the steel industry in Hamilton just below the escarpment. Limestone has been quarried along the crest of the escarpment in some places. Tourists come in large numbers, not only to Niagara Falls, but also to other scenic locations along the escarpment. The Bruce Trail, an attraction for hikers and campers, extends from the Niagara Peninsula to the Bruce Peninsula on Georgian Bay.

Efforts have been made for many years to control the spreading development along the Niagara Escarpment, but success has been limited. Since 1930 much of the most sought-after land close to the escarpment has been urbanized. Finally, in 1985 the Ontario government approved the **Niagara Escarpment Planning and Development Act.** This act was the product of twelve years of careful planning by the Niagara Escarpment Commission. During this time many interest groups and organizations, as well as the general public, were fully consulted.

The Niagara Escarpment Plan takes priority over other provincial policies. The plan controls land use and development in the area shown in Figure 12.5.

Figure 12.5 Niagara Escarpment plan area

Niagara Escarpment plan area
Niagara Escarpment future planning area
County and regional municipal boundary
Township and area municipal boundary

Bruce Peninsula National Park
Lion's Head
Lake Huron
Georgian Bay
Wiarton
Owen Sound
Nottawasaga Bay
Collingwood
Shelburne
Orangeville
CALEDON
HALTON HILLS
MILTON
Toronto
N
FLAMBOROUGH
BURLINGTON
Lake Ontario
DUNDAS
ANCASTER
HAMILTON
STONEY CREEK
GRIMSBY
0 20 km
LINCOLN
ST. CATHARINES
NIAGARA-ON-THE-LAKE
PELHAM

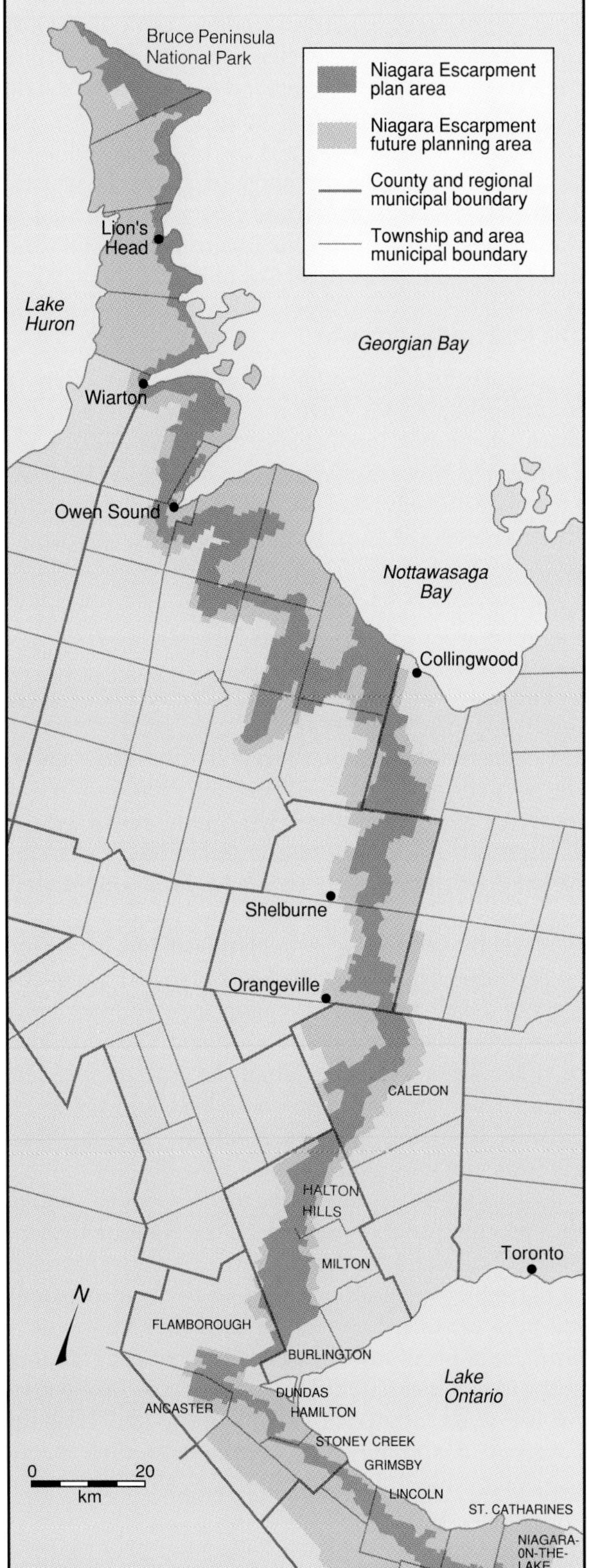

Reprinted with permission of the Niagara Escarpment Commission.

Actual land-use decisions are largely made by the municipalities in accordance with criteria set out in the plan.

The Niagara Escarpment zone has no less than 105 parks along its total length, most of which are connected by the Bruce Trail. The many agencies that manage these parks are coordinated by the Ministry of Natural Resources. Some new land is to be acquired by the government through this ministry, mainly to complete the Bruce Trail.

The implementation of the Niagara Escarpment Plan was funded by the government of Ontario at the rate of $2.5 million (CDN) per year until 1995. Donated funds are collected by the Ontario Heritage Foundation. Overall, the work of overseeing the plan is coordinated by the Niagara Escarpment Commit-

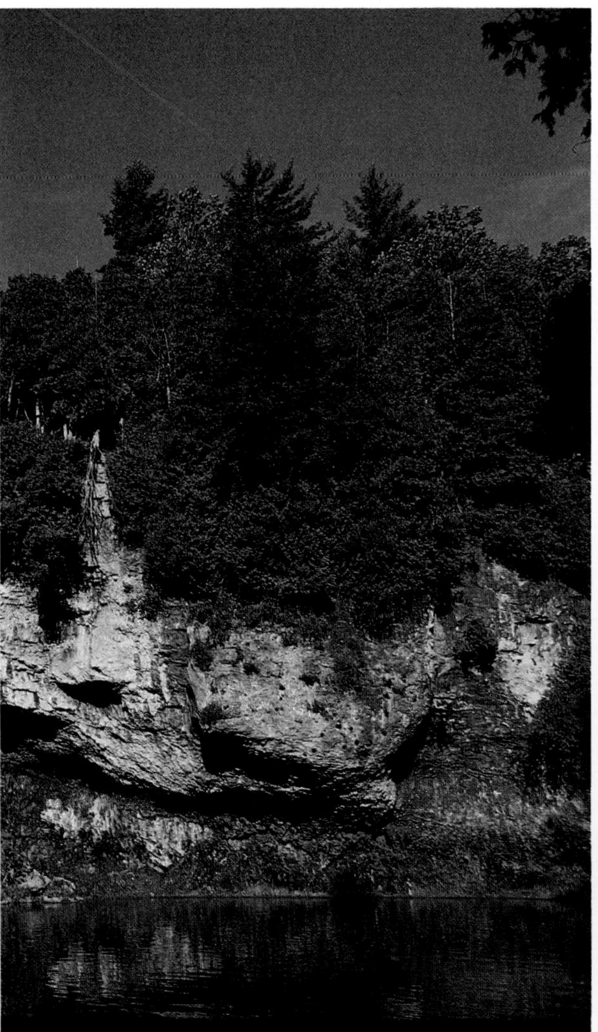

The Elora Gorge is part of the scenic beauty of the Niagara Escarpment, which stretches for 700 km in Ontario.

tee, working with the Ministry of Natural Resources and the Natural Heritage League of Ontario.

Howe Sound

The Niagara Escarpment is an area that has been threatened by competing demands for its valuable land resources. Howe Sound in British Columbia is one of Canada's most scenic coastal areas. Forested mountains border this sheltered inlet, which lies only a short distance north of Vancouver. It has traditionally been used for inshore fishing and by shellfisheries.

Two large pulp and paper mills are located on Howe Sound. (See Figure 12.6.) Both mills release emissions into the air and water. The mills use the **kraft pulp process**. In this process the bleaching releases chlorine, which combines with organic matter to form organo-chlorides. In the late 1980s these two mills dumped 120 000 kg of organo-chlorides into Howe Sound each day. The greatest threat to health is when contaminants in the pulp wash combine with chlorine in the bleach to form dioxins and furans. (See page 13.)

Dioxins and furans are highly toxic to both animals and humans. Fish experience reproductive failure and often show evidence of liver damage and cancerous tumours. These effects were observed up to 10 km from the mills. Shellfish, being filter feeders, tend to concentrate toxic chemicals in their fatty tissues.

The situation came to a head in 1989 after the environmental organization **Greenpeace** tested the waters close to the mills and found dangerous quantities of dioxins and other toxic chemicals. Government tests confirmed the results. In June 1989 all fisheries in Howe Sound were closed down by order of the federal government. In November 1989 all shellfisheries near BC pulp mills were closed indefinitely.

Beautiful Howe Sound, north of Vancouver, is being threatened by air and water pollution created by pulp and paper mills.

The mills have been slow to comply with government safety standards. Yet they have seldom been fined for exceeding the pollution standards. In effect the victims (the fisheries) have been punished, while the polluters (the mills) have gone free.

In May 1992 the Government of Canada introduced regulations governing the discharge of dioxins and furans from pulp and paper mills. In response to these regulations the BC pulp and paper industry stepped up their investment program to reduce these discharges. Between 1989 and 1994 the levels of dioxins in coastal pulp mill effluent fell by 93 percent and furans by 99 percent. All mills met the dioxin regulatory limit of 20 parts per quadrillion (10^{12}). As a result, about 40 percent of the shell fisheries and some non-commercial crab fisheries in upper Howe Sound were reopened in 1995. However, it will be years before Howe Sound recovers fully from the volume of toxic waste that has been dumped into it in the past.

Figure 12.6 Howe Sound, showing the location of the two pulp mills

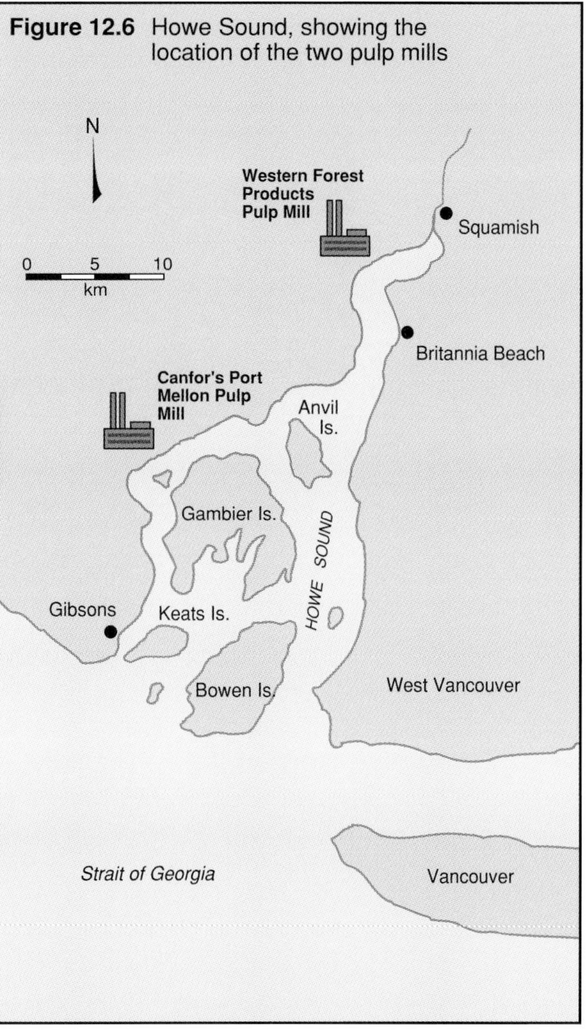

Antarctica

The continent of Antarctica is one of the largest land masses, larger than India and China put together. Although remote and covered by thick ice sheets, it contains large deposits of coal. A deep drilling venture by the United States in 1973 indicated that Antarctica may also contain deposits of oil and gas.

The dangers of exploiting Antarctica are clear. The ecosystem is a fragile one. Oil spills take much longer to disperse in the frigid waters and garbage does not decompose. Should the ozone layer continue to decrease, the supply of Antarctic phytoplankton could be reduced. This would reduce the population of krill, which feed on the phytoplankton. The populations of fish, whales, and penguins would suffer.

Antarctic wildlife has already been drastically reduced by whale and seal hunting, some species to the point of extinction.

Treaties relating to Antarctica

To protect this last true wilderness on earth, several treaties have been drawn up. (See Figure 12.7.) In 1959 the **International Antarctic Treaty** was signed by twelve countries, including the United States, the Soviet Union, and other countries that claimed a slice of Antarctic territory. It was ratified in 1961. The treaty "froze" the claims of various countries to their piece of Antarctic territory for a period of thirty years. It was declared that the Antarctic "shall continue forever to be used exclusively for peaceful purposes and shall not become the scene or object of international discord." Protection of Antarctic life was given top priority.

The provisions of this treaty ended in 1991. Antarctica, therefore, had to be protected by a new treaty. In 1988 several nations produced a Minerals Treaty, known as the Wellington Convention, that would allow future exploitation only on a strictly controlled basis. This convention requires the signatures of sixteen countries and has not been ratified. It was firmly rejected by conservationists on the grounds that it would not necessarily prevent a possible ecological disaster in Antarctica.

In 1989 Australia and France called for Antarctica to be made the world's first international wilderness park in which no country could own any territory.

Figure 12.7 Antarctica

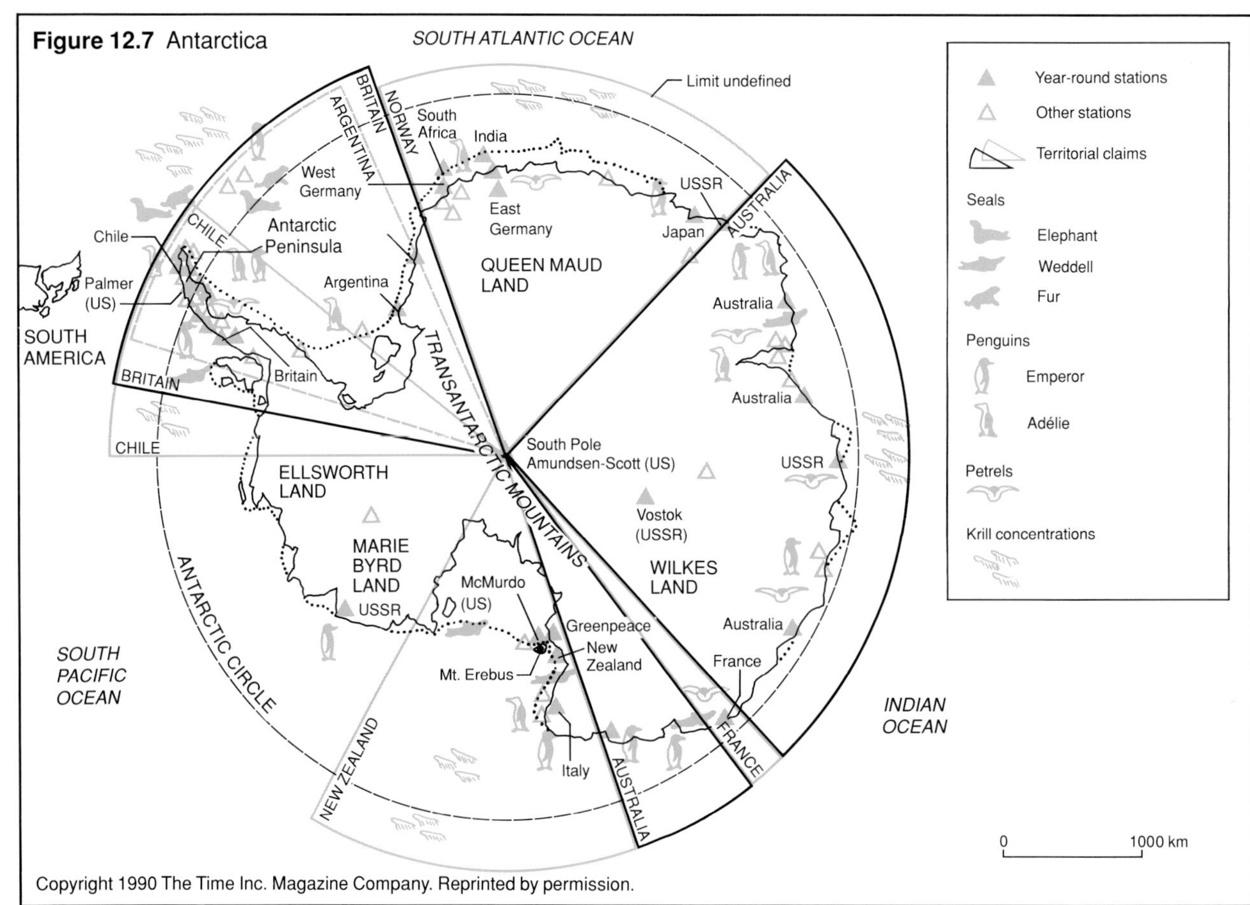

World conservation programs

Nature recognizes no political boundaries. It is not surprising, therefore, that the conservation movement is truly international. The **United Nations Environment Program (UNEP)** was established in 1972. It is based in Nairobi, Kenya. UNEP provides funds for many activities, including desertification control and environmental monitoring. It also maintains a register of toxic chemicals and pesticides.

Another international organization in the conservation field is the International Union for the Conservation of Nature and Natural Resources (IUCN). The IUCN was founded in 1948 by conservationists in Switzerland and France. This body coordinates the efforts of conservation organizations in many countries.

The World Conservation Strategy

In 1980 the IUCN, together with UNEP and the **World Wildlife Fund (WWF)**, set up the **World Conservation Strategy (WCS)**. The objectives of the WCS emphasized **sustainable development** seven years before the phrase was widely publicized in *Our Common Future*. The main objectives of the WCS are as follows:

1. to maintain essential ecological processes and life support systems;
2. to preserve genetic diversity; and
3. to ensure the sustainable utilization of species and ecosystems.

From the International Union for the Conservation of Nature and Natural Resources, *World Conservation Strategy*, 1980.

The WCS is a clear statement of the priorities that need to be adopted to resolve the world's main environmental problems. Canada endorsed the strategy in 1981.

Later in the decade, the Canadian government set up the National Task Force on Environment and Economy (1986). The task force was asked to consider both the WCS and the Brundtland report, *Our Common Future*. They encouraged each province to set up a provincial task force, or "Round Table," so that Canada would have a conservation strategy on a provincial as well as on a national basis.

The World Heritage Convention

The IUCN was also responsible for drafting the **World Heritage Convention**, which was adopted by the United Nations Educational, Scientific, and Cultural Organization (UNESCO) in 1972. Out of this came the **World Charter for Nature**, a system of **biosphere reserves**, and a program for wetlands protection.

Canada is one of more than 100 countries that are members of the World Heritage Convention. The convention binds member countries to assist one another in protecting their heritage sites, which include cultural areas and areas of natural beauty. To date almost 300 sites have been placed on the World Heritage list. Canada has eleven sites. Five are national parks and two are urban centres.

Canadian World Heritage Sites

Nahanni National Park (Northwest Territories)

Dinosaur Provincial Park (Alberta)

Kluane National Park (Yukon)

Four Mountain Parks (Alberta and British Columbia)

Wood Buffalo National Park (Alberta and Northwest Territories)

Gros Morne National Park (Newfoundland)

L'Anse-aux-Meadows National Historic Park (Newfoundland)

Anthony Island Provincial Park (British Columbia)

Head-Smashed-In Buffalo Jump (Alberta)

Québec City (Québec)

Lunenburg (Nova Scotia)

Other World Heritage Sites include areas as unique as the Grand Canyon in the United States, the Great Barrier Reef in Australia, and the Taj Mahal in India.

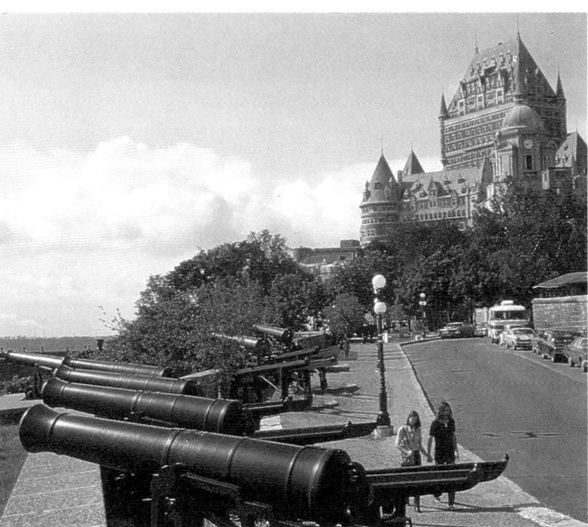

Historic Québec City is one of Canada's eleven world heritage sites.

The Biosphere Reserves Program

In 1971 UNESCO launched the **Man and the Biosphere Program (MAB)**. The aim was to encourage a sustainable relationship between people and their environments throughout the world. MAB is centred on protected areas known as biosphere reserves.

Biosphere reserves are designed to conserve the major ecosystems throughout the world, including both land and coastal/marine areas. They are designed for research, education, and the monitoring of the natural environment. MAB seeks to find solutions to the problems of meeting human economic needs while conserving natural resources and biological processes.

Biosphere reserves are planned to include a core area, buffer zone, and transitional area. (See Figure 12.8.) The core area consists of a section of one of the earth's biomes that has not been greatly affected by human activities. The core areas are strictly protected. Only passive research can go on — in other words, no experimentation with the ecosystem can take place.

The buffer zone acts as a protective area surrounding the core. Activities within it are also regulated, but MAB allows what it calls "manipulative research." Traditional land uses are allowed, and the land can be rehabilitated if necessary.

There were 324 biosphere reserve sites in 82 countries worldwide in 1995. Only six are in Canada. They are Charlevoix and Mont St. Hilaire in Québec, Long Point and the Niagara Escarpment in Ontario, Riding Mountain National Park in Manitoba, and Waterton Lakes National Park in Alberta. Examples from other countries include Manu National Park in Peruvian Amazonia and the Changbai Biosphere Reserve in China.

The future agenda

Biosphere reserves underline an idea that is the theme of the book *Endangered Spaces*, edited by Monte Hummel of the World Wildlife Fund (Canada). The point is made that we have rightly become concerned with the loss of species, both plants and animals, throughout the world. However, the real answer to preserving *species* is to preserve the *spaces* that they inhabit. In other words, we need to emphasize an ecosystem approach. Ecosystems can be eroded from all sides and eventually disappear. As Harold Eidsvik puts it (in *Endangered Spaces*): "Behind every square kilometre sits a lawyer and a plan."

In Ontario, for example, there are over 3000 plants and 600 vertebrates. Yet to preserve these, a significant area of each of the thirteen ecosystems of the province must be maintained. The only chance of the long-term survival of a variety of species is the preservation of these natural ecosystems.

Future national parks?

A Gallup poll taken in 1987 shows that more than 95 percent of Canadians approved of government spending to protect Canada's wilderness areas. Much remains to be done, however. The parks and wilderness system is only 54 percent complete, if we accept the Brundtland report's target that 12 percent of a country should be protected as wilderness. To date, Canada has only 6.3 percent.

If we divide Canada into thirty-nine types of ecosystems, only twenty-one of them contain national or provincial parks. (See Figure 12.9.) Several of these ecosystems can never have the parks they need. Space no longer permits the 50 000 ha that a park in south-

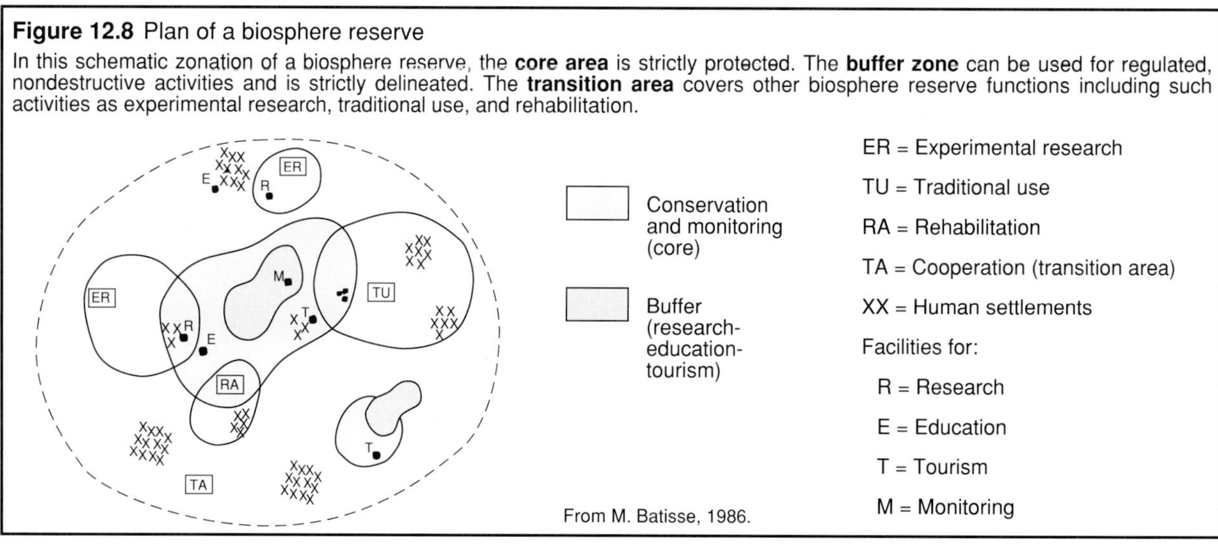

Figure 12.8 Plan of a biosphere reserve

In this schematic zonation of a biosphere reserve, the **core area** is strictly protected. The **buffer zone** can be used for regulated, nondestructive activities and is strictly delineated. The **transition area** covers other biosphere reserve functions including such activities as experimental research, traditional use, and rehabilitation.

Figure 12.9 Canada's national parks and ecological zones

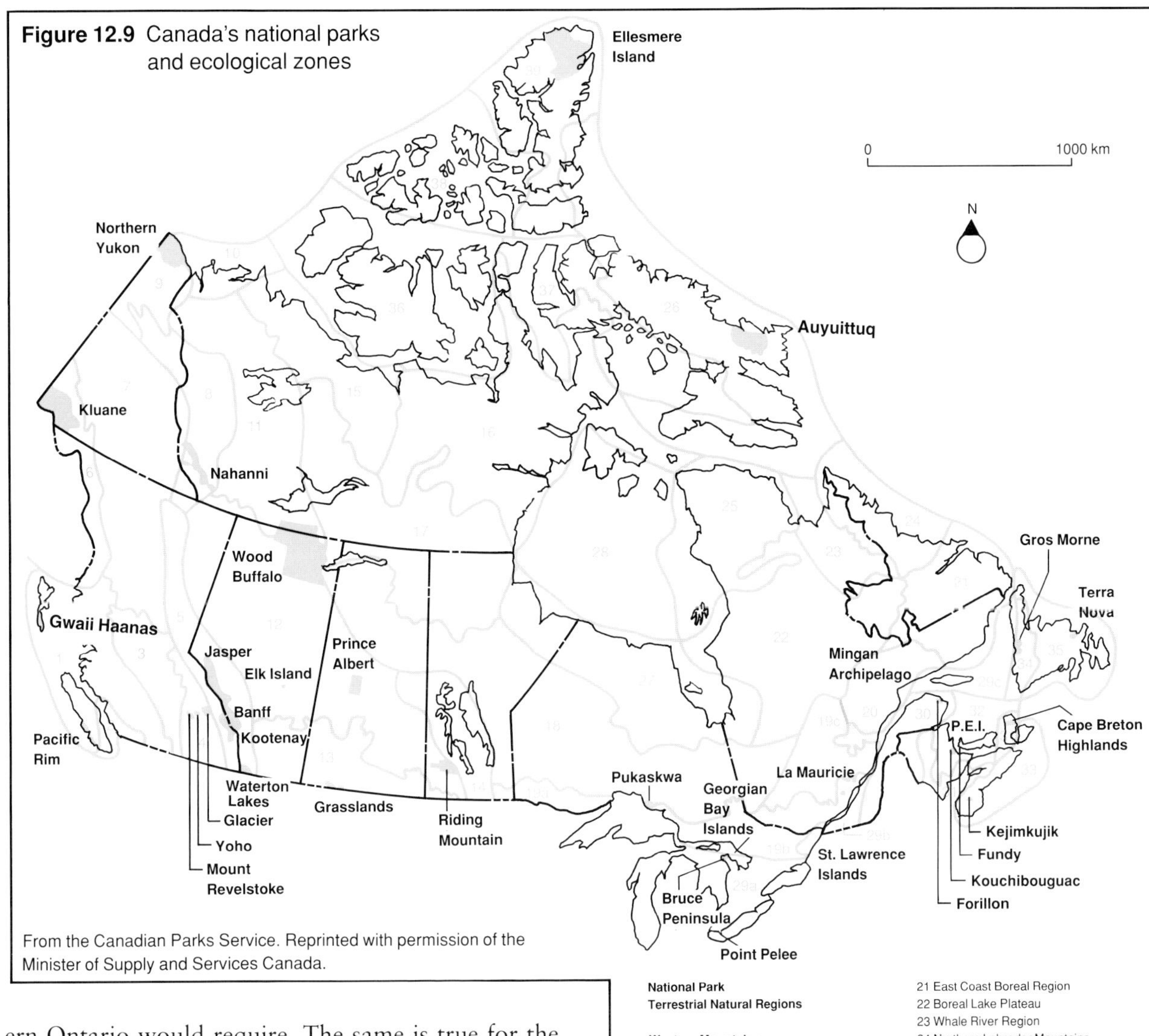

From the Canadian Parks Service. Reprinted with permission of the Minister of Supply and Services Canada.

National Park
Terrestrial Natural Regions

Western Mountains
1 Pacific Coast Mountains
2 Strait of Georgia Lowlands
3 Interior Dry Plateau
4 Columbia Mountains
5 Rocky Mountains
6 Northern Coast Mountains
7 Northern Interior Plateaux and Mountains
8 Mackenzie Yukon Region
9 Northern Yukon Region

Interior Plains
10 Mackenzie Delta
11 Northern Boreal Plains
12 Southern Boreal Plains and Plateaux
13 Prairie Grasslands
14 Manitoba Lowlands

Canadian Shield
15 Tundra Hills
16 Central Tundra Region
17 Northwestern Boreal Uplands
18 Central Boreal Uplands
19 (a) West Great Lakes-St. Lawrence Precambrian Region
(b) Central Great Lakes-St. Lawrence Precambrian Region
(c) East Great Lakes-St. Lawrence Precambrian Region
20 Laurentian Boreal Highlands
21 East Coast Boreal Region
22 Boreal Lake Plateau
23 Whale River Region
24 Northern Labrador Mountains
25 Ungava Tundra Plateau
26 Northern Davis Region

Hudson Bay Lowlands
27 Hudson-James Lowlands
28 Southampton Plain

St. Lawrence Lowlands
29 (a) West St. Lawrence Lowland
(b) Central St. Lawrence Lowland
(c) East St. Lawrence Lowland

Appalachian
30 Notre Dame-Megantic Mountains
31 Maritime Acadian Highlands
32 Maritime Plain
33 Atlantic Coast Uplands
34 Western Newfoundland Island Highlands
35 Eastern Newfoundland Island Atlantic Region

Arctic Lowlands
36 Western Arctic Lowlands
37 Eastern Arctic Lowlands

High Arctic Islands
38 Western High Arctic Region
39 Eastern High Arctic Glacier Region

ern Ontario would require. The same is true for the long grass Prairies of Manitoba and old growth forests in the Maritime provinces.

Canada has forty-five national wildlife areas, but a further ninety-nine sites have been identified. These are not yet protected. Only two of twenty-nine identified marine park areas are now protected. We should remember that even areas that are legally protected may still suffer from poaching. This is well illustrated in the African game parks, where the slaughter of elephants and other species continues in spite of legal protection. The enforcement of protection demands large sums of money, which most of the world's parks do not have.

Monte Hummel pleaded for all provinces of Canada to have parks plans in place by the end of 1990. His timetable suggested that plans should be implemented in stages and fully completed by the year 2000.

Figure 12.10 A topographic map of the Lake Louise area

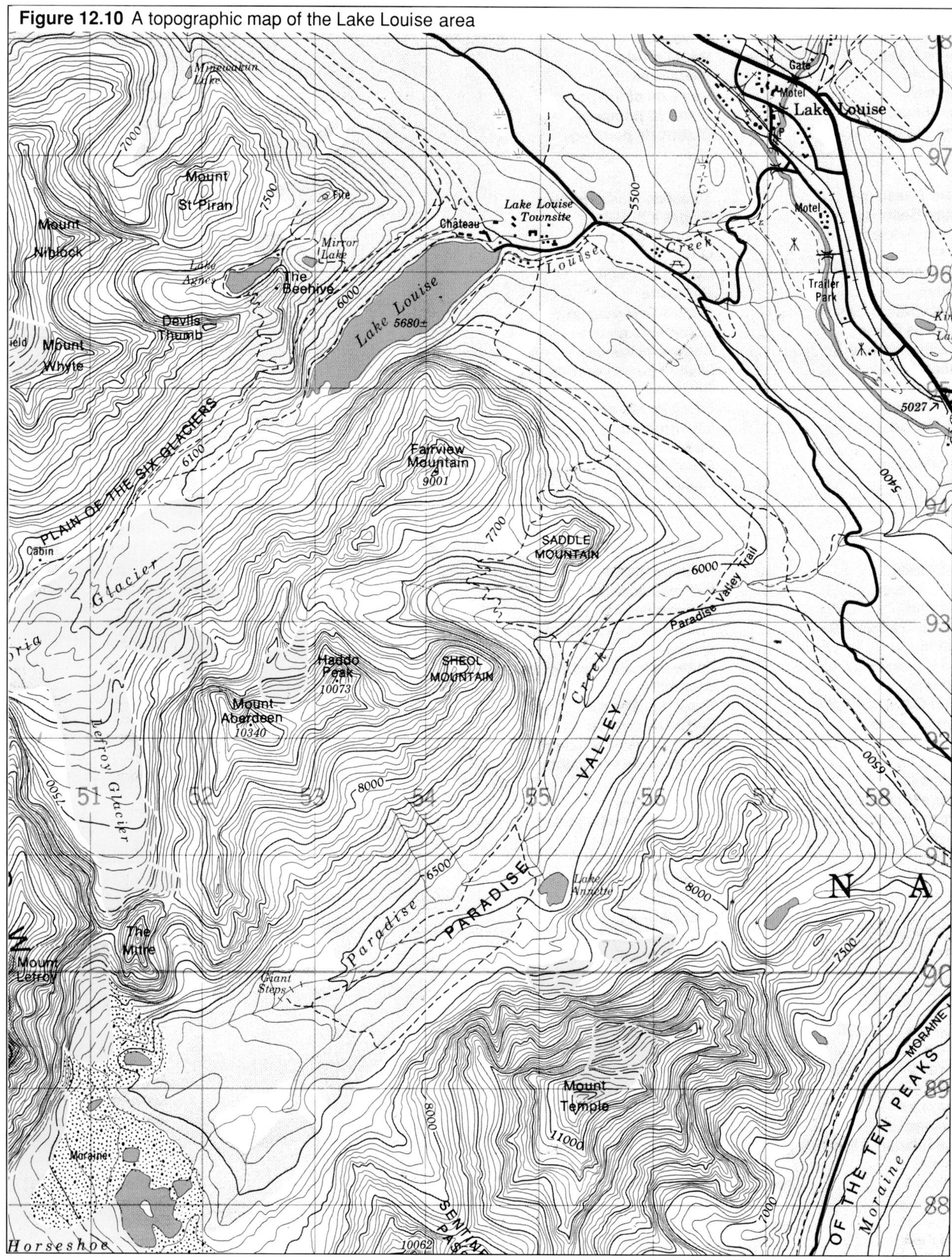

Looking back

1. What is the difference between preservation and conservation?
2. List the pressures placed on Algonquin Park that you think might be found along the Highway 60 corridor.
3. (a) Compare biosphere reserves with Canada's national parks system.
   (b) Describe the different zones in each biosphere reserve and their purpose.
4. List the reasons why the Niagara Escarpment has been so attractive for development.
5. Why is it important that each of Canada's thirty-nine types of ecosystems should have a national or provincial park to protect it?

Applying your knowledge

1. Write a short essay outlining whether or not you think wildlife conservation is important. Give reasons for your position.
2. Examine Figure 12.10 and identify the following:
   (a) the main physical features;
   (b) the height of the mountains;
   (c) the lakes, rivers, and icesheets; and
   (d) any recreational facilities.
   Explain why this land should be protected in a national park.
3. Prepare an argument either in favour of or against the plan to conserve the Niagara Escarpment.
4. (a) List the reasons why an environment might be considered at risk.
   (b) Which of these reasons fits the environment of Howe Sound?
   (c) Describe the actions you think should be taken to prevent further pollution of Howe Sound.
5. In a class discussion identify the ways in which the management of a wilderness park in Antarctica would differ from that of a wilderness park in North America. Keep a record of the discussion in your notes.
6. Explain why preserving *spaces* is essential if we are to preserve *species*.

Extending your thinking

1. Visit a wilderness area near you. Prepare a photo essay that identifies the features this area was designed to protect. Under each picture, outline the importance of these features.
2. Identify a specific environment in your local area that is endangered. Find out what pressures threaten the area and write a letter to your government representative with your recommendations on how to protect it.
3. Choose three World Conservation Programs. Research each one in depth and present a comparison analysis of the objectives, methods, and accomplishments of each. Report your findings to the class.
4. Prepare a case for or against one of the following statements:
   - National parks should be used primarily for the conservation of wildlife, not for recreational or economic activities.
   - The federal government should allocate more money to the creation and development of national parks even though money for social spending is scarce.

13 URBAN MANAGEMENT

Many of the environmental problems that we face today are concentrated in our cities. The high density of population and economic activity in cities leads to air and water pollution as well as waste disposal problems. A city, as we saw in chapter 4, is a highly artificial ecosystem. Plant and animal life is limited by the number of buildings and the intensity of human activities.

In historic times the Greeks held the city in high esteem. The people of the city-state of Athens created the following oath, showing how highly they valued their city:

> We will ever strive for the ideals and sacred things of the city, both alone and with many; we will unceasingly seek to quicken the sense of public duty; we will revere and obey the city's laws; we will transmit this city not less, but greater, better and more beautiful than it was transmitted to us.
>
> From "Promoting Health in the Urban Context," WHO Healthy Cities Project, Paper No.1, Denmark 1988.

Throughout history, cities have acted as magnets for people. Migration from country to town has occurred in every nation. People, particularly young people, have left the country to seek better jobs and a more exciting lifestyle in the cities.

Cities have played a crucial role in human affairs. Great works of music and literature have been written in cities, and political movements and events have occurred there. Cities have been the nerve centres of societies and the birthplace of ideas. Not surprisingly, many people find city life stimulating and rewarding.

The ugly side of cities

We pay a price, however, for the benefits of city life. Athenian ideals have not been achieved during much of the history of cities. Today Athens has one of the worst records of air pollution in Europe, causing the ancient Greek monuments to decay at a rapid rate. On badly polluted days the number of deaths in Athens rises sixfold. But the Industrial Revolution in northern Europe was even worse. An eyewitness describes part of Manchester, England, in 1832:

> [There were] squat houses, [and] wretched streets of brick under red roofs crossing each other in all directions and leading down to the river...narrow alleys and dusty yards were foul with the smell of rotting old clothes and decorated with rags and linen hung out to dry...The houses [were] generally of a single storey, low, dilapidated, kennels to sleep and die in...The impression is not one of debauchery, but of abject, miserable poverty.
>
> From Norman Longmate, *Alive and Well: Medicine and Public Health, 1830 to the Present Day* (London: Penguin Books, 1970).

Fortunately, the dirt and disease of the Industrial Revolution have been largely overcome with the help of clean water supplies and proper sewage facilities. Cities in the Western world are now much cleaner than they were in the mid-nineteenth century. However, some new environmental problems have surfaced in cities because of the volume of emissions released into the urban atmosphere. Other problems relate to the psychological stresses that may accompany urban lifestyles.

In this chapter we shall look at some of the environmental problems of urban living, including polluted air, traffic issues, and urban lifestyle problems. We will also consider how to manage these problems.

Air pollution

Clean air is usually the first casualty in the development of a city. The Worldwatch Institute reports that 150 million people live in parts of the United States where, according to the Environmental Protection Agency (EPA), the air is considered unhealthy. Breathing the air in some cities in the developing world, such as Bombay and Mexico City, is equivalent to smoking more than a pack of cigarettes a day.

According to 1990 reports, the air was so bad in some towns that were formerly part of East Germany that people had to leave because of persistent illness. The problem was caused by widespread burning of brown (dirty) coal. Much the same problem occurs in China. A letter written in Beijing makes the following observation:

> Everyone uses a cheap kind of coal, which is available locally but also contains much sulphur. Air pollution is awful. We normally could see only five or six streets from our hotel window. The rest is bluish smog. And that despite few cars and trucks. Beijing has 10 million people and 7 million bicycles. Goodness knows what will happen when the Chinese start riding motor cycles, or cars!
>
> From a letter to Stewart Dunlop from Manfred Harpe.

One of the adverse effects of dirty air in cities is the frequency of winter fogs. In the coal-burning days of the 1950s, London, England, suffered several "pea-soup" fogs. These were associated with high-pressure weather systems, during which the air hung so heavily over the city that smoke and exhaust fumes could not escape. The thick, choking fog usually led to a large number of deaths from respiratory diseases and pneumonia. About 4000 people are estimated to have died prematurely as a direct result of the 1952 London fog. (See Figure 13.1.) Similar killing fogs have occurred in Donora, Pennsylvania, and the Meuse Valley, Belgium.

Serious health problems occur today in some developing countries and in eastern Europe because of the dependence on coal. Many of their power stations are using outdated technology with no scrubbers to remove pollutants.

Figure 13.1 Deaths related to air pollution during the London fog of December 1952

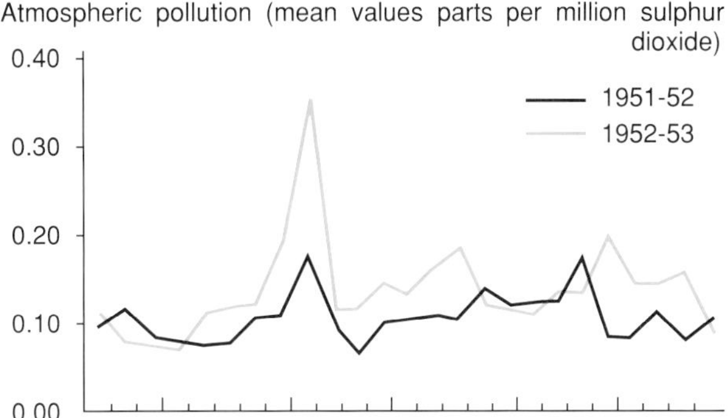

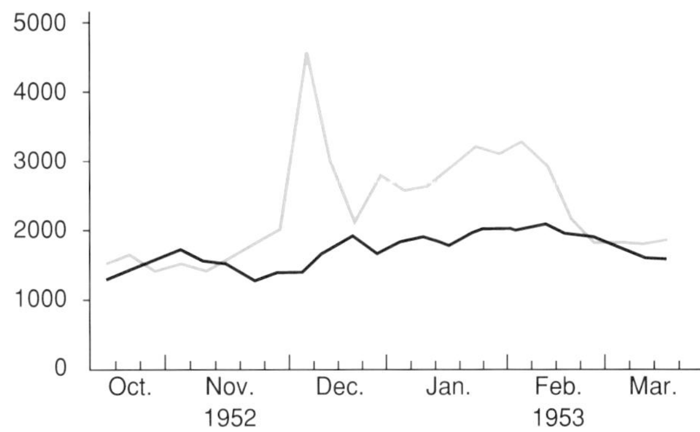

From J. N. Morris, *Uses of Epidemiology*, 2nd ed., (Edinburgh: Churchill Livingstone, 1964.)

Air pollution in eastern European countries like Poland is among the worst in the world.

Cleaning up the air

On the whole, the Western world is making some progress in improving air quality. Many cities have introduced by-laws to limit the burning of coal, wood, and other fuels that discharge dust and soot into the atmosphere. In some cases city councils have embarked on a program of cleaning up stonework that has been blackened by smoke over many years. For instance, the stone buildings in the city of Glasgow, Scotland, for years had been covered by a layer of grimy soot. After stone cleaning they now look clean and bright.

In the United States progress has been made in the control of atmospheric dust (particulates) and sulphur dioxide, but nitrogen oxides remain a problem. The global problem of the greenhouse effect also remains. The use of fossil fuels and the burning of the rain forests continue to release enormous amounts of carbon dioxide into the atmosphere.

Heritage buildings in cities like Glasgow, Scotland, are being cleaned and restored to their original beauty.

Figure 13.2 A comparison of energy use by mode of commuting

MODE OF TRANSPORT	FUEL OR ELECTRICITY USE (L/100 KM)	NUMBER OF COMMUTERS	ENERGY USE MJ/PERSON-KM
Automobile	15	1	4.74
Automobile	15	4	1.19
Van	20	15	0.42
Diesel bus	56	40	0.52
Subway	2.6 kWh/km	75 (per car)	0.13
GO Rail	761	810	0.35

From Environment Canada

Traffic problems

Cars have helped to shape our lifestyles and the layout of our cities. The car has become the symbol of freedom, enabling us to travel almost anywhere without having to rely on bus schedules or infrequent trains. Most drivers feel a great sense of freedom and power when sitting behind the wheel. Driving appeals to our egos, and to many people cars are an important status symbol.

The car plays a very important role in the modern world, especially in Canada and the United States. It has caused more changes in the way we live than any other innovation in the twentieth century. Take, for instance, the effects that cars have had on our modern cities. If we had to rely on public transport today, the suburbs would be confined to narrow strips along transit routes. Before the automobile, this was in fact how our cities originated.

By the middle of the twentieth century, car ownership was widespread. The suburbs quickly spread outwards filling in the gaps between public transit routes. For most of the past half century, little legislation was passed to stop the outward spread of cities. The result is that our cities have eaten up large areas of some of the best agricultural land. Anything from 25 to 50 percent of the urban landscape in North America is devoted to the car.

If the density of housing is low, as in many US cities, most journeys are made by car. In low density suburbs the energy costs of commuting by car are high, as Figure 13.2 shows. In Europe, the population density is much higher, leading to greater use of public transport. Toronto has been one of the more successful Canadian cities in encouraging the use of public transit, resulting in the less rapid spread of low density suburbs.

The price we pay for using our cars

On a world scale, car ownership continues to rise dramatically, as Figure 13.3 shows. But we pay a high price for the convenience of owning and driving cars.

The 465 million cars (1993) in the world use almost half of our fossil fuels, creating more pollution than any other single activity. Close to 1 billion tonnes of carbon enter the global atmosphere from car exhausts every year. Cars also contribute to the problem of toxic urban runoff. According to the Southam Environment Project, about 300 million litres of engine oil are discarded into the Canadian environment each year. This is eight times more oil than was spilled by the *Exxon Valdez*. Oil may seep into groundwater and contaminate drinking water.

Figure 13.3 Automobiles in use worldwide

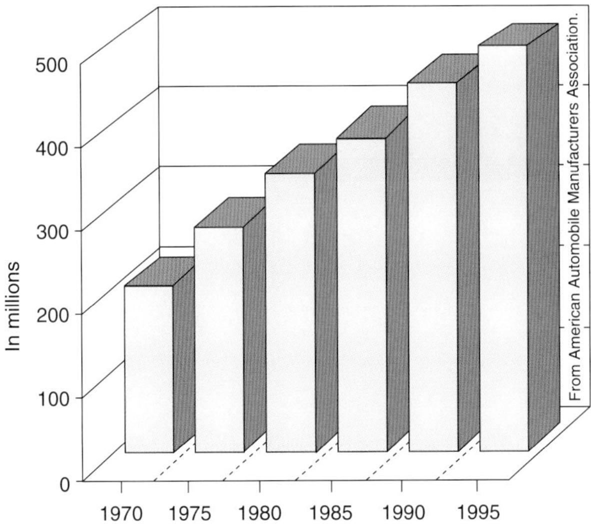

Cars are the main source of photochemical smog. When smog levels are high the health of millions of people, especially children and the elderly is at risk. Childhood asthma has risen significantly in cities where ozone smog is high. The cost of traffic jams, measured by wasted gasoline, lost work time, and stress on drivers may run into billions of dollars in Canada alone. At least 250 000 people die in road accidents worldwide yearly—more than all other accidental deaths combined.

Government legislation since the 1970s has led to lower emissions from cars of gases such as nitrogen oxides and carbon monoxide. Figure 13.4 shows that the reduction per vehicle in Canada is greater than the total reduction in emissions because of the larger number of cars on the roads. Atmospheric lead has also been sharply reduced since many countries, including Canada, have phased out leaded gasoline. Yet the reduction in the use of lead has caused an increase in the use of other toxins. Fumes emitted in refineries and at service stations also create a health hazard. The incidence of leukemia near refineries and among refinery workers is significantly higher than normal.

Controlling the use of cars

The long-term future of the car may be in doubt. Darrell Richards of Transport 2000 Canada predicts that "lone individuals driving into major urban centres will just not be tolerated." He thinks a change in attitude will some day make driving in the city, other than in specially designed cars, socially unacceptable.

There are three ways of encouraging people to be less dependent on their cars. The first method is to

Figure 13.4 Total annual and per vehicle emissions of No_x, VOCs (volatile organic compounds), and CO from personal-use passenger cars, 1980–1988

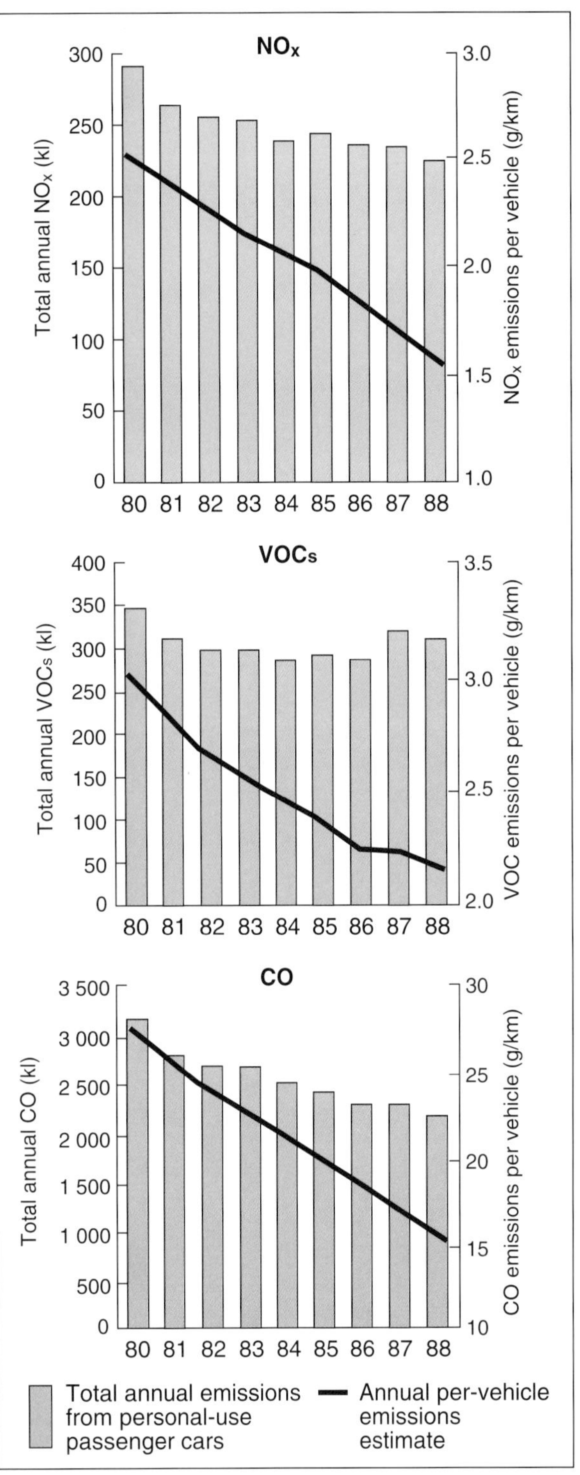

From: Statistics Canada (1991); unpublished data, Environment Canada, Industrial Programs Branch, Transportation Systems Division.

price cars and gasoline much higher. Ontario has put a $5 tax on tires, although the money raised goes into general revenue rather than into a fund for the environment. Unfortunately, high taxation on gasoline has the effect of penalizing people with low incomes. However, a differential tax on cars could be useful, with a higher rate of tax on cars with poor gas consumption or high emission levels.

A second method is to ensure that public transit is efficient and cheap. Buses and rapid transit systems create only about one-eighth of the pollution caused by cars measured on a per capita basis. Some cities heavily subsidize public transit systems. In so doing, they save on road repairs and expansions and help to reduce air pollution. Car pooling also increases the occupancy rate of cars, reducing the per capita amount of pollution. Some cities, such as Seattle, Washington, provide lanes for use only by buses or by cars with more than one occupant.

The third method of controlling cars is through regulations. When traffic reaches a saturation point and air pollution severely threatens our health, the use of cars is likely to be restricted. We may then expect to find cars excluded from our city centres. This has happened already in some cities. Either cars have been excluded outright, or the cost of visiting the city centre has been made so expensive that people choose public transport instead. Singapore, for example, imposes a heavy tax on cars entering the city centre. Parking in the city centre can also be made very expensive. In Geneva, Switzerland, parking is prohibited altogether at places of work in the centre of the city, forcing people to use public transport.

New car technology may help to resolve some of the problems caused by cars. Electric cars are quieter and are adequate for city use, which is where most of our journeys are made. At the present time battery technology limits the use of electric cars for longer journeys. These cars would help to reduce emissions, but only if their batteries are charged overnight, when electric power is relatively unused and cheap.

It is becoming increasingly common in urban centres to create pedestrian-only areas where once cars ruled the roads. In Strasbourg, France, large parts of the city centre have been reserved for people rather than automobiles.

Problems of urban living

There are many problems with living in cities apart from pollution and traffic. Studies show that mental and physical health in cities is related to the residential environment, in particular to the **density of population**. In some areas of Montréal, Toronto, and Vancouver population density may exceed 20 000 per km^2. A high density of population per square kilometre, especially in developing countries, appears to be related to the incidence of diseases, such as tuberculosis and gastro-intestinal disorders. There is also a correlation between population density and social disorders, such as juvenile delinquency.

Overcrowding

Population density can also be measured by the number of people per room. If a house has more than 1.5 occupants per room (excluding kitchens and bathrooms), it may be said to be overcrowded. In overcrowded areas there is a greater threat of disease, since ventilation may be poor and concentrations of bacteria are higher. Studies have shown that infectious diseases and accidents are about one-third higher in low-quality housing.

Overcrowding in developing countries

In developing countries, cities are growing at an alarming rate. Much of the growth is due to migration from rural to urban areas. People are leaving rural poverty in search of a better life in the cities. Such migrants know that the cities often have better (though still inadequate) health and education facilities. They also feel that there is a better chance of finding a job. So they arrive in large numbers every day. Mexico City receives 1000 migrants daily from rural Mexico, and the situation is similar in cities such as Cairo, Egypt, and Jakarta, Indonesia. Many of the migrants set up homes in makeshift squatter settlements or shantytowns.

Lack of freshwater and sewage facilities make the shantytowns breeding grounds for many kinds of disease. Elephantiasis, marked by acutely swollen legs, is caused by a type of mosquito that breeds in sewage and other polluted water. Typhoid and cholera are other diseases that are common when freshwater and sanitation facilities are lacking. Many countries are now making the effort to provide basic sanitation and health amenities in urban slums.

Urban stress

In cities of the developed world, the above health problems are now relatively rare, although in the past tuberculosis was a common urban disease. The health problems that stem from overcrowding are more to do with mental health. Psychologists tell us that each of us lives in a kind of invisible bubble, which is our own personal space. Living in overcrowded conditions leads to the loss of our sense of privacy. Prolonged exposure to the problems of overcrowding can damage both mental and physical health.

Stress is something we all have to live with. In small amounts it is probably good for us. However, living in cities increases the amount of stress for many people. This is partly because of overcrowding. Traffic jams, which have led to the modern term **gridlock**, clearly increase stress. So does the pressure of modern business. A farmer may have weeks to plan his farming operations, but a foreign currency trader has to react to minute-by-minute changes in financial affairs. Air traffic controllers also work under continual pressure. Stress has been associated with ulcers, high blood pressure, colitis, and asthma, all of which are more common in urban than in rural areas.

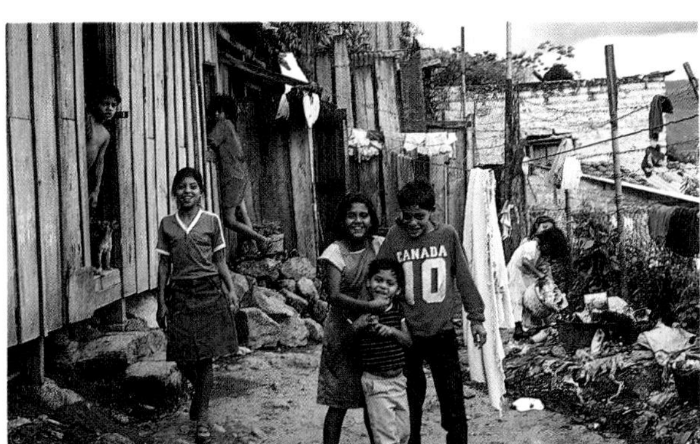

In urban areas in developing countries, many people live in overcrowded shantytowns.

Currency traders are among the many workers who experience high levels of pressure in their jobs.

High-rise living

One type of urban stress may be related to living in high-rise apartments. Many cities built high-rise apartments in the 1950s and 1960s. If you live in a high-rise apartment you may have adjusted to it. But if you only visit one occasionally you may be struck by how impersonal it is. Often you announce your arrival through an intercom before being summoned to enter by a buzzer. An elevator, small and confining by nature, then carries you to your floor. The hallways and doors are usually identical, and the spaces people live in seem like boxes.

Some people feel insecure in high-rise buildings because of the height and others may not trust the elevators, which they find claustrophobic. To many people, apartments can be less appealing than houses.

High-rise living in cities such as Winnipeg is a way of life for many people.

The possible hazards of electromagnetism

Scientific evidence today increasingly shows that the electromagnetic fields emitted from power cables and wires may damage the nervous system or even cause cancer. These sources of electromagnetism are present in all our homes, but higher levels are emitted from power lines. Experiments indicate that cells are affected by low-level electromagnetic fields.

We do not know if the adverse effects of electromagnetic fields are real. However, scientists at Carnegie-Mellon University suggest that hydro companies take steps to route power lines farther from residential areas. Within the home they recommend that electric blankets be used only to preheat the bed and that electric alarm clocks be kept as far away from the bed as possible.

Noise pollution

Transportation is the leading cause of noise pollution in cities. Noise is measured in decibels. Figure 13.5

Reprinted by permission of Alberta Environment.

shows familiar noises on the decibel (dB) scale. Heavy city traffic registers about 90 dB. Several other urban sounds are even higher on the scale. Your hearing may be damaged if noise stays above about 85 dB for any length of time. Needless to say, our stereos blast out music well above the danger level. Exposure to excessive noise can also interfere with speech patterns and the efficiency of your daily performance.

Noise is also an environmental hazard near airports, especially near the ends of frequently used runways. Most airports are paying close attention to the problem. Vancouver International Airport, for example, maintains a monitoring system with eight noise recorders attached to a central computer. The information is used both to enforce existing noise abatement laws and to help plan the future growth of the airport.

Figure 13.5 The noise pollution scale (in decibels)

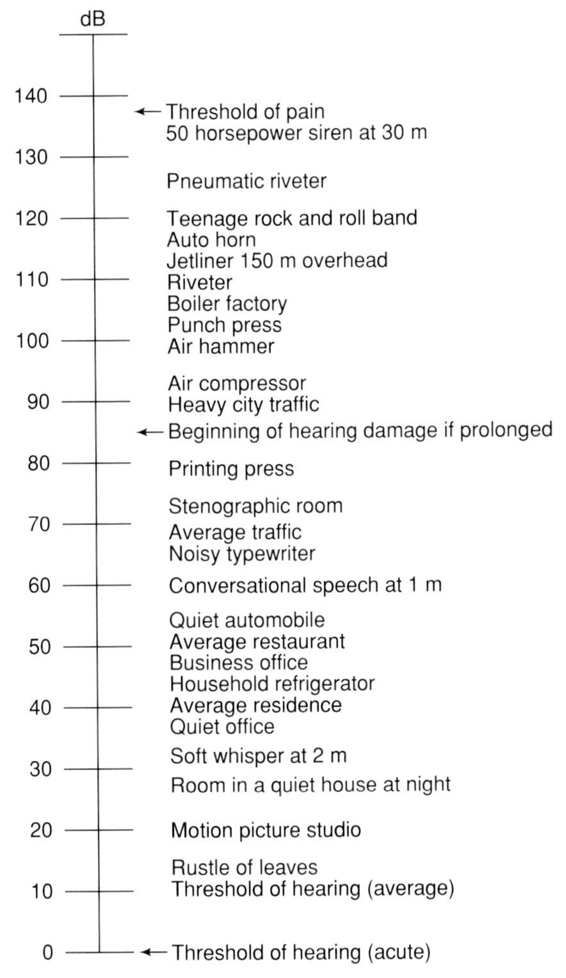

Improving the urban environment

Since the early 1980s a new emphasis has been placed on environmental health. In Canada the origin of this concern was a report entitled *A New Perspective on the Health of Canadians*. The importance of environmental health was emphasized by the World Health Organization in *The Healthy City*. Publications like these claim that medical science alone cannot solve all of our health problems. The physical, social, and economic aspects of the environment in which people live have a great deal to do with the quality of life, including our health. This is particularly true for people who live in cities.

What is a good urban environment?

According to Kevin Lynch, a noted authority on city life, a good urban environment consists of "sustenance, safety, design, and ecological stability." These features mean that a city should have an adequate supply of food, energy, clean water, and fresh air. Hazards from poisons and diseases should be absent or effectively controlled. As well, the environment of the city should be designed so that it is in harmony with its citizens. For example, a city should be neither jarring to the senses nor repetitive. Its layout should promote physical exercise and reduce the harmful effects of noise and indoor air pollution. Finally, an ecologically stable city should enhance the genetic diversity of species that are useful to people. The environment should also provide for the stability of the whole ecological community.

Making the city a healthier place is not just a matter of curing or preventing diseases. According to the World Health Organization, many groups can contribute to a healthier urban environment. Architects, planners, environmentalists, social workers, and voluntary groups can all help to create a good urban environment. For example, tree-planting initiatives have been undertaken by companies such as McDonald's and by Earth Day volunteers. Community and voluntary organizations have an important role in pressing for and maintaining improvements in our cities.

Improving the appearance of a city can be as simple as increasing the amount of greenery. Planting trees and shrubs immediately improves the appearance of most cities. Greenery also has a dramatic effect on the quality of city air. (See Figure 13.6.) Plants cleanse the air by collecting dust. A mature tree can trap 50 to 100 kg of dust on its leaves, which will be removed by the next heavy rainshower. Trees can also remove some toxic gases from the air.

Figure 13.6 How trees reduce air pollution

Plants clean the air by collecting airborne particles, which are periodically removed by heavy rainfall. Streets with trees have considerably less dust pollution than streets without trees.

STREET WITH TREES

1000 to 3000 dust particles per litre of air

STREET WITHOUT TREES

10 000 to 12 000 dust particles per litre of air

Livable streets

Most of our streets are entirely devoted to the car. This can have serious effects on the social life of people who live there, as well as on the number of traffic accidents. A study done in San Francisco showed the differences between streets with light compared with heavy traffic volumes.

The questionnaires dealt with the effects of traffic on the quality of life of people living on the street. Questions were asked about stress from noise pollution, the danger of accidents, the amount of social interaction, and the general environmental quality of the streets. Finally, respondents were asked to write down how they felt about their streets. Figure 13.7 illustrates some of the responses.

By redesigning some of our streets as "people places" our cities can be greatly improved. Instead of being dangerous places, where you breathe in exhaust fumes or risk getting hit by a car, streets can become centres of social activity and places to relax.

Figure 13.7 Effects of light and heavy traffic on the quality of life and the environment

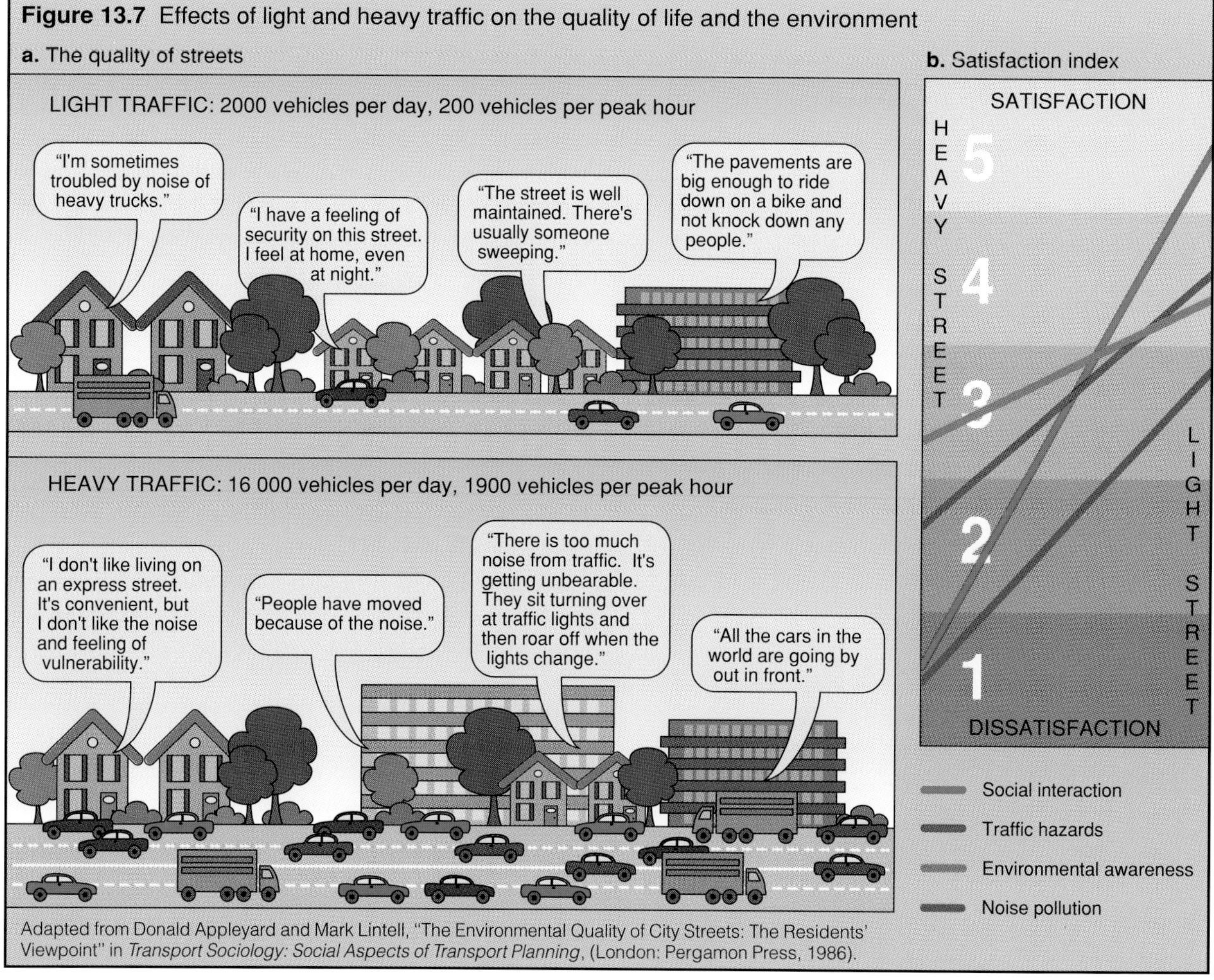

a. The quality of streets
LIGHT TRAFFIC: 2000 vehicles per day, 200 vehicles per peak hour
"I'm sometimes troubled by noise of heavy trucks."
"I have a feeling of security on this street. I feel at home, even at night."
"The street is well maintained. There's usually someone sweeping."
"The pavements are big enough to ride down on a bike and not knock down any people."
HEAVY TRAFFIC: 16 000 vehicles per day, 1900 vehicles per peak hour
"I don't like living on an express street. It's convenient, but I don't like the noise and feeling of vulnerability."
"People have moved because of the noise."
"There is too much noise from traffic. It's getting unbearable. They sit turning over at traffic lights and then roar off when the lights change."
"All the cars in the world are going by out in front."
b. Satisfaction index
SATISFACTION
HEAVY STREET
LIGHT STREET
5
4
3
2
1
DISSATISFACTION
Social interaction
Traffic hazards
Environmental awareness
Noise pollution

Adapted from Donald Appleyard and Mark Lintell, "The Environmental Quality of City Streets: The Residents' Viewpoint" in *Transport Sociology: Social Aspects of Transport Planning*, (London: Pergamon Press, 1986).

Healthy cities projects

Several Canadian cities have responded to the World Health Organization's healthy cities project, among them Toronto and Edmonton.

Toronto 2000

Toronto is a good example of a healthy city by world standards. But it has only attained this standard by some dramatic improvements in health over the past century. For example, the average age at death was only twenty-six in 1881. By 1993 it had risen to seventy, seventy-six for women and sixty-five for men. The change was largely due to a drop in the **infant mortality rate** from 193 infant deaths per 1000 live births in 1908 to 6.3 per 1000 in 1993. Similar improvements have taken place in most cities of the Western world. The main reasons are due to improvements in water supply, sewage disposal, nutrition, education, housing, and immunization against infectious diseases.

The overall result was a substantial movement away from infectious diseases toward noninfectious diseases, such as heart disease and cancer. (See Figure

Figure 13.8 Positive and negative behaviours relating to health in Ontario (% of total population)

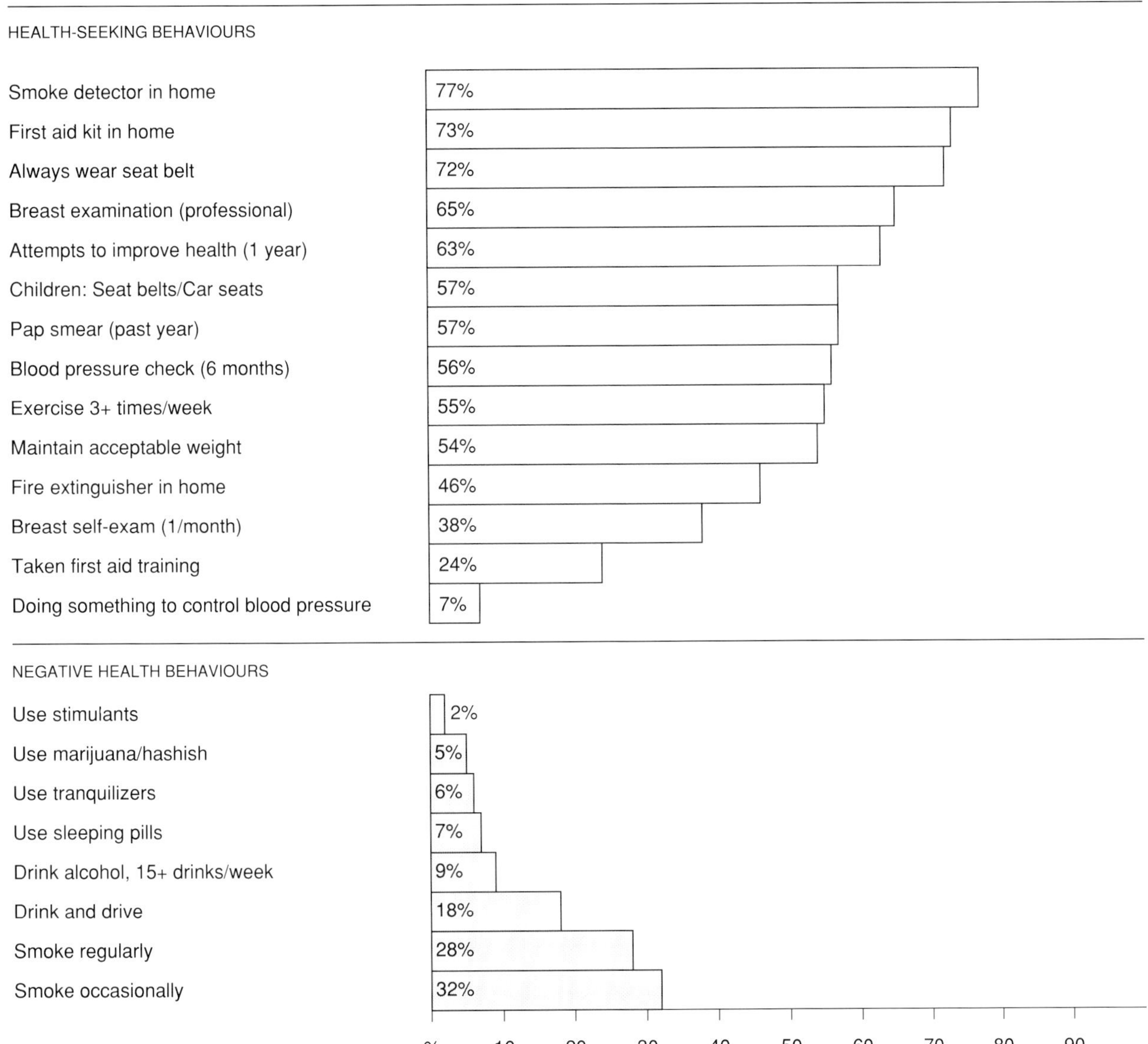

From Health and Welfare Canada, 1985. Reproduced with permission of the Minister of Supply and Services Canada.

11.1.) Toronto's total death rate has continued to fall.

In spite of its falling death rates, environmental health in Toronto could be improved. In 1988 the Board of Health published a report entitled *Healthy Toronto 2000*. The "roadblocks to better health" listed in the report include homelessness, pollution, poor nutrition, unemployment, and safety and security.

The number of homeless in Toronto rose from 3500 in 1982 to possibly 30 000 in 1993. High real estate prices have forced many people out of owned or rented housing. Homelessness is related to poor health. The homeless are also more likely to suffer from problems such as violence or substance abuse.

The report listed air pollution, waste disposal, and the pollutants in Lake Ontario as the main environmental problems in Toronto. In the summer of 1988 the city had twenty-six days of "moderate to poor air quality" though it has improved since. Overflows from storm sewers pollute the Don and Humber rivers. Levels of PCBs, DDT, and mirex in Lake Ontario are decreasing, but are still high enough for the report to advise against eating certain types of fish, especially women of childbearing age and children.

A good diet, according to the report, is a prerequisite for health. Yet one in twenty citizens required the help of food banks. Inadequate or unbalanced diets are increasing the incidence of cancer, diabetes, and weight problems.

Since work is not merely a source of income but a vital part of our well being, the report deplores the high level of unemployment, especially for young people. Unemployment leads to both loss of income and self-esteem.

Violence has risen in cities everywhere. Toronto is no exception, although its rates are below those of Montréal and Vancouver. Assaults more than doubled in the 1980s. Violence is often related to drugs or the excessive use of alcohol.

The *Healthy Toronto 2000* report was issued with a discussion-response paper to many people in the community. The responses were revealing. The leading concern of people by a large margin was the physical environment. Safety, peace, and nonviolence came second. Safety was a word that came up frequently in the responses. Affordable housing came third, followed by the need for green space in the city. Overall, the report was widely accepted as an agenda for the concluding years of the twentieth century. Many urban improvements are costly, however. Taxpayers face important choices if the necessary improvements are to be made to our cities.

Edmonton's KidsPlace project

Like Toronto and several other Canadian cities, Edmonton adopted a healthy cities project in 1987. One element of the project was setting up a food council, which deals with all aspects of the food supply system, including food banks.

More attention, however, has been focused on other aspects of the project. The city set up a **KidsPlace project** similar to one tried a few years earlier in Seattle, Washington.

Students were asked to make a map of their neighbourhoods as they saw them. They were given a list of positive and negative adjectives to describe places in each neighbourhood. From responses, such as "too many stray dogs" and "older kids chasing younger ones out of parks," a set of issues was prepared.

Students in a low-income area were surveyed and asked what they would like to have changed in their local community. Interviewers went on walkabouts with kids and visited their homes to get first-hand experience of their needs. The information from young people was integrated with information from police and other social service departments to form the basis of community action.

Many practical steps have been taken in the city. Neighbourhood watches have been set up. Crosswalks and street lighting have been improved. New safe meeting places after school have been opened.

The KidsPlace method has been a successful way to encourage public participation in the planning of large cities.

Figure 13.9 Satisfaction ranking of Canadian Cities in a North American survey

CITY	SATISFACTION WITH CITY (RANK)	CITY	SATISFACTION WITH CITY (RANK)
Toronto	4	Victoria	112
Vancouver	11	Winnipeg	127
Québec City	30	Windsor	128
Montréal	48	Saskatoon	129
Halifax	57	St. Catharines	132
Hamilton	57	Regina	190
Ottawa Hull	63	Oshawa	209
St. John's	63	Trois-Rivières	224
London	70	Saint John	256
Calgary	83	Thunder Bay	272
Kitchener	91	Sudbury	303

Adapted from *Places Rated Almanac*.

Vancouver, British Columbia, is considered a beautiful city and ranks high on lists of livable cities.

Rating our cities as places to live

Guidebooks, such as *Places Rated Almanac*, rank our cities as places to live. This book ranks 333 North American cities according to several criteria. These include climate, facilities (health care, education, recreation, transportation, and the arts), and indicators (crime, cost of living, housing, and jobs). Generally, smaller centres rank higher on the *indicators*, because these places have a lower crime rate and cost of living. Larger cities, with their variety of educational, recreational, and entertainment opportunities, usually rank highest in the *facilities* categories.

In the 1993 *Places Rated Almanac*, Toronto was the highest ranked Canadian city, ranking fourth in North America. It received high scores for the arts, jobs, and education. Vancouver was the second-highest rated Canadian city, placing eleventh overall in North America. It had high ratings for climate, jobs, and recreation. Québec City ranked thirtieth in North America, and received the third-highest score among Canadian cities. It was highly rated for recreation and health care. Altogether, eleven Canadian centres ranked in the top 100 cities in North America.

Looking back

1. Explain why a city is a highly artificial ecosystem.
2. (a) How would you rate the quality of the air in your region?
   (b) What are the causes of any air quality problems that occur?
   (c) What solutions or controls are in practice in the region?
3. (a) Study Figure 13.2 and explain why the use of public transport is more energy efficient and less damaging to the environment than travel by private car.
   (b) What pollution problems would the continued increase in car ownership, as shown in Figure 13.3, create throughout the world?
4. List the environmental problems that can arise in overcrowded urban areas. Examine the photograph on page 205 to find clues for your answer.
5. (a) List the aspects of the KidsPlace project that you like.
   (b) Identify any problems you think the implementation of the project might pose.

Applying your knowledge

1. Brainstorm a list of suggestions on how public transit can be improved in your area. Share your list with a classmate and then the class. Determine the three most important suggestions from the class list and write a letter to the local transit authority asking for comment on them.
2. With a partner, analyse Figure 13.4 and write an explanation of the changing causes of lead emissions in the atmosphere.
3. Prepare an organizer of the environmental problems of your town or city using the following headings: The Physical Environment; Waste Disposal; Traffic; and The General Quality of Life. Make suggestions as to how these problems may be solved.
4. Write a short essay outlining why "healthy city" projects are relevant for Canada and not just for cities in the developing world.
5. You are considering moving to one of the cities listed in Figure 13.9. Select five possibilities from the list and find out more about each of these places. Use a decision-making organizer to decide in which city you would prefer to live. Explain the reasons for your choice.

Extending your thinking

1. Prepare an organizer to show the differences between a natural and a built (urban) environment.
2. Prepare a report on the system in place in your community to dispose of surplus water such as storm runoff. Use a large-scale map, air photographs, and information gathered from visiting water works sites in your area. In your report, indicate whether or not the system is adequate; if it is not, find out how it could be improved. Also discuss whether the system contributes to or solves environmental problems.
3. In small groups discuss the causes of urban stress. Prepare a list of your findings and make suggestions as to how these types of stress can be managed.
4. Draw up a questionnaire using the questions listed here to find out how the volume of traffic affects the quality of life in your town or city. Select a "light traffic" street and a "heavy traffic" street. At each checkpoint, observe the number of vehicles that pass by during specific five-minute periods. Then ask at least twenty people in each street to respond to your questionnaire. The first four questions should be answered by a number from 5 (best) to 1 (worst). In question 5 respondents are asked to express how they feel about their street. (If you wish, you may add your own questions to the questionnaire.)

Questionnaire on traffic in residential streets

Give a score of 1 (lowest rating) to 5 (highest rating) to your street for each question. For example, if you are only a little troubled by traffic noise, answer 4 or 5. If you are very troubled, answer 1 or 2.

Name of street:

1. Are you ever troubled by traffic noise and/or vibration?
2. Do you feel threatened by traffic on this street?
3. Is it easy to visit friends who live on this street?
4. Is this street environmentally attractive?
5. How would you describe living on this street?

Average the results of your questionnaires for each street and create a graph of the responses similar to that shown in Figure 13.7(b). Use the responses to question 1 for "noise pollution," to question 2 for "traffic hazards," to question 3 for "social interaction," and to question 4 for "environment."

5. Rank your town or neighbourhood according to the environmental index listed below. For each of the ten indicators, rate your community on a scale of 1 (the lowest evaluation) to 10 (the highest evaluation). To assess your community properly, you will need to research some of the data.
   (a) air, water, and land pollution;
   (b) the amount of green space;
   (c) the variety of flora and fauna;
   (d) the degree of traffic congestion;
   (e) the provision of social services;
   (f) cultural facilities;
   (g) personal security and the crime rate;
   (h) recreational facilities;
   (i) the economy;
   (j) the provision of medical services.

   When you have assigned a score for your community for each category, add up your total. You will now have an environmental index rating out of 100 for your community.

14 THE ENVIRONMENT AND YOU

We have examined the causes of many of today's environmental problems. All of us are clearly part of the problem. Now we must consider how we can become part of the solution.

In this final chapter, we will summarize, how to eliminate or reduce our polluting habits and how we can encourage other people to do the same. Our contributions can lead to a cleaner and healthier planet.

Bathrooms are one of the most environmentally wasteful rooms in the house.

Our homes

We like to think of our homes as safe and clean. Yet they are centres of pollution, second only to factories and power stations. In our homes we use and discard the products of industry. The more we use, the more the world's forests, waters, and minerals are exploited.

An environmental tour of the home

Every part of our home has an impact on the environment. For example, bathroom tissue contains dioxins that are produced in the bleaching process. A shower uses up to 15 L of water per minute, while leaving the tap running when you brush your teeth can use 8 L. With care, you can brush equally well using only 1 L. A dripping faucet can waste water at a rate of over 10 000 L per year. But the main problem in the bathroom is the toilet. In an average year each of us generates about 30 000 L of sewage from the toilet alone. Only 2 percent of this is waste; the rest is treated water that comes from the same source as our drinking water. This sewage may or may not be treated before disposal into rivers, lakes, or oceans.

The kitchen is another source of environmental pollution. Detergents and household cleansers run through the drainage system and end up in the sewage stream. CFCs, which have been used in the cooling systems of refrigerators, may leak into the air and rise upward to the ozone layer when these appliances are discarded. Cupboards made from particle board emit fumes and vapours from the glue that binds the wood particles together. Traces of dioxins can be found in kitchen paper towels and in coffee filters.

The amount of paper products we use in our kitchens adds to our environmental problems.

Keeping the thermostat set low can save energy in the home.

Figure 14.1 Costs and savings of selected appliances

	ADDITIONAL COSTS ($CDN)	SAVING ($CDN/YEAR)
Energy-efficient refrigerator	200	30
Energy-efficient light bulbs (each)	25	6
Double-glazed windows	25% more	105
Washing clothes in cool water	—	30
Water-saving shower head	8	30
Energy-efficient water heater	35	24
Other energy-efficient appliances	various	24
Turning down nighttime heat 5°C		30

From *West Magazine*. Reprinted with permission of *The Globe and Mail*, Toronto.

Kitchen appliances also consume large amounts of energy. Most of these appliances now come with an energy rating or "Energuide." A carefully set thermostat can also save a great deal of energy in a home. Your local hydro office can advise you on how to reduce your consumption of electricity.

Living rooms and bedrooms usually contain furniture with foam padding. The millions of tiny air bubbles in the foam may contain CFCs, which slowly leak out, especially when the articles are exposed to the weather at dump sites.

Throughout the house the air contains traces of vapours from paints, carpets, cleaning agents, solvents, and moth repellents. We have already noted the dangers of indoor cigarette smoke. The better a house is sealed or draftproofed, the more these vapours are retained within the house and inhaled by the people who live there. This is the one disadvantage of having a well-insulated home.

Finally, the house releases valuable energy into the atmosphere through windows, walls, and the roof. In most cases this energy involves the burning of fossil fuels, which is a major cause of air pollution. Any ways in which we can save energy will have a positive effect on the atmosphere.

How you can save money — and the environment

Figure 14.1 shows how to improve your home in ways that benefit the environment. A fully energy-efficient home, often referred to as an **R-2000 home**, is virtually airtight, with double- or triple-glazed windows and air-vapour barriers in the walls. Windows are concentrated on the south side to take advantage of passive solar heating. R-2000 homes have efficient heating systems that recover heat from outgoing air to help heat incoming fresh air. Such homes normally cost 5 to 10 percent more than ordinary homes, but the savings in energy costs eventually exceed the higher purchase price. The costs to the environment are also significantly reduced by energy efficient homes.

Practical advice for the home

Several environmental organizations prepared the following list of ways in which people can reduce the threats to the environment created in their own homes.

Take your chemicals to a toxic waste depot Up till now we have been pouring an average of 40 L of toxic waste down our sinks every year. Paint thinners and brush cleaners should not be disposed of in this way. Call your municipal office to find out the correct way to dispose of them.

Use refillable bottles Where possible we should buy beverages in returnable bottles. Reuse is better than recycling. Where returnable bottles are not available, make sure that the bottles or cans are recycled. Try to avoid using plastic bottles.

Plastic bottles do not degrade easily.

Use low watt electric bulbs Bulbs are now available that use only about 8 watts of electricity to provide the same light as from a normal 60 watt bulb. They cost about $25, including an adapter, but since they last 10 000 hours and use much less electricity they pay for themselves in time.

Use cloth rather than disposable diapers This will save money since disposable diapers are an expensive item in the budgets of families with young children. Most disposable diapers use chlorine bleached pulp fluff that creates dioxins and furans in its manufacture. Some diapers are now made using hydrogen peroxide, thus avoiding the dioxin problem. If used, the contents of disposable diapers should be flushed down the toilet as much as is possible to reduce the bacterial content in landfills.

Use re-refined oil Every year, Canadian motorists produce 425 000 000 L of used engine oil. Most of this is disposed of in an unsatisfactory way. This oil can be re-refined to produce a good quality oil, thus saving our valuable supply of crude oil and reducing a serious waste disposal problem.

If you can't reuse, recycle Buy products that come in containers that can be recycled. Be especially careful to recycle paper, which takes up the most space in landfill sites. Old fridges, stoves, and televisions may be recycled or given to charitable causes if they still work.

Avoid excessive packaging Much unnecessary packaging is used by our manufacturers. Try to buy goods that come in a sensible, but not excessive, amount of packaging. Make your views on excess packaging known to the stores where you shop. Take old shopping bags with you to reuse them when you shop.

Cut down on water consumption Every litre of the 285 L we use at home every day has been purified and treated. For most people water conservation is easy. Avoid brushing your teeth with the tap running continuously, and don't peel vegetables under running water. Both toilets and showerheads can be modified to use less water. With a 4 L space filler in toilet tanks a family can save tens of thousands of litres of water a year. Our water bills would go down as a result, and we would need to build fewer dams and reservoirs.

Get your lawn off drugs The spraying of chemicals on lawns can be dangerous, especially to children with bare feet. The person spraying also is likely to inhale some chemical vapours. The main selective weedkiller used on lawns is 2,4-D, which has been found to be a

Poisons abound in the garden.

health hazard among Prairie farmers. Organic composts will help to feed your lawn. Weeds can be reduced by regular mowing or removed by hand.

On-line information The Internet can give you excellent up-to-date information on the environment. Try searching using names such as Environment Canada, the Worldwatch Institute, or the United Nations Environmental Program (UNEP); or for topics like "global warming" and "endangered species."

Our schools

You spend a great deal of your lives at school, where you consume a lot of paper. You can reduce the demand for trees simply by saving and recycling this paper. You can also become more environmentally responsible in other ways. You can encourage your school not to use disposable cups and to start a recycling program for glass or aluminum beverage cans. Homes in the school neighbourhood could also be involved in these recycling campaigns. Your school could also develop compost kits and sell them to local residents, together with instructions explaining to people how they should be used. An excellent piece of publicity for your school is a "clean up" of a local beach, stream, or public area.

Within your school, you could organize competitions, such as a prize for the best environment song—or even for the most often used lunch paper bag! With the help of your teacher, you could arrange for visits by Environment Canada or provincial environment department experts. You can plan events and activities for Canadian Environment Week, which usually takes place in the first week of June.

Resources of all kinds are available to you. Some provinces supply conservation or environment kits. All will supply sources of information on environmental topics. Many books and magazines are also available. Consult your school or local library for these.

Outdoor education in environmental studies is now growing in Canada. For example, the Scarborough Board of Education in Toronto runs environmental courses at its centre in the Almaguin Highlands northeast of Parry Sound, Ontario. The courses offered earn high school credits and provide an effective, practical experience of the environment for urban students.

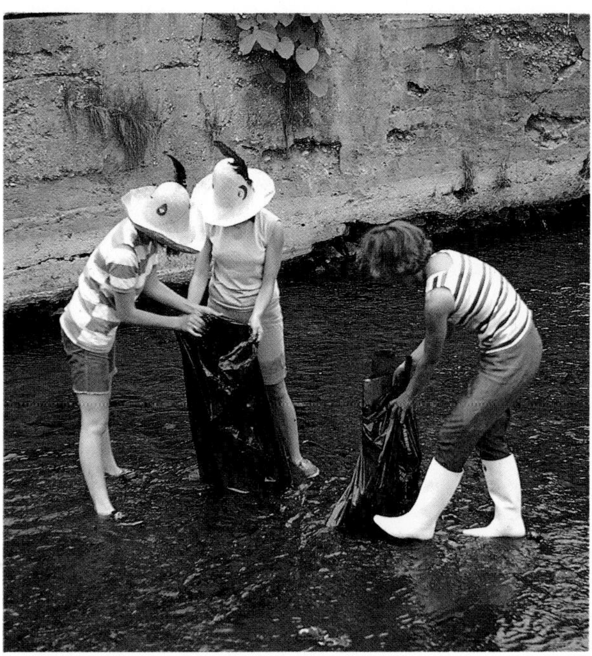

Students in Peterborough, Ontario, pitch in to clean up the environment.

Environment fairs can help us to learn more about the environment.

Environment fairs

Many schools already hold science fairs, in which projects and experiments are prepared in large displays for the benefit of fellow students and parents. Some Canadian schools have begun holding environment fairs.

These fairs can include a variety of projects suitable for different grade levels. Younger students can examine different species of organisms. You can draw or photograph them and locate them on a map. Using library resources, you can write stories and anecdotes about most plants and animals. In this way you can learn a great deal.

Relationships between organisms and their immediate environment can also be examined. Why is moss found on one side of a roof and not on the other? The amount of sunlight, temperature, moisture, and soil conditions all have a bearing on the distribution of plants and other organisms.

For senior students, a good approach is to show through experiments or examples how human actions modify or upset the relationship between plants and their environments. This could be done using local examples. Projects could also be prepared on global environmental issues.

Action 21

Action 21 is an Environment Canada program that encourages Canadians to take action in their communities in support of healthy environments. It has two components: a public awareness initiative, and a community funding program to support non-profit groups to carry out environmental projects.

The kinds of programs include:

- air issues: reducing air pollution from vehicles and reducing emissions from other sources;
- toxic substances: reducing use of pesticides and promoting safe disposal of hazardous wastes;
- ecosystems: conserving or rehabilitating natural areas such as wetlands, lakes or coastal areas;
- biodiversity: protecting wild animals and preventing their loss of habitat.

The Applicant's Guide "Action 21" is available from Environment Canada or one of its regional offices. Applicants should call to discuss their proposals. Then a registration form has to be filled in and the proposal submitted. The proposal has six parts:

A Need for the Project
B Project Objectives
C Project Work Plan
D Detailed Project Budget
E Evaluation Plan
F Appendices (including partners and letters of support)

Action 21 is available through Environment Canada's "Green Line" on the Internet at http://www.doe.ca

The "green" consumer

As consumers, we have enormous power in our society. Canadians spent $213 billion (CDN) on retail purchases in 1995 — an average of $7350 per person. Market researchers spend tens of millions of dollars trying to find out what consumers want to buy. In this way, manufacturers learn what to produce from how we spend our money. Thus consumers who are aware of environmental issues can greatly influence manufacturing. We can also tell local supermarkets what we do *not* want to buy and why. Alternatively, we can write to manufacturers about their products.

It is everyone's responsibility to make sound environmental choices when shopping.

According to *The Canadian Green Consumer Guide*, there are six key issues for the environmentally conscious consumer. The "green" consumer should avoid products likely to:

- endanger the health of the consumer or others;
- cause significant damage to the environment during manufacture, use, or disposal;
- cause unnecessary waste, either because of over-packaging or because of an unduly short useful life;
- use materials derived from threatened species or from threatened environments;
- involve the unnecessary use of — or cruelty to — animals, whether for toxicity testing or for other purposes;
- adversely affect other countries, particularly in the Third World.

From the Pollution Probe Foundation, *The Canadian Green Consumer Guide*. Used by permission of the Canadian Publishers, McClelland & Stewart, Toronto.

"Green" products

Retail companies have responded to consumer pressure by labelling goods that are "environmentally friendly." However, as consumers, we must read carefully to make sure that claims are not merely ploys to sell the products. To help consumers reduce the burden on the environment, products and services may be certified with the EcoLogo* symbol now owned by Terra Choice Environmental Services. A product may be certified with the EcoLogo* because it is reusable or made in a way that improves energy efficiency, reduces hazardous by-products, uses recycled materials, or in some other way is environmentally sensitive. For example, we will be able to identify phosphate-free detergents or cleaning agents based on baking soda rather than on powerful chemicals.

It is also possible to make many of our own cleaning agents. Simple instructions are available for using nonhazardous materials such as baking soda, vinegar, and lemon juice.

A key to green shopping is avoiding excess packaging and buying articles in reusable containers wherever possible. For example, eggs should be bought in paper cartons, not in polystyrene foam containers. Consumers can also complain about products that have an excessive amount of packaging. Or we can simply not buy them. Eventually the manufacturers will get the message.

Environment Canada's EcoLogo is reserved for products that meet high environmental standards.

Further suggestions for improving the environment

A handbook entitled *What Atlantic Canadians Can Do for Their Environment* was produced by Environment Canada and the environment ministries of the Atlantic provinces. It contains hundreds of suggestions that are appropriate for all Canadians. Below is an abbreviated list of the most useful ideas.

Acid rain and air pollution

Use unleaded gasoline in all cars built since 1973. Avoid idling your engine for long periods, and keep the engine regularly tuned and the tires properly inflated. Reduce your total amount of driving, as car exhausts are a major cause of acid rain and other forms of air pollution. Use public transportation and car pools. In the home, use well-seasoned wood in your stove. Maintain a high-temperature fire and do not let the fire smoulder. Smouldering fires are the worst polluters.

Energy conservation

Reuse as many articles as possible. This saves the energy required to produce new articles. Keep your home a degree or two below normal temperature. Consider insulating your home. Wash clothes in cold or cool water, using full loads. Use the shortest cycle for dishwashers.

Hazardous wastes

Shop wisely for nonhazardous alternatives. If you must purchase hazardous materials, keep them sealed in their original containers. Make use of hazardous waste collection days and never flush these wastes down the sink or toilet.

Land pollution

Do not use salt to melt ice on sidewalks or driveways. Instead use sand to prevent slipping. Minimize the volume of what you throw out as waste, thereby reducing the demand for space in landfills. Use organic materials as compost where possible.

Ozone depletion

Avoid using styrofoam cups, unless you know that they do not contain CFCs. Never buy car or home-repair products in aerosol cans. Aerosol containers should never be burned, crushed, or punctured.

Toxic chemicals

The advice given under the heading of hazardous wastes also applies here. Use nonhazardous cleaners, solvents, waxes, paints, and varnishes. Avoid spray-can oven cleaners, or use them only with excellent ventilation. In your house or garden, use insecticidal soaps rather than toxic chemical sprays to deal with insects. If you are scraping off old paint, remember that it may contain lead. Double bag the old paint in plastic and put it out with your ordinary garbage. Use plastic gloves, goggles, or masks when dealing with any dangerous chemicals or with new wood that has been pressure treated with preservatives.

Conservation

Even a dripping tap uses a great deal of water every year. Repair all leaks. Conserve water in the kitchen and bathroom. Insulate your water heater and pipes. Water your lawn and garden only when they begin to show signs of drought. An occasional heavy watering is better than frequent short waterings. If you are stocking a new garden, use less thirsty plants. Drip watering systems make the most efficient use of irrigation water.

Water pollution

Never pour chemical wastes down the sink or toilet. Use detergents with little or no phosphorus content. If you have a septic tank, have it checked annually and have the sludge removed every three to five years. If you have an oil storage tank, watch for signs of leaks. One litre of oil can contaminate up to 2 000 000 L of water.

Wildlife safeguarding

Keep a bird feeder during severe winter weather. Grow bushes and trees that give birds shelter and maintain a bird bath. On the water, never throw any trash or plastics overboard. Do not drive all-terrain vehicles along beaches or through marshes. Observe notices and regulations concerning wildlife.

How can you influence governments?

You are a member of the greatest power in the country — the people. Individually and collectively people can make a great difference to the actions of all levels of government.

Governments are swayed by public opinion. They know that they depend on the votes of people. Most governments will change their most cherished policies rather than be forced out of office. You can take action by being informed about the issues and by contacting your elected government representative.

Read all you can about an environmental issue that

concerns you. Almost always, there are two or more sides to such issues. You should know what the other points of view are.

Write to your provincial and/or federal legislative member about the government's views on the issue. The government may already be planning some action that could help to resolve your own particular problem. It is believed that one citizen who writes a letter of enquiry or protest achieves as much as 400 people who do not bother to write. Remember, we cannot right wrongs unless we are all willing to make a contribution.

Environment Canada gives some advice on writing letters on the environment. "The most effective letters are (a) brief, (b) devoted to one environmental topic per letter, (c) not overly emotional, (d) clear about views and positions, and (e) designed to require a reply."

From Environment Canada, *What We Can Do for Our Environment: Hundreds of Things to Do Now*, Ministry of Supply and Services Canada, 1990, p. 24.

Cadmium, mercury found in flesh of Arctic whales

Two million Chernobyl victims have to be moved

Where's the wildlife gone?

Must we go on being the dustbin of the world?

Africa refuses to be international dumping ground for toxic waste

Ozone over Toronto getting thinner?

Take back your PCBs, Welsh insist

Mediterranean pollution at crisis point

Will the Med soon be dead?

The environment is frequently headline news.

Solutions: can they be found?

Environmental pollution can destroy us. It has already been responsible for many deaths. Consider some of the disasters of the 1980s — the accident at the Chernobyl nuclear power plant, the *Exxon Valdez* oil spill, the hole in the ozone layer, and the PCB scare. All of these events are symptoms of the breakdown of world environmental systems. As economic growth increases, environmental systems are unable to meet our demands.

Unfortunately, most of the attention seems to be devoted to treating the *symptoms* of environmental mismanagement rather than the *processes* that cause it. For example, a company will try to control its effluent rather than use materials and adopt processes that do not create effluent in the first place.

The main reason that we face so many problems is that since the Industrial Revolution we have adopted technology that makes intensive use of energy. As a result, the carbon and other materials in fossil fuels have been removed from the ground and released into the atmosphere on a massive scale. We have come to depend on fossil fuel energy in most aspects of production.

Solutions to environmental problems must focus on the reasons for the damage. Some of these reasons are the growth of population, the generation of energy, the demands of transport, the exploitation of soils, and the pressures on ecosystems that lead to the extinction of species.

Reordering our goals

The main goal of Western economies since the Industrial Revolution has been economic growth. It is a natural ambition. We all want to improve, or at least maintain, our standards of living. But the economic growth of the past two centuries has treated resources as if they will last forever.

For example, the forestry industry in North America used the "cut and run" technique for at least seventy years. During this period reforestation was not taken seriously. This happened because people operated on a short-term profit motive. Figure 14.2 illustrates the fact that, in the short term, forestry profits may indeed be higher if reforestation is ignored. But the cost to the environment is heavy. The result is that future generations will find limited timber and increased soil erosion.

Many people — especially young people — are beginning to appreciate the scarcity of the planet's resources. More people are becoming worried about the way in which resources are squandered recklessly.

Figure 14.2 The difference between a short-term and a long-term view

Forest overcutting can create a short-term profit but leads to a long-term loss.

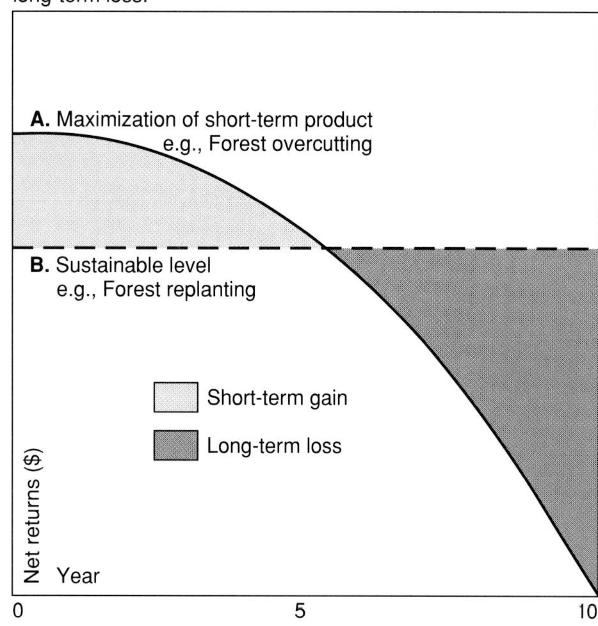

From Edward W. Manning, "Towards Sustainable Land Use: A Strategy," 1986. Reproduced with permission of the Minister of Supply and Services Canada, 1990.

To solve our environmental problems, we have to consider our goals first, then select the processes that will achieve these goals. Only then will the symptoms of environmental breakdown decrease. First, we must change our goal of short-term economic growth. This means changing how money is spent. If governments could also be persuaded to change their goals, we would make much more rapid progress toward solving our environmental problems.

Figure 14.3 shows an estimate of how much money would be required to achieve sustainable development in the decade from 1990 to 2000. The cost is small compared to the $600 billion (US) spent on car sales and the $1000 billion (US) spent on arms worldwide each year.

In 1989 and 1990, dramatic political changes transformed eastern Europe, leading to the prospect of a more peaceful world. Perhaps billions of dollars can now be saved in defence spending. These savings are known as the **peace dividend**. A 10 percent saving in arms expenditures worldwide would be more than enough to solve several key environmental problems. As well, the problems of starvation in famine areas could be greatly reduced. Unfortunately, it is difficult to reorder spending priorities from high-technology defence systems to the environment. Many major industries would have to shrink while other industries develop. Such a shift would take time and a great deal of political will.

Figure 14.3 The cost of achieving sustainable development

ESTIMATES OF ADDITIONAL EXPENDITURES REQUIRED TO ACHIEVE SUSTAINABLE DEVELOPMENT BETWEEN 1990 AND 2000 (BILLIONS OF DOLLARS)

YEAR	PROTECTING TOPSOIL ON CROPLAND	REFORESTING THE EARTH	SLOWING RATES OF POPULATION GROWTH	RAISING ENERGY EFFICIENCY	DEVELOPING RENEWABLE ENERGY	RETIRING THE DEBTS OF DEVELOPING COUNTRIES	TOTAL
1990	4	2	13	5	2	20	46
1992	14	4	22	15	8	40	103
1994	24	6	28	25	12	50	145
1996	24	6	31	35	18	30	144
1998	24	7	32	45	24	10	142
2000	24	7	33	55	30	0	149

Cost of achieving sustainable development in ten years, estimated by WorldWatch Institute, includes expenditures to reduce rates of population growth and to restore and maintain global resources. The figures should be weighed against the world's military expenditures, which alone total close to $1 trillion a year.

From "Strategies for Sustainable Economic Development" by Ian Worpole.

Are we making progress?

Although reversing the process of environmental degradation will take a long time, we have made some progress in recent years. This is particularly true of river pollution. Fish now live again in many of our rivers as a result of reduced amounts of raw sewage and phosphates entering the water. We have also made progress in conserving some endangered species of wildlife, such as the whooping crane and the wood bison.

The atmosphere has become cleaner and brighter over many Western cities, thanks to the control of emissions. Nevertheless, the problem of the future industrialization of developing countries leaves the overall global atmosphere seriously threatened. There appears to be little chance of reducing the total amount of carbon entering the atmosphere until low-cost renewable energy becomes widely available.

Progress has also been made in regulating many of our polluting industries. Although the practices of our forest industries in Canada are still widely criticized, it was not too long ago that virtually no restrictions existed. Today, trees are used more efficiently, increased reforestation is taking place, and the emissions from pulp and paper mills are being reduced. In 1996 the Canadian government announced that it had eliminated the production of CFCs ahead of the commitment made in the Montréal Accord and in line with the 1992 Copenhagen Conference.

Perhaps our greatest achievement, however, has been to increase the awareness of the damage we have been doing to the environment and to ourselves. Much remains to be done, however, in all areas of the environment. One of the great challenges is the reduction in the use and disposal of toxic chemicals. Another is the problem of soil erosion, as the loss of soil in parts of the world's farming regions increases at an alarming rate.

Citizens concerned about the environment can get involved in a clean up of their communities.

Is sustainable development possible?

Everyone seems eager to protect and sustain the environment. Governments have rushed to pass laws, produce reports, and set up task forces. We are continually under pressure to save the rain forest, conserve energy, protect the ozone layer, and recycle waste. There are so many environmental issues facing us today that it is possible to become confused and to lose all hope.

For this reason we should look at the larger picture. According to most forecasts, by the year 2030 the world population will be about 9 billion people rather than the 5.7 billion it was in 1995. This rapidly growing population contributes to our environmental problems. Everyone wants to share in greater economic development. The three-quarters of the world's population that are less developed economically will not be content to remain so. They will demand action to reduce the gap between themselves and the rich minority. And this will put acute pressure on the global environment.

Many people predict that an environmental breakdown will have occurred by 2030, causing death by starvation for millions of people. To avert this crisis we have to achieve sustainable development. The world's economic systems will have to produce the required goods and services without destroying the environmental system. This means that we will have to make changes in our lifestyle and find alternatives to the resources we use so freely today. *The State of the World 1990* raised some of the questions that we must face in creating this sustainable world:

> Building a more environmentally stable future clearly requires some vision of it. If not fossil fuels to power society, then what? If forests are no longer to be cleared to grow food, then how is a larger population to be fed? If a throwaway culture leads inevitably to pollution and resource depletion, how can we satisfy our material needs? In sum, if the present path is so obviously unsound, what picture of the future can we use to guide our actions toward a global community that can endure?
>
> From Lester R. Brown, Christopher Flavin, and Sandra Postel, "Picturing a Sustainable Society," in *State of the World, 1990*, Worldwatch Institute, 1990.

What is necessary to achieve a sustainable world by the year 2030, according to Worldwatch? Here are some of the essential features.

Our responsibility to future generations

We have to recognize that, for the sake of future generations, we must leave the world's natural resource systems as productive as we found them. During the time since the Industrial Revolution this goal has been ignored in the ceaseless drive to exploit resources. Now is the time for conservation to be taken seriously.

Fossil fuels must give way to renewable energy

Very soon there must be a major shift from the use of fossil fuels to an energy technology based on renewable resources. To stabilize the global climate, carbon emissions should be reduced to a mere 2 billion tonnes per year from the present 6 billion tonnes. Allowing for the world's population growth, this goal is equal to a world average of about one-eighth of the emissions created by each person in western Europe today.

This reduction in carbon emissions can be achieved by making energy savings in buildings, industry, and transport. Much of the technology already exists today for these savings. We will also need to make large-scale use of renewable energy sources, such as solar power.

A transport revolution

Transportation will also have to be revolutionized to create a sustainable society by 2030. Gas-guzzling cars will be confined to museums. In urban areas we should have "city cars," powered by batteries or hydrogen and creating no urban smog. Public transit is likely to make a major comeback. The bicycle may become the most common form of transportation, as it is in China today.

Electric cars can save scarce oil resources.

Reuse or recycle

The recycling of materials on a large scale will be necessary to avoid a resource crisis by 2030. This will not only save energy but will reduce pressure on nonrenewable resources. More than half of all our materials will be recycled in a sustainable society.

Restoring the biological base

The world's biological base will have to be restored to sustain the population by 2030. The spread of desertification will have to be stopped and much desertified land restored. Even then, less than 0.2 ha of productive land will be available per head of world population. Farming will become more intensive, yet without the overuse of chemicals. New farming practices will have to be adopted, such as **agroforestry** and the use of new types of crops. **Aquaculture** and **hydroponics** are likely to become more common. People in the more affluent parts of the world will probably have to "move down the food chain." That is, we will have to consume less animal and more vegetable products to allow enough food to be produced for all the world's population.

Other changes

The establishment of a sustainable world system will involve many changes in all our lives. It will affect the types of jobs available to us. Fewer people will exploit resources and many more will reuse and recycle them. A sustainable world system may change the balance between urban and rural living. The present flow of migrants to the cities could dwindle to a trickle as people use more of their own energy to produce food. Successful food production will make **land reform** necessary in many parts of the world. This would allow more of the world's people to own their own small pieces of land.

Some of these changes we can make ourselves. Others will have to be imposed on us by the collective decisions of society. But these changes are necessary to avoid a breakdown of the earth's productive systems, which could lead to disasters such as large-scale famine. Protecting and caring for our planet is in our own best interests and is essential for the well being of future generations. Achieving these goals is the responsibility of us all.

Hydroponics can grow food for an expanding population.

Looking back

1. (a) List the main rooms in your house and describe how each could be made more environmentally friendly.
   (b) If you use 8 L of water brushing your teeth with the tap on and 1 L of water brushing with the tap off, calculate how much water you would save in a year if you brushed your teeth with the tap off twice a day.
   (c) Since water is a renewable resource, why should we worry about water losses from such things as leaky faucets?
2. List the ways in which we can become more environmentally responsible in our schools.
3. (a) Explain what is meant by the term *green consumer*.
   (b) List the ways in which we can become green consumers.
4. Rank the suggestions for improving the environment given on page 218 in the order in which you feel you can personally make a contribution.
5. What are the problems of reallocating government funds from defence spending to programs that will help the environment?
6. Explain the term *sustainable development*.

Applying your knowledge

1. Develop a project to reduce the consumption of one of the following in your home for one month: electricity, water, or heating fuel. Learn how to measure consumption in your home. Examine old records to determine how much was consumed during the same month in previous years. Determine what steps are necessary to reduce consumption. Convince your family to take part. At the end of the month, analyse the results and report your findings to the class.
2. Invite the principal to visit your class. Prepare a presentation to convince him or her to promote some of the suggestions you created in question 2 in the Looking Back section.
3. (a) Brainstorm a list of products that you think should not be purchased, according to the six key issues for the environmentally conscious consumer.
   (b) Visit supermarkets in your area and prepare a list of products with the EcoLogo. How do the prices for these products compare with those for products without the logo?
   (c) If prices are higher for EcoLogo products, do you think this is justified if it means less damage to the environment? Write a brief editorial in support of your position.
4. Write a short essay explaining how a *symptom* of an environmental problem differs from the *cause*. Give three specific environmental problems as examples.
5. Prepare and debate a question on the following topic: "Our responsibility to future generations."

Extending your thinking

1. As a class, devise an Action 21 plan. This may involve consulting a local environmental group to identify a particular need. Make a detailed plan of how the project could be implemented and estimate all the costs involved.
2. (a) Evaluate our society's management of the environment by grading our attitudes, efforts, and progress towards the issues listed below. In a table, list the issues down the left column and create three columns for Attitudes, Efforts, and Progress. Assess a grade from between 1 and 10 (with 1 representing the lowest evaluation) for each issue for each of the three categories.
   (i) Exposure to toxic substances;
   (ii) Industrial water pollution;
   (iii) Radioactive waste;
   (iv) Disposal of garbage;
   (v) Pesticide residues;
   (vi) Water pollution from farm runoff;
   (vii) Industrial air pollution;
   (viii) Destruction of the ozone layer;
   (ix) Contamination of the oceans;
   (x) Vehicle exhaust;
   (xi) Tanker oil spills;
   (xii) Acid rain;
   (xiii) The greenhouse effect;
   (xiv) Indoor air pollution.

(b) Discuss your evaluation with a classmate. Which issues do you think are the most serious? What do you think needs to be done to improve the rate of progress for each issue?
(c) In a class discussion, suggest ways in which governments, industries, and individuals must all do their part to protect the environment.

3. As a class, create an agenda for an international conference on the environment. Choose six topics to be discussed. Working in groups, choose one topic and prepare a background paper for presentation at the conference.

4. (a) Prepare a case to support the following assertion: "Sustainable development must be achieved by the year 2030 in order to prevent a major environmental disaster."
(b) Discuss the changes in lifestyle, particularly in the Western world, that will be necessary if we are going to create sustainable development.

5. Using specific examples, write an essay to show how your awareness, attitude, and personal practices with regard to the environment have changed as a result of this course.

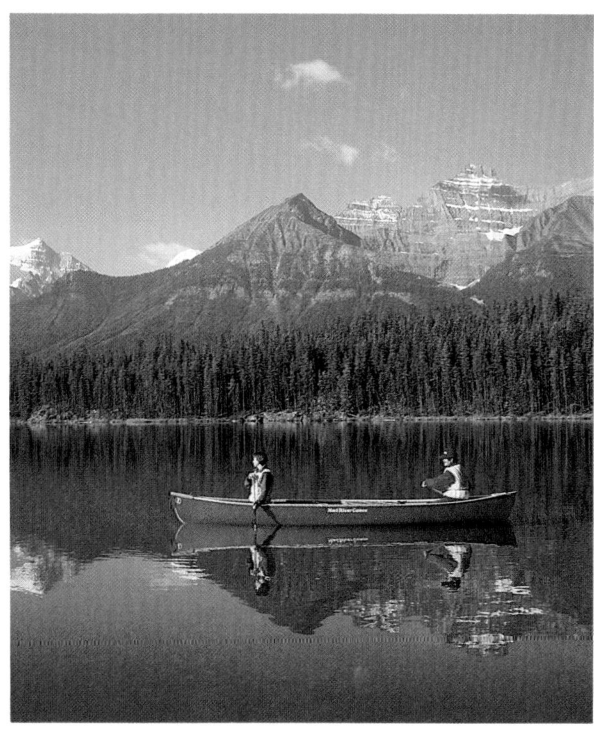

Can we look after our planet so that scenes like this will still be here for future generations to enjoy?

GLOSSARY

Glossary terms are in **bold** in the text.

Abiotic. The non-living components of an ecosystem; applies to inorganic elements.
Acid deposition. All forms of acidity coming from the atmosphere, including acid precipitation and dry matter.
Acid rain. Precipitation with a pH level of less than 5.6.
Acid shock. Spring meltwater made acid by the melting of acidic snow.
Active layer. The surface layer above permafrost that thaws each summer and refreezes each autumn.
Active solar energy. The use of solar energy devices to heat water or buildings.
Aftershock. A lesser shock that occurs after an earthquake.
Agricultural Land Reserve. Land in BC preserved by the government for agricultural use.
Agroforestry. The practice of integrating forestry and cultivated crops.
Air Quality Index (AQI). An index used to monitor the amount of ozone and other pollutants in the air.
Alkaline chlorination. The adding of an alkaline solution to oxidize toxic chemicals such as cyanide.
Alley cropping. The growing of crops interspaced with trees.
Alluvium. Sediment deposited by rivers.
Anaerobic bacteria. Bacteria that survive without oxygen — the opposite of aerobic.
Annual allowable cut. A formula used to determine the amount of timber that can be cut while maintaining sustainable yield.
Anopheles mosquito. Species of mosquito that is the main vector for malaria.
Anthracite coal. Hard coal with a high carbon content; burns relatively cleanly.
Aquaculture. The harvesting of fish in a controlled environment.
Aquifer. A water-bearing layer of rock.
Arable. Land that is suitable for growing crops.
Arctic haze. Low-level air pollution in the Arctic, originating in temperate industrial regions.
Artesian well. A well in which water is trapped by an impermeable cap rock, usually under pressure.
Atoll reef. Circular coral reef fringing an island that has been submerged by a rise in sea level.

Backcountry. Areas in parks inaccessible by modern transportation.
Barrier reef. A long coral reef that lies some distance from shore and that is separated from it by a lagoon.
Base metal. A metal of relatively low value (e.g., iron).
Bilharzia. A parasitic disease in which parasites from standing water enter the body through the skin. (Also known as **schistosomiasis**).
Bioaccumulation. The accumulation of a foreign material such as a toxic chemical in living tissue. Usually increases in degree as one moves up the food chain.
Biochemical oxygen demand (BOD). The amount of oxygen that would be used if the organic wastes in a litre of polluted water were broken down by decomposing organisms in that water; a useful measure of organic pollution.
Biodegradable. Materials that revert to inorganic constituents over time.
Biogeoclimatic zone. A large-scale vegetation zone associated with a world climate region and regional geology.
Biological control. Method of pest control that makes use of the natural predators, parasites, or diseases of pests or of naturally produced chemicals such as insect pheromones.
Biological degradation. The decomposition of organic compounds into inorganic chemicals.
Biological magnification. The increased concentration of toxic material at consecutive levels in an ecosystem.
Biome. Large-scale ecological system dominated by a particular type of natural vegetation.
Biosphere. The zone on or close to the earth's surface where life is found.
Biosphere reserve. An ecosystem that is preserved under UNESCO's Man and the Biosphere program.
Biota. All of the living organisms (fauna and flora) found within a given region.
Bituminous coal. A soft coal that produces tar when it burns as well as much smoke and ashes; does not burn cleanly.
Boreal. Northern (usually applied to coniferous forest).
Bund. A low earth wall or dike built to retain water.

Canadian Shield. An area of ancient hard rock in northern and eastern Canada.
Capillary action. Movement of water through small pore spaces, usually upwards.
Captive breeding program. The breeding of endangered species in captivity.
Carbon cycle. Movements of carbon and its compounds between earth, oceans, atmosphere, and organisms.

Carnivore. An animal that eats flesh.
Check dam. A dam constructed in a gully to trap silt and eventually fill the gully.
Chlorofluorocarbons (CFCs). Chlorinated compounds widely used in refrigerators and air conditioners; a cause of the depletion of the ozone layer.
Cinder cone. A volcanic peak made of cinders and other materials ejected from a volcano.
Clay soil. Soil in which the dominant particles are less than 0.002 mm in diameter.
Clearcutting. A method of timber harvesting whereby the trees in a given area are completely cleared.
Climax vegetation. The vegetation that can be supported by the climatic conditions of an area over the long term.
Closed system. A self-contained system that does not have inputs and that does not produce outputs. *See also* Open system.
Cogeneration. The use of fossil fuels to generate electricity and create usable heat at the same time.
Combined heat and power (CHP). *See* Cogeneration.
Commensalism. A relationship between two species in which the "guest" species benefits from living with the "host" species but the latter neither benefits nor is harmed by the former.
Commons. Elements of the environment that are shared by people (e.g., air and water).
Community forestry. The planting and managing of forests by local communities to provide fuel wood and help soil conservation.
Composite cone. A volcanic peak consisting of alternating layers of lava and ash or cinder.
Composting. The degrading of organic wastes, often producing a soil mulch.
Conservation. The management of natural resources to protect their long-term survival.
Continental shelf. The shallow submerged zone of the oceans adjacent to the continents.
Corn Belt. The part of the American Midwest where corn is the leading crop.
Crop rotation. The growing of different crops in succession to maintain soil fertility.

"Debt for nature" swap. An agreement to cancel the debt of a developing nation in return for a guarantee that certain aspects of the environment will be protected.
Deciduous. The seasonal shedding of leaves.
Decomposers. Organisms that cause decay, including bacteria and fungi.
Demand-side management. The use of conservation measures to counteract increases in demand for energy.
Detoxification. A chemical process that renders a compound no longer toxic.
Dioxins. Toxic compounds created by the incomplete combustion of organo-chlorides.
DNA. Deoxyribonucleic acid, the chemical that contains the genetic code that transmits the hereditary information for all cells.
Drip irrigation. The application of water by controlled dripping from pipes at the roots of plants.
Dry farming. A method of farming that conserves water by frequent fallowing, working the soil after rainfall, cross-ploughing, and controlling soil erosion.

Ecology. The study of the relationship between organisms and the physical environment.
Ecosystem. A biological community and its physical environment.
Ectoparasites. Parasites living outside the bodies of their hosts.
Endangered species. Species classified as being in danger of extinction.
Endoparasites. Parasites living within the bodies of their hosts.
Estuary. A wide river mouth or body of water open to the sea.
Eutrophication. The enrichment of water by nutrients such as nitrogen and phosphorus, resulting in excessive growth of organisms and oxygen depletion.
Evapotranspiration. Water returned to the atmosphere by evaporation and transpiration.
External costs. Costs borne by society at large rather than by a specific polluter of the environment.
Extinct. A species that no longer survives anywhere in the world.
Extirpated. A species that no longer survives in a particular country or region.

Fallow. The resting of land by leaving it uncultivated for a period of time.
Fauna. Animals living in a region.
Feral. Animals that have reverted to a wild state from domestication.
Filter feeders. Animals that obtain food by filtering it from water.
Fiord. A deep inlet of the sea caused by the flooding of a glacial valley.
Flora. Plants living in a region.
Fluidized bed combustion. The addition of limestone to the burning of coal to reduce emissions.
Food chain. The transfer of food through a sequence of organisms, each feeding on the previous one.
Food chain concentration. The tendency of a foreign material to become more concentrated at the higher levels of the food chain.
Food pyramid. A diagram of the feeding relationships in an ecosystem with photosynthesizers at the base and omnivores at the top.
Food web. The food link between organisms in a community. *See also* Food chain.
Fossil fuels. Coal, oil, and other hydrocarbons deposited in a previous geological age.
Fossil groundwater. Groundwater trapped over a long period of time.
Fringing reef. A coral reef that grows directly offshore with no deep lagoon between it and the shore.

Frontcountry. The areas of parks that are accessible by road.
Furans. A group of organo-chlorides, similar to dioxins.

Gene pool. The total of all the genes in a population.
Gene splicing. The introduction of a foreign gene into an organism.
Genetic clones. Offspring produced by the asexual reproduction of a single individual. Members of a clone are genetically identical.
Genetic engineering. The manipulation of genes between species.
Green Revolution. The rapid spread of scientifically bred high-yielding crops beginning in the 1960s.
Greenhouse effect. The raising of atmospheric temperature by the trapping of heat by carbon dioxide, methane, and other gases.
Gridlock. Traffic congestion, particularly at intersections, in which vehicles are unable to move.
Gross National Product (GNP). The value of the goods and services produced in a country in one year.
Groundwater. All subsurface water that participates in the hydrological cycle.
Guano. Bird excrement that is used as fertilizer because of its abundance of nutrients.
Gully erosion. The formation of deep channels on sloping ground as a result of runoff.

Habitat. The physical environment in which an organism lives.
Hazardous waste. Refuse that could present dangers as a result of the contamination and pollution of the environment.
Heavy metals. Metals with a high atomic mass that are capable of disrupting biological processes (e.g., lead, mercury, silver, cadmium, copper, tin, and zinc).
Herbivores. Animals that eat plants.
High-yielding variety (HYV). A crop produced by cross-breeding to ensure higher yields.
Horizon. A visually recognizable zone in a soil.
Host. An organism that provides a habitat for parasites.
Humus. Organic material in soil.
Hurricane. Tropical storm with strong winds spiralling around a low pressure centre.
Hydrocarbon. A compound of carbon and hydrogen.
Hydrological cycle. The circulation of water between the atmosphere and the earth's surface.
Hydrophyte. A plant that lives in water.
Hydroponics. The cultivation of plants in water without soil.
Hydrosphere. Water at or near the earth's surface.

Incineration. The disposal of refuse by burning.
Industrial smog. Atmospheric pollution consisting of emissions of industrial gases and particulate matter.
Infant mortality rate. The number of infants that die before reaching a specific age (usually one year) per thousand live births.
Infectious disease. A disease that is transmitted from person to person.
Integrated Pest Management (IPM). A method of controlling pests by using fewer chemicals and nonchemical methods.
Intercropping. The growing of different crops in alternate rows.
Intertidal zone. The area between high and low tides.
Irradiation. A technique used to sterilize insects as a means of controlling reproduction.

Kraft pulp process. The manufacture of wood pulp using sulphur compounds to separate wood fibres. Chlorine bleaching is also used in this process.
Krill. A small, shrimp-like organism that is a major component of the diet of baleen whales.

Land reform. The reallocation of large estates into smaller holdings.
Landfill. A site used to dispose of solid waste.
Leaching. The removal of soluble chemicals by downward movement of water in soils.
Legume. A type of plant that is capable of fixing nitrogen from the atmosphere (e.g., peas, beans, and clovers).
Lignite. A soft brownish-black coal, relatively low in carbon content.

Malaria. A parasitic disease caused by the protozoan *Plasmodium* affecting the blood; carried by the female *Anopheles* mosquito.
Mangroves. A group of trees and shrubs that inhabit tidal marshes and river mouths in the tropics.
Mean sea level. The average of the levels reached by high and low tides.
Methyl-mercury. A highly toxic compound of mercury.
Microhydro. A small-scale hydro development.
Microlayer. The top 1 mm of the ocean.
Monoculture. The practice of cultivating a single crop.
Mutation. A sudden change in the DNA of cells, which then changes the genetic information carried.
Mutualism. A relationship between two organisms of different species which benefits both.

Natural environment. The environment without modification by people.
Natural resources. Materials existing in nature that are useful to people.
Night soil. Human excrement used as a fertilizer.
NIMBY (Not In My Back Yard). Opposition to waste disposal in residential areas.
Nitrogen cycle. The movement of nitrogen between the atmosphere, organisms, and the earth.
Nongovernmental organizations (NGOs). Agencies not controlled by the government.
Noninfectious disease. A disease that cannot be transmitted from person to person.
Nonrenewable resource. A resource that cannot be replaced by natural processes in a short time.
Nuclear fission. A nuclear reaction in which an atomic nucleus (e.g., uranium) splits, releasing large quantities of energy.

Nuclear fusion. A nuclear reaction in which two light atomic nuclei combine to form a single heavier nucleus, releasing large quantities of energy.

Old growth forest. A natural forest ecosystem that has never been logged.
Omnivore. An animal that eats both plants and flesh.
Open pit mining. The removal of minerals by digging a pit from the surface.
Open system. A system that receives material from external sources and releases materials to the outside.
Organic. A chemical compound containing carbon; having characteristics of or being derived from living organisms.
Organo-chloride. A compound that contains carbon and chlorine.
Organo-phosphate. A compound that contains carbon and phosphorus.
Ozone depletion. The loss of ozone from the ozone layer caused by CFCs and other chemicals.
Ozone layer. A layer in the stratosphere that contains high concentrations of ozone, which helps absorb harmful solar ultraviolet radiation.

p-dichlorobenzene (p-DCB). A chemical compound often used in moth repellents.
Parasite. An organism that lives on or in another organism, causing harm to that organism.
Parasitism. A relationship in which one organism lives as a parasite on another organism.
Passive solar energy. The design of buildings to maximize the use of solar energy.
Pastoral. Relating to the keeping of animals.
Pathogen. An organism that causes disease.
Peace dividend. Government money available for spending as a result of lower defence costs.
Permafrost. Permanently frozen ground.
pH scale. A measure of acidity or alkalinity based on hydrogen ion concentration; a pH below seven is acidic and above seven is alkaline.
Photochemical smog. A form of pollution caused by the build up of hydrocarbons and nitrogen oxide with water vapour in the presence of ultraviolet sunlight.
Photoperiodic. A plant that is sensitive to the lengths of day and night.
Photosynthesis. The process by which solar energy is used to turn carbon dioxide and water into sugar and other carbohydrates, releasing oxygen in the process.
Photovoltaic cells. Silicon cells designed to convert solar rays into electricity.
Phytoplankton. A microscopic plant found in bodies of water.
Pioneer community. Plants that colonize an area from which the original vegetation has been removed.
Pivot irrigation. A circular irrigation system in which the water is sprayed from a boom that rotates around a central pivot.
Plant association. A group of plants commonly found together in an area.
Plate (tectonic). An almost rigid piece of the earth's crust that covers a large area.
Podzols. An acid soil with a grey upper horizon, commonly associated with coniferous forests.
Polychlorinated biphenyls (PCBs). Chlorinated organic compounds widely used in the past as insulating fluids in electrical transformers.
Prairie. Literally "meadow"; usually applied to the mid-continental grasslands of North America.
Primary treatment. The treatment of sewage by screening only.
Producer. An organism that produces organic compounds from inorganic compounds by photosynthesis or chemosynthesis.

Rad (radiation absorbed dose). A measure of nuclear radiation.
Radiation. Energetic nuclear particles and waves that are capable of damaging living tissues.
Radionuclides. Radioactive particles.
Radon. A radioactive gas produced by the decay of uranium 238.
Recombinant DNA. DNA with genes from different organisms.
Recombining genes. The process of combining genes from different organisms.
Recycling. The process of reusing materials that would otherwise be wasted.
Red tide. A periodic bloom of algae (dinoflagellates) on the west coast of Canada. If concentrated in shellfish, toxins in the red tide can lead to paralytic shellfish poisoning.
Refuse derived fuel (RDF). The use of combustible materials in garbage as a source of energy.
Rem (roentgen equivalent in man). A measure of nuclear radiation.
Renewable resource. A resource that is renewed by natural processes.
Resource recovery. Recovery of useful materials from waste.
Respiration. The process whereby a living organism or cell takes in oxygen and food and converts these to water and carbon dioxide, producing usable energy.
Richter scale. A scale to record earth tremors.
River basin. Land draining into a single river and its tributaries.
Ruminants. Cud-chewing animals that have a four-chambered stomach (e.g., cattle, deer, sheep, antelope, goats).

Sahel. Land located on the southern margin of the Sahara Desert.
Sanitary landfill. A landfill engineered to prevent hazardous wastes from leaking into the environment.
Savanna. A grassland region of the tropics and subtropics.
Scattergraph. A graph relating two variables by means of plotted points.
Scrubber. A device to remove sulphur and other impurities from chimneys.
Secondary treatment. The treatment of sewage by degrading its organic content.

Seedbank. A bank of seeds, often frozen, kept in storage to preserve genetic information.
Selective logging. The removal of selected trees in an area of forest.
Sewage. Waste discharged in liquid form from households and industries.
Sewage effluent. Liquid waste after the solids have settled.
Sheet erosion. Erosion by water flow over a sloping land surface.
Shelter belt. Trees or bushes planted to reduce the force of winds.
Shield volcano. A volcano with a low profile consisting of basic lava.
Shifting agriculture. A system of farming in which fields are cultivated for a few years then abandoned.
Silviculture. The science of forestry.
Slash and burn. The removal of forest by cutting and burning.
Sludge. Solid waste after the removal of fluids from sewage.
Smog. Gases and particulate matter in the air caused by transport and industrial pollution.
Soft energy. Energy obtained from renewable resources.
Soil erosion. The removal of soil by the action of water and/or wind.
Soil profile. The vertical arrangement of layers in a soil.
Soil structure. The tendency of particles in a soil to stick together.
Soil texture. The size of soil particles.
Solar thermal energy. The generation of electricity by using heat from solar mirrors to drive steam turbines.
Solid waste. Non-liquid waste discharged by households and industries.
Source separation. The separation of wastes into categories of materials before disposal.
Species. A distinct kind of organism consisting of a group of individuals that have a high degree of similarity and can generally interbreed only among themselves.
Sprinkler irrigation. Irrigation by means of overhead sprinklers.
Steppes. Normally applied to the short grass prairie found in the Soviet Union.
Stomata. An opening or pore in the leaf of a plant that allows movement of gases.
Strip farming. Alternate strips of crop and fallow across the line of the prevailing wind.
Strip mining. *See* Open pit mining.
Stubble mulching. A dry farming system in which stubble is left on the surface during fallow.
Subduction. The movement of one tectonic plate beneath another.
Subsurface cultivator. A machine designed to cut the roots of weeds on fallow fields, leaving stubble on the surface.
Succession. A series of changes through which a plant community passes before reaching its maximum possible development.
Surface irrigation. Irrigation water applied from channels on the borders of a field.
Sustainable development. The use of resources in a manner that maintains the resource supply for future generations.
Sustained yield. The exploitation of a renewable resource so that the amount taken is at least balanced by the amount replaced naturally.
Symbiosis. The close association of dissimilar species. *See also* Commensalism, Mutualism, and Parasitism.
Syndrome. A number of symptoms occurring together that characterize a particular disease or condition.
Synergy effect. The unknown effect of two or more chemicals acting together.

Taiga. Northern (boreal) forest.
Tailings pond. A pond constructed to allow mine wastes to settle rather than run into rivers.
Temperate. Pertaining to mid-latitude regions with moderate climates.
Terracing. The creation of level step-like features to reduce runoff and erosion.
Tertiary treatment. Complete treatment of sewage enabling the recovery of some materials.
Tornado. A violent, rotating, land-based cyclone capable of causing great destruction.
Toxic. Poisonous.
Toxic rain. Precipitation containing toxic chemicals.
Transpiration. Moisture released by vegetation.
Trash farming. *See* Stubble mulching.
Tree line. A narrow zone separating tundra and northern coniferous forest.
Trichloroethylene (TCE). A toxic chemical used in dry cleaning and other activities.
Tropical cyclone. *See* Hurricane.
Tsunamis. A seismic sea wave (often incorrectly called a tidal wave) caused by an earthquake.
Typhoon. *See* Hurricane.

Underground mining. The use of shafts and tunnels to mine mineral ores.
Urban heat island. The build up of heat in an urban environment resulting from buildings and energy consumption.
Urbanization. The spread of urban centres.

Vector. An organism that carries disease.

Water cycle. *See* Hydrological cycle.
Water erosion. Erosion caused by water flowing over the ground.
Water table. The upper limit of the saturated zone in the ground.
Wetland. A bog or marsh area frequently covered by shallow water.
Wind erosion. The removal of soil by wind action.
Wind tunnelling. The acceleration of wind by channelling between buildings.
Windbreak. Trees or bushes planted to reduce the force of the wind.

Xerophyte. A plant adapted to withstand dry conditions.

Zooplankton. Microscopic animals found in bodies of water.

INDEX